ANGLO-EGYPTIAN RELATIONS
1800 - 1956

A HISTORY OF
MODERN EGYPT
AND ANGLO-EGYPTIAN RELATIONS
1800 - 1956

by

John Marlowe

SECOND EDITION

ARCHON BOOKS
HAMDEN, CONNECTICUT
1965

TO
RICHARD USBORNE
FOR MANY ACTS OF FRIENDSHIP

First Published 1954
SECOND EDITION
©Copyright 1965, John Marlowe

Library of Congress Catalog Card Number: 65-10972
Printed in the United States of America

CONTENTS

PREFACE

TO SECOND EDITION

This book was written in 1953 and first published in the Spring of 1954. I have often regretted that, lacking the gift of prophecy, I did not delay writing it for another three or four years, when I should have been able to bring the story to a well-rounded end with the Suez expedition of October-November 1956. This new edition of my book, coming at a time when the passions aroused by the Suez expedition have, to some extent, died down, gives me the opportunity to add a postscript bringing the story of Anglo-Egyptian relations down from 1953 to the climax of November 1956. Apart from the postscript, the book appears exactly as it was originally written. I have resisted the temptation, on the one hand to use the benefit of hindsight to re-write any of the original text, or on the other hand to carry the postscript beyond 1956. The Suez expedition provides a natural end, not of course to Anglo-Egyptian relations as such, but to that long process of more or less intimate Anglo-Egyptian involvement which started with Nelson's victory at the Battle of the Nile.

JOHN MARLOWE

Dedham,
Buckinghamshire
January, 1964

CHAPTER ONE

THE FIRST BRITISH OCCUPATION

BY the end of the eighteenth century the three hundred years of oppressive and inefficient government from which Egypt had suffered since the Ottoman conquest had reduced that country to the lowest depths of economic and cultural decay. The once prosperous overland transit trade between Europe and the East had almost vanished. The irrigation canals had become silted up and the drainage had been neglected, with the result that large areas of land, once cultivated, were reverting to desert and swamp. The evils of governmental rapacity were unredeemed by any compensating advantages of security or stability. The incursions of Bedouin from the desert were a constant menace both in the towns and in the cultivated areas. The once great city of Alexandria had sunk to a small town of some 15,000 inhabitants. The whole population of Egypt numbered a little over 2,000,000. The native Egyptians, both Moslems and Copts,¹ had no responsible share in the government of the country, and cowered in utter subjection beneath the rapacity and violence of the Mameluke² beys, who, under the usually nominal suzerainty of the Turkish sultan, were the real masters of the country.

To trace the origin of the Mamelukes it is necessary to go back to the end of the twelfth and the beginning of the thirteenth centuries, when Salah-ed-Din al Ayyubi and his descendants ruled in Egypt. Finding the docile and peace-loving peasantry of Egypt unsuitable as soldiers either for guarding their persons or for prosecuting their wars, the Ayyubi rulers recruited their armies from slaves, most of whom were of Turcoman origin. With the decline of the

7

Ayyubi Dynasty, this foreign slave army developed into a military oligarchy of which the leaders were more powerful than their nominal masters. In 1249 the Ayyubi Sultan al-Salih died, leaving an infant son. His widow, Shajaret-ed-Durr,[3] herself a freed slave, reigned in his stead as Sultana for eighty days, the only woman who has ever sat as a sovereign on a Moslem throne. The Mamelukes then completed their usurpation of supreme authority by electing one of their number, Izzedin Aybak, as Sultan. Shajaret-ed-Durr, deserting the cause of her infant son, married the usurper and, profiting by her husband's absorption in war with the Ayyubi partisans in Syria, continued herself to exercise supreme power in Egypt. But before long Shajaret-ed-Durr's feminine frailty asserted itself over her masculine resolution and, in a fit of sexual jealousy, she had her Mameluke husband murdered. Aybak was speedily avenged by the slave-women of his first wife, who seized Shajaret-ed-Durr and beat her to death with wooden clogs. From then on Egypt was ruled in name as well as in fact by the Mameluke military oligarchy. The Mameluke sultans were at all times more or less dependent on the oligarchy of which they were members and by which they were elected. The degree of dependence varied with the political and military capacity of the sultan. Occasionally an exceptional sultan, such as Beybars, made himself sufficiently independent of his electors temporarily to establish an hereditary sultanate. But the tenure of the majority of the Mameluke sultans was a precarious one. The rule of the earlier, or Bahri[4] Mameluke sultans, who originated with the slave bodyguard of the Ayyubi al-Salih, and who derived their name from the barracks which they had originally occupied on the Nile island of ar-Roda, was culturally fruitful and militarily successful. Among the twenty-five Bahri sultans are numbered Beybars, who transferred the fainéant Khalif from Baghdad to Cairo; Qalaun, who extinguished the last remnant of Crusader power in Syria; and al-Nasir, whose reign marked the height of the Mameluke culture which has given to

8

Cairo the most noble of her ancient buildings. After al-Nasir the power of the Bahri Mamelukes, who were mostly of Turcoman origin, began to decline, and towards the end of the fourteenth century the Bahris were succeeded as Egypt's rulers by an oligarchy of Circassian Mamelukes, originating from Qalaun's bodyguard; this new dynasty became known as the Burjis[5] from the towers of the Citadel, which had been their first barracks. None of the Burji sultans attained the same independence of their electors as had been attained by some of the Bahri sultans, and the administrative anarchy which had marked the last years of Bahri rule was accelerated during the 134 years of Burji supremacy. Power was attainable and thereafter maintained only by intrigue, violence and spoliation. The Mameluke senior officers, or beys, organized themselves into factions, each with their own bodyguard of slaves. Fighting and intrigue between rival beys became endemic, making organized administration impossible. Occasionally a strong Sultan would temporarily assert his authority. On such occasions the beys usually came together in a precarious alliance to depose and murder him. The whole conception of a strong central government disappeared amid the confusion of an endemic state of civil war. In these circumstances, the Mameluke dominions, which still included Syria, provided an easy prey for the Ottoman Sultan Selim I, who invaded Syria in 1516. The Mameluke Ghuri-al-Qansuh, who happened to be one of the strongest and best of the Burjis, showed a bold face to the invader. But the inferiority of Mameluke arms and the treachery of the Mameluke beys[6] were too much for him. Crippled at the last moment by the desertion of two of the beys and their followers, his army was overwhelmed and he was killed on the field of al-Dabiq, near Aleppo. Syria hastened to make its peace with the victorious Selim, who within a few months had crossed Sinai and was advancing on Cairo. Tuman, Ghuri's successor, offered a stubborn resistance, but the majority of the beys had already determined to make their peace

9

with Selim. Tuman was captured and executed, Egypt annexed to the Ottoman dominions, and the puppet Khalif transferred from Cairo to Constantinople. Mameluke sovereignty was at an end. But Mameluke rule in Egypt continued, subject to the payment of an annual tribute to Constantinople, and subject to the usually nominal control of a resident Turkish governor.

Egypt was of interest to the Ottomans mainly as a source of tribute. Under the Ottoman dispensation all land in Egypt was confiscated to the State and farmed out to *multazimin*[7] who were made responsible for the collection of Miri (tribute derived from a land tax) and for local administration, in that order of importance. These concessions were farmed out to the Mameluke beys, who thus became provincial governors, and who soon compensated themselves in wealth for what they had lost in political importance. Although a Turkish pasha was the nominal head of the administration, it came about in practice that the real power was divided between a Mameluke Shaykh-al-Balad (Governor of Cairo) and a Mameluke Amir-al-Hajj (literally leader of the annual Pilgrimage to Mecca, actually Commander of the Army). These officers were elected by the Grand Divan, an Assembly of Mamelukes which was established by Suleiman the Magnificent. Its original purpose was to assist the Turkish pasha in government; its actual function was to provide a forum for the intrigues of the Mameluke beys.

As the power of the Ottoman Empire declined, so the rapacity and insubordination of the Mameluke beys increased. In the early days of the Ottoman conquest a Turkish garrison had been maintained in Egypt, but the Mameluke military hierarchy had been retained as part of the Turkish garrison. Later the Turkish troops were withdrawn, and with them the only effective means of Ottoman control. The Mamelukes continued to recruit their numbers by the purchase of slaves, mostly of European and Christian origin, in the same way as the Ottomans recruited their janissaries, and were able to make and unmake Turkish pashas almost at will. The only source of influence left to the Ottoman representative was the admittedly fruitful one deriving from the endemic state of discord existing between the Mamelukes. Nevertheless, the spectacle of a herald clothed in black, unattended and mounted on a donkey, proceeding to the Citadel with the intimation that the pasha's services were no longer required became an increasingly frequent one, and it was rare for the pasha to dispute the terse command *Inzil ya Pasha* (Descend, O Pasha) with which the herald was wont to announce his mission.

For two hundred and fifty years Egypt endured this state of anarchic misrule. Nothing but a despotism could have improved matters. But no sufficiently strong man arose, either among the pashas to destroy the Mamelukes or among the Mamelukes to oust the Turks and subdue his fellow beys. But in 1769, Ali Bey, the Mameluke Shaykh-al-Balad, established a sufficient ascendancy over the other Mameluke beys to enable him successfully to rebel against the Ottomans, to capture Mecca, and to declare himself 'Sultan of Egypt and Lord of the Two Seas'.[8] For a few years Egypt experienced the rule of a single and reasonably benevolent master. The fame of Ali Bey spread beyond the bounds of Egypt. Russia offered him assistance against his Ottoman suzerain. He invaded Syria. While he was away, his chief lieutenant, one Abu Dahab, encouraged by Constantinople, revolted against him. Ali Bey returned hot-foot from Damascus to deal with this revolt, but was defeated and killed by the rebels at Salhiye. Abu Dahab was made Pasha of Egypt by Constantinople as a reward for having got rid of Ali Bey, but he did not long survive his promotion. Within a few weeks of his death, Egypt was in the throes of civil war. Two leading beys, Ibrahim and Murad, rose in revolt against Ismail, the Shaykh-al-Balad, who was supported by the Turkish Pasha. Ismail and the Pasha were driven out of Cairo by Ibrahim and Murad, who, as soon as they had disposed of their common enemies, started quarrelling with each other. Murad was driven out of Cairo by Ibrahim and set up a separate government in Upper Egypt. The threat of Ottoman hostility drove them to a reconciliation. Ibrahim became Shaykh-al-Balad and Murad Amir-al-Hajj.

The rapacity of Ibrahim and the inhumanity of Murad would not by themselves have provoked the Turks to intervention. But they committed the unforgivable crime of repudiating the tribute. This was the one action which was almost certain to move Constantinople to act resolutely. A Turkish fleet was despatched to Alexandria and a Turkish army to Rosetta. Murad marched towards Rosetta to meet the Turks and was defeated. The rest of the beys hastened to desert to what, for the time being, appeared to be the winning side, and Murad and Ibrahim fled to Upper Egypt. The Ottoman Captain-General entered Cairo, restored Ismail Bey as Shaykh-al-Balad and made him Pasha of Egypt. Ismail died in 1790 and Ibrahim and Murad returned to Cairo. Their second period of power may be said to mark the climax even of Mameluke misgovernment. The *'ulema*⁹ and the *fellahin*, united in action for the first and last time, joined in a revolt which succeeded in wringing a few concessions out of the two tyrants. Many of the foreign consuls, together with the members of their communities, unable to trade or even securely to live under the conditions prevailing, left Egypt. Baldwin, the British Consul, who left in 1796, wrote: 'I do not conceive that Egypt can be much longer tenable by the Franks owing to the excessive tyranny of Murad Bey who latterly has given them to understand . . . that the Capitulations mean nothing to him, and that he shall extract and exact, as in fact he has done, without respect to anyone. The same spirit invades the whole body of Mamelukes.'

Such was the situation on the eve of the French invasion in 1798: a country ruled by two major and a host of minor tyrants who had no common ties of blood or interest with the local inhabitants and who were able, by means of their military organization, to plunder the country very much at their will. In their capacity of *multazimin*, most of the cultivable land of Egypt was in the grip of the beys, who lived in splendid palaces in Cairo on the proceeds of the peasants' toil, retiring to their estates when political vicissitudes drove them forcibly from the capital. Capricious and oppressive taxation, combined with endemic neglect and insecurity, were destroying the country's agricultural resources. Foreign trade was almost at a standstill. Justice was administered by the Grand Qadi[10] and by his subordinates, in theory according to the Shari'a Law, in practice according to the financial interests of the judges. Even in the Ottoman dominions it would have been difficult to discover a people more grievously oppressed, an economy more sorely decayed.

It is not easy to point to any convincing reason for Bonaparte's Egyptian expedition, in spite of the volumes of information on the subject which are available. It is clear that the inspiration came from Bonaparte and that the Directory were not unwilling to see him occupied at a comfortable distance from France. Among the reasons adduced by Bonaparte were: (*a*) a desire to revive the French overland trade with the East, which had been destroyed by the Mamelukes under British influence (There is in fact no evidence that the Mamelukes were any less arbitrary in their treatment of the British than they were in their treatment of other foreigners; in fact, while the British Consul had left in 1796, the French Consul, M. Magellon, had stayed on, and his advice was a powerful factor in persuading the Directory to agree to the expedition.) (*b*) a desire to cripple British overland trade with the East (This trade had already become almost non-existent by reason of the extortions of the Mamelukes.) (*c*) a desire to establish contact with Tippoo Sahib in order to help him make trouble for the British in India (*d*) a desire to establish a French Empire in the East which would surpass and perhaps supersede that of the British in India. Whichever was the most powerful of these reasons, it is evident that they were all primarily motivated by a desire to strike a blow at England.

This is understandable in view of the fact that Bonaparte selected Egypt as the site of his next adventure only after he had been compelled to advise the Directory that their plans for the invasion of England were impracticable.

Perhaps the main attraction of an Egyptian campaign was the certainty of an easy conquest. The Mameluke military organization, although adequate for maintaining a domestic tyranny, was ludicrously inadequate when confronted with a European army. Moreover, the beys enjoyed no popular support in the country, the inhabitants of which had recently been in revolt and would, according to the calculations of Bonaparte and M. Magellon, be prepared to welcome the French army as deliverers.

The main disadvantage was the possibility that Turkey would regard the invasion of Egypt as an act of hostility to herself. In the event, and stimulated thereunto by Great Britain and Russia, Turkey did so regard the French invasion, but before the invasion it was not impossible to believe that the resources of French diplomacy would be able to convince the Sultan that the subjection of Ibrahim and Murad, who were in rebellion against the Porte, could not in any way be regarded as a hostile act against Turkey. On the contrary, it was not unreasonable to suppose that a French promise to ensure punctual payment of the tribute would be regarded in Constantinople as adequate compensation for any technical breach of sovereignty.

So the expedition proceeded. From the military point of view, there was no miscarriage. The expedition was conveyed safely to the Egyptian coast, capturing Malta on the way, landed without opposition, and entered Alexandria in the face of negligible resistance. Within three weeks of the landing the Mameluke forces under Murad Bey had been completely routed at the Battle of the Pyramids[11] and Cairo had surrendered. Murad fled to Upper Egypt, Ibrahim to Syria. Then Bonaparte's troubles began. Barely a week after the occupation of Cairo the French fleet, at anchor in Abuqir Bay, was attacked and destroyed by Nelson. With the news of Bonaparte's landing, British diplomacy had also gone into action. Spenser Smith, the British Minister at Constantinople, was instructed to open negotiations with the Porte for an Anglo-Turkish alliance against France which would have as its main object the expulsion of the French from Egypt. The Russian Government was also pressing Constantinople for an alliance against France, and the efforts of the French Minister to persuade the Porte of French friendliness were of little avail. In December 1798 a Russo-Turkish alliance was concluded, followed in January 1799 by an Anglo-Turkish alliance. This was astonishingly quick moving by Constantinople, and argues either great dexterity on the part of the British and Russian negotiators or else a singular lack of dexterity on the part of the French ones. Under the terms of the Anglo-Turkish treaty, the Porte agreed to supply 100,000 troops and the whole Turkish Navy for fighting the French in Egypt, and England undertook to keep a 'respectable fleet' in the eastern Mediterranean and not to lay down arms until the integrity of the Ottoman Empire had been assured.

In its negotiations with Turkey it is uncertain how far the British Government was actuated by a general desire to harass the French wherever they might be as part of the grand strategy of war against France, and how far it was actuated by a specific desire to prevent the French from establishing themselves in Egypt. But it is apparent that at least one member of the British Cabinet had already appreciated the strategic importance of Egypt from the point of view of British imperial possessions. Dundas, the Minister of War, in the course of a memorandum to Lord Grenville, the Foreign Secretary, wrote: 'The possession of Egypt by any independent Power would be a fatal circumstance to the interests of this country.' This is probably the first explicit and official statement of the policy which has governed British relations with Egypt for the last 150 years, and it is interesting to note this expression of opinion by a British Minister seventy years before the Suez Canal was constructed and at a time when the overland transit traffic through Egypt was almost at a standstill.

After the Battle of Abuqir, Nelson had left Captain Hood with three ships to blockade the coast of Egypt. At about the same time Commodore Sir Sidney Smith, brother of the British Minister at Constantinople and a naval officer with a brilliant if rather unorthodox record, was sent to the eastern Mediterranean with the warship *Tigre* and instructions 'to take command of such of H.M.'s ships as he may find in those seas, unless by any unforeseen chance it should happen that there should be among them any of H.M.'s officers of superior rank', and 'to act with such forces in conjunction with the Ottoman and Russian squadrons for the defence of the Ottoman Empire and the annoyance of the enemy in that quarter'. It was always Sir Sidney Smith's practice to take a large view of the instructions given to him, and his first act on arrival in the eastern Mediterranean was to proceed to Constantinople to assist his brother in negotiations with the Turks. Between them, as has been seen, they brought the negotiations to a successful conclusion just before the arrival of Lord Elgin, the new British Ambassador to the Porte. No time was lost in pushing the Turkish Government into active operations. Part of the Turkish fleet joined a Russian squadron in operations against the French in the Adriatic, and another part was despatched to join Hood in the blockade of Egypt. In March 1799 another British officer, Colonel Koehler, arrived in Constantinople with a mission to help prepare the Turkish Army for operations against the French in Egypt. At the same time the Turkish Government, on its own account, was making other warlike preparations. Ibrahim Bey, after his defeat at the hands of Bonaparte, had taken refuge with Jazzar Pasha, the Governor of Akka. He was followed to Akka by several other of the Mameluke beys. Jazzar Pasha was a notable figure. It is uncertain whether his name, which means 'butcher', derives from his father's profession or from his own cruelty. He was a Bosnian of humble birth who had risen to power by the usual methods of violence and intrigue. At the time of Bonaparte's invasion of Egypt he was Pasha of Akka in name, and ruler of most of Palestine and southern Syria in fact. He had, however, found it convenient to keep on friendly terms with his nominal suzerain in Constantinople. He was encouraged by Constantinople to champion the cause of the defeated Mamelukes and, with Turkish assistance, made preparations for an attack on Egypt. He advanced as far as al-Arish, and the menace of Egypt from that quarter became so serious that Bonaparte was compelled in February 1799 to embark on his ill-fated Syrian expedition.

The story of that expedition, the capitulation of al-Arish and Ghazze, the storming of Jaffa, the massacre of the surrendered Jaffa garrison on the beach, and the abortive siege of Akka, need not be told in these pages. Suffice it to say that Jazzar, supported from the sea by the guns of a British squadron under the command of Sir Sidney Smith, and sustained on land by the versatility and determination of that eccentric but brilliant adventurer, succeeded in holding Akka against Bonaparte's assaults until the spread of disease and discontent in his army caused him to raise the siege and return to Egypt in May 1799.

The first year of the French occupation of Egypt had not justified Bonaparte's expectation that the native inhabitants would welcome the French as their liberators from Mameluke tyranny. He had underestimated the influence of the Moslem fanaticism which caused the Egyptians to hate and distrust the French as infidels. His clumsy attempts to show sympathy with Islam exacerbated rather than diminished this prejudice. He neglected to consider the unpopularity which was bound to accrue from the financial levies imposed for the maintenance of his army after it had been cut off from France by Nelson's victory at Abuqir. He was surprised at the extent to which the native Egyptians were incapable of and apathetic towards any measure of self-government. He did not appreciate the instinctive Oriental suspicion of nearly all forms of governmental activity, and did not realize that sinister motives would be attributed even to actions beneficent in their intentions. A revolt in Cairo in the autumn, headed by the '*ulema* and occasioned by a French attempt to impose a house tax, cured Bonaparte of his illusions. The revolt was suppressed without much difficulty and order restored without the exercise of undue severity. But the honeymoon period of the French occupation was over. There was no more talk of liberation, no more flirtation with Islam. Desaix was sent to Upper Egypt with a column to deal with the guerrilla resistance still being offered by Murad. French military governors were appointed to supervise the administration in Cairo and in the provinces of the Delta. By the time Bonaparte had returned from Syria, Desaix had completed a fairly successful campaign against the Mamelukes in Upper Egypt, during the course of which he had penetrated as far as Aswan; but most of the Delta provinces were in revolt, and communications between Cairo and Alexandria were continually being interrupted by marauding Bedouin.

But Bonaparte was given no leisure to develop internal administration. In July a Turkish force landed in Abuqir Bay accompanied thither by Sir Sidney Smith, who lay off Alexandria in the *Tigre*. The Turkish force was ignominiously defeated and compelled to re-embark, but Bonaparte was by this time weary of his Egyptian adventure. He was, moreover, alarmed at the reverses which were being suffered by the Directory in Europe, news of which was conveyed to him by Sir Sidney Smith. Whether this was an example of eighteenth-century courtesy towards a foe or whether it was a ruse designed to induce Bonaparte to leave Egypt for France and so risk capture by the British fleet is uncertain. The effect appears to have been to confirm Bonaparte in his determination to return to France, and in August 1799 he quitted Egypt for ever, leaving Kléber in command of the Army of the East.

The position of the new Commander-in-Chief was not an enviable one. The British fleet rendered the despatch of reinforcements and provisions from France almost impossible. A Turkish army, under the command of the Grand Vizier, was on its way through Syria to attack Egypt. The population of Egypt was discontented, and in some districts in open revolt. His troops were discouraged and homesick. He himself felt, not unreasonably, that he had been left in the lurch by Bonaparte. In these circumstances Kléber lent a ready ear to Sir Sidney Smith's proposals for negotiations with a view to an armistice and evacuation. Sir Sidney Smith was greatly exceeding his powers in initiating these negotiations, but within a few weeks he had succeeded in establishing himself as a mediator in official negotiations between Kléber and the Grand Vizier, who had by this time reached and captured al-Arish. In January 1800 an agreement, known as the Convention of al-Arish, was arrived at under the terms of which the French army was to evacuate Egypt in transports provided by the Turks and was to be granted a safe passage through the Mediterranean by the British fleet. Smith appears neither to have sought nor to have received any instructions from higher authority during the course of these negotiations, but Lord Elgin, British Ambassador at Constantinople, recommended acceptance of the terms of the Convention to His Majesty's Government. The British Government, however, unwilling to see the French forces in Europe reinforced by the Army of the East, instructed Admiral Keith, C.-in-C. Mediterranean Fleet, to refuse the safe conduct. Some weeks later the Cabinet, under pressure from Dundas, changed its mind, but it was too late. Fighting had broken out again. The Grand Vizier had advanced on Cairo and been defeated at Heliopolis by Kléber, who had been roused to pugnacity by the failure of the al-Arish negotiations. The Porte, annoyed by the British refusal to accede to the al-Arish Convention, then withdrew the Grand Vizier's army from Egypt. At the same time Murad, who had allied himself and subsequently quarrelled with the Grand Vizier, made his peace with Kléber and was allowed to retire to his estates in Upper Egypt. Any chance of getting the French out of Egypt by negotiation appeared to have evaporated for the time being.

The British Government's vacillation over the Convention of al-Arish is illustrative of the two schools of thought about Egypt in the Cabinet. There was, on the one hand, Dundas, who regarded the consolidation of the French occupation of Egypt as an ultimate threat to the British position in India, and who was prepared to risk disadvantages nearer home in order to get the French out. On the other hand, there was most of the rest of the Cabinet, who were inclined to regard the presence of French forces in Egypt as a not unwelcome diversion of strength from French forces in Europe.

It soon became clear that Dundas, Elgin, and Sidney Smith had been right about the Convention of al-Arish and the majority of the British Cabinet wrong. In the following year it became necessary to despatch a considerable military expedition to Egypt in order to accomplish what Sidney Smith had accomplished single handed at al-Arish. In spite of the assassination of Kléber in June 1800, and the incapacity of his successor, Menou, the French continued to consolidate their position in Egypt. By the beginning of 1801 the British Cabinet had come round to Dundas's view that the perils inherent in a permanent French occupation of Egypt more than outweighed the advantage of diverting French effort from Europe. In February an expedition 15,000 strong under the command of Sir Ralph Abercrombie sailed for Alexandria and arrived in Abuqir Bay at the beginning of March. A landing was made on the Abuqir Peninsula against light French resistance and an attempt made to take Alexandria by storm. This attempt, which cost about 1,000 British casualties, was repulsed, and a fortnight later the French counter-attacked in an attempt to drive the British back into the sea. The French counter-attack failed, but the British Commander, Abercrombie, was killed. He was succeeded by his second-in-command, General Hutchinson, who abandoned any attempt to take Alexandria by assault. He isolated the town from the east by cutting a canal across the narrow strip of land between Lake Mariut and Abuqir Bay, and blocked it from the west by landing a small force under General Coote at Marabout on the western approach to Alexandria, near where Bonaparte had landed just three years before. Hutchinson then turned east and with his main force captured Rosetta, at the mouth of the west branch of the Nile. This enabled a force of 4,000 Turks to land at Rosetta and join Hutchinson in an advance up the Nile towards Cairo. The first objective of this advance was to cut off communications between Cairo and Alexandria, and so to prevent the possibility of Alexandria being relieved from Cairo. The second objective was the capture of Cairo itself.

By this time three separate columns were converging on the Egyptian capital. First, there was the Anglo-Turkish force advancing from Rosetta. Secondly, a Turkish force under the Grand Vizier was on its way from Syria. And, thirdly, a force of 6,000 British Indian troops under General Baird had landed at Qusair[12] on the Red Sea and were moving across the desert to the Nile Valley at Qena, preparatory to an advance on Cairo from the south. The only chance for the French in Cairo was to go out and attack the converging columns while there was still time and space to deal with them separately. But the chance was lost, and Hutchinson and the Grand Vizier were allowed to join forces on the Nile a few miles north of Cairo. Meanwhile, Ibrahim Bey (Murad had recently died) had mobilized the Mameluke beys and their followers, but avoided intervention until he could see how events were shaping. When he had satisfied himself that the French were making no serious attempt to oppose the advancing columns, he presented himself to General Hutchinson as an ally, and soon afterwards 1,200 Mamelukes, under the command of Osman Bey al-Bardissy, joined the Anglo-Turkish forces at the apex of the Delta. The position of the French in Cairo was now hopeless, and the French Commander, General Belliard, asked for and obtained an armistice on 18 June 1801. By the terms of the armistice, the French forces in Cairo were to surrender, but were to be allowed to evacuate Egypt and be given a safe conduct back to France. Evacuation on the same terms of all the French forces in Egypt had been agreed to at al-Arish eighteen months previously without the necessity of employing a British expeditionary force at all.

Alexandria was still holding out under Menou, the French Commander-in-Chief. In spite of a bitter denunciation of Belliard's surrender, Menou himself accepted the same terms for the Alexandria garrison on 3 September. The French occupation of Egypt, which had lasted for a little over three years, was at an end.

It is interesting to speculate on the extent to which the 'Westernization' of Egypt during the nineteenth century owed its peculiarly French bias to the fact that the initial contact with the West was through the medium of the French occupation. There is no doubt that the French occupation made the process of Westernization possible by breaking the power of the Mamelukes. Although their *coup de grâce* was not administered until about twelve years later by Mohamed Ali, the long domination of the Mamelukes had in fact come to an end at their first serious clash with Western arms in the plain of Embaba in June 1798. It is pathetic to read of the richly caparisoned horses, the gold ornaments, the body armour, the jewelled sabres, and the complete lack of artillery with which the beys so confidently faced the Army of the Revolution. The Mamelukes were a survival from the Middle Ages and had only persisted as a result of the complete isolation from Europe which they had imposed on Egypt. Once this barrier of isolation had been broken by the rude clash of arms, nothing could have restored their authority. It remained for some source of authority to replace the Mamelukes and to create a new social and political order on the ruins of the medievalism which had so suddenly collapsed. During the period of the French occupation nothing was done permanently to fill the gap. The experiment of developing indigenous

22

government was tried and had failed. Thereafter military preoccupations had prevented any progress being made in laying the foundations of a Westernized civil administration under French control. The short period of the occupation and the hostility of the inhabitants had prevented the spread of any Western social or cultural influences. It is in fact unreasonable to suppose that the normal behaviour of European troops of occupation at the end of the eighteenth century was likely to influence Moslems in favour of a relaxation either of the harem system for women or of the Prophet's prohibition of fermented liquors for men.[13]

With the departure of the French there was no recognized source of authority in Egypt except for the Anglo-Turkish occupying forces. The British Government had before it three possible courses: continuing the occupation for an indefinite period or handing over the problem to the Turks or setting up an indigenous administration. The first course was bitterly opposed by the Allied Powers, whose representatives were by this time assembled at Amiens for the purpose of negotiating peace with France. The Russian representative told the Conference that 'any concession to England in Egypt must be common to all nations in amity with Turkey, that the restitution of Egypt by England was no favour, for Europe would not permit her to remain there'. The second possibility—that of leaving Egypt to Turkey—was at first strongly favoured by the British Government. Huskisson, the Under-Secretary for Foreign Affairs, wrote a private letter to Hutchinson in which he advised him to maintain strict neutrality in what he described as 'Turkish domestic affairs', meaning the administration of Egypt. The advantages of this course were considerably vitiated by Russia's action in refusing to agree to Turkish representation at Amiens and by Turkey's consequent reaction of signing a separate peace, which almost amounted to an alliance, with France, whose diplomatists were not slow to take advantage of Turkish resentment at the slight put upon her. Thus the attention of the

British Government became concentrated on the third possibility of setting up an indigenous administration in Egypt. This was the solution which from the beginning had been favoured by the military authorities on the spot. Before landing in Egypt, Abercrombie had sent a friendly message to Murad, and Sidney Smith, still Ambassador-at-large in the eastern Mediterranean with undefined powers, was cultivating relations with the Mameluke beys through various agents. After landing, the political sympathies of the expedition began to move strongly in favour of a restoration of Mameluke power with British guidance and assistance. This pro-Mameluke feeling was strengthened by the British dislike of their Turkish allies, by the realization of the practical impossibility of a genuinely Egyptian administration, and by the assistance, albeit somewhat belated, which the Mamelukes gave to the British expedition. Hutchinson wrote to Dundas saying that he thought 'no event so unlikely as that Egypt would long continue to belong to Turkey'. And to Elgin: 'The Turks, without money, without provisions of any kind, pillage and plunder everything that falls into their hands. Any interference would arouse their enmity and any acquiescence would alienate the natives from the British.' Hutchinson's general theme, as developed in despatches to Dundas and Elgin, was that since Turkey was incapable of holding Egypt by reason of her administrative inefficiency and the hatred she inspired in the inhabitants, and since a permanent British occupation was politically impracticable, then Great Britain should sponsor Egyptian independence under Mameluke rule.

Under these circumstances, it is not surprising that the Mamelukes were encouraged to believe that the British intended to restore them to power and that the Turks accused the British of intriguing against them with the Mamelukes. Hutchinson endeavoured to mediate between the Turks and the Mamelukes, who were already openly quarrelling while Alexandria was still in French hands. It was agreed (a) that the Turks would appoint a Pasha as formerly, (*b*) that the annual tribute would continue to be paid, and (*c*) that the Mamelukes should be reinstated in their properties. This agreement was, however, repudiated by the Turks almost as soon as it was made.

In their efforts to arrive at a solution for Egypt's future, the British Government sent Mr. J. P. Morier of the British Embassy in Constantinople to study and report on the position in Egypt. Mr. Morier produced three possible solutions: (*a*) British occupation, (*b*) indirect rule through the Mamelukes while continuing to recognize Turkish sovereignty, and (*c*) the destruction of Egypt by inundation. All these suggestions were rejected by the British Government, which then sent a statement of policy to Lord Elgin, on the basis of which he was instructed to open negotiations with the Porte to settle the future of Egypt. This statement of policy proposed that Great Britain should co-operate with Turkey in the following:

(*a*) Rights and privileges of the Mamelukes to be ascertained and fixed and made conditional on the performance of fixed services.

(*b*) The revenue of the country to be properly assessed.

(*c*) A fixed proportion of the revenue to be set aside for military training under British officers.

(*d*) Alexandria to be garrisoned by the British for the duration of the war with France.

(*e*) Rest of Egypt to be evacuated forthwith by British troops.

(*f*) Turkish sovereignty to remain and the Porte to continue to appoint a Pasha and to receive tribute.

The statement of policy envisaged what would have been an Anglo-Turkish condominium over Egypt. In fact, it did nothing more than to provide a starting-point for a series of inconclusive wrangles between Elgin, Hutchinson, the Ottoman Government, and the Mamelukes. The Turks complained to Elgin of Hutchinson's intrigues with the beys. Hutchinson complained of treacherous attempts by the

Capitan-Pasha to murder the leading beys. Elfi Bey, who, with Bardisi Bey, had succeeded Ibrahim and Murad in the leadership of the Mamelukes, encouraged by Hutchinson's attitude, advised the Mamelukes to put themselves openly under British protection. Lord Elgin, who clearly felt that Hutchinson was becoming too deeply committed to the Mamelukes, and who had written to the Foreign Office that 'no engagement of Sir John Hutchinson's would be right if of a nature to endanger the authority of the Porte', sent Mr. Straton, a member of the Embassy staff, to Egypt with instructions to try to persuade the beys to leave the country, and to offer them asylum in either India or England, with guaranteed pensions. Lord Cavan, who had replaced Hutchinson as Commander-in-Chief in Egypt, and who could not have been particularly pleased at Mr. Straton's intervention, refused either to use violent means to induce the beys to leave Egypt or to curtail their liberty while they remained in Egypt. Not for the first nor for the last time the British civil and military authorities were each pursuing separate and contradictory policies and each spending a good deal of time intriguing to defeat the policy of the other. Meanwhile, Hutchinson, who had returned to England, was endeavouring, with some success, to swing the British Government and popular opinion over to the support of the beys. Public opinion was shocked by Hutchinson's revelations of Turkish attempts to murder the beys, and impressed by the romantic attributes of the Mamelukes. The British Government was becoming disturbed at the increasingly close relations between France and Turkey.

By this time the Peace of Amiens had been signed and the war was over for the time being. Under the terms of the Peace the British Government had agreed to evacuate Egypt, and it was becoming urgently necessary for this agreement to be honoured. Sir John Stuart was sent out to replace Lord Cavan and arrange the evacuation. He was instructed to call at Constantinople on the way and, in concert with Lord Elgin, to try to make some suitable arrangement with the Turks for the administration of Egypt. In fact, the British Government had arrived at a policy which was to leave the Turks in control of Egypt, but to claim rights of protection over the Mamelukes. This would give the British Government an excuse to intervene in Egypt at any time and also give England a *point d'appui* for political manœuvring inside Egypt. From the point of view of this policy, the weakness of the Mamelukes was an advantage rather than a disadvantage. In pursuance of this policy, Elgin and Stuart approached the Porte with proposals, first for the restoration to the Mameluke beys of all their properties and, when this had been rejected, for the restoration of their properties in Upper Egypt. But the Turks insisted on the expulsion of the beys from Egypt, and negotiations broke down.

Stuart then proceeded to his command in Egypt. Soon after his arrival, his enthusiasm for the Mamelukes was temporarily diminished by the discovery that Elfi and Bardisi had established contact with one Sebastiani, a French agent who had been sent by Bonaparte to Egypt to fish in troubled waters. This discovery had the effect of bringing the British Government nearer to the Turkish viewpoint, and before many weeks a compromise agreement was negotiated by which the Porte agreed not to take any punitive action against the beys and to assign to them the province of Aswan in return for the evacuation of British troops from Egypt. From the point of view of British Government policy as described above, the agreement was not an unsatisfactory one, since it provided the British with a plausible excuse for re-entry into Egypt in defence of Mameluke interests. From the point of view of the British High Command in Egypt, the agreement was less satisfactory, since, in view of the support given by them to the Mameluke cause and in view of the fact that no reliance could be placed on Turkish undertakings, the Mamelukes might, not unreasonably, have accused them of breach of faith.

The British forces were evacuated in March 1803, after an occupation of just two years. Before departing, Stuart did what he could for the Mamelukes. He supplied them with arms and ammunition. He took Elfi Bey with him to England to plead his cause. And he left a British Agent in Egypt (there had been no British consular representative in Egypt since Baldwin's departure in 1796), a certain Major Misset, who, as time was to show, could be relied upon to support Mameluke interests in every possible way.

The British military occupation, after having accomplished its primary task of expelling the French from Egypt, had been almost entirely occupied in defending Mameluke interests against the Turks, and had made no direct contribution to the administration of the country, which, in so far as it was administered at all after the French evacuation, was administered by the Turks. The British had therefore come little into direct contact with the inhabitants, and left on the country no permanent impress of their occupation.

NOTES ON CHAPTER ONE

1. Copts. Members of the Monophysite or Coptic Church of Egypt. The Coptic Church seceded from the Orthodox Church after the Council of Chalcedon had declared Monophysitism heretical. At the time of the Moslem invasion it was the National Church to which nearly all Egyptians belonged. In 1800 they probably made up about 10 per cent. of the population of Egypt. There were a large number of Copts employed as clerks in government service, since in early Moslem times they had established a monopoly of keeping the government accounts.

2. Mameluke. The Arabic word *mamluk* means 'owned', and the name was derived from the slave origins of the Mamelukes. There were twenty-four Mameluke beys according to the twenty-four provinces into which the Turks had divided Egypt.

3. Shajaret-ed-Durr means 'spray of pearls'.

4. Bahri derives from *bahr*, meaning sea, a word colloquially applied to the Nile. Hence Bahri means 'of the Nile'.

5. Burji from *burj*, meaning 'tower'.

6. One of the beys, Khair Bey, was presented by Selim with a robe of honour, the Governorship of Cairo, and his name was changed to Khain (traitor) Bey.

7. *Multazimin*. Singular, *multazim*, meaning contractor.

8. Presumably the Mediterranean and Red Seas.

9. *'Ulema*. Singular, *'alim*, meaning 'learned man'. The religious dignitaries of al-Azhar, the great Moslem university and theological centre in Cairo.

10. Qadi, meaning 'judge'; properly speaking, a Judge of the Shari'a or Quranic Laq.

11. Battle of the Pyramids. This battle was fought in the plain of Embaba on the west bank of the Nile, opposite the port of Bulak and just west of the village of Embaba. The Pyramids would have been plainly visible from the battlefield, a few miles to the south-west.

12. Qusair. The route from Qusair to Qena is one of the oldest commercial routes between Europe and Asia. The Romans made a port at Myos Hormos, some miles north of Qusair, from which a fleet set out annually to Ceylon in search of spices and silks. When the fleet returned to Myos Hormos the cargo was conveyed across the desert to the Nile valley, by a road which is still visible, and floated down the Nile to the Mediterranean. In Moslem times Qusair, together with Jedda on the Arabian coast, was used instead of Suez as a.port of discharge for Eastern cargoes owing to the contrary winds prevailing in the Gulf of Suez. After the invention of the steam vessel and the digging of the Suez Canal, the route fell into disuse, but during the Second German War a military railway was constructed between Safaga (near Qusair) and Qena. There is also a motor road between Qena and Qusair.

13. Bonaparte devoted a certain amount of attention to 'welfare'. He was only prevented by the British blockade from anticipating E.N.S.A. and bringing variety artistes from France to entertain the troops.

CHAPTER TWO

GREAT BRITAIN AND MOHAMED ALI

WITH the evacuation of British troops from Egypt, responsibility for British interests there became divided between the British Ambassador in Constantinople and Major Misset, who had been left behind in Cairo by Sir John Stuart as an unofficial British Agent. It has already been noted that throughout the period of the British occupation there had been a marked divergence of opinion between the British Embassy in Constantinople and the British High Command in Cairo as to the policy to be pursued in Egypt. With the disappearance of the immediate practical problems created by the occupation this divergence became even more marked. On the one hand, Drummond, who had replaced Elgin as Ambassador, was writing to the Foreign Office that 'it can never be consistent with our policy to leave the Beys in independent possession of Egypt . . . any connexion which we may desire to keep with Egypt may be more effectively and easily maintained through the medium of the Porte. . . . While Egypt continues to be an integral part of the Ottoman Empire its invasion by a foreign Power is less likely to happen than if it were subject to the Mamelukes. . . . I am inclined to lament that measures were not effectively taken to secure the sovereignty of Egypt to the Turks since it was deemed expedient to recall British troops.' On the other hand, Misset, backed by Stuart and Elfi Bey, who were conducting a strenuous Mameluke propaganda campaign in London, was actively and openly encouraging the Mameluke beys in their revolt against the Turkish Pasha, Khusrev Pasha, which broke out within a few weeks of the British evacuation.

The Turks were garrisoning Egypt with a mixed force of Turkish and Albanian troops which would have been sufficient to deal with the Mameluke revolt had not the Albanian troops, under Taher Pasha, the Turkish Vice-Governor, mutinied and joined the Mameluke rebels. Taher Pasha was killed almost immediately, and the leadership of the Albanian mutineers devolved on Mohamed Ali, an Albanian officer who had landed at Rosetta with the Turkish expedition in 1801.[1] The Mamelukes and Albanians deposed Khusrev Pasha, who fled to Damietta, where he was captured by the Mamelukes under Bardisi Bey. At this point British activity in Egypt had got into such a tangle that one serving British officer, a Major Hayes, was assisting Khusrev Pasha, while Major Misset, another serving British officer, was assisting the rebellious beys.

Shortly after Khusrev's capture, Elfi Bey, puffed up by his reception in London, returned to Egypt on board a British frigate, and immediately started quarrelling with Bardisi Bey. This Mameluke split played into the hands of Mohamed Ali, whose potentialities appear to have passed completely unrecognized by Major Misset. Mohamed Ali first allied himself with Bardisi, whom he assisted in driving Elfi and his followers out of Cairo and into the desert. He then turned on Bardisi and demanded, as the price of his help, the arrears of pay owing to his Albanian soldiers. Bardisi, as Shaykh-al-Balad, attempted to raise the money from the inhabitants of Cairo in order to satisfy the Albanians. Whereupon Mohamed Ali incited the inhabitants of Cairo to revolt in protest against Bardisi's rapacity. (It will be recalled that the Cairene revolt against the French in 1798 was occasioned by an attempt to raise taxes from an urban population which had been accustomed to see the whole burden of taxation resting on the shoulders of the cultivators.) It was now Bardisi's turn to flee to the desert, whither he was accompanied by the aged Ibrahim Bey. Having disposed of Elfi and Bardisi, there remained only the Turkish Governor, Khurshid Pasha, who had replaced

Khusrev Pasha, and who had remained inactive and impotent in the Citadel while Mohamed Ali had been dealing with the Mameluke leaders. The popular rising against Bardisi was easily diverted against the Pasha; Khurshid was deposed by popular acclamation in favour of Mohamed Ali, who proclaimed himself Pasha of Egypt, at the same time acknowledging his dutiful submission to the Sublime Porte (May 1805).

The Porte, faced with Mohamed Ali's *fait accompli*, first of all tried to tempt him to leave Egypt by offering him the Pashalik of Salonika. That attempt having failed, the Capitan-Pasha was sent to Egypt to report on the situation. Having studied and rejected the possibility of engineering a Mameluke revolt against Mohamed Ali, the Capitan-Pasha, more clairvoyant than the British Agent, recommended to Constantinople that Mohamed Ali should be recognized and confirmed as Pasha. This recommendation was accepted, and in November 1806 Mohamed Ali became, in name as well as in fact, Pasha of Egypt.

This acceptance of Mohamed Ali by Constantinople removed any difficulty which the British Embassy might have felt about the attitude to be adopted, and Arbuthnot, the British Ambassador, peremptorily instructed Misset to abandon his intrigues with Elfi. Within a few weeks of Mohamed Ali's confirmation as Pasha, such chance as there might have been of a Mameluke revival was extinguished by the deaths of Elfi and Bardisi within a few days of each other.

Meanwhile, war had broken out again in Europe. The Battle of Trafalgar had finally ended Bonaparte's prospects of invading England. The battle of Austerlitz had brought Austria to her knees. Russia, who persisted in combining hostility to Bonaparte with hostility to the Sultan, had thrown Turkey into the French camp, thus sharpening British fears of a second French occupation of Egypt. These fears were duly played upon by that section of British military opinion which was still smarting from the defeat of its

Egyptian policy by Mohamed Ali. Misset, who had apparently come to realize that a Mameluke restoration was out of the question, was agitating for the annexation of Egypt by England in order to prevent it from falling into the hands of France. He appears both to have under-estimated Mohamed Ali's strength and to have over-estimated his willingness to identify himself with Turkish policy. If England had been ready to protect him from the consequences and to guarantee his position in Egypt, there is little doubt that Mohamed Ali would have been prepared to co-operate with England in keeping the French out of Egypt. Instead, the British Government, relying presumably on Misset's advice, made preparations for the despatch of an expeditionary force to Egypt.

The record of General Fraser's expedition is one of the most melancholy in British military history. In March 1807 General Fraser landed in Egypt with 5,000 men and captured Alexandria without any serious resistance being offered. Misset attached himself to the expedition as a kind of unofficial political officer after having given Shahin Bey, the leader of the surviving Mameluke beys, to understand that the purpose of the expedition was to depose Mohamed Ali. As a result of this intimation, the remnants of the Mamelukes started mobilizing in Upper Egypt, but soon desisted when they saw that no encouragement was forthcoming from General Fraser. Mohamed Ali, who realized that he would not, in the long run, establish himself in Egypt in face of British hostility, was not prepared, if he could help it, to incur that hostility in defence of the sovereign rights of his suzerain. He therefore made friendly overtures to Fraser, which were rejected, by Misset's advice, on the ground that friendship with Mohamed Ali would alienate the local inhabitants. (It does not seem to have occurred to Misset that Mohamed Ali's position *vis-à-vis* the local inhabitants was precisely the same as that of the Mamelukes, in that he was an usurper of foreign blood, but professing the Moslem faith, who had imposed himself on the country by means of military force in the same way as the Mamelukes had done.) Mohamed Ali, having thus unceremoniously been thrust back into the arms of his suzerain, proceeded to oppose Fraser's advance into the Delta. Again acting on Misset's advice, Fraser attempted to capture Rosetta (a reasonable operation on the assumption that the object of the expedition was to deny Egypt to the French), but two attacks, under Generals Wauchope and Stuart respectively, were repulsed with fairly heavy casualties. Mohamed Ali then proceeded to drive the British forces into Alexandria and to invest the town.

The whole face of European affairs was then changed by the news of the signature of the Treaty of Tilsit between Bonaparte and the Czar of Russia. The situation was analogous to that created in August 1939 when Hitler and Stalin made the Pact which precipitated the Second German War. As far as Europe as a whole was concerned, the effect of the treaty was to make the balance of power swing temporarily and precariously in favour of France. But in the eastern Mediterranean the effect was to send Turkey scuttling out of the French and into the British camp. It was clear that one of the implications of the treaty was a free hand for Russia against Turkey, and in these circumstances Turkey was compelled to sue for British friendship. This sudden development robbed the Fraser expedition of any justification which it might originally have possessed, and it was evacuated from Alexandria in September 1807. Mohamed Ali made no attempt to oppose the evacuation, and released such British prisoners as had fallen into his hands. All that was left in Egypt to commemorate this futile expedition were the heads of a number of decapitated British soldiers adorning the pleasure grounds of Ezbekieh on the western outskirts of Cairo. Major Misset accompanied the evacuating troops. The record of events has rendered judgement of his diplomacy superfluous.

Within a year of Fraser's departure, Mohamed Ali completed the ruin of the Mamelukes with his famous party at the Citadel, at which the remaining Mameluke beys and their followers were treacherously slaughtered almost to a man.[2] The Mameluke domination of Egypt had been ended by Bonaparte at the Battle of the Pyramids in 1798. The possibility of Mameluke rule in Egypt under Turkish or British protection had been destroyed by Mohamed Ali's coup in May 1805. But they still remained a potential nuisance, in spite of a preliminary purge carried out by Mohamed Ali in September 1805, when a number of the beys were ambushed and slaughtered near the Bab-ez-Zuweila[3] in Cairo. After their attempted rising in Upper Egypt on the occasion of Fraser's landing, Mohamed Ali determined to exterminate them once and for all. His first act after Fraser's departure was to deprive the beys of their rights as *multazimin*, but he blunted the edge of their resentment by enabling them to live in peace and comparative affluence in their Cairo palaces. Having thus herded them together into the capital, and having lulled them by fair treatment into a false sense of security, he administered the *coup de grâce*. Deprived of their peasant followers, shorn of their warlike attributions, and softened by urban life, the Mamelukes were an easy prey.

Mohamed Ali was now undisputed ruler of Egypt under the suzerainty of the Sultan. But already his ambitions were reaching out beyond Egypt, and he was dreaming of recreating an Empire coterminous with that ruled over by his Fatimid and Mameluke predecessors. He was quick to realize that the attainment of such an empire depended on the goodwill of England, who would never permit, and who was in a position to prevent, the rise of a hostile power on the western land approaches to her Indian possessions. Mohamed Ali was therefore resolved never to be provoked by resentment at British methods to any display of hostility towards England. He was too far-sighted to make the mistake of measuring England by the silliness of Misset's diplomacy or by the weakness of Fraser's army.

From the British side, the establishment of a stable

government in Egypt under a ruler who appeared to be disposed to accept Turkish suzerainty represented an ideal solution to the Egyptian question now that the menace of a Franco-Turkish alliance had been removed. Mohamed Ali's campaign against the Wahhabis[4] (1809–15), ending in the capture of the Wahhabi capital of Dariya and the execution of the reigning Sa'udi Amir, was watched with wary but not unfriendly eyes by the British in the Persian Gulf. His expedition to the Sudan in 1820 in search of ivory, gold-dust, and slaves was viewed without serious concern. The powers were not yet interested in Central Africa. So long as Mohamed Ali confined his ambitions to the deserts of Arabia and the jungles of Africa, he could rely on continued British benevolence. But in 1821 a Greek revolt broke out against Turkey which was destined once more to make the eastern Mediterranean a theatre of European rivalry and once more to bring Mohamed Ali into conflict with Great Britain.

The Greek insurrection developed into a bitter and prolonged struggle marked by appalling atrocities on both sides. In their attempts to crush the rebels the Turks suffered a severe disability from their weakness at sea. The Greeks seized command of the Aegean, and so denied to the Turks their most convenient road of approach to Greece. The Sultan called upon his vassal Mohamed Ali to assist him with the resources of the Egyptian Navy, created by Mohamed Ali in the new shipyards which he had constructed at Alexandria. This request caused Mohamed Ali some embarrassment. The Greek revolt had already attracted the attention of the powers. Russia, who had long regarded herself as having rights of protection over the Greek Orthodox subjects of the Sublime Porte, was certain to try to take advantage of a favourable opportunity to put pressure on Constantinople and to create an independent but Russian-protected State on the Mediterranean. Great Britain and France were determined not to let Russia intervene unilaterally on behalf of Greece. Public opinion in all these countries was in favour of Greece. It was certain that any act of assistance by Mohamed Ali to the Sultan would be most unfavourably regarded by the powers. On the other hand, the Sultan, who had been most suspicious of Mohamed Ali's motives in building a fleet, made it clear that refusal to use that fleet in the service of his suzerain would be considered as an act of rebellion. If Mohamed Ali had been able to rely upon the support of the powers in such an act of rebellion, it is possible that he would have defied the Sultan. But his experience of the powers had warned him that, after having used him to help settle the Greek question, they were quite capable of assisting the Sultan to depose him by way of compensation for having compelled the Sultan to yield to the Greeks. So, reluctantly, and after long delays and complicated evasions, Mohamed Ali sent sixteen warships into Greek waters to assist his suzerain.

Meanwhile, the diplomatic wrangles of the powers had crystallized into a conference in London at which it was decided to inform the Sultan that autonomy must be granted to the Greeks and that the powers were prepared to mediate between Turkey and the Greeks on that basis. The Sultan refused to negotiate and called on Mohamed Ali for more help. After some bargaining, Mohamed Ali obtained from the Sultan the promise of the Pashaliks of Crete, Damascus, Tripoli, and Syria in return for the despatch of an Egyptian force to occupy the Morea. Once again the powers had to choose between what amounted to support for Mohamed Ali's imperial ambitions and a prolongation of the Greek war. After some delay, Mohamed Ali, having no promise of support from the powers equivalent to that which he had been promised by the Sultan, despatched his son Ibrahim Pasha at the head of 5,000 troops to the Morea (1825).[5]

Mohamed Ali had burnt his boats in a more literal sense than he realized. Russia, impatient at the Sultan's obstinacy, and at the same time anxious to take unilateral advantage of it, concentrated troops on the Russo-Turkish frontier. A British naval squadron was sent into Greek waters. Concerted pressure by the powers would undoubtedly have brought the Sultan to heel without the necessity for any fighting. But Great Britain and Russia were mutually suspicious, and were each anxious to turn the situation to their own advantage. In the event, each of the two powers, without consulting the other, took violent action against Turkey. The British squadron under Admiral Codrington, which was cruising in Greek waters, attacked and destroyed the Turco-Egyptian fleet while it was at anchor in the harbour of Navarino. The Russians overran Moldavia and Wallachia and reached the Danube. The British Government was not prepared to follow up the victory at Navarino (which appears to have embarrassed the British Government almost as much as it dismayed the Turkish and Egyptian Governments) with further naval or military action. The Russians pursued their advance on Constantinople, forced the Turks to treat for peace and, at the Treaty of Adrianople, secured sovereign independence for a Greek state. Great Britain, who, in her nineteenth-century dealing with the Ottoman Empire, was to perfect the technique of depriving Russia at the conference table of what she had won on the field of battle, joined France in a protest at the Treaty of Adrianople as being a breach of the undertakings given at London to the effect that none of the powers would make a separate settlement with the Porte over the Greek question. Russia was compelled to submit the Treaty of Adrianople for ratification at a second conference of the powers held in London. At this conference the Adrianople terms were revised so as to exclude Thessaly from the boundaries of the new Greek state, and to substitute autonomy for the independence agreed to at Adrianople. Thus ended a course of disputation, fighting, and bargaining from which none of the principals, except the Greeks themselves, emerged with very much moral or material credit.

Mohamed Ali had suffered twice from British displeasure as a result of co-operation with the Sultan. He was in the future destined to suffer a great deal more British displeasure as a result of opposition to the Sultan. This opposition developed from the Sultan's refusal to honour the promises made to Mohamed Ali as the price of Egyptian assistance in Greece. Mohamed Ali had not only lost his fleet and incurred the enmity of the Powers as the result of that assistance, but had, by that assistance, saved the Sultan from a humiliating defeat at the hands of the Greeks. He was not unnaturally insistent on obtaining the promised reward as compensation for his losses and as payment for his services. The only reason for his continued loyalty to the Sultan had been his feeling that the Sultan was able to offer him more for his money than he could have obtained elsewhere. It now appeared that a point had been reached at which the Sultan considered that Mohamed Ali had achieved the maximum of power compatible with continued subordination to Turkey. In other words, loyalty to the Sultan had exhausted its usefulness.

The time was favourable for successful rebellion against Turkey. The Sultan, Mahmud II, had just followed Mohamed Ali's example and exterminated the Janissaries, who had long played in Turkey the same role as the Mamelukes had played in Egypt. This step paved the way for a reorganization of the Turkish Army on more modern lines, but caused, for the time being, a severe weakening of Turkish military power. France, whose Eastern ambitions had not evaporated with the fall of Bonaparte, seemed disposed to regard the aggrandisement of Mohamed Ali as a means of furthering her designs. Great Britain, with her growing commercial and strategic interests in Egypt, while viewing with some uneasiness the possible extent of Mohamed Ali's ultimate ambitions, was unwilling immediately to pick a quarrel with the man who was to all intents and purposes absolute master of Egypt.

With these considerations in mind, Mohamed Ali placed his son, Ibrahim Pasha, who had commanded the Egyptian expeditions to the Nejd against the Wahhabis and to the Morea against the Greeks, at the head of an army of some 40,000 men, which set out across Sinai for the invasion of

Syria (1831). After the reduction of the fortress of Akka, the key to Syria from the south, Ibrahim Pasha overran all Syria without difficulty. If he had stopped there, it is unlikely that any serious opposition would have been encountered from the powers. But, flushed with victory and desirous of preventing the possibility of a Turkish counter-stroke, Ibrahim Pasha advanced into Asia Minor, defeated the Turks at Konya, and continued his advance westward as far as Brusa. By this time the powers had become seriously alarmed. The Ottoman Empire seemed on the point of dissolution. The Russians, who had acquired considerable influence in Constantinople since the Greek War, moved first and landed an army at Constantinople to protect the capital. Great Britain and France, horrified as usual at any unilateral action by Russia in the affairs of the Ottoman Empire, hastily followed with assurances of diplomatic and, if necessary, armed support. Mohamed Ali was not prepared to challenge this formidable combination. A conference was arranged, as a result of which it was agreed that Mohamed Ali should withdraw from Asia Minor in return for confirmation in the Pashaliks of Egypt, Crete, Syria, Damascus, and Tripoli for the period of his lifetime. The Russians withdrew their troops from Constantinople, and another eastern European crisis was over. Mohamed Ali had extorted from the Sultan the redemption of his promises in full and had, for the time being, secured the goodwill of the powers on account of his moderate and reasonable behaviour in front of Constantinople.

Although France joined Great Britain and Russia in bringing Mohamed Ali to a halt in front of Constantinople, she had not abandoned her ideas of establishing French supremacy in the eastern Mediterranean by means of an alliance with Mohamed Ali which would substitute French protection for Turkish suzerainty in Egypt.

French interest in the Levant dated back long before the Bonaparte expedition, which was an incident in and not the origin of the history of French connexions with the Levant.

France had always regarded the Crusades as having been specifically a French enterprise,[6] and found some justification in this from the fact that during the time of the Crusades, and indeed for several hundred years afterwards, Europeans in the Levant were usually referred to under the generic name of 'Franks'. France had been the first state, with the exception of Venice, to establish diplomatic relations with the Ottoman Empire. A treaty which was the origin of the system of capitulations had been signed between Francis I and Sulayman the Magnificent in 1535, and until well on into the seventeenth century France had been, in both diplomacy and commerce, the foremost European nation in the Levant. Thereafter her influence had declined, both absolutely as a result of British and Dutch competition, and relatively as a result of the decline of the overland and the development of the Cape route to the East. The loss of her Eastern possessions in the Seven Years' War had accelerated the decline of France's Levant trade and prestige, and by the end of the eighteenth century the traditional French connexions with the Levant had almost entirely disappeared.

But there was still one important source of contact. In Syria the French had, since the beginning of the seventeenth century, been closely identified with the Roman Catholic religious houses which played such a prominent part in the creation of the Uniate Churches[7] later in the century. This identification had caused France to claim for herself the same rights of protection over Uniate Christians in the Ottoman Empire as the Russians had secured at the Treaty of Kainarji over Orthodox Christians. This French right had never been recognized by treaty, but became recognized *de facto* by most of the European powers during the course of the nineteenth century.

Bonaparte's expedition to Egypt caused a revival of French interest in the Levant which not only survived Bonaparte, but became a permanent and prominent feature of French foreign policy for the next 150 years.

In these circumstances, it was not surprising that Great

Britain should view with disfavour the French diplomatic approaches to Mohamed Ali. The strategic and commercial importance of the Levant was becoming revolutionized as a result of the invention of the steam vessel. The possibilities of the Suez-Alexandria overland route had been greatly circumscribed in the days of sail owing to the difficulties experienced by sailing vessels in combating the prevailing north winds in the Gulf of Suez. So great was this difficulty that sailing vessels bound from the East usually discharged their cargoes either at Jidda for transhipment by the caravan route to Syria or at Qusair, where the cargo was conveyed by caravan across the desert to the Nile Valley and thence down the river to the Mediterranean. Owing to the considerable difficulties attending the proper organization of the latter route, the route via Jidda had achieved something of a monopoly, a fact which induced the Sultan to attempt to forbid the transhipment of cargo at Suez when the advent of the steamship made this route more expeditious than the Jidda one.

The steamship similarly opened up opportunities of developing the overland route to and from the East via Aleppo and the Euphrates,[8] although in the event the advantages of this route were completely eclipsed by the rapid development of the Suez route under the aegis of Mohamed Ali.

Within a few years of the invention of the steamship the average length of time taken by a passage from England to India had been reduced to forty days by the overland route as compared with an average of five months via the Cape (which in the early days of steam was only practicable by sailing ships, as the paddles of the early steamers were liable to damage in the high seas of the Atlantic). Great Britain's interest in these new possibilities of rapid communication was obvious, both from the commercial and from the strategic points of view. The necessity of ensuring that no European rival should place herself athwart these new lines of communication became imperative. The invention of the steamship was followed by intensive British diplomatic and naval activity in the Red Sea and Persian Gulf with a view to ensuring safety of access to and navigation on these waterways for British ships. Piracy in the Persian Gulf was brought under control. A British Consulate was established at Jidda in 1825. The island of Socotra was occupied in 1835, and Aden in 1839.[9]

Meanwhile, in 1830 the first steam voyage had been made between Bombay and Suez, and in 1836 the Oriental Steamship Company started a regular service of steamers between London and Alexandria. In 1834 an Englishman named Waghorn started to organize a regular transit service for passengers and goods between Alexandria and Suez. The continuation and development of all this British-inspired activity was, of course, dependent on the existence in Egypt of a government friendly to British interests. It was not only the development of trade, the convenience of passengers, and the celerity of mails which were at stake. The establishment of another European power in Egypt and Syria would have meant that that power would have been in a position to send troops to India from Europe quicker than any British troops could be despatched to India from England. It is in the light of this significant fact that British suspicions of French approaches to Mohamed Ali can best be appreciated.

Mohamed Ali was by no means unaware of British anxieties, and would probably at any time have been willing to exchange French for British support had any indication of British support been forthcoming. But Great Britain, apprehensive as she was of French designs, was not disposed to try and outbid France in competing for Mohamed Ali's favours. The encouragement of Mohamed Ali's ambitions would almost certainly have led to the disintegration of the Ottoman Empire, and while in that event Mohamed Ali might well have inherited the eastern part of the Empire, Russia would have almost certainly have annexed the western part, including Constantinople. In this way one danger would have been averted only at the expense of creating another. It therefore became the aim of British policy on the one hand to detach Mohamed Ali from France and on the other hand to preserve the Ottoman Empire from his ambitions. These apparently irreconcilable objectives were both successfully realized.

In 1838 Mohamed Ali, with French encouragement, withheld payment of the annual tribute in respect of his pashaliks. The Ottoman Army was still in no position to fight Mohamed Ali, but, against the advice of Lord Ponsonby, British Ambassador at Constantinople, a Turkish force under Hafiz Pasha was sent into Syria and was decisively defeated by Ibrahim Pasha at Nezib, near Aleppo, in May 1839. A worse disaster was to follow. A Turkish fleet, under the command of Ahmed Fevzi, the Capitan-Pasha, which had set out from the Dardanelles for Syria, changed course in mid-voyage and steered for Alexandria, where the Capitan-Pasha deserted with his fleet to Mohamed Ali. The course of events now depended on whether Russia would defy Great Britain and attempt to partition the Ottoman Empire with Mohamed Ali, or whether she would co-operate with Great Britain in the maintenance of Ottoman integrity. Great Britain's naval power was sufficient to persuade her to take the latter course. Diplomatic conversations were initiated by Russia with the British Government, of which Lord Palmerston was Foreign Secretary. A general agreement was reached between the two countries to the effect that Ottoman integrity was to be safeguarded and that Mohamed Ali was to be made to restore the Turkish fleet and to evacuate Syria. The Ambassadors of the two countries at Constantinople were instructed accordingly. At the same time the newly-appointed British Consul-General in Egypt, Colonel Hodges, was instructed to warn Mohamed Ali of the British and Russian attitude, to inform him that Austria had associated herself with Great Britain and Russia, and to advise him to restore the fleet and evacuate Syria forthwith (January 1840). The peremptoriness of the British attitude may be judged from the following extract from

44

Palmerston's instructions to Hodges: '. . . to a garrison which capitulates in time honourable conditions are granted, but a garrison which insists on being stormed must take the chances of war'. Nothing could have been clearer. But Mohamed Ali refused to yield. On Hodges's asking him what he intended to do with the Turkish fleet, he replied that he intended to keep it until his 'differences' with the Turks had been settled. There seems little doubt that Mohamed Ali's obstinacy was the result of French encouragement, which inclined him to believe that France was able to drive a wedge between Great Britain and Russia. This the French, whose diplomacy at Constantinople was almost traditionally inept, failed to do. A Conference of Ambassadors, consisting of the representatives of Great Britain, Russia, and Austria at Constantinople, drew up a convention by the terms of which Mohamed Ali was promised the hereditary Pashalik of Egypt and the life term of the Pashalik of Akka in return for the immediate restoration of the Turkish fleet and the evacuation of northern Syria. If this offer were not accepted within ten days, that part of the offer relating to Akka was to be withdrawn; if it were not accepted within twenty days, he was to be deposed from the Pashalik of Egypt as well. (It is to be noted that Sultan Mahmud II had died just after the Battle of Nezib, and that for the next few critical weeks the Conference of Ambassadors virtually directed the policy of the Ottoman Empire.) An Ottoman envoy was sent to Egypt to acquaint Mohamed Ali with the terms of this ultimatum, which were also confirmed to him by the Consuls of Great Britain, Russia, and Austria. Mohamed Ali, still acting under French advice, returned a series of evasive answers until the stipulated twenty days had elapsed. On the expiry of this period the Porte declared his deposition from the Pashalik of Egypt, and the three Consuls departed from Alexandria (August 1840).

Military action now succeeded diplomatic negotiation. A combined British-Austrian-Russian-Turkish naval squadron arrived off Beirut escorting an Anglo-Turkish military force.[10] This force, under the command of Sir Charles Smith, was landed in Junieh Bay on 3 September 1840. The French, who had long-standing and intimate connections with the Maronite inhabitants of the Lebanon, tried to persuade them to resist the invaders. But the rule of Ibrahim Pasha had been too oppressive for the inhabitants to be prepared to fight for the privilege of seeing it maintained. A second Anglo-Turkish force was landed at Saida, and the Amir Beshir Shihab, the semi-autonomous ruler of the Lebanon, who was bound by ties of gratitude to Mohamed Ali and who had supported the régime of Ibrahim Pasha, was deposed. Ibrahim Pasha himself was defeated in the mountains above Junieh, and the towns of Tripoli and Beirut surrendered. The naval squadron moved south and bombarded and captured Akka. France, who had tried to bluff Great Britain and Russia into believing that she would take up arms on behalf of Mohamed Ali, had in the event taken no action at all except for her abortive attempt to stimulate the Maronites to what would have been a futile and costly resistance. Their diplomatic failure and military inactivity were bitterly resented by Mohamed Ali, who complained publicly to the French Consul that he had been led to disaster by listening to French advice and that he had not received any effective help from France.

In November 1840 Commodore Napier arrived off Alexandria with the British part of the Allied squadron which had been operating in Syrian waters. He had with him a copy of a despatch written by Lord Palmerston to Lord Ponsonby expressing the British Government's view that, if Mohamed Ali were to submit to the Sultan, return the fleet, and evacuate Syria, he should be granted the hereditary Pashalik of Egypt under the Sultan's suzerainty. Commodore Napier exercised a wise discretion in communicating the contents of this despatch privately to Mohamed Ali, together with his personal advice that he should offer his submission in accordance with the terms of the British proposal.

Mohamed Ali's position was hopeless. Tripoli, Beirut, Saida, and Akka were in British or Turkish hands. Ibrahim Pasha had been driven out of the mountains and was trying to regroup his forces in the plain of the Biq'a. There was no assistance to be expected from the French. A British squadron was lying off Alexandria. After an interview with Napier, he signified his willingness to accept Palmerston's terms provided that they were confirmed by the Porte. A temporary difficulty then arose in that Stopford, the Commander-in-Chief of the Mediterranean fleet, and Smith, the Commander of the Anglo-Turkish forces in Syria, disapproved of Napier's initiative. But the British Government, possibly remembering a similar situation which had arisen forty years previously with Sir Sidney Smith over the Convention of al-Arish, supported Napier, and authorized him to tell Mohamed Ali that, although they were not in a position to dictate to the Porte, and although they had no intention of bargaining with the Porte on his behalf, they were prepared to recommend that he should be granted the hereditary Pashalik of Egypt provided that he restored the fleet and evacuated Syria forthwith. As a result of this communication, Mohamed Ali ordered Ibrahim Pasha to return to Egypt with his army, and at the same time released the Turkish fleet, which was still lying at anchor in Alexandria Harbour. Sir Charles Smith secured from his Turkish allies, not without difficulty, the unmolested withdrawal of Ibrahim Pasha and his army from Syria; Admiral Walker, a British naval officer seconded to the Turks, had the satisfaction of hoisting the Turkish flag on the Turkish flagship *Mahmudieh* in Alexandria harbour (January 1841). A month later, on 4 February, the appointment of Mohamed Ali as hereditary Pasha of Egypt was officially gazetted in Constantinople.

Great Britain had won a notable diplomatic victory. She had avoided the partition of the Ottoman Empire in circumstances which would have inevitably divided that Empire into spheres of Russian and French influence. She had utterly discredited French influence at the Court of Mohamed Ali, and thus removed the threat of French domination of the overland route to India. She had earned the goodwill of Mohamed Ali, in spite of the measures which she had initiated against him, by securing for him the hereditary Pashalik of Egypt at a time when, without such support, he would almost inevitably have been deposed. In the attainment of these objectives she had secured the collaboration of Russia without having to acquiesce in any concession to Russia at the expense of the Ottoman Empire. On the debit side she had incurred the enmity of France, which was, however, appeased by allowing that country freely to pursue her imperial ambitions in North-West Africa as compensation for the frustration of her schemes in the Levant.

The differences which had arisen between Great Britain and Mohamed Ali over Greece and Syria had been unaccompanied by any undue display of rancour on either side. Diplomatic disputes and even martial clashes had not interrupted the steady development of British commercial interests in Egypt, nor had they prevented Mohamed Ali from employing British experts in many of his schemes of modernization. We have already described how the invention of the steamship increased the importance of, and stimulated British interest in, the overland route to and from the East via Alexandria and Suez. Mohamed Ali at all times whole-heartedly supported British enterprise in the development of this route. He defied the Sultan's *firman* which attempted to create a monopoly of the transit trade for Jidda by forbidding the unloading of eastern cargoes at Suez. He arranged for the construction and policing of a coach-road between Cairo and Suez, assisted in the establishment of rest-houses at various stages along the route[11] and organized a system of semaphore signalling between the two towns.[12] In 1819, at the suggestion of an Englishman named Samuel Briggs,[13] he caused the Mahmudieh Canal[14] to be dug from Alexandria to Atf on the Rosetta branch of the Nile, thus connecting Alexandria directly with Egypt's

48

main traffic artery. By 1841 a regular service of steamboats run by the P. & O. Company was plying between Alexandria and Cairo. With the advent of the steamship, Mohamed Ali organized a series of camel caravans for the transport of coal from Alexandria to Suez, which enabled coal to be sold to steamships at Suez for £3 per ton. In 1834 he arranged for a survey to be made by a British engineer named Galloway, who had already constructed a foundry for Mohamed Ali at Bulaq, for the construction of a railway between Cairo and Suez. (Many of the materials for the construction of this railway were actually purchased and landed in Egypt when Galloway's death put an end to the scheme for the time being.)

As a result of all these developments, the overland route via Egypt became established as the normal method of passenger travel between England and India. In 1840 275 passengers travelled by the overland route; in 1845 2,300; in 1846, 3,000. By this time it was possible to travel from Alexandria to Suez in three days at a cost of £15 by a combination of steamboat from Alexandria to Cairo and stage coach from Cairo to Suez.

Very great importance was attached by the British Government to the development of this route, not only for reasons of commerce and convenience, but also in view of the strategical implications which have been indicated. This importance was reflected in the care that was always taken to try to respect the dignity and prestige of Mohamed Ali even when it became necessary to oppose his expansionist ambitions. For his part, Mohamed Ali displayed, on the whole, a sagacious understanding of British imperial necessities. Any deficiencies in the extent of that understanding were repaired by the events of 1839–41, which also appear finally to have convinced Mohamed Ali of the essential identity of interest between himself and Great Britain. A striking illustration of this is to be found in his refusal to lend any encouragement to the various French-inspired schemes for the construction of a canal across the

Isthmus of Suez on the ground that the construction of such a canal would bring Egypt into conflict with Great Britain, whose control of communications to the East would thereby be endangered.

It is impossible even to begin to visualize the Egypt of the second half of the nineteenth century without an understanding of what Mohamed Ali accomplished in the way of economic development during the first half. When Mohamed Ali was proclaimed Pasha by the '*ulema* of al-Azhar in 1805, Egypt had a population of about two and a half millions. In 1847, two years before Mohamed Ali's death, the population of Egypt was four and a half millions. During the same period the population of Alexandria increased tenfold, from 15,000 to 150,000. In 1800 the cultivated area of Egypt amounted to 3,200,000 *feddans* (1 *feddan* equals 1 acre approx.); by 1852 it had increased to 4,150,000 *feddans*. In 1798 the Government revenue amounted to an equivalent of £1,203,500, of which £1,052,450 was from land tax. In 1846 the revenue amounted to £4,200,000, of which about half was derived from land tax. Between 1800 and 1840 exports rose from a value of about £200,000 annually to a value of something over £2,000,000. Imports over the same period rose by about the same amount. (It is interesting to note that by the end of Mohamed Ali's reign Great Britain bought about half of Egypt's total exports and supplied Egypt with about one-third of her total imports.)

This development, which was all the more remarkable in view of the almost continual wars in which Mohamed Ali was engaged, came about mainly as the result of improvements in irrigation which made possible the cultivation of summer crops in general and cotton in particular, and which also minimized the effects of exceptionally high or exceptionally low flood seasons. The essence of Egypt's traditional system of irrigation had been the direction of flood water into enclosed basins of cultivated land, and the subsequent draining off of water from the basins after the silt in suspense had been deposited on the soil. The 'basin' system involved the construction of canals from the river leading into and out of a series of basins through which the water, controlled by sluices in the earth walls of the basins, proceeded by force of gravity until finally it drained off again into the river. In the Delta, where the fall of the water was insufficient to allow for the filling and drainage of basins, the land was irrigated by means of canals led off from the river, out of which the water was lifted on to the fields by means of primitive irrigation engines, such as the *shadoof*, the *saqia*, and the Archimedes screw. Under the Mamelukes this system, which required continual and careful maintenance, had fallen into disrepair. The basin walls had not been maintained and the canals had silted up. The neglect of man had been unable entirely to nullify the bounty of Nature, but as a result of this neglect Egypt had become unable in any way to mitigate the periodical incidence of drought as the result of low, and flood as the result of high, Niles, and had been unable to prevent much cultivated land from becoming swamp through lack of drainage.

One of Mohamed Ali's first acts after his assumption of power was to abolish the old system of *multazimin* (who had started as tax-farmers and had ended up as semi-autonomous provincial governors) and to declare all the land of Egypt as belonging to the State. This apparently arbitrary measure was in fact an indispensable preliminary to an urgently necessary reform of the system of land tenure. Having taken over all the land in the name of the State, and having dispossessed all the previous owners (who mostly consisted of the Mameluke beys), he distributed part of it in estates to members of his family and entourage, but retained most of it as State property cultivated by the previous tenants. In course of time these tenants became, to all intents and purposes, the owners of the land they cultivated, provided that they paid their taxes. For example, in 1854, provision was made for the registration of land in the name of the occupier on the evidence of his taxation receipts, and in 1858 the Moslem law of inheritance was made officially applicable to land so registered. These two types of ownership—land granted by the State in return for services rendered (*sic*), and land accruing to the occupier as the result of continued occupancy—were known as *ushuri* and *kharaj* respectively. The *ushuri*[15] lands were exempt from half the land tax in virtue of the terms on which they were originally granted to their owners. The *kharaj* lands were thus the main source of the land tax, from which was derived the annual tribute paid to Constantinople. (Hence the name *kharaj*, meaning 'that which goes out'.)

The system of tax farming was abolished, and instead Mohamed Ali created a hierarchy of officials, depending from the central government, who were responsible for the collection of taxes, for the control of irrigation, and for the maintenance of public security. Under this system (which in its essentials still exists in the Egyptian provinces), Egypt was divided into provinces, each under a *mudir*, or governor. These provinces, or *mudiriyas*, were subdivided into *markazes*, each under a *mamur*, who had under him the *umdas*, or headmen, of the various villages.

Having thus brought the cultivated land under his direct control, Mohamed Ali was able to proceed with his irrigation works. He caused the basin walls to be repaired and the canals to be redug. But he did not stop there. The traditional system only provided for irrigation during the time of high Nile. There was no water available for summer crops during the time of low Nile, when the land, perforce, lay fallow. For this reason it was impracticable to grow the sub-tropical crops for which the climate of the Egyptian summer was, in other respects, suitable. Mohamed Ali, who had a keen eye for industrial developments in Europe, and who knew all about the boom in textiles resulting from the invention of mechanical spinning and weaving, quickly saw the possibilities of cotton cultivation in Egypt.[16] The climate was suitable. Transport to the sea-coast was cheap and easy. European markets were not too far distant. A profitable export crop would provide the money necessary for the Western goods and services which he was determined to introduce into Egypt. The only thing lacking was summer water. This was obtainable both by the digging of canals deep enough to enable the water to be led off from the low Nile, and by the construction of dams to raise the level of the low Nile. Both these expedients were adopted by Mohamed Ali. He chose the Delta for his cotton-growing experiment, presumably owing to its proximity to the seaboard. Deep canals were cut by forced labour. Steam pumps were used to raise the level of the summer water on to the fields, since the difference in level was too great for the primitive *saqias* and *shadoofs*. In 1834 a start was made on the construction of the Delta Barrage at the branching of the Rosetta and Damietta channels, some twelve miles north of Cairo. But work was soon abandoned, and only renewed, under French engineers, in 1847. It was hardly completed during Mohamed Ali's lifetime, and was thereafter neglected and allowed to fall into desuetude, until it was rehabilitated by British engineers some forty years later.

Cotton was not the only crop introduced into Egypt through the development of summer irrigation, which, by making it possible to grow two crops a year on one piece of land, increased the productivity of the land to a far greater extent than is indicated by the figures showing the increase in cultivated area. The indigo plant was brought from India and was an important agricultural product until the development of chemical dyes killed the indigo trade. Tobacco flourished until its cultivation was forbidden under the British occupation in the interests of the Customs revenue. Maize became an important summer crop and provided a valuable cereal supplement to the traditional winter crops of wheat and barley. The country's food supply was further augmented by the development of summer rice cultivation in the north-eastern Delta. These summer food crops in turn permitted a certain amount of winter cultivation to be turned over to *bersim* (a kind of clover) for animal fodder.

This had the effect both of helping to preserve the fertility of the land and of enabling the land to support a larger population of livestock. The advent of the steam pump, which pumped water from the subsoil, made it possible for much of the land in the basin areas of Upper Egypt to be cultivated in the summer.

Such was Mohamed Ali's anxiety to obtain the maximum of profit from the export crops which were his main, if not only, source of exchange needed for the industrialization of the country, on which he had set his heart, that he established a series of monopolies under which the cultivator was denied a free market for his produce and was forced to sell it to the State at prices fixed by the State. These State monopolies, which were imposed on cotton, tobacco, indigo, and other export crops, were extremely oppressive. The cultivator's produce was forcibly requisitioned at a fraction of the market price, and sold by Mohamed Ali's agents at an enormous profit to the European merchants in Alexandria. But in 1838 a treaty was signed between Great Britain and the Porte, under the terms of which British merchants were allowed freely to trade in all the Ottoman dominions. Great Britain took the view that this treaty, signed with Mohamed Ali's suzerain, enabled British merchants in Egypt to disregard the monopoly. Since Great Britain was Egypt's largest customer, and since Great Britain, at all events after 1841, was in a position to have her wishes respected, it came to pass that the 1838 treaty proved the death-blow of the monopolies, to the benefit both of the cultivators and the foreign brokers.

Mohamed Ali's régime was oppressive to the cultivator in other respects. The considerable irrigation and other public works—such as the digging of the Mahmudieh Canal— were accomplished with forced labour. This was no new thing in Egypt, but the extent of Mohamed Ali's public works made it an exceptional burden. It was estimated that in the year 1825 a total of 355,000 men were employed for four months of the year on forced labour digging canals. At

54

that time the total population of Egypt was about 3 million. A population of 3 million, in a country where there is a low expectation of life and a high birth-rate, means an able-bodied adult male population of about 750,000. Thus in that year about one-sixth of the total labour force available was engaged on forced labour. Since the *corvée* was taken entirely from the villages, the proportion of the agricultural labour force employed must have been even higher. It is true that much of the forced labour was of direct benefit to the agricultural community, and it is true that the forced labour was mostly during low Nile, when ordinary agricultural work was slack; nevertheless, forced labour, which was unpaid and which was extorted on an ever-increasing scale, constituted a grievous burden on the agricultural population.

In addition to forced labour, the incidence of taxation was heavy. Between 1798 and 1846 the amount collected from land tax increased twofold, while the area under cultivation increased by only one-third. It is true that the productivity of the agricultural area had also increased, but as against this the *ushuri* lands, which represented about one-third of all agricultural lands, were partly exempted from the land tax. It is difficult to arrive at any accurate comparison, but it is probable that the cultivator was as heavily, if not more heavily, taxed at the end of Mohamed Ali's reign than he had been at the beginning.

Mohamed Ali's schemes of industrialization were less successful than his agricultural projects. Apart from the successful establishment of several cotton ginning and pressing factories, most of his schemes of industrial development came to naught.[17] Numerous sites all over the country, housing derelict and rusting machinery, provided melancholy evidence of the failure of enthusiastically conceived but ill-founded plans for the establishment of spinning and weaving factories, silk-mills, tanneries, dye-works, etc. This failure was partly because Egypt possessed neither indigenous metals nor fuel, but mainly because the attempted rate of progress outstripped the rate at which trained engineers, foremen, and mechanics could be produced in a predominantly agricultural and educationally backward country. It is impossible to assess how much money was squandered by Mohamed Ali in his abortive industrial experiments, but, in view of the prodigality of his successors, it is noteworthy that he died without having pledged the State's credit to the extent of a single piastre.

The development of Alexandria during Mohamed Ali's reign was indicative of the growth of trade connexions with Europe. The construction of the Mahmudieh Canal concentrated all the import and export trade, which had previously been shared with Damietta and Rosetta, on Alexandria, now connected by water with the markets of Cairo and the villages of Upper Egypt and the Delta. A large proportion of the increased population consisted of foreigners of all nationalities, but mostly Greeks and Italians, who settled in Alexandria as a result of their connexions with the foreign trade of the port. By the end of Mohamed Ali's reign about 6,000 of the permanent residents of Alexandria consisted of foreigners. Their wealth and importance was out of all proportion to their numbers, and before Mohamed Ali died Alexandria was well on the way to becoming a European city, more akin to Marseilles, Genoa, or Barcelona than to Cairo.

Up to the time of Mohamed Ali, the citizens of the towns were more or less exempt from direct taxation, and we have already seen how the citizens of Cairo revolted on two occasions against attempts to impose direct taxation on them. But Mohamed Ali succeeded in imposing a head tax—known as *Jazieh*—on the town-dwellers. This became a part of the regular State revenue. As a result of this tax, together with the Customs and other duties and dues accruing from the increased foreign trade, the land tax, which had at the beginning of the century provided nearly all the revenue, only provided about half the revenue at the end of Mohamed Ali's reign, although the amount collected on account of land tax was more than doubled.

All this considerable economic development was only made possible by the extensive employment of foreign experts. In the selection of these Mohamed Ali does not appear to have let himself be affected by political considerations. As a result, probably, of the interest in all aspects of Egyptian life which had been stimulated in France by the Institut d'Egypte which Bonaparte had founded, a large proportion of the experts were Frenchmen, but there were a number of Englishmen and other Europeans as well. Mohamed Ali's schemes were carried out almost exclusively by means of what we should now call State capitalism. The money was found by Mohamed Ali and the work done by servants, Egyptian and foreign, hired by Mohamed Ali. No foreign concessions were granted, no foreign capital borrowed. The fruits of success accrued to the State, the penalties of failure were paid by the State (or rather passed on to the *fellahin*). In Mohamed Ali's day foreigners were the servants and not the masters of the Egyptian state. Politically, Mohamed Ali was compelled from time to time to acknowledge his dependence on the powers. Economically, he remained his own master. It was an example that his successors would have done well to follow.

Mohamed Ali's schemes of Westernization were not confined to Egypt's economy. Early in his reign he realized the necessity of modernizing the Egyptian Army, or, rather, of creating an Egyptian Army to replace the Mameluke feudal levies. For this purpose he engaged the services of a Colonel Seves, a French artillery officer who had been with Bonaparte's expedition, and who subsequently became known as Soliman Pasha. With the assistance of Soliman Pasha, Mohamed Ali founded an infantry school at al-Khanka, a cavalry school at Giza, and a school of artillery under a Spaniard named Colonel Seguira. His first attempt at creating a navy ended disastrously at Navarino, but in 1829 he had a new naval arsenal constructed at Alexandria and employed British and French instructors in shipbuilding. Social services were not entirely neglected, and it is to the credit of a French physician, Clot Bey, that bubonic plague, which had been a terrible scourge in Egypt during the time of the Mamelukes, ceased to be a serious menace from about 1840 onwards. (The rapid increase in population after that date is partly due to this fact.) Mention must also be made of the growth of the new science of Egyptology, which, by making Egyptians conscious of their tremendous past, must have played no small part in stimulating their ambitions for an independent future. Egyptology was developed almost entirely through French initiative, starting with Denou, a member of the Institut, who explored the ancient monuments of Upper Egypt, and inspired many of his fellow countrymen to the task of unravelling from Egypt's monuments the secrets of her past.

In spite of the importation of Western experts and Western techniques, it does not appear that the manners and customs of the West made very much headway, even among the urban upper classes, during the reign of Mohamed Ali. The Viceroy[18] and his family all dressed and lived in the traditional manner, and gave no encouragement to the boulevard pseudo-culture which invaded Egypt during the reigns of Said and Ismail. It appears from the writings of Lane, who was living in Cairo during the latter part of the reign of Mohamed Ali, that the capital was at that time an entirely Oriental city in respect both of its appearance and of the manners and customs of its inhabitants. So far from Egypt adopting European ways of life, it was usual for Europeans living in Egypt to adopt Egyptian ways of life in such matters as food, dress, and accommodation. Mohamed Ali was no lover of Westernization for its own sake, and during his reign Egypt was spared from such things as frock-coats, advertisement hoardings, competitive examinations, and the intricacies of European table cutlery.

It must remain doubtful whether Mohamed Ali's development schemes did very much to raise the standards of health, wealth, and happiness of the inhabitants of Egypt as a whole. At the end of his reign the average cultivator was working harder, but was probably no less indigent, than he had been under the Mamelukes. Public security had improved, but conscription for foreign service was a doubtful improvement on perpetual embroilment in civil war. The hierarchy of *mudirs, mamurs,* and *umdas* was probably no less oppressive and no less corrupt than the *multazimin* and their understrappers. It is perhaps too early, even yet, to pass final judgement. The Industrial Revolution in England was for many decades an unmitigated curse to the majority of the people of England. It was only gradually that the benefits of increased productivity seeped down to the masses. In any case, Mohamed Ali's object was not human happiness for others, but power for himself and his descendants. The next chapters will describe how these descendants threw away the power which Mohamed Ali bequeathed to them.

NOTES ON CHAPTER TWO

1. Mohamed Ali had also landed with the abortive Turkish expedition to Abuqir Bay in 1799. During the evacuation of the Turkish force on that occasion, he had been nearly drowned, and was rescued by a boat belonging to one of the British warships lying off Alexandria.

2. There is an erroneous tourist's legend to the effect that Hassan Bey escaped by jumping his horse over a parapet. The curious observer can see the alleged site of the jump, which would have been a considerable feat for both man and horse. In point of fact, Hassan Bey had the good fortune to miss the party, being ill in bed at the time.

3. One of the remaining gates of the Fatimite city of al-Qahira. Also known as the Bab-al-Metwalli.

4. The Wahhabis are a puritanical Moslem sect professing the austere Hanbali rite. The sect rose to power in Central Arabia during the second half of the eighteenth century under the aegis of the house of Ibn Sa'ud, the rulers of Nejd. At the beginning of the nineteenth century the Wahhabis drove out the Sherif of Mecca and occupied the Holy Cities. The consequent predominance of the Sa'udi family in Arabia was a menace to Ottoman influence in the Peninsula, and Mohamed Ali's Arabian expedition was made at the instance of the Sultan, who perhaps wished to see his two most powerful vassals exhaust themselves by fighting each other. If so, his expectations were disappointed. The result of Mohamed Ali's expedition was temporarily to destroy both Sa'udi dominance and the influence of the Wahhabi faith in Arabia.

5. The real and alleged atrocities committed by Ibrahim Pasha in the Morea were a powerful influence in mobilizing British public opinion against his rule in Syria fifteen years later. Ibrahim Pasha was Mohamed Ali's eldest son and his principal general. He predeceased his father by a year. Shortly before his death he paid a visit to England.

6. Some French historians go further back and date French interest in the Levant from an alleged treaty between Charlemagne and Harun-al-Rashid, the Khalif of the *Arabian Nights*.

7. 'Uniate' is the generic term applied to those Eastern Churches in communion with, but liturgically separate from, the Roman Catholic Church. Most of the Uniate Churches were founded as the result of 'break-aways' from the Greek Orthodox and other Eastern Churches during the second half of the seventeenth century. These 'break-aways' came about mainly from the missionary efforts of the Jesuits. For example, a Greek Catholic Church was founded by converts to Rome from the Greek Orthodox Church, a Syrian Catholic Church by converts from the Monophysite or Jacobite Church. In addition to these break-aways, the Maronite Church, which had been separated from the Orthodox Church in the sixth century, had been recognized as being of the Roman Communion since the twelfth century, although it retained both liturgical and administrative independence.

8. For various reasons, the Euphrates proved unsuitable for steam navigation. A regular British-owned steamer service was, however, established on the Tigris between Basra and Baghdad, and the overland telegraph route to India was laid along the Euphrates route. Up to the beginning of the nineteenth century Aleppo was, as far as British trade was concerned, a far more important entrepôt for the Eastern trade than either Cairo or Alexandria. It was largely owing to Mohamed Ali's encouragement of the Suez-Alexandria route that much of this trade was diverted from Aleppo.

9. Aden was required for use as a coaling station.

10. This squadron consisted mostly of steamships. It is probably the first instance of steamships having been used in a warlike action.

11. There was a rest-house and a staging post at intervals of ten miles in the eighty-mile journey.

12. There were sixteen signal stations, the ruins of some of which can still be seen at the side of the present Cairo-Suez road.

13. Samuel Briggs was senior partner in the firm of Briggs and Thorburn, probably the first British firm of cotton-brokers to be established in Egypt.

14. The Mahmudieh Canal also became the principal means of supplying Alexandria with fresh water.

15. In theory, and perhaps to a certain extent in practice, *ushuri* lands were undeveloped lands reclaimed from the desert which needed a certain amount of capital for their development. The remissions in land tax were granted in order to encourage such development.

16. The cotton plant had been cultivated on a small scale in Egypt for many centuries before the time of Mohamed Ali. But it was of inferior quality and was not exported. It was used mainly for stuffing divans, saddles, etc. In 1819 a Frenchman named Jumel discovered a specimen of a cotton plant, imported from India, growing in a Cairo garden. This cotton plant, to be known as *mako*, after the proprietor of the garden in which it was discovered, was developed commercially at Jumel's instigation and was the first variety of cotton to be exported from Egypt. In 1840 American Sea Island cotton was also introduced into Egypt. Most of the modern commercial grades have been developed from one or other of these varieties.

17. For example, Mohamed Ali started a number of textile factories for the manufacture of Army uniforms and *galabiya* (peasants' smocks) from Egyptian cotton. Twenty-four of these factories, employing 20,000 operatives, were established. Three years after Mohamed Ali's death, all that remained of this enterprise was one factory worked by steam and two worked by ox-power.

18. Mohamed Ali's official title was *wali*, meaning governor.

CHAPTER THREE

THE SUEZ CANAL

A CANAL from the Nile to the Red Sea by way of Wadi Tumulat, along what is now the Ismailia Canal, was started by the Pharaoh Necho in the seventh century B.C. and completed by Darius I after Egypt had been conquered by the Persian Emperor Cambyses. This canal appears to have fallen into disuse, to have been redug by Ptolemy I in the third century B.C., and again by Amr ibn-al-As, the Arab conquerer of Egypt in the seventh century A.D. By the time of the Fatimids it had again become silted up and forgotten, and was no more heard of it until Bonaparte's invasion of Egypt at the end of the eighteenth century. During the French occupation military engineers started making a survey for a canal connecting the Red Sea with the Mediterranean, and in the course of their work found traces of the old canals. As a result of their surveys, the French engineers came to the erroneous conclusion that there was a difference of level between the Red Sea and the Mediterranean large enough to make a direct cut across the Isthmus of Suez impracticable. They therefore confined themselves to the consideration of a canal linking the Red Sea with the Nile, and so with the Mediterranean, in the same way as the earlier canals had done.

The French evacuation of 1801 prevented any material progress from being made with the scheme, but the idea of a canal from the Red Sea to the Mediterranean took root in France. As we have seen the invention of the steamship had diverted much of the eastern traffic from the Cape to the overland route and thus greatly enhanced the commercial possibilities of such a canal. The overland route,[1] while convenient for passengers and mail, was less convenient for merchandise owing to the necessity for expensive transhipment. A canal would obviate this, and so give to the shorter Egyptian route an overwhelming advantage over the Cape route for merchandise as well as for passengers and mail.

In 1834 a Frenchman named Fournel applied for, but was refused, a concession to build a canal. Mohamed Ali, in spite of his passion for modernization, was to the end of his life a resolute opponent of the canal scheme, accurately realizing that such a canal would not only be of no benefit to Egypt, but would make it impossible for Egypt to remain independent.

Twelve years after the refusal of a concession to Fournel another Frenchman, named Enfantin, formed a Société d'Etudes pour le Canal de Suez, in which a number of his fellow countrymen, including a certain Ferdinand de Lesseps, a French consular official in Egypt, became interested. Mohamed Ali maintained his opposition; his original objection to the Fournel scheme had been fortified by the knowledge that Great Britain would look with disfavour on what she was already beginning to regard as a French scheme for undermining Great Britain's ascendancy in the Levant. Mohamed Ali's grandson and successor, Abbas, also opposed the scheme, in the same way as he opposed all other forms of Westernization and Western encroachment.

In 1854 Abbas died after a short reign and was succeeded[2] by his Uncle Said, who was one of the youngest of Mohamed Ali's numerous progeny of sons. In his youth, Said had formed a friendship with Ferdinand de Lesseps, whose father had been French Consul-General in Egypt, and who had himself at that time been an *élève* Consul. It was a friendship destined to have momentous consequences. Ferdinand de Lesseps had been dismissed from the Consular Service, for reasons which have remained unknown, on the accession of Napoleon III. He left Egypt, where he had become a convert to Enfantin's enthusiasm for the canal, and retired to a farm in France waiting for the day when his friendship with Said might enable him to transform his dreams of the canal into a reality. For although the idea of a canal had not been his, his adoption of the scheme was so enthusiastic, his energy so intense, and his imagination so vivid that the construction of the canal became the ruling passion of his life. Like Cecil Rhodes, who so greatly resembled him, he was an idealist who was at the same time practical, able, and unscrupulous.

Immediately on hearing of Said's accession, de Lesseps hurried back to Egypt. Said had not forgotten his old friend, and within a few months he had granted de Lesseps a concession for the construction of a canal from the Red Sea to the Mediterranean (November 1854). De Lesseps appears to have realized the importance of reconciling Great Britain to his concession and to have relied on his powers of persuasion being equally effective with the British as with Said. Before any public announcement of the concession had been made, he went to see Bruce, the British Consul-General, and told him about the scheme, representing himself as Said's technical adviser. Bruce appears to have been noncommittal. Said then summoned his Ministers and the European Consuls and formally advised them of his intention to grant de Lesseps a concession for the construction of a canal from the Red Sea to the Mediterranean. (It had not then been decided whether the canal was to be cut straight through the Isthmus of Suez or whether it was to go via the Wadi Tumulat to the Nile.) The concession, which was for a period of ninety-nine years, was officially promulgated in May 1855, together with an intimation to de Lesseps that work was not to start until the concession had been ratified by the Sultan.

The publication of the concession was followed by a spate of diplomatic activity. The British Government, which regarded the whole scheme as a French political move to establish their supremacy in Egypt, made it clear that it was opposed to ratification. At that time the endemic nineteenth-century skirmishing between the powers over the Ottoman

Empire had erupted into a war in which Great Britain and France were allied with Turkey against Russia. The French Government was therefore rather less than normally disinclined to respect the wishes of the British Government, and was, moreover, not yet in any way committed to de Lesseps's scheme. The French Government therefore returned a soft answer to the British Government's objections. At the same time, Lord Stratford de Redcliffe, British Ambassador at Constantinople, and a powerful influence in the councils of the Ottoman Empire, made it clear to the Porte that the British Government viewed the canal scheme with disfavour.

De Lesseps, who was not in good odour at the French Court, came to England to see the Prime Minister, Lord Palmerston. Palmerston told him forcibly that he did not regard the Canal as a commercial proposition, and that he consequently distrusted it as a political one. He added, with great frankness, that he was afraid that the creation of a new channel of trade might completely upset the commercial and maritime advantages which Great Britain then possessed, and that it might seriously jeopardize Great Britain's friendly relations with France. De Lesseps also saw Lord Clarendon, the Foreign Secretary, who was equally discouraging. He reported the result of his interviews to the Quai d'Orsay, but does not appear to have made any attempt to obtain French diplomatic support for his venture.

De Lesseps then set about forming an International Commission to examine and report on the technical aspects of the project. The British Government refused to nominate any members, but three British engineers agreed to serve independently. The Commission went out to Egypt and, in January 1856, issued their Report recommending the scheme. Their principal findings were as follows: (a) that the Wadi Tumulat route was impracticable owing to the expense involved; (b) that there was no insurmountable difficulty about the direct route across the isthmus; (c) that suitable ports could be constructed at each end of the Canal;

(*d*) that the whole project would not cost more than £6,000,000.

This expert Report completely changed the aspect of the scheme, and the Canal became elevated to the rank of a business proposition. The British Government continued to oppose it, but many British business and public men, including Bright, Cobden, Gladstone and Lord John Russell were attracted by it. The Government was asked in the House of Commons whether it considered it desirable to persevere in opposition to a scheme which was viewed with favour by all the nations of Europe. Disraeli, then Chancellor of the Exchequer, replied that the Canal was futile and impossible of execution and that 'the operation of nature would in a short time defeat the ingenuity of man.'

Meanwhile the original concession had been replaced by a more detailed concession given to the Compagnie Universelle du Canal Maritime de Suez in which it was provided, *inter alia* (*a*) that in addition to a concession for the construction of a maritime canal through the isthmus, the Company was to be given for the period of the concession a strip of land in the Wadi Tumulat linking the area of the concession with the Nile for the purpose of digging a sweetwater canal to meet the needs of the canal zone; and (*b*) that the Company was to be freed from taxation in respect of this strip and was to enjoy the benefits deriving from its cultivation.

The financial arrangements were as follows: the Egyptian Government was to be allotted an issue of preference shares entitling it to 15 per cent. of the nett profits of the Company; 10 per cent. of the nett profits were to go to the holders of founder shares, to be allocated at the discretion of the Company. The remaining 75 per cent. of the nett profits were to go to the holders of ordinary shares.

A secret codicil was added to the concession by which the Egyptian Government undertook to supply on demand labour according to the requirements of the Company for the construction of the Canal.

It is astonishing to contemplate the extent to which Said had committed himself to the Company. Not only had he alienated from the Egyptian State, for the period of the concession, a strip of potentially cultivable land extending into the heart of Egypt, but he had pledged the Egyptian State to provide an unlimited quantity of manpower for the construction of the maritime and sweet-water canals. He had in fact undertaken to provide almost everything required for the construction of the canal in return for a promise of 15 per cent. of the nett profits. And this, as will be seen, was not the limit of his folly.

In October 1858 the subscription list for the Company's ordinary shares was opened. The capital was fixed at Fr. 200,000,000 (£8,000,000) divided into 400,000 shares of Fr. 50,000 each; 207,111 shares were taken up in France and 96,517 by the Egyptian Government. When the subscription list was closed at the end of November, 85,506 shares, which had been allotted to Great Britain, U.S.A., and Russia, but which had not been taken up in those countries, were left unsold. It was from this point that the financial irregularities in connexion with the Canal may be said to have started.

Mention has already been made of the founder shares, the holders of which were to receive 10 per cent. of the nett profits of the Company. The names of the holders of these founder shares have never been divulged, but there is no reasonable doubt that de Lesseps distributed the majority of them in Paris in such a manner as to secure for the Company the strong diplomatic support of Napoleon III's Government. Up to the time of the opening of the subscription list, the French Government had remained strictly neutral over the Canal, and had in fact made an agreement with the British Government by which both parties bound themselves to refrain from exercising any pressure in Constantinople for or against the project. Napoleon III himself was, up to the autumn of 1858, unenthusiastic about it, in view of his desire to keep on good terms with Great Britain. Moreover, as has been related, de Lesseps was *persona non grata* in Third Empire circles. During October–November 1858 a significant change took place, and thereafter de Lesseps appears to have been able to rely on the unwavering support of the French Government.

When the subscription list had officially been closed, de Lesseps announced that Said had agreed to take up the 85,506 shares which had remained unsold, bringing his total shareholding (or, rather, the total shareholding of the Egyptian State) to 182,023 shares at a cost of Fr. 91,011,150, or about £3¾ million sterling. At the same time he informed the French Government (the Company was registered in Paris and subject to French law) that the share capital had been fully subscribed. Said, by means of a formal note circulated to all the foreign consuls, denied that he had agreed to take up the unsold shares. He also warned de Lesseps for the second time that work on the Canal was not to start until the Sultan had ratified the Concession.

By this time de Lesseps was able to rely on the full support of the French Government, which not only ignored the contradiction between de Lesseps's affirmation and Said's denial about the unsubscribed shares, but also, in defiance of its agreement with the British Government, proceeded to exert pressure on the Sultan for the ratification of the concession. So sure was de Lesseps of the efficacy of this support that, in April 1859, he started work on the Canal in defiance both of the Sultan and of Said. He then not only succeeded in becoming reconciled with Said, who had not unnaturally broken off relations with him after the affair of the unsubscribed shares, but also persuaded Said to take up those shares. How he did this is unknown, but there is no doubt that by this time Said had drifted into a dangerous state of subservience, not only to de Lesseps, but to the French Government, with which de Lesseps was now so closely identified.

Having secured his position in Egypt, de Lesseps went to Paris and made it doubly secure by arranging for the dismissal of the French Consul-General in Egypt who had shown a certain lack of enthusiasm in furthering de Lesseps's interests. He then proceeded to Constantinople to try to expedite the ratification of the concession by the Sultan. He discovered that the principal obstacle to this ratification was the British Ambassador, Sir Henry Bulwer, who was pressing the Sultan both to refuse ratification and to insist on Said's enforcing a cessation of work on the Canal. De Lesseps's persuasiveness failed to have any effect on Bulwer, and he left Constantinople with the Sultan still vacillating between the opposing counsels of the British and French Ambassadors.

Back in Egypt de Lesseps succeeded in persuading Said to implement the codicil to the concession by which the Company's requirements of labour for the Canal were to be met by the Egyptian Government. This, of course, meant forced labour—or, in plain words, slavery. (It was one thing to force the Egyptian peasant to work on the irrigation canals, which were necessary for the life of Egypt, and which only required labour at a time when agricultural work was slack. It was quite another thing to recruit forced labour all the year round for a work from which the Egyptian peasant could derive no immediate or ultimate benefit, and which frequently meant his forcible transportation to a point several hundred miles from his native village.) The British Government was quick to take advantage of the forced labour issue, and mainly as the result of its protest, work on the Canal almost came to a standstill. So matters remained until the beginning of 1863, when Said, worn out by the continual badgering to which he had been subjected by de Lesseps, the French Government, the British Government, and the Sultan, died.

Said was succeeded by Ismail,[3] a grandson of Mohamed Ali and the son of Ibrahim Pasha. He was about thirty-two years of age at the time of his accession and a prince of considerable ability and astuteness. There appeared to be no good reason why he should honour his predecessor's agreement to the preposterous codicil to the 1856 concession, nor indeed was there any good reason why he should acknowledge the concession at all, since it had not yet been ratified by the Sultan. He was, however, anxious to keep as even a balance as possible between the British and French in Egypt, and was unwilling to commit himself unreservedly to the protection of either country. He therefore confined himself, for the time being, to an intimation to the French Consul-General that he was in favour of the Canal, but that the terms of the concession would have to be radically changed. He then went to Constantinople for his Investiture. While in Constantinople he was warned by Sir Henry Bulwer that the British Government not only objected to the use of forced labour on the Canal, but objected to the construction of the Canal by any means whatsoever.

On his return to Egypt, Ismail appears to have decided to co-operate with de Lesseps. He agreed to take up the 85,506 shares which had been forced on Said, as well as the 96,516 shares originally allocated to the Egyptian Government, and arranged for an issue of bonds to cover the whole of his ordinary shareholding. He then sent his Armenian Minister, Nubar Pasha, to Constantinople and Paris charged with the task of negotiating a revision of the concession in respect both of the supply of labour and of the Wadi Tumulat lands. In March 1864, Nubar Pasha, presumably with Ismail's approval, agreed to submit the 1856 concession to the arbitration of the Emperor Napoleon, who by this time could hardly be regarded, even by the most uninstructed, as being a disinterested party. An all-French arbitration committee was appointed, and in due course made its award as follows: (a) it found that Said had contracted to supply *corvée* labour according to the Company's requirements and that Ismail should pay £1,520,000 in compensation for having refused to do so; (b) it declared that the Sweetwater Canal concession, which Ismail considered detrimental to Egypt's independence, should be abandoned against a payment by Ismail to the Company of £1,840,000.

Great Britain, under a Liberal Government which appears to have lost all interest in the fortunes of the Canal, made no effective protest against this award. This quiescence was presumably taken by the Porte as an indication that Great Britain had retired from the contest. At all events, in April 1865, the Sultan, acting under considerable pressure from the French Government,[4] issued a *firman* authorizing the construction of the Canal.

All the financial and political objections had now been cleared away. The physical obstacles were puny in comparison. Within four years the Canal was completed. The ceremonial opening, at which Eugénie, Empress of the French, was the guest of honour, took place in November 1869 in the presence of representatives from all nations, and amid scenes of extravagant ostentation partaking about equally of the barbaric generosity of Ismail and the opulent vulgarity of the Third Empire. France had gained a diplomatic victory in Egypt which appeared to have more than offset the ascendancy which Great Britain had established during the reign of Mohamed Ali. The gun-flashes of Napier's squadron had seemingly been eclipsed by the peaceful illuminations on the ships gathered at Port Said for the opening of the Canal.

Let us briefly examine the nature of this French triumph. The opening of the Canal had virtually killed the Cape route and substituted the Canal route as the principal channel of trade between Europe and the East. Previous to the opening of the Canal, the overland route via Egypt had been quicker than the Cape route for passengers and mail, but had been unable to challenge the Cape route for heavy merchandise owing to the expense of transhipment. In short, the Canal greatly increased, but did not create, the importance of Egypt from the point of view of British imperial commerce, communications, and strategy. The Canal was owned by French interests to the extent of over 50 per cent. of its ordinary shares, and to the extent of most (probably) of its founder shares. Most of the remaining ordinary shares, as well as all the preference shares, were held by Ismail, who was, temporarily, a satellite of France. The Canal was administered entirely by French personnel. In fact, the Canal was a French concern. But French ownership and French operation of the Canal did not, in themselves, confer on the French effective control of the Canal. Whoever had effective control of Egypt also had effective control of the Canal, irrespective of who operated or owned it. French diplomacy had temporarily triumphed over British diplomacy, not as a result of having secured the ownership and operation of the Canal, but as a result of having acquired a temporary political ascendancy over the Government of Egypt. This political ascendancy had made possible the construction of the Canal under French auspices, but the construction of the Canal did not, in itself, guarantee the continuance of that ascendancy.

The final cost of the Canal, which very greatly exceeded the £6,000,000 estimate of the expert Commission, has never been irrefutably established, but appears to have been in the neighbourhood of £16,000,000. Of this some £4,500,000 was subscribed by the ordinary shareholders other than the Government of Egypt. The balance was paid for by Said and Ismail. The details of the disbursements made by them in connexion with the Canal (excluding interest on money borrowed for the financing of the Canal) are approximately as follows:

	£
Amount of ordinary shareholding . .	3,750,000
Compensation as per Arbitral Award . .	3,500,000
Expenses in connexion with construction of Sweetwater Canal	3,250,000
Expenses of opening ceremony plus sundry expenses of Missions, etc. in connexion with the Canal	1,000,000
Total	£11,500,000

(The Sweetwater Canal, although it remained the property of the Egyptian State as a result of the Arbitral Award, and although Egypt benefited to the extent of the cultivation made possible by its construction, was an integral part of the Canal scheme in that the construction of the maritime Canal scheme necessitated bringing supplies of fresh water from the Nile.)

Thus, apart from their purchases of Ordinary shares, Said and Ismail paid a total of about £8,000,000 in return for the 15 per cent. share in the nett profits of the Canal provided by the allocation of the preference shares to the Egyptian Government under the 1856 concession. Since the ordinary shareholders were to receive 75 per cent. of the nett profits in return for a similar investment, it is clear that the £8,000,000 spent by the Egyptian Government could not be said to have been well invested even if it had not been necessary to borrow the whole of the sum so invested on ruinous terms. (It has been calculated that the total interest paid up to September 1873 on account of sums borrowed by the Egyptian Government in connexion with the Canal exceeded £6,000,000.)

But if the bargain was a bad one financially, it was a disastrous one politically. As Mohamed Ali had foreseen, the existence of the Canal proved incompatible with Egyptian independence. It was vital for Great Britain that no power should be in a position to close the Canal to her ships. The French were in a position to do so unless either (a) French influence in Egypt was counterbalanced by equal British influence, or (b) French influence was supplanted by British influence, or (c) French influence was replaced by direct international control, or (d) if French influence was neutralized by indirect international control in the form of a revival of effective Turkish overlordship. The Canal made it impossible for Great Britain to leave Egypt alone. It made it impossible for Egypt to be neutralized without some form of international control. Previously it had been possible to neutralize Egypt by keeping foreign powers out. But now a foreign power was there in the form of an *imperium in imperio*. The influence of this power could only be counter-balanced by adding the equal influence of another power or consortium of powers or eliminated by substituting the influence of another power or consortium of powers. Ismail's indebtedness became the excuse rather than the reason for the intensification of foreign interference with Egypt which marked the years following the opening of the Canal. The real reason for such interference was the existence of the Canal itself.

At first it did not appear as if the Canal would prove a financial success. By 1871, two years after the opening, the ordinary shares had dropped from a par value of Fr.500 to Fr.208. There were suggestions that the British Government should take advantage of the slump to try to buy up the shares. But the Liberal Government in power was not interested. Whether they failed to realize the importance of Egypt or whether they appreciated that financial ownership was immaterial to the effective control of the Canal is uncertain.

Meanwhile, the Franco-Prussian War had been fought and lost, and Napoleon III had been deposed. The support which de Lesseps had been accustomed to receive from the French Government was no longer forthcoming in its old generous measure. Ismail, always in want of ready money, was looking round for a buyer for his ordinary shares. In the summer of 1874 he gave an option to a certain M. Dervieu, a French banker, for the purchase of the Egyptian Government's holding at a price of £3,680,000. (The par value of the shares was about £3,750,000; the market value of the shares in 1874 was Fr. 422 per Fr. 500 share.) Ismail then arranged that the British Government should hear indirectly about the Dervieu option. By this time a Conservative Government, with Disraeli as Prime Minister, was in power, and Disraeli duly received news of the option. After asking for and obtaining confirmation from the British Consul-General in Egypt, he informed the French Government that the British Government would object to Ismail's shares being taken up by French interests, since this would result in virtually 100 per cent. French ownership of the Canal. The French Government, still suffering from the chastening effects of national defeat, acquiesced, and the Dervieu option was allowed to lapse. As soon as the option had lapsed, Disraeli, with a characteristic theatrical flourish, bought the shares for £4,000,000.[5] Ismail's calculated indiscretion had gained him over a quarter of a million sterling, about the only profitable financial transaction he ever made with a foreigner; the British Government had acquired something like 40 per cent. of the Company's ordinary shares and had become the largest ordinary shareholder. But Disraeli had overlooked two important points. The first point was that Article 51 of the Company's bye-laws laid down that twenty-five shares entitled the holder to one vote, but that no one shareholder could have more than ten votes. The second point was that by a decision of the Suez Canal Company Board in 1871, Ismail was deprived of any voting power in respect of his shares until 1894 as a result of his having hypothecated his dividends until that date. Disraeli had been duped by Ismail, who, by waving the Dervieu option in front of him, had induced him to pay substantially more than the market price for shares which gave the British Government no voice in the management of the Canal, although this was Disraeli's avowed object in purchasing them. Even on the false assumption that an effective voice in the management of the Company was a relevant factor in the strategic control of the Canal, Disraeli had made a blunder. He had spent £4,000,000 of his country's money without having asked Parliamentary sanction beforehand, without telling Parliament the true facts of the case subsequently, and without having bothered to ascertain what he was receiving in return. In the light of the cold facts, it is difficult to know whether to be amused or disgusted at Disraeli's childish and mendacious boast to the Queen ('It is yours, ma'am'). Since by the time that he made that remark he almost certainly knew that he had bought the shares under a misapprehension, it is probable that, to most minds, disgust at the mendacity of a Prime Minister will predominate.

De Lesseps was not slow to take advantage of Disraeli's blunder. Rightly surmising that Disraeli would give much to avoid the political consequences which would follow upon a publication of the true facts of the transaction, he resisted the British Government's attempt to claim a participation in the direction of the Canal commensurate both with the British Government's shareholding and with British contributions to the Canal's revenue (about 80 per cent. of the tonnage passing through the Canal was British). After some negotiation, he agreed (a) to a restoration of the ten votes which Ismail had forfeited and (b) to an allocation of three British seats out of twenty-four on the Canal's Board of Directors. On Disraeli's assumption that effective control of the Canal was a matter of ownership and management, his bargain would have been an even worse one than was ever struck by Said or Ismail.

Thus ended the comedy of Disraeli and the Canal shares. Disraeli's excursion into the realm of high finance had not in any way affected the relative positions of Great Britain and France in Egypt. But these relative positions had already been affected by France's defeat in the Franco-Prussian War and by the deposition of Napoleon III. France was a defeated nation. She could no more have closed the Suez Canal against Great Britain than she could have closed the Straits of Gibraltar. If she had attempted to do so, Great Britain could have landed an armed force on the banks of the Canal without any possibility of effective French interference. It was this fact which made the purchase of the Canal shares such an unnecessary piece of buffoonery from the political point of view. Financially, the transaction proved, in the long run, to be a good investment. Fifty years after the purchase, the British Treasury was receiving dividends to the tune of about £1,500,000 a year in return for the original investment of £4,000,000. But the object of

75

the transaction was, of course, not financial, but political. It was rather as if a batsman, intending to make a full-blooded drive, had mistimed the ball and scored an ignominious boundary through the slips.

Commercially, the transaction was not a fortunate one for British shipping. The British Government's financial interest in the revenues of the Canal was at perpetual war with the interest of British shipping in low Canal dues. As usual, the Treasury won and British shipping suffered. If Great Britain had not been the largest shareholder in the Canal, she would have been in a much better position, as the Canal's largest customer, to force down the dues, which have always been exorbitantly high.

But if Disraeli's transaction did little to benefit his country, it at least did very little materially to harm it. But what is one to say of the part played by Said and Ismail in the construction of the Canal? Said's case is simple. He was the victim of a confidence trick played by a master of the art. We, who are not under the spell of de Lesseps and who can only guess at the real or simulated pressure applied by the French Government, find it difficult to imagine how Said could have given to de Lesseps *carte blanche* over the supply of labour for the Canal, and how he could have forgiven de Lesseps for his trickery over the unsubscribed shares, even to the extent of relieving de Lesseps's embarrassment by taking up these shares himself.

Ismail's case was different. He was not a fool. He was quick to realize the impossible terms of the concession in so far as they applied to the provision of forced labour and the cession of the Wadi Tumulat lands. He was too cynical to have been bemused by de Lesseps's charm. Nevertheless, he not only took up the unsubscribed shares, but never attempted to make the taking up of these shares conditional on a revision of the concession. Instead, having agreed unconditionally to take up the shares, he agreed to the concession being arbitrated by people whom he knew must have a financial interest in the Company, and agreed to abide by an award which involved his having to pay nearly a quarter of the total cost of the Canal as compensation for the cancellation of two clauses in the Concession which he could never have been forced either by law or international pressure to accept. What is the explanation? Was there some sinister form of financial pressure at work? Or was it simply that de Lesseps kept on telling Ismail that, unless he agreed to this and that, the work on the Canal would have to stop, and the shares (including the Egyptian Government's Preference shares) would become valueless, and that both he and Ismail would become figures of fun in the eyes of Europe in general and in those of Great Britain in particular? There is no doubt that Ismail had come to regard his prestige in the eyes of Europe as being bound up with the successful completion of the Canal, on which so many doubts had been cast. There is no doubt that he had a sovereign contempt for money and that he was unlikely to attach very much importance to the expenditure of a few millions more or less on a project on which he had set his heart. It is also possible that he thought that his share of the future profits of the Canal would be sufficiently important to make it more than worth his while to keep the Canal alive by such additional contributions as were necessary after the original ordinary share capital had been exhausted.

In the long run, Ismail's investment would have been a profitable one for Egypt financially, had Egypt retained a financial interest in the Canal. But she did not retain her financial interest long enough to enable her to benefit from the large profits which the Company began to earn in later years.[6] Ismail's ordinary shares were, as we have seen, sold to the British Government in 1874 for £4,000,000. There remained the preference shares—entitling the Egyptian Government to 15 per cent. of the nett profits of the Company—which represented the Egyptian Government's royalty on the concession. The facts regarding the disposal of these shares did not become generally known for some time, and it was assumed that Ismail must have disposed of them in the course of the frenzied quest for ready money which marked the last years of his reign. In fact, these preference shares were still the property of the Egyptian Government at the time of his deposition, and passed, together with other assets, into the hands of the Anglo-French Controllers, who sold them to the Credit Foncier for £880,000. The background of this transaction will be dealt with in the next chapter, but it is obvious that the Controllers made an exceedingly bad bargain on behalf of the country whose finances they were supposed to be recuperating. The income deriving from the preference shares was later to amount to about £500,000 per annum, and would, if they had been retained by Egypt, have provided a not inadequate return for the sums which Ismail had expended on the Canal.

But even if Egypt had retained the whole of her financial interest, the profits deriving therefrom would not have compensated her for the political disadvantages of the Canal's existence. Geographically, the Canal is a highway between Europe and the East. Politically, it has proved a highway from Europe to the heart of Egypt.

NOTE ON THE INTERNATIONAL STATUS OF THE SUEZ CANAL

(This Note anticipates events dealt with in later chapters of this book, but it is subjoined, for convenience, to this chapter.)

The international status of the Suez Canal was first defined in the Constantinople Convention of 1888, to which Great Britain, Austria-Hungary, France, Germany, Holland, Italy, Russia, Spain, and Turkey were signatories. Proposals for the 'internationalization' or 'neutralization' of the Canal had been made from time to time before, during, and after its construction. The principle of free navigation of the Canal for merchant ships of all nations had been stipulated in the *firman* approving the concession, and had always been tacitly recognized; in 1873, during a conference on the calculation of tonnages for the assessment of Canal dues, a declaration was issued admitting this principle and extending it to warships and military transports. In 1878, when Russia was at war with Turkey (Egypt was still legally part of the Ottoman Empire and the Canal was therefore in Turkish territorial waters), the British Government asked and obtained from Russia an undertaking to refrain from any action which would interfere with free navigation of the Canal. In 1882, British forces, acting on the authority of a Khedival decree, occupied the Canal and for a few days stopped navigation along it. Failing a specific international agreement, the position was that control of navigation through the Canal was *de jure* in the hands of Turkey as being in Turkish territorial waters and *de facto* in the hands of Great Britain as being the predominant naval power in the eastern Mediterranean. This position was not materially altered by the British occupation of Egypt, except that this occupation increased the desire of the other powers for an agreement which would bind Great Britain to respect the

79

freedom of the Canal. After various abortive suggestions and negotiations, a convention was signed at Constantinople in October 1888, but made subject to the proviso that it was not to become effective until the end of the British occupation, which at that time was still assumed to be temporary. This convention provided, *inter alia*: (*a*) That the Suez Canal should always be open in time of war as well as in time of peace to every vessel, commercial or military, without distinction of its flag. The signatories agreed not to disturb in any manner whatsoever the free use of the Canal either in time of peace or in time of war, and never to subject the Canal to blockade (Article I). (*b*) That the Egyptian Government was responsible for the defence of the Canal, and that this responsibility should devolve on the Ottoman Empire if Egypt were unable to discharge it.

In 1904, as part of the Anglo-French Agreement which recognized the British occupation of Egypt, Great Britain agreed to give effect to the 1888 convention, thereby making herself responsible to the powers both for the defence of the Canal and for the security of free navigation through it. In the next year, during the Russo-Japanese War, Russian warships *en route* for the Pacific were allowed to use the Canal, despite the fact that Japan was Great Britain's ally.

The entry of Turkey into the First German War on the side of Germany and against Great Britain posed a pretty international problem, summarily solved by a unilateral British declaration of a protectorate over Egypt which put an end to the formal suzerainty of the Ottoman Empire. It was apparent that in the event of a war involving the Power *de facto* in control of the Canal, the responsibility for the defence of the Canal might well become incompatible with the duty of securing free navigation for ships of all nations wishing to use it, since the defence of the Canal was obviously incompatible with the admission to it of enemy shipping. During the First German War Great Britain treated the Suez Canal in precisely the same manner as she treated any other waterway under her control, seizing enemy ships and subjecting neutral vessels to the same restrictions as were imposed in British territorial waters.

The 1922 Declaration of Independence which gave Egypt the status of an independent sovereign state affected the status of the Canal in so far as it became a part of Egyptian territorial waters. The defence of the Canal and, by implication, the safeguarding of free navigation through it remained reserved to Great Britain in accordance with the four 'reserved points' of the Declaration.

The international status of the Suez Canal again came into prominence during the autumn of 1935, when Italian transports and warships were allowed to pass through it on their way to East Africa, where Italy was preparing for the war of aggression which she subsequently launched against Ethiopia. After the invasion of Ethiopia started, and in spite of the fact that Italy was condemned as an aggressor by the League of Nations, of which Great Britain was a member, no steps were taken to deny the transit of the Suez Canal to Italian warships and transports. As the defence of the Suez Canal was not immediately in question, this case could reasonably be regarded as on all fours with the transit of the Russian fleet in 1905, and Great Britain probably had legal justification for her attitude.

The signature of the Anglo-Egyptian Treaty in 1936 affected the international status of the Canal in one important respect. In accordance with Article 8 of the treaty, the Suez Canal was recognized as an integral part of Egypt, and it was provided that Great Britain would co-operate with Egypt in the defence of the Canal and in safeguarding its free navigation until such time as the Egyptian Army should be in a position 'to ensure by its own resources the liberty and entire security of navigation of the Canal'. This defined the position until 1956, at the end of which time the future guardianship of the Suez Canal was to be decided by the League of Nations.

During the Second German War, Great Britain, in conjunction with Egypt, took up the same position as in the

First German War, and the right of free navigation of the Canal was subordinated to the necessities of defence.

The Palestine 'war', when the states of the Arab League attacked the newly proclaimed state of Israel, posed yet another problem in the international status of the Canal. During the course of the fighting (no war was officially declared), the Egyptian Government imposed restrictions on the transit through the Canal of ships and cargoes with a view of preventing supplies reaching Israel by way of the Canal. These restrictions principally consisted in the denial of passage through the Canal to oil tankers bound from the Persian Gulf to Haifa, whose normal source of supply, by means of the pipeline from Kirkuk, had been cut off by Iraq's refusal to allow exports of oil to Haifa through the pipeline. No serious legal or other objection was, nor could reasonably have been, raised against the Egyptian restrictions, either by Great Britain or by any other power, during the actual course of the fighting. Egypt was, jointly with Great Britain, responsible for the defence of the Canal, and it could reasonably be held that the denial by Egypt of supplies destined for a country at war with Egypt was a necessary part of the defence of Egypt, and consequently of the Canal. But after the fighting had ceased, Egypt still maintained a blockade against Israel which involved the denial of transit through the Canal of tankers bound for Haifa. This denial drew forth a stream of protests both from Great Britain and from other interested powers. (Great Britain was principally affected, as the prohibition of exports of oil through the pipeline from Kirkuk to Haifa meant that the continued operation of Haifa Refinery—an important source of sterling oil—was dependent on the tanker import of crude oil to Haifa, of which the only conveniently available source of supply was the Persian Gulf.) The legal position was debatable, but it was difficult for Egypt diplomatically to justify the continued breach of one part of the Convention—the right of free navigation—as a necessary means of complying with another part of the Convention—the defence of the Canal—when this defence took the form of an attempted economic blockade of a neighbouring state with which Egypt had signed a truce, but the existence of which she did not officially recognize. Apart from the British interest in Haifa Refinery, the British Government was deeply concerned as a co-guarantor with Egypt of the right of free navigation through the Canal. At the time of the 1936 treaty it had not presumably been contemplated that Egypt would take unilateral action in respect of her responsibility for the defence of the. Suez Canal. Apart from the question of Egypt's responsibility under the 1936 treaty for observance of the Convention, it was clear that Egypt, as a sovereign State, could take what steps she liked against Israel within her own territorial waters. The question was the extent to which her sovereign rights were limited by her responsibilities for the observance of the Convention. Obviously, if Egypt—or Great Britain— had the unfettered right of judging what restrictions, if any, on free navigation were necessary for the defence of the Canal, the Convention became a dead letter, and the Suez Canal was in the same position as any other territorial waters. On the other hand, what body had the right of limiting or reversing the judgement of either or both of the guarantors? As far as Great Britain was concerned, it would not have been desirable to admit or to create any such limitation to a judgement which she might at any time wish freely to exercise on her own behalf. It was probably this consideration which led Great Britain to be very chary about applying pressure to Egypt to compel her to restore the right of free navigation. So long as Great Britain is a co-guarantor of the security of the Suez Canal, it obviously suits her to take as wide a view as possible of the freedom of action permissible to the guarantors.

NOTES ON CHAPTER THREE

1. The speed and convenience of the overland route was increased by the completion of the Alexandria-Cairo Railway in 1856 and the Cairo-Suez Railway in 1857. The Alexandria-Cairo Railway was built by George Stephenson, a son of Robert Stephenson, the inventor of the steam locomotive. It was

started in 1851, and completed as far as Kafr-az-Zayat, on the Rosetta branch of the Nile, by 1853. It was extended to Tantah in 1855 and to Cairo in 1856. At first the Nile crossing at Kafr-az-Zayat was made by ferry. Later a suspension bridge was built. The Cairo-Suez Railway, by the direct desert route, fell into disuse when the Suez Canal was opened, and was not rebuilt until 1934.

2. Until 1866 the succession in Egypt was regulated by Ottoman law under which the eldest living male of the family succeeded. In 1866 Ismail purchased from the Sultan the title of Khedive (a Persian word meaning 'Lord'), together with the right of succession for his heirs by primogeniture.

3. Ismail was the second son of Ibrahim Pasha. Up to the year 1858 the Heir Apparent had been his brother Ahmed, the eldest son of Ibrahim Pasha. In 1858 Ahmed was killed in a railway accident. A special train on its way from Cairo to Alexandria, bearing a number of princes of the Royal Family and their entourage, crashed into the Nile as a result of the Kafr-az-Zayat Bridge (see note 1, above) having been left open. Gossip inevitably accused Ismail of responsibility for the accident which gave him the throne of Egypt. It is interesting to speculate on the extent to which this accident may have changed the course of history. Ahmed, who, if he had lived, would have been Viceroy on Said's death, was parsimonious to the point of miserliness, and would never have got into Ismail's financial difficulties.

4. Napoleon III 'cut' the Turkish Minister on an official occasion, and made it known that his action was due to the Sultan's delay in ratifying the concession.

5. Actually, the British Government paid £3,976,582 for 177,642 shares. The difference between this and Ismail's nominal shareholding of 182,023 shares never seems to have been accounted for.

6. With the disposal of the preference shares the Egyptian Government forfeited the last remnant of its financial interest in the Canal, and from 1880 to 1936 the Egyptian Treasury received no share in the very large profits being made by the Canal Company. In May 1836 the Company made an agreement with the Egyptian Government by which the latter received an *ex-gratia* payment of £E.300,000 per annum, and by which two Egyptians were nominated to the Board of the Company. Later the agreement was amended to enable the Egyptian Government to receive 7 per cent. of the nett profits of the Canal Company, which in 1950 came to £E.22,000,000, of which Egypt's share worked out at £E.1,540,000.

CHAPTER FOUR

INTERNATIONAL CONTROL

SINCE the sixteenth century, Europeans in Egypt had enjoyed extra-territorial privileges, known as the Capitulations, which were conferred on certain European nationals as a result of treaties concluded between the Sultan of Turkey and the governments of various European states. The original purpose of these privileges had been to confer upon European Christian communities such immunities from the Shari'a Law, and such autonomy in matters of personal status, as to enable them to live with reasonable freedom and convenience in the Ottoman dominations. The Capitulations were in no sense a derogation from Ottoman sovereignty imposed by superior force; they were privileges granted as a result of treaties freely negotiated between equals. The first of these treaties was in 1535 between Suleiman the Magnificent and Francis I of France. This treaty, *inter alia*, gave to French and French-protected subjects residing in the Ottoman Empire the right (*a*) to have disputes between themselves and matters of personal status adjudicated by their own consuls, (*b*) to immunity from the criminal jurisdiction of the Ottoman Empire except in answer to a specific and written charge, (*c*) to the presence of a consular representative in the event of their being tried before the Ottoman courts as per (*b*), and (*d*) to the presence of a consular representative in the event of a domiciliary search. Similar treaties were subsequently concluded between the Porte and most other European powers until, by the middle of the nineteenth century, Capitulatory privileges were possessed by the nationals of all the principal European states, and by those of the U.S.A.[1]

Up to the end of the eighteenth century European communities in Ottoman towns lived together in one quarter of the town under the leadership and protection of their consul. The privileges granted were no more than were essential for the proper regulation of relations with each other and with the native inhabitants; in fact, they were in general accord with the Milla system, by which non-Moslem Ottoman subjects were permitted a certain degree of autonomy under the leadership of their elected or hereditary chiefs. On the whole, the system worked without serious abuse on either side, fitting smoothly into the well-worn pattern of Ottoman administrative usage.

It was only during the nineteenth century, when Egypt became more and more separated from the Ottoman Empire, that the Capitulations in Egypt began to take the form of a compulsory limitation on the legislative and executive powers of a state. This change was due, first, to a change in the foreign mercantile communities in Egypt, and, secondly, to the pressure which European powers were able to exert on Mohamed Ali and his successors. Up to the end of the eighteenth century European merchants in Egypt had kept themselves to themselves and had seldom become the owners of land or of any immovable property in the country. The question of their position with regard to taxation, and to the civil law generally, had not therefore arisen in any acute form. But foreign property ownership inevitably led to litigation both with European and with Ottoman nationals, and to the assessment of liability to local taxation on such property. Diplomatic pressure usually brought about *ad hoc* settlements of these matters and, as a result of this pressure, the Capitulations for the first time took the form of an imposed limitation on the powers of the indigenous government in its dealings with European nationals. For example, although civil cases between European and Ottoman nationals were normally settled by arbitration, the result of the arbitration was settled more often by diplomatic pressure than on the actual merits of the case.

Similarly, although immunity for Europeans from land taxation had been expressly waived by the consuls, it became in fact difficult to collect taxes on immovable property owned by foreigners owing to the privileges claimed and enforced by the consuls. This derogation from state sovereignty extended to the criminal law, in which the right of a European national to be tried before his own consul, instead of being merely represented by his own consul, gradually became established. This acquired right led to serious abuses, since many consuls were sufficiently unscrupulous as to connive at various criminal acts performed by their own nationals. In the same way, the old Capitulatory privilege of having consular representation at domiciliary searches came to amount in practice to a veto on such domiciliary searches. This veto was particularly serious in suspected cases of smuggling, and resulted in smuggling becoming rife among the foreign communities.

Whereas the abuse of Capitulatory privileges in respect of criminal law merely led to injustice, abuse of these privileges in respect of civil law led to more practical inconveniences, which demanded more immediate remedies. From 1850 onwards, the increasing trade of the country and the increasing part taken by foreigners in that trade, made it imperatively necessary to bring the Ottoman Capitulations into line with existing conditions. For example, what was the correct procedure in the frequent event of two Europeans of different nationalities being involved in civil litigation? The existing procedure was that the case was tried before the defendant's consular court. This was unsatisfactory. The arbitration usually resorted to when a European was involved in litigation with an Egyptian was almost equally unsatisfactory, since it was difficult to find an impartial arbitrator, and in important cases foreign diplomatic intervention took the place of arbitration. Various attempts to create courts to deal in a judicial manner with these 'mixed' cases were made, but were defeated by the foreign consuls, jealous of their acquired privileges, and conscious

87

of the monetary advantages which their nationals derived from them. The plethora of foreign investment and the influx of foreign residents which took place during the reign of Ismail made chaos of existing legal relations between foreigners and Egyptians on the one hand, and between foreigners of different nationalities on the other. A solution was essential if the process of Europeanization and foreign investment was to continue. Fortunately, a man well fitted to find a solution was at hand. Nubar Pasha, the son of an Armenian *négotiant*, and a Minister of Ismail's, was destined by chance and fitted by ability and temperament for the task of establishing a *modus vivendi* in Egypt between East and West. In 1869 an international conference was convened in Cairo at which Great Britain, Austria-Hungary, Germany, France, Italy, Russia and U.S.A. were represented, for the purpose of considering a proposal by Nubar Pasha for the abolition of the Capitulations and for the unification of the various civil and criminal jurisdictions of Egypt into a single hierarchy of courts, staffed by both Egyptian and foreign judges. He proposed that these 'mixed' courts should replace the national courts, the consular courts, and the various courts of arbitration. In order to try to secure the assent of the powers to his proposal, Nubar Pasha was even prepared to concede a majority of European judges in the proposed mixed courts. The British Government was prepared to accept Nubar's proposals. But the French and Italian Governments, influenced by the clamorous protests of their nationals living in Egypt who were unwilling to forego the immunities conferred on them by the existing state of affairs, secured their rejection. Nubar Pasha, whose main object was to rescue financial and commercial transactions from legal anarchy, then watered down his proposals so as to provide for the establishment of mixed courts for the trial of civil cases between Egyptians and foreigners and between foreigners of different nationalities, leaving the consular courts in existence for the trial both of criminal cases and of civil cases involving foreigners of the same nationality. A

88

second conference, held in Constantinople in 1873, agreed (with France dissenting) to the establishment of mixed courts for a trial period of five years on the basis of Nubar's amended proposals. The charter for the new mixed courts was then drawn up, in spite of French objections. The most important and far-reaching provision of the charter was that defining the position of the Egyptian Government *vis-à-vis* the mixed courts. Contrary to the usual practice by which the head of the state and his ministers are immune from the civil law in respect of their public duties, it was provided that the 'Government, the Administration, and the estates of H.H. the Khedive and the members of his family shall be subject to the jurisdiction of the Courts in litigation with foreigners'. It has been stated that Nubar's object in agreeing to this provision was to place a limit on the despotic power then being exercised by Ismail. This explanation seems improbable, in that the provision did not affect the despotic powers being exercised by Ismail in respect of his own subjects. A more probable explanation is that Nubar considered the jurisdiction of the mixed courts preferable to the exercise of diplomatic pressure over disputes between foreigners and the Egyptian Government. Another provision laid it down that, while the mixed courts were entitled to award damages to a foreign plaintiff against the Egyptian Government in respect of action by the Government damaging to the plaintiff, they were not entitled to restrain the Government from that action. Even with this qualification, it soon became apparent that a power had been conferred on the mixed courts analogous to that possessed by the Supreme Court of the U.S.A., in that it was in a position to veto actions by the Executive. As in the case of the Supreme Court, the extent to which this position was abused was dependent on the extent of extra-legal pressure applied from time to time on the mixed courts. Nubar Pasha, so far from eliminating diplomatic pressure, had provided a convenient channel for its exercise.

The Mixed Courts Charter also provided for a majority

of foreign judges, who were to be appointed by the Egyptian Government from the nationals of the Capitulatory states on the unofficial recommendations of the governments of these states. The appointments were for life, and the courts were divided into two sections, civil and commercial. These courts were originally intended as a modification of the Capitulations, and their jurisdiction was originally confined, by implication, to the nationals of the Capitulatory States. But in practice it was soon extended to all foreigners. Provision was made for the limitation of the jurisdiction of the mixed courts under martial law. The language of the mixed courts was to be either French, English, Italian, or Arabic, but in practice French came to be the only language used. The mixed code was based on French law. Nubar Pasha was not in Egypt to see his creation inaugurated in 1875, as by that time he was in exile, as a result (probably) of Ismail's displeasure at his having been made subject to the jurisdiction of the new courts in his relations with foreigners.

As has been pointed out, the regulation of the juridicial status of foreigners in Egypt had been made necessary by the increasingly important part being played by foreigners in the economic life of the country. In 1850 there had been 6,000 Europeans resident in Egypt, mostly in Alexandria. Twenty-five years later there were 100,000, of whom about one-half were in Alexandria, one-quarter in Cairo, and one-quarter in Port Said, Suez, Ismailia, and the provinces. These foreigners had been attracted to Egypt by the Westernizing policy of Said and Ismail, which had created lucrative opportunities for European administrators, technicians, and merchants, as well as for a cloud of professional adventurers. The material progress achieved during the reign of Ismail was enormous. Nearly 1,000 miles of railway, 8,000 miles of canals, and 5,000 miles of electric telegraph line were constructed between 1863 and 1879. During the same period the cultivable area was increased from 4,000,000 to nearly 5,500,000 *feddans*, the population from 4,800,000 to 5,500,000, the average annual value of imports from £2,000,000 to

£5,500,000, the annual value of exports from £4,500,000
to just under £14,000,000. A large sugar-growing and refin-
ing industry had been established in order to provide an
additional export crop after the cotton prices had slumped
from the high levels attained during the American Civil
War. A modern harbour was constructed at Alexandria.
A system of public education was established and some
4,500 schools opened.

Unfortunately, the immediate value to Egypt of all this
development was almost completely nullified both by the
volume of unproductive expenditure which was incurred
simultaneously, and by the fact that both productive and
non-productive expenditure was mainly financed by foreign
loans contracted on ruinous conditions. At the time of Said's
death the Egyptian Treasury was in debt to the extent of
some £7,000,000, consisting of a foreign loan of £3,000,000
raised from the firm of Fruhling and Goschen in 1862, and
a floating debt of £4,000,000 secured by Egyptian Treasury
bills. By 1876 Egyptian foreign loan indebtedness amounted
to about £68,000,000, her internal loan indebtedness to
about £14,500,000, and her floating debt to about
£16,000,000. Of this total of nearly £100,000,000, it is
computed that Said and Ismail had not received more than
about £65,000,000, the balance having gone on discounts
and commissions, which were exaggerated and inflated to
the verge, and beyond the verge, of fraudulence. The 7 per
cent. interest payable on the nominal sums borrowed
amounted to something like 12 per cent. on the sums
actually received. Even if the loans had been raised entirely
for productive purposes, the conditions would have been
ruinous. As it was, they were clearly impossible of fulfilment.
By 1873 the interest on Egypt's foreign loans amounted to
nearly £5,000,000 per annum, or more than the whole of
Egypt's annual revenue during the reign of Said. Ismail,
partly by extortionate taxation, and partly by the undoubted increase of productivity brought about by his
expansionist policy, had more than doubled Egypt's revenue,

91

but this was still insufficient for the triple burden of ordinary administration, debt services, and new extravagances. So Ismail looked for further loans. The European money market drew in its horns and proved unwilling to advance any more money at any price, rightly guessing that it would have its work cut out to exact its pound of flesh on the sums already advanced. Ismail had already started raising money nearer home on terms even more ruinous than those on which he had borrowed from Europe. The Muqabala Loan of 1871 was a masterpiece of improvidence. Ismail offered to Egyptian landowners the option of halving their land tax in perpetuity by paying on the spot six years' land tax in advance. Landowners had enjoyed a prosperous time during the previous decade as the result of high cotton prices prevailing during and after the American Civil War, and they responded readily to what was, from their point of view, an exceedingly profitable investment. The Muqabala Loan raised £9,500,000 at the price of depriving future Egyptian administrations of land tax in respect of some 1,000,000 *feddans* of cultivated land. In 1874 Ismail raised another indigenous loan, known as the Rouznameh, from Egyptian magnates. This loan was for a nominal sum of £5,000,000, bearing 9 per cent. interest. The Treasury only received about £2,000,000 of this. In point of fact, the Rouznameh was rather a forced levy than a loan. No security was given for the money advanced, and no regular interest was paid.

There could only be one end to this rake's progress. The inevitable end was delayed for a short time by the sale of the Canal shares to Disraeli for £4,000,000. Disraeli's eagerness to purchase these shares appears to have persuaded Ismail that the British Government might be prepared to assist him with his finances in return for some measure of control over State expenditure. He therefore invited the British Government to supply him with a British financial adviser. The British Government appears to have been willing to consider something of the sort. But before committing itself it required some information about the state of Egypt's finances. A certain Mr. Stephen Cave, M.P., was sent to Egypt at the beginning of 1876, not as Financial Adviser, but charged with the mission of conducting an enquiry into the financial position. His enquiry appears to have been a cursory one, for he was back in England in less than two months, and his report was issued before the end of March.

The Cave Report made it clear that Egypt's finances were in a critical state, but attributed the crisis 'almost entirely to the ruinous conditions of loans raised for pressing requirements'. It also stated that 'Egypt is well able to bear the charge of her present indebtedness at a reasonable rate of interest, but she cannot go on serving floating debts at 25 per cent. and raising loans at 12 per cent. to 15 per cent. to meet additions to her indebtedness which do not bring a single piastre into her Exchequer'. There was nothing in the Report to precipitate panic among Egypt's creditors, for the precarious state of Egypt's finances was well known. In fact, the Report would have been a reassuring one to reasonable creditors with no political axe to grind. But the Cave Mission, following on the purchase of the Canal shares, had alarmed the French Government, in spite of the British Foreign Secretary's announcement that the Mission 'must not be taken to imply any desire to interfere in the internal affairs of Egypt'. It seemed to France that this was precisely what the Cave Mission did imply. Bismarck, preoccupied at that time with the desire to keep Great Britain and France quarrelling in order to avoid the possibility of their combining against Germany, added fuel to the flames. European financial circles became alarmed at the prospect of British financial control in Egypt, which would in all probability result in a drastic scaling down of the extortionate loan terms. Egyptian stocks slumped on the European bourses, and Ismail could no longer get his paper discounted. On 8 April 1876 he was forced to suspend payment on his Treasury bills.

In May 1876 Ismail issued two decrees embodying his

proposals to his creditors. The first decree, dated 2 May, provided for the creation of an international Caisse de la Dette Publique, with one British, one French, one Italian and one Austrian member, which was to be empowered to supervise the collection and administer the distribution of the annual sums required for the service of the Debt, which sums were to be raised from specific items of revenue. The second decree, dated 7 May, embodied a plan for the funding of the entire bonded and floating debt at £91,000,000, bearing interest at 7 per cent.

These proposals would not have been unacceptable if the foreign debt-holders and their backers had really wanted a settlement. In fact, the terms of the proposed settlement were unwarrantably generous both as regards the capital value of the debt and the proposed rate of interest. The security of an international debt-collecting agency and the 'affectation' of certain revenues were unexceptionable. It was, however, unlikely that it would be physically possible to extract enough money from the *fellahin* to service the debt on these terms, and there is some reason to believe that Ismail only proposed the settlement in order to provide himself with a breathing space until he could think of some way of out-witting his creditors. However that may be, the bond-holders rejected the proposed settlement out of hand on the ground that the claims of the bond-holders should be given priority over the claims of the floating debt-holders, whereas under Ismail's scheme both were classed together as unsecured creditors. There was some substance in this, since most of the foreign loans had been contracted on the security of some specific source of revenue, such as Railway receipts. As a result of negotiations between Ismail and the bondholders, a Mission headed by Messrs. Joubert (France) and Goschen (British) arrived in Egypt in the autumn of 1876 charged, on behalf of the bond-holders, with the task of drawing up a revised settlement.

The Goschen-Joubert Enquiry, which was enlivened by the disappearance and suspected murder of Ismail Pasha

Sadiq,[2] Ismail's Chief Inspector of Finances, arrived at the conclusion that Egypt's maintainable revenue amounted to just under £11,000,000 per annum, and her minimum necessary expenditure to just under £4,000,000 per annum, leaving about £7,000,000 per annum for the debt service. The mission arranged for the funding of the bonded debt into three categories: the Preferred Debt, the Daira Debt, and the Unified Debt.[3] Two Controllers were appointed— one British and one French—one to supervise the collection of revenue, the other to control the flow of expenditure. An International Board was appointed to manage the State Railways, the State Telegraphs, and Alexandria Harbour, the revenues from which were earmarked for the service of the Preferred Debt. The revenue from part of Ismail's estates was earmarked for the service of the consolidated Daira Debt. The service of the Unified Debt was secured on the balance of general revenue.

The British Government was careful to disassociate itself from any responsibility for the Goschen-Joubert Mission. Goschen, although a British subject, was not appointed by the British Government and was merely a representative of the British bond-holders. Similarly, the British Government refused to appoint a British Controller or a British representative on the Railways Board. The two Englishmen appointed, Mr. Romaine and Colonel Marriott, were appointed as private individuals. At this time the British Government was undoubtedly in favour of an independent as opposed to an internationalized Egypt. Her object seems to have been to restrain France sufficiently to enable Ismail, with a certain amount of European assistance, to recuperate his shattered finances at the expense of the Egyptian peasantry without the necessity for European intervention. This object was not achieved.

The immediate cause of the failure of the Goschen-Joubert settlement was the reaction to it of the excluded floating debt-holders. Several of these sued the Egyptian Government in the newly-created mixed courts, and won their cases.

95

The Goschen-Joubert plan had provided no machinery for the settlement of such claims. The powers were faced with the conflicting demands of the bond-holders backed by the Goschen-Joubert settlement and of the floating debt-holders backed by the judgements of the mixed courts. At the same time it became apparent that the Goschen-Joubert Mission had overestimated the maintainable revenue and under-estimated the essential expenditure of the Egyptian state, with the result that the 'affected' revenues were insufficient to cover the service of the Preferred and Daira Debts, and the balance of the revenue was insufficient to cover both the ordinary expenses of administration and the service of the Unified Debt. The settlement therefore became unworkable, and the members of the Caisse de la Dette[4] urged on the powers the necessity for an international commission of enquiry to revise it.

In February 1878 M. Waddington had addressed to Lord Derby, British Foreign Secretary, a communication on Egypt's debts which stated that if Great Britain and France did not act in concert the matter was in danger of slipping out of their hands. Lord Derby replied that the British Government would 'be happy to co-operate with that of France in any measures not inconsistent with the Khedive's independent administration of Egypt'. At the end of March 1878, as a result of British and French pressure, a Commission of Enquiry was appointed by Khedival decree. The nominal President of the Commission was, for some extra-ordinary reason, M. de Lesseps, but the *de facto* President was an Englishman, Mr. (later Sir) Rivers Wilson, of the British Treasury, who had been in Egypt for a few weeks in 1876 on an abortive mission as Financial Adviser after the publication of the Cave Report. The other members were the four Commissioners of the Debt and an Egyptian ex-Minister, Riaz Pasha.

The new Commission[5] was in a much stronger position *vis-à-vis* Ismail than the Goschen-Joubert Mission had been, since it enjoyed the full support of the British and French

Governments, acting for once in accord. The implacable mood of Egypt's foreign creditors, as well as Great Britain's temporary subordination to France in Egyptian matters, had been clearly shown over the half-yearly coupon of the funded debt, which fell due for payment at the end of April. The Caisse de la Dette was disposed to waive collection on the ground of Egypt's inability to pay. Vivian, the British Consul-General, made it clear to his Government that any attempt to enforce payment would lead to the most appalling injustice and oppression. The French Government insisted on the ground that Ismail had sufficient hidden assets[6] to pay the coupon. The required amount was flogged out of the Egyptian peasantry and the coupon was duly paid.

Ismail was quick to realize the position, and decided that the time had come to *reculer pour mieux sauter*. Now that he could no longer evade the supervision of his finances, he determined to make a show of willingness to submit himself to such supervision and by this means to transfer from himself to his creditors the odium of the economies and extortions resulting from such supervision. He therefore recalled Nubar Pasha from exile, and in August 1878 astonished the world by dismissing his Prime Minister, Riaz Pasha (who had resigned from the Commission of Enquiry in order to become Prime Minister after the previous Prime Minister, Sherif Pasha, had resigned in order to avoid giving evidence before the Commission), and by appointing an international Government with Nubar as Prime Minister, Rivers Wilson as Minister of Finance,[7] and de Blignieres[8] as Minister of Public Works. This novel experiment in government, which had the blessing of Great Britain and France, superseded the financial administration of the Anglo-French Controller, whose functions were taken over by Rivers Wilson and de Blignieres.

The Commission of Enquiry had been sitting for four months before its metamorphosis into the Government of Egypt. During that period it had come to the conclusion that one of the main reasons for Egypt's financial plight was the confusion between the State accounts and Ismail's private expenditure, which enabled Ismail to draw without limit on the Treasury for his own personal extravagances. The Commission therefore proposed to separate that part of the royal estates, amounting to about 500,000 *feddans*, not already pledged to the service of Ismail's foreign loans, and to place it under an international administration, which became known as the Domains Administration, and to raise a loan on the security of these Domains to meet Egypt's immediate financial requirements. Rivers Wilson was in process of negotiating such a loan with Rothschild's when he became Minister of Finance. (A loan of £8,500,000 bearing 7 per cent. interest and conditional on the international administration of the Domains was eventually arranged. The Egyptian Treasury only received about £6,000,000 of this amount, bearing an effective rate of interest of about 10 per cent. In spite of the international safeguards with which this loan was hedged, Rivers Wilson was unable to secure terms less extortionate than those which Ismail previously had managed to get for himself. It is interesting to note that 'internationalism', the professed object of which was to put Egypt's financial house in order, started its career by saddling Egypt with yet one more international loan negotiated on the same extortionate terms as the previous ones.)

To all appearance, Ismail was now a prisoner in the hands of his creditors. Wilson and de Blignieres were to all intents and purposes the representatives of the British and French Governments. It was made clear to Ismail that these Governments would view with concern any attempt to remove them from their position as controllers of Egypt's purse-strings. Egypt appeared to be a Franco-British protectorate, with Great Britain as France's junior, not to say sleeping, partner in the enterprise. (Rivers Wilson was an ardent Francophile and at least as much under the influence of the French as he was under that of the British Government.)

But Ismail was not finished yet. For another year he was

to display all his considerable resources of ingenuity and intrigue in fighting a losing battle against the powerful forces arrayed against him.

The international Government did not have an easy passage. First, the Domains Loan was held up as a result of claims made on the Domains estates by creditors in the mixed courts. This difficulty was not finally settled until after Ismail's deposition. Secondly, the necessity for economy led to the retrenchment of a number of Army officers and civilian officials. This was widely resented, the more so since many of the officers and officials did not receive the arrears of pay due to them. Thirdly, it was believed that Rivers Wilson intended to abolish the privileges purchased by the subscribers to the Muqabala Loan. This alienated the large and powerful body of landowners who had subscribed to the loan in legitimate expectation of the promised remission of land tax. Another powerful body of landowners was alienated by the Government's believed intention to raise the tax on *ushuri* lands, which up to that time had enjoyed preferential treatment. [9]

These difficulties were immensely increased by the fact that Nubar was an Armenian Christian and Wilson and de Blignieres European Christians. The latter two made things more difficult for themselves by making no attempt to conform to Egyptian customs, even to the extent of refusing to wear the tarbush. Ismail fanned the flames of discontent. He was determined to show who was the real master of Egypt. To all complaints he made the reply that it was not he himself, but Nubar and the European Ministers who were responsible. When asked by his Ministers for his assistance, he replied that they had insisted on his being a constitutional monarch and that he proposed to behave like a constitutional monarch and leave the business of governing the country to them. If they thought that they could do better than he had done, by all means let them try and see.

Ismail's calculated unhelpfulness went beyond mere non-co-operation. There is reason to believe that he instigated

99

a demonstration of dismissed Army officers in February 1879, when both Nubar Pasha and Rivers Wilson, who had come to his assistance, were assaulted and manhandled on their way to their offices. They were rescued from their predicament by Ismail in person, who was thus able to make an impressive demonstration of his personal authority. There is little doubt that he organized the demonstration for that purpose. He then felt strong enough to dismiss Nubar Pasha, which he did next day on the ground that it would be impossible to guarantee public security if Nubar remained in power. It was a bold step, and one to which Great Britain and France might have been expected to react strongly. The British Government was in favour of insisting on Nubar's reinstatement, but the French Government, with whom Nubar was, for some reason, unpopular, refused to intervene. So Ismail was able to appoint his son and heir, Taufiq, as President of the Council of Ministers, sugaring the pill by giving Wilson and de Blignieres, who remained in office, the right of vetoing any Government measures.

Encouraged by the success of his first step towards the liquidation of European control, Ismail proceeded almost immediately to the second. At the end of May, profiting by the signs of dissension which had been apparent in the divergent British and French attitudes over Nubar's dismissal, and encouraged by the marked hostility shown by Vivian, the British Consul-General, towards the Anglo-French Ministers, he organized another 'popular' demonstration and dismissed Wilson and de Blignieres from office. This was a far bolder step than the first one, since the British and French Governments had made it clear that they expected to be consulted before any question of removing these Ministers arose. But the French and British Governments took no action. It seemed that Ismail had won another victory. A new Government was formed by Sherif Pasha, who had resigned office the previous year, and Nubar and Riaz Pasha were sent into exile. Ismail then decreed a refunding of both the bonded and floating debts and announced his proposals a few days in advance of the Report of the Commission of Enquiry,[10] which was published shortly after the dismissal from office of the two principal authors, Wilson and de Blignieres. Ismail's decree was similar to the Commission's proposal in that both recommended a drastic scaling down of capital and interest. But while the Commission's proposal provided for a complete divorce between the finances of Ismail and his family and those of the State, and the granting of a fixed Civil List to the former, Ismail would have regarded any suggestion of personal non-access to the whole of the State revenue as an intolerable infringement of his prerogative.

But both schemes were doomed to be of academic interest only. Rivers Wilson, on his return to Europe, told the Rothschilds that there was a grave danger of Ismail's repudiating the Domains Loan which had been negotiated with the Rothschilds by Wilson. The Rothschilds, having failed to get any action out of the French Government, approached Bismarck. It has been mentioned that several judgements had been obtained against the Egyptian state by foreign creditors suing in the mixed courts. The judgements had remained pending during the sittings of the Commission, but after the dismissal of Wilson and de Blignieres the creditors became restive. It so happened that among these creditors were some German nationals. Bismarck, who had hitherto shown little interest in the fortune of Egypt's European creditors, now informed Great Britain and France that unless they were prepared to intervene effectively in Egypt to protect the interest of these creditors, then Germany would be compelled to take such steps as she considered necessary to this end. This announcement had the calculated effect of throwing Great Britain and France into a panic.

Vivian, the British Consul-General, who was generally regarded as a champion of Ismail against his foreign creditors, was replaced by Sir Frank Lascelles who, in conjunction with his French colleague, began to press upon Ismail the desirability of abdication in favour of his son Taufiq. Taufiq's accession was secured by the *firman* of 1866 by which Ismail had been granted the right of succession by primogeniture in place of the Ottoman law of succession, by which the eldest male member of the family succeeded. Taufiq was believed to be an amiable young man and likely to be amenable to Anglo-French control. For this reason, Great Britain and France were anxious that Ismail should abdicate of his own accord, rather than that he should be deposed by the Sultan, who would probably have insisted on the revocation of the 1866 *firman* in order to secure the succession of Ismail's uncle Halim, the successor under the Ottoman law and an Ottoman protégé, living at Constantinople under the Sultan's protection.

Ismail rejected the advice of the two Consuls-General, and at the same time spent money freely in Constantinople in an attempt to avert a *firman* of deposition. He decreed that the strength of the army should be raised to 60,000 men, refused to accept the mixed court judgements in favour of the floating debt-holders, and repudiated Egypt's liabilities under the Goschen-Joubert funding arrangements. But the sands were running out. Sherif Pasha, the Prime Minister and a man by no means sympathetic to European influence, tried to persuade Ismail to abdicate in order to avoid deposition. But Ismail, with a gambler's optimism, insisted on seeing the game out. He had not long to wait. Satisfactory arrangements were made in Constantinople regarding Taufiq's accession and on 25 June 1879 Ismail received a *firman* of deposition from the Sultan. The same courier brought another *firman* appointing Taufiq as his successor. Two days later Ismail left Alexandria in the royal yacht *Mahroussa*, accompanied by his harem and a considerable store of treasure. He was never to see Egypt again.

The character and achievement of Ismail have been the subject of acute controversy. At one end of the scale are Cromer, Milner, and Colvin, who were at pains to contrast the vices of Ismail's reign with the virtues of their own enlightened despotism. At the other end of the scale is Judge Crabites, to whom Ismail is a chevalier *sans reproche*. In fact, Ismail was neither the monster of depravity depicted by Milner nor the paragon of virtue lauded by Crabites. He was a curious mixture of barbarism and enlightenment. On the one hand, he tolerated the use of flogging in order to wring the last piastre of taxation out of the *fellahin*; on the other hand, he made a real attempt to fight illiteracy. He employed Baker and Gordon to put down the slave trade in the Sudan, yet cultivated his own estates entirely by forced labour. He employed European experts in his administration; he had his Chief Inspector of Finances secretly murdered. He had all the application of a European man of affairs, together with all the capriciousness of an Oriental despot. He combined the financial ingenuousness of an Uckridge with the raffish acumen of a Dr. Smart Alec.

His contribution to Egypt's material progress was enormous. He laid the foundations on which British administrators were later to build so successfully. But his financial recklessness, pushed to the uttermost extremes of folly, resulted in Egypt being deprived of the fruits, while being burdened with the labour and expense, of all his enterprises. If ever a man sold his country it was Ismail. The fact that his creditors were unscrupulous was an aggravation of his folly, for he should have realized their unscrupulousness before he had put Egypt in pawn to them. An absolute ruler has the responsibilities as well as the privileges of power.

Without in any way lightening the burdens of toil and taxation which Mohamed Ali had placed on the inhabitants of Egypt, Ismail mortgaged the proceeds of their toil and taxation by engaging in enterprises which, although good in themselves, were entirely beyond Egypt's financial capacity. What should have been spread over half a century was crowded into a decade without any attempt at equating income with expenditure. His financial irresponsibility was stupendous; he was a very prince of spendthrifts. And he had

something of the personal charm which so often accompanies
financial extravagance. His authority in Egypt was absolute,
his actions unquestioned. His rewards and his punishments
alike were regarded as irrevocable dispensations from on
high. He was Effendina—Our Lord. He was neither good
nor bad. He was above judgement. He could say with Louis
XIV—and with more truth than Louis XIV—'*L'Etat c'est
moi*'. During his reign public morality might have deteriorated; but public security improved. His government might
not have been respectable; but it was respected. His was the
mind that directed; his was the will to be obeyed. His
Ministers were lackeys, liable, like lackeys, to summary
dismissal at the will of their master. When he went the whole
authoritarian structure of the Egyptian State collapsed, and
there was nothing ready to put in its place. The Arabi
rebellion would have been unthinkable under Ismail. His
departure marked something more than the triumph of
European intervention. It marked the beginning of Egyptian
nationalism.

The circumstances of Taufiq's accession would have made
it difficult even for a man of strong character to assert his
independence of Anglo-French control. He had been placed
on the throne by the instrumentality of the British and
French in the expectation that he would be more amenable
to their wishes than his father had been. Such authority as
he had in the country was derived from the support given
to him by the British and French. In the modern idiom, he
was an Anglo-French stooge.

The British Government, having assisted the French in
securing Ismail's departure, was not at first disposed to
accept the implications of its action by joining France in
establishing a virtual protectorate over Egypt. It did not
realize that, by deposing Ismail, it had destroyed indigenous
authority to an extent which made such a protectorate
inevitable. Apparently believing that the main object of
intervention had been secured by the deposition of Ismail,
the British Government tried to persuade France to leave

Egypt alone. M. Waddington wrote: 'You must think that I am very short-sighted if you imagine that I am going to surrender the vantage-ground we have gained in Egypt. The great achievement of my diplomacy has been the acquiring for France in Egypt the influence on the administration of the country to which she is justly entitled, and this influence I am not going to throw away because it does not suit the convenience of England to follow out our common policy.' M. Waddington's appreciation was realistic. There would have been no object in deposing Ismail unless it had been intended to establish a European protectorate over Egypt. To depose Ismail and then to have left Egypt alone would have been childish, because Egypt was no longer capable of standing alone.

The British Government accepted the French viewpoint. After a short and academic argument as to whether Great Britain and France should exercise their protectorate by means of Anglo-French Ministers or Controllers, the latter alternative was chosen, and Major Baring and M. de Blignieres appointed. Major Baring had been the British member of the Caisse de la Dette. M. de Blignieres had been Minister of Public Works in the Nubar Government. (The fact that Rivers Wilson was not chosen as British Controller was probably due to the French who wanted de Blignieres to be *primus inter pares*. They underestimated Major Baring.) It was provided that the Controllers had the right to be present at Cabinet meetings, to demand information, to give advice, to appoint inspectors in the Ministries and in the provinces, and to report to their diplomatic representatives in the event of refusal to accept their advice. Sherif Pasha, President of Ismail's Council of Ministers, was dismissed, and a Government formed by Riaz Pasha, who had been a member of the 1878 Commission of Enquiry and subsequently exiled by Ismail.

The embarrassments facing the Controllers, who were the real rulers of Egypt, were no less acute than those which had faced the international Government the year before. Their first task was to settle the conflicting claims of the Domains estates, which on the one hand had been pledged to the Rothschilds as security for a loan of £8,500,000, and on the other hand were encumbered by judgements delivered by the mixed courts in favour of various unsecured creditors. The matter was settled by a compromise which settled all judgements given in the courts up to the time of the floating of the loan, and obtained the cancellation of all judgements against the estates given after that date. But the main task of the Controllers was to enforce or to amend the debt settlement recommended by the Commission of Enquiry. The Controllers proposed to amend it, but Germany, Italy, and Austria objected to any amendment being made except after consultation with them. As a result of their objections, an International Commission of Liquidation was appointed whose task it was to draw up a final settlement of the Egyptian Debt.

The Commission[11] was composed of two Englishmen, two Frenchmen, one German, one Austrian, and one Italian, under the presidency of Sir Rivers Wilson. Its terms of reference were (a) to assess the total maintainable revenue; (b) to assess the minimum essential State expenditure; and (c) to allocate the difference between (a) and (b) among the creditors. It was clear that the findings of the Commission would be largely conditioned by the attitude of the Controllers, on whom the Commission would have to rely for most of the information about Egypt's finances. In this matter Major Baring, the British Controller, received instructions which indicated that Great Britain was at last beginning to emerge from that subservience to France which had marked British policy in Egypt for the previous eighteen months. Backed by the British Consul-General, Major Baring took the attitude that the interests of the Egyptian people, as well as those of the bond-holders, must be considered in arriving at a settlement, and that Egypt should not be mulcted up to the extreme limit of her ability to pay regardless of any other consideration.

The Commission found that Egypt's maximum maintainable revenue amounted to £8,500,000 per annum (compared with the Goschen-Joubert estimate of £10,500,000). Of this sum, £4,500,000 was reserved for the essential expenses of administration (about £750,000 more than the Goschen-Joubert figure), leaving £4,000,000 per annum for the service of the Debt (compared with the Goschen-Joubert figure of £7,000,000). The bonded debt was re-funded at £80,000,000, consisting of £14,000,000 Preferred Debt, £9,500,000 Daira Debt, £8,500,000 Domains Loan, and £48,000,000 Unified Debt.[12] A new issue of £5,600,000 preferred stock was made in order to pay off the Floating Debt. The following arrangements were made for the servicing of these debts:

(a) *Preferred Debt.* The revenues of the State Railways, the State Telegraphs and Alexandria Harbour. Interest fixed at 5 per cent.

(b) *Daira Debt.* The Daira lands were placed under an Anglo-French administration and the profits earmarked for the service of the Daira Debt. Interest 4 per cent.

(c) *Domains Loan.* The international administration stipulated by Rothschild's as a condition of the loan was continued, but the interest scaled down to 4 per cent.

(d) *Unified Debt.* Receipts from Customs, tobacco dues, and the land tax revenues from the provinces of Gharbis, Menufia, Behera, and Assiut, after meeting any deficit in the service of the Preferred Debt, were earmarked for the service of the Unified Debt, on which the interest was fixed at 4 per cent.

In addition to the arrangements for repaying foreign indebtedness, a sum of £150,000 was earmarked for the payment of compensation to the holders of the Muqabala Loan, whose promised land tax exemptions were repudiated. No provision was made for repayment of the Rouznameh Loan, for which there were no proper receipts, and which was to all intents and purposes a forced levy rather than a loan.

The settlement was avowedly based on the maximum payments which could be expected from Egypt without ruining her whole economy. The fact that the sum allocated to the service of the debt was little more than half that allocated by the Goschen-Joubert Mission (in spite of the fact that an additional £8,500,000 worth of indebtedness had been incurred) is evidence, not of the generosity of the Law of Liquidation (the decree in which the findings of the Commission were promulgated), but of the utter impracticability of the Goschen-Joubert proposals. It is clear, however, that the Controllers, in their capacity as guardians of Egyptian finances, did exercise a moderating influence on the Commission and did secure a settlement which, according to the ethics of international finance, was not an extortionate one.

The foreign creditors had nothing to grumble about. The foreign loans had been floated on grossly extortionate terms in the first place. The security afforded by the Anglo-French control was ample compensation for the scaling down of principal and interest, particularly as the process was mainly a matter of squeezing out water. The only creditors (apart from the Rouznameh creditors) who really did have anything to complain about were the subscribers to the Muqabala Loan.[13] Ismail had obtained £9,500,000 from this loan, and the sum of £150,000 set aside as compensation for what amounted to a complete loss of capital was, in comparison with the treatment of the foreign bond-holders, grossly inadequate. But the worst feature of the settlement was a provision by which any surplus revenue, after the deduction of the 'standard' administrative revenue and the sum set aside for the service of the Debt, was to be paid into a Sinking Fund for the eventual liquidation of the debt. In other words, any increase in Egypt's productivity was to be for the benefit, not of the Egyptian people, but of Egypt's foreign creditors. Whatever Egypt's material progress, her expendable revenue was to be limited to a sum quite inadequate for the development of social services, public works, etc., until such time as Egypt's total indebtedness had been paid off. The Law of Liquidation[14] presupposed the continued administration of Egypt's finances by the representatives of Egypt's creditors, for by no other method was it likely that the machinery of the Egyptian state would continue to work for the exclusive benefit of its creditors. It is probable that this provision was insisted on by the Commission as a *quid pro quo* in exchange for an immediate reduction in the burden of annual payments. It is an open question whether an increase in the immediate burden would not have been preferable to an indefinite mortgaging of Egypt's future prosperity.

It became the duty of the Controllers to administer the finances of Egypt in accordance with the provisions of the Law of Liquidation. It became the duty of the Caisse de la Dette to collect and distribute the sums laid down by the Law of Liquidation and to act as guardians of the Sinking Fund. Such a régime, operating behind the façade of a puppet Sovereign and a complaisant Government, could not fail to be oppressive.[15] But there was no longer an Ismail to exploit the situation. Instead, opposition began to make itself felt from bodies of opinion which were, as the result of Ismail's deposition, able to express themselves for the first time. The powers, by driving out Ismail, had made room for other and potentially more formidable adversaries, who were to transfer the affairs of Egypt from the field of diplomacy to the field of battle and, in so doing, inadvertantly to restore to Great Britain that initiative in Egyptian affairs which she had lost since the accession of Said.

NOTES ON CHAPTER FOUR

1. The Capitulatory Powers at the time of the inauguration of the mixed courts in 1875 were: Great Britain, France, U.S.A., Germany, Austria-Hungary, Belgium, Denmark, Russia, Spain, Greece, Italy, Holland, Portugal and Sweden. Norway was added in 1905 when the Swedish and Norwegian Crowns were separated. Russia ceased to be a Capitulatory Power after

the 1917 Revolution, and Germany and Austria-Hungary after the 1914–18 War.

2. Ismail Pasha Sadiq, known as the Mufattish, was a sinister figure, being Ismail's chief instrument for the extraction of money from his people. He also made an enormous fortune for himself. His disappearance created a nine days' wonder in Cairo. He walked into Gezira Palace one afternoon and was never seen again. Some days after his disappearance a boat left for Upper Egypt in which it was said that the Mufattish was confined as a prisoner, bound for exile in the Sudan. Some weeks later it was announced that he had died in Upper Egypt. It is probable that he never boarded the boat alive, and that he had been murdered at Ismail's orders in order to prevent his giving evidence to the Goschen-Joubert Mission.

3. This funding arrangement, which was later replaced by the decree embodying the Law of Liquidation represented a modification of Ismail's proposal for a Unified Debt of £91,000,000. The arrangement consisted of: (a) a preference stock of £17,000,000 bearing interest at 5 per cent.; (b) a Daira Loan of £9,500,000 bearing interest at 5 per cent., which amalgamated two loans, the Daira Khassa and the Daira Sanieh, which had been raised on the security of Ismail's estates; (c) a Unified Debt of £59,000,000 bearing interest at 6 per cent. A sum of approximately £6,500,000, representing the floating debt, was left unfunded.

4. The Caisse de la Dette was set up as a result of Ismail's decree of 2 May 1876. It became responsible for the execution first of the Goschen-Joubert settlement and later of the Law of Liquidation. The first British representative on the Caisse was Major Baring, later Lord Cromer.

5. The principle on which the Commission proceeded, to quote the words of the Report, was that 'no sacrifice should be demanded of the creditors until every reasonable sacrifice has been made by the debtors'. The Commission appears to have found no incongruity between the sacrifice of a bond-holder compelled to accept a lower rate of interest, and the sacrifice of a peasant whose crops were seized in order to pay that interest.

6. It is suggested by Judge Crabites in his *Spoliation of Suez* that the assets referred to by the French were the Canal Company's preference shares, which were later (1879) sold to the Credit Foncier by the Anglo-French Control. Crabites alleges that the French attitude was dictated by a desire to force Ismail to disgorge these shares in order to meet the coupon.

7. Rivers Wilson was a Commissioner of the National Debt and a British civil servant. Permission from the British Government was required before he could accept a Ministerial appointment in Egypt. This permission was granted by Lord Salisbury, the Foreign Secretary, who emphasized that the appointment was in Great Britain's interest.

8. M. de Blignieres was the French representative on the Caisse de la Dette.

9. In 1879 *Kharaj* lands paid from 120 to 170 piastres per *feddan* per annum in land tax. *Ushuri* lands paid an average of only 30 piastres per annum.

10. The Report of the Commission of Enquiry formed the basis for the final settlement subsequently decreed in the Law of Liquidation.

11. One English, one French, and the Austrian and Italian members were, as members of the Caisse, *ex officio* members of the Commission.

12. As compared with the Goschen-Joubert settlement, the principal of the Preferred Debt was reduced by £3,000,000, and the rate of interest maintained; the principal of the Daira Debt was maintained and the rate of interest reduced

from 5 per cent. to 4 per cent.; the principal of the Unified Debt was reduced by £11,000,000 and the rate of interest reduced from 6 per cent. to 4 per cent.

13. The money to pay the Muqabala compensation was found by raising the land tax on the *ushuri* lands.

14. The decree embodying the Law of Liquidation was assented to by six powers—Great Britain, France, Russia, Germany, Italy, and Austria-Hungary. These powers guaranteed the assent of the other eight Capitulatory Powers. This set a precedent which was afterwards generally followed for all international arrangements in connexion with the Debt.

15. It is fair to mention that a great many reforms were instituted and implemented by the Dual Control. The poll tax was abolished; agriculturalists were relieved from payment of the professional tax; many *octroi*, highway, and market dues were abolished. The method of collecting land tax was regularized and sums due from each cultivator fixed instead of being assessed arbitrarily. The system of extorting land tax in advance was abolished, and the due date of payment fixed so as to cause a minimum of hardship to the cultivator. The salt tax was abolished and replaced by a salt monopoly.

CHAPTER FIVE

THE SECOND BRITISH OCCUPATION

THE Egyptian nationalism which started to manifest itself for the first time after Ismail's deposition consisted of three separate elements. First, there was the school of Islamic modernism founded by Jamal-ad-Din Afghani, and developed in Egypt by his pupil and successor, Mohamed Abdu. Islamic modernism was an attempt to rescue Islam from the disputatious sterility in which it was sunk, and to equate the basic principles of the Quran with the new conditions created by material progress. It was a liberal movement in that it did not insist on a literal interpretation of the Shari'a Law;[1] it was a conservative movement in that it did seek to call a halt to the boulevard culture which was sapping the foundations of traditional Islamic conduct. During the latter years of Ismail's reign, Islamic modernism in Egypt attained a fair measure of influence among the younger *'ulema* at al-Azhar and among the more serious-minded intellectual laymen who were disturbed both by the social trends of Westernization and by the apparent inability of Islam to combat these trends by other than obscurantist methods. The Islamic modernists were bitterly opposed both to the Royal Family and to the Turkish ruling class generally, regarding them as responsible for the Western secularism with which Egypt had been overrun. They were sensible enough to realize that this secularism could be combated only by a restatement and a reimplementation of the principles of Islam.

The second component of Egyptian nationalism, which can conveniently be termed 'Constitutionalism', was made up of a number of European-educated magnates, whose personal objection to European control operating behind a mask of Khedival absolutism was reinforced by theoretical admiration of liberalism, picked up in the course of their European education and travel. The leader of the Constitutionalists was Sherif Pasha, a polished gentleman of Turkish extraction and French education who had gained considerable popularity in Egypt as the result of his refusal to give evidence before the 1878 Commission of Enquiry. Their strength was dependent on the support which they might expect to receive from the Chamber of Notables, a consultative body of provincial magnates set up by Ismail in 1866, and representing the only organized body of public opinion then existing in Egypt.

The third component was the native Egyptian element among the Army officers. There was still in Egypt a very definite distinction between Turks, Circassians, and Albanians on the one hand, and native Egyptians on the other. Most of the ruling class was still Turkish, Circassian, or Albanian, occupying the same position *vis-à-vis* the native Egyptian as the Norman must have occupied *vis-à-vis* the native Englishman in the early years after the Norman Conquest. The process of assimilation had advanced far enough to make the Egyptians resent their feeling of inferiority, but not far enough to eliminate the fact of inferiority, either in respect of ability or social position. The resultant jealousy was particularly marked among the Egyptian-born officers of the Army.

While Ismail ruled, his iron hand was sufficient to silence discontent. With the accession of Taufiq, the personal influence of the Throne was weakened, and the causes of discontent were multiplied.

The discontents arising from the Dual Control represented the only common ground between the three nationalist groups. Statesmanship on the nationalist side might have used the discontents to weld the diverse elements together into a disciplined group with a constructive programme of action. Statesmanship on the part of Great Britain and

France might, by judicious guidance, have built up a new Egyptian state on the basis of these nationalist elements. But statesmanship was lacking on both sides.

The incidence of the Dual Control affected the three nationalist groups, as it affected the country as a whole, in varying degrees. The strict implementation of the Law of Liquidation meant a continuance of heavy taxation, nearly half of the proceeds of which were devoted to the service of the Debt. The ever-increasing number of highly-paid European officials (at the end of 1881 there were 1,325 Europeans in the Egyptian Service, drawing total annual emoluments of £373,704) introduced by the Dual Control not only displaced a great many Egyptian officials from their posts, but also represented an increasingly heavy burden on that static part of the revenue that remained at the disposal of the Treasury. Such administrative economies as were made were apt to be resented when they were accompanied (as they usually were) by the appointment of Europeans at high salaries to do what had previously been done by Egyptians at low salaries. Together with the influx of foreign officials there was a great increase in the number of non-official foreign residents, traders and others, who too often abused their Capitulatory privileges at the expense of the native inhabitants.

The Islamic modernists were incensed at the debauching of Egyptian life that was going on under cover of the Capitulations.[2] The Constitutionalists were frustrated by the Dual Control's policy of using the Khedive as an authoritarian *homme de paille* for their own dictatorial administration. (Soon after Taufiq's accession, Sherif Pasha resigned as a result of the refusal of the Controllers to concede constitutional government. He was replaced as Prime Minister by Riaz Pasha, an orthodox Moslem and confirmed reactionary, who hated constitutionalism even more than he hated foreign control.)

But it was the Egyptian officers of the Army who were foremost in giving voice to their grievances. As has been related, Ismail, just before his deposition, had been in process of raising the strength of the Army to 60,000 men. The *firman* authorizing Taufiq's accession had stipulated the limitation of the Army to 18,000 men. The Dual Control, for reasons of economy, insisted on a reduction even below this figure. The result was wholesale retrenchment of officers and men. The men were doubtless only too pleased to be allowed to return to their fields and families. The officers were in a different case. The Army was their career. The Egyptian officers were the first to be retrenched. This, coming on top of their other grievances, brought matters to a head.

During the course of 1881 a group of Egyptian Army Colonels, headed by one Ahmed Arabi, succeeded first in having a Circassian Minister of War replaced by one of their own nominees (Mahmud Sami), and later in forcing the Khedive to dismiss Riaz Pasha, to invite Sherif Pasha, the leader of the Constitutionalists, to form a Ministry, and to summon the Chamber of Notables. The fact that the Khedive was unable to resist these demands made it apparent that he commanded no organized body of support in Egypt, and that his prestige was insufficient to prevent organized opposition from manifesting itself and getting its way. He had not even the support of the Sultan, who favoured his uncle Halim. He was only kept on the throne by Anglo-French influence, operating through the Consuls-General and the Controllers, who were without the backing of any armed force.

Although the efforts of the military malcontents were immediately directed against the Khedive, it was clear that their ultimate object was the power behind the Khedive—the Anglo-French Controllers and foreign influence generally. The military movement, deeply influenced by the *'ulema*, was, in fact, specifically anti-foreign. The Circassians in the Army were the first objects of their nationalist hatred. As successive mutinies caused the gradual elimination of the Circassians from positions of authority, the scope of the attack broadened to embrace, first the Turkish ruling class, then the Controllers, and finally foreigners in general.

In the circumstances it was clear that the existing position of the Khedive and the Controllers could not be long maintained. Fear and ambition drove the Colonels from mutiny to successful mutiny, and the Khedive and the Controllers had the force neither of arms nor of public opinion with which to oppose them. Their authority was diminishing to vanishing-point. The British and French had four clear-cut alternatives before them: (a) abandonment of Dual Control and the Law of Liquidation; (b) the reinforcement of Dual Control by an Anglo-French military occupation; (c) a request to the Sultan for a Turkish military occupation; (d) an accommodation with one of the Egyptian nationalist groups.

Of these alternatives the fourth seemed to be the most immediately promising. The Sherif Government and the Chamber of Notables were alarmed at the insubordination of the Army, and were in consequence disposed to be accommodating towards the Dual Control as the lesser of two evils, provided that the Dual Control was prepared to come out from behind its Khedival façade and make some concession in the direction of constitutional self-government. The opportunity for such a concession came when the Chamber of Notables, which had assembled towards the end of December, demanded the right to vote that part of the Budget not specifically assigned to the service of the Debt. A concession in this direction would have cemented the alliance between Sherif and the Notables, would have encouraged the Notables in their opposition to the Army, and would have provided the Dual Control with a basis on which to build up some permanent alternative to Khedival absolutism.

The opportunity was not taken. Towards the end of December a change of Ministry in France had brought M. Gambetta into power. Gambetta, who had very definite views about Egypt, succeeded in making the British Liberal

116

Government (which had come into power in March 1880) almost as subservient to French policy in Egypt as its Conservative predecessor had been.

By refusing reasonable concessions demanded peacefully, France and Great Britain made armed intervention inevitable. They destroyed any possibility of co-operation with moderate Egyptian nationalism and, by making the position of moderate nationalists impossible, conferred on Arabi a monopoly of indigenous authority in the country. It was unfortunate that Lord Granville, the British Foreign Secretary, had neither sufficient strength of character nor sufficient breadth of view to form a proper appreciation of the situation. Instead, egged on by Gambetta on the one hand and by Malet and Colvin on the other, he caused the Liberal Government to drift into an Egyptian policy which, had Mr. Gladstone been in opposition instead of being head of the Government, would have drawn from him an impressive harangue on international morality.

While Gambetta was almost openly in favour of creating a situation in Egypt which would make armed intervention imperative, Lord Granville inclined to the view that a Turkish occupation was the least objectionable alternative if it should prove impracticable to let things 'dawdle' on as they were. (In view of Mr. Gladstone's public utterances about Turkey a year or two before, his Foreign Secretary's advocacy of this solution of the Egyptian question is not without humour.)

Had Lord Granville been allowed to have his way and let things 'dawdle' on, it is just possible, although not probable, that fear of the Army would have kept the Notables sufficiently united and sufficiently moderate to secure a precarious equilibrium on which the Dual Control could have continued to function. But M. Gambetta did not approve of dawdling. He conceived the idea that a display of Anglo-French solidarity would frighten both Army and Notables into acquiescence with the authoritarian ideas of the Dual Control. He therefore prepared the text of a joint note for submission to the Egyptian Government. The text, which was in the form of an instruction to the British and French representatives in Cairo, read as follows:

You have been instructed on several occasions to inform the Khedive and his Government of the determination of England and France to afford them support against the difficulties of various kinds which might interfere with the course of affairs in Egypt. The two powers are entirely agreed on the subject, and recent circumstances, and especially the meeting of the Chamber of Notables convoked by the Khedive, have given them the opportunity for a further exchange of views. I have accordingly to instruct you to declare to the Khedive that the British and French Governments consider the maintenance of His Highness on the throne, on the terms laid down in the Sultan's *firman* and officially recognized by the two Governments, as alone able to guarantee, for the present and future, the good order and development of general prosperity in Egypt in which France and Great Britain are equally interested. The two Governments, being closely associated in their resolve to guard, by their united efforts, against all causes of complication, internal or external, which might menace the order of things established in Egypt, do not doubt that the assurance publicly given of their fixed intention in this respect will tend to avert the dangers to which the Government of the Khedive might be exposed and which would certainly find England and France united to oppose them. They feel certain that His Highness will derive from this assurance the confidence and strength which he requires to direct the destinies of Egypt and his people.

Assuming M. Gambetta to have been correctly informed of the state of affairs in Egypt, it is impossible to avoid the conclusion that the despatch of such a note was intended to create a situation in which armed intervention would become imperative. To refuse concessions to the Constitutionalists was one thing; to make a formal declaration of root-and-branch opposition to Constitutionalism, either immediately or in the future, was quite another. The joint note was a calculated slap in the face to Sherif Pasha and the Notables, who at that time alone stood between Egypt and armed insurrection.

Lord Granville did not, apparently, see the matter in that light. He agreed to Gambetta's draft, with the characteristic reservation that the British Government 'must not be considered as committing themselves to any particular mode of action, if action should be found necessary'. Consequently, on 6 January 1882, the joint note, according to the above text, was communicated to the Egyptian Government by the British and French representatives.

The result might have been foreseen. The Chamber of Notables swung over to support of the Army, and became exigent in their demands both for control of the Budget and an increase in the size of the Army. Sherif Pasha, who had reluctantly supported the Dual Control in its attitude towards the Chamber's demands over the Budget, lost his hold on the Notables when they saw how his co-operation had been rewarded. The attitude of the Army appeared to have received conclusive justification.

The hostile reception accorded to the note caused the British Government to consider whether it would not be politic to make some concession to the demands of the Chamber. But it was now too late for concessions, even if the French had been disposed to agree to them. The foundations of Sherif's Government, which represented the only possible bridge between the Dual Control and Egyptian nationalism, had been ruthlessly knocked away.

On 3 February Sherif Pasha resigned, and Mahmud Sami became Prime Minister, with Arabi as Minister for War. (Mahmud Sami had been Minister and Arabi Under-Secretary for War in the Sherif Government.) The military were in the saddle and the horse was about to run away.

Four days before Sherif's resignation, Gambetta had himself gone out of office, and had been replaced by M. de Freycinet, who was even more opposed than Lord Granville to military intervention in Egypt.

Events now moved quickly. A situation had been created

in which something more than the financial interests of the bond-holders had become dependent on the maintenance of some measure of European authority in Egypt. While the situation prior to the despatch of the joint note might be said to have jeopardized the interests of the European creditors, the situation after the despatch of the joint note developed in such a way as to jeopardize the lives of European residents. Religious fanaticism and its concomitant xenophobia, fanned by the more unscrupulous of the *'ulema*, had always been a potent feature in Egyptian nationalism, as indeed it must be in any popular movement in the Moslem world.

It is fair to state that the New Government appears to have done nothing to incite its more irresponsible supporters. But, like many Egyptian politicians after him, Arabi, the real head of the Government, was the prisoner of his own propaganda. A Government which has come into power as the result of the successful defiance of authority inevitably finds it difficult to maintain its own authority. The ability of a revolutionary government to do so is a test of its quality. By this standard, the Sami Government was not impressive. The Army, thoroughly Egyptianized by this time, sated itself with the spoils of office. New battalions were raised; pay was increased; hundreds of officers were promoted without reference either to their ability or to the Army establishments. Troops in the provinces pillaged the inhabitants and carried on an active trade in firearms.

The Controllers were in no position to control the new Government. Their power had been dependent on their ability to arrive at an accommodation with Egyptian nationalism; they had failed to do so, and had become powerless in consequence. There was nothing for them to do but to join the Consuls-General in passively observing the situation which their own lack of prescience had helped to create. De Blignieres resigned; Colvin remained, on instructions from the British Government.

Meanwhile, the British and French Governments were

considering ways and means of extricating themselves from the situation in which M. Gambetta's precipitancy had placed them. Lord Granville and M. de Freycinet were at one in their desire to avoid armed intervention. Since it appeared that some form of outside intervention would soon become necessary in order to protect the lives and property of European residents in Egypt (consideration for the interests of the bond-holders was temporarily in abeyance), both Governments began seriously to consider the desirability of Turkish intervention.

But the Sultan was in no hurry to intervene in order to restore the authority of Taufiq. He had for some time, through his emissaries, been in contact with Arabi, and may even have been considering an accommodation with the military party which would have involved the deposition of Taufiq and his replacement by Halim. Furthermore, M. de Freycinet was still wavering in his consent to the principle of Turkish intervention.

Eventually the British and French Governments agreed to send naval squadrons to Alexandria. On 19 May Admiral Seymour[3] arrived off Alexandria in the battleship *Invincible*, escorted by two gunboats. On the same day the French battleship *La Gallionière* arrived, also escorted by two gunboats. The rest of the two squadrons remained at call in Suda Bay, Crete. The British Admiral had instructions to contact the British Consul-General and to co-operate with the French force in the support of the Khedive's authority and for the protection of British and European residents to the extent of landing a force should this prove to be necessary. The French Admiral was merely instructed to give moral support to the Khedive, but to abstain from any warlike action unless attacked. The French were already pulling out of the imbroglio created by M. Gambetta.

The Turkish Government now apparently considered that the English and French had become sufficiently *brulés* in Egypt to enable it to intervene independently. Two Turkish Commissioners were therefore sent to Egypt, the senior,

Darwish Pasha, with instructions to support the Khedive, and the junior, Essad Pasha, with instructions to place himself in contact with Arabi. There is, in fact, little doubt that the Ottoman Government, while making a show of co-operation with Anglo-French policy, was paving the way for the deposition of Taufiq.

But events were moving too fast for the tortuous diplomacy of the Sublime Porte. Arabi considered himself sufficiently powerful to be able to dispense with any assistance, official or unofficial, from Constantinople. Those Notables who did not actively support him kept quiet for the sake of their own safety. The Khedive no longer possessed even the outward semblance of authority. The Dual Control had ceased to exist.

On 10 June the situation in Egypt was forcibly brought to the notice of the outside world by an anti-foreign outbreak in Alexandria which resulted in the murder of some fifty Europeans.[4] This massacre, which was accompanied by similar outbreaks in the provinces, was the natural outcome of the religious fanaticism and xenophobia which had increased *pari passu* with increasing nationalist extremism. Arabi was able to demonstrate both his authority and his increasing sense of responsibility by his successful use of the Army to restore order. During the course of the next few days most of the members of the foreign communities in Alexandria were embarked on the numerous European ships which had now arrived in the harbour.[5]

A conference of the powers met at Constantinople. As the necessity for intervention became more apparent, the unwillingness of the powers to intervene became more marked. It was clear that the melancholy sequence of injudicious intransigence followed by extorted concessions had built up Arabi's influence to an extent which made it possible that intervention might prove to be a long-drawn-out and costly operation if it were to achieve its object of restoring the power of the Khedive and the Dual Control. The Ottoman tradition was to compound with successful rebellion, not to fight it. The French, Germans, and Austrians likewise veered round in favour of an accommodation with Arabi. The British Government found itself alone in advocating his overthrow.

There was no more time to be lost. It was necessary either to open negotiations with Arabi or to call a halt to his activities. For the first time in its dealings with Egypt since 1840, the British Government made a firm decision and firmly acted on it.

At the beginning of July the Egyptian garrison at Alexandria was reinforced and work on the fortifications and coastal batteries, which had ceased on the Sultan's order at the beginning of June, was recommenced. On 3 July Admiral Seymour, who had been heavily reinforced since his arrival at Alexandria and now had under his command eight ships of the line, one torpedo boat and five gunboats,[6] was instructed to prevent the continuance of work on the fortifications and to open fire if his representations were not complied with. These instructions were communicated to the French Government. On 5 July M. de Freycinet told the British Ambassador that he could not instruct the French Admiral at Alexandria to associate himself with Admiral Seymour's instructions. On the same day M. de Freycinet informed the French Chamber that no act of hostility would be committed by France in Egypt without the consent of the Chamber. On 9 July, as work on the fortifications had not ceased, Admiral Seymour announced that if the forts were not surrendered to him within twenty-four hours, he would open fire on them. This decision was communicated to the foreign consuls and to the various European governments. The French squadron sailed for Port Said.

At 7 a.m. on 11 July the bombardment of the forts started, and continued throughout the day until the shore batteries had been silenced. The next day the town of Alexandria was observed to be in flames.

The Khedive,[7] who had previously refused a British offer

to embark him at Alexandria, had remained with his Government and had actually given the order to reply to Admiral Seymour's fire. He was at Ras-el-Tin Palace during the bombardment, and accepted the protection of the British fleet the following day when Arabi and his army had started to withdraw in the direction of Kafr-al-Dawar, on an isthmus connecting the Peninsula of Alexandria with the mainland of the Delta.[8]

The origin of the Alexandria fire has never been satisfactorily explained. It was variously alleged to have been caused by Seymour's shells and by Arabi's retreating army. What is certain is that Arabi deliberately left Alexandria to the mercies of fire and loot. Seymour, who was apparently unaware that Arabi had withdrawn, considered that he could not spare a sufficient force to effect a landing in face of probable resistance. As a result, Alexandria, deserted by the Egyptian Army and unoccupied by the British Navy, suffered these disasters for several days until it became apparent to Admiral Seymour that no resistance was to be apprehended. Small naval parties were then landed to deal with the situation as best they could pending the arrival of the expeditionary force which the British Government had decided (on 20 July) to send to Alexandria under Sir Garnet Wolseley.

On 22 July the Khedive, now under the protection of the British fleet, declared Arabi a rebel for having disobeyed his command to return to Alexandria.[9] Of more immediate moment was the meeting of a 'National Council' in Cairo which declared its support of Arabi.

Meanwhile, diplomatic negotiations were proceeding in Constantinople. The Porte, which had been impressed by the degree of popular support enjoyed by Arabi and by the lack of unanimity among the powers, refused to commit itself either by declaring Arabi a rebel or by associating itself with the British intervention. The French refused a British invitation to co-operate in the occupation of the Suez Canal. Italy and Austria alone unequivocally supported the British intervention, without either desiring or being asked to participate in it.

Towards the end of July, the British Navy, acting under the nominal authority of the Khedive, occupied Port Said, Ismalia and Suez, in spite of the protests of the French Government and of M. de Lesseps, who apparently considered the Canal as a sovereign State of which he himself was the dictator. On 8 August the de Freycinet Government fell and was replaced by a Government which was even more opposed to adventures in Egypt than its predecessor. On 15 August Sir Garnet Wolseley arrived at Alexandria with his expeditionary force. The larger part was almost immediately re-embarked and landed at Ismailia. (Arabi, relying on the fatuous assurances of de Lesseps to the effect that he could successfully prevent a British landing in the Canal, had made no attempt to occupy the Canal Zone himself.) There followed an almost unopposed advance by the British force along the Sweetwater Canal. The Battle of Tel-al-Kebir (13 September), the flight of Arabi, the occupation of Cairo, and the collapse of the rebellion followed.

The Ottoman Government, which had refused British requests for intervention until it was certain which way the cat was going to jump, veered round in favour of the British as soon as it realized that they were sincere in their determination to crush Arabi. But since Great Britain's object in seeking Turkish intervention had been to avoid the necessity for acting herself, it is not surprising that the British Government should no longer have welcomed Turkish action after earlier Turkish refusals had made British intervention necessary. So, during the first fortnight of September, Turkish and British roles in Constantinople became reversed. The Turks were anxious to intervene; Lord Dufferin, the British Ambassador, procrastinated until such time as the news of the Battle of Tel-al-Kebir demonstrated that this had become superfluous.

At the end of September Great Britain was in absolute and undisputed possession of Egypt. There was probably not a single person outside Great Britain who did not believe that this had been accomplished as the result of a deep-laid and Macchiavellian plot designed to oust any other power from any share in the control of Egypt. The real facts were as follows: (*a*) it was France and not Great Britain who had taken the initiative in the policy which had made foreign intervention inevitable; (*b*) it was France and not Great Britain who had persistently opposed Turkish intervention; (*c*) it was France who, in the most unequivocal terms, had refused to join with Great Britain in the bombardment of Alexandria or in the occupation of the Suez Canal.

The valid criticisms of the British Government's policy in the events leading up to the occupation are: (*a*) that it neglected to seek an accommodation with moderate nationalism in the days of the Sherif Government, but instead, at French instigation, consolidated and united Egyptian nationalism against the Dual Control by means of the joint note; (*b*) that having, by the joint note, created a violent, united and hostile Egyptian nationalism, it did not devote sufficient attention to the possibility of treating Arabi as the accredited representative of the Egyptian nation.

The possibility of treating with Arabi does not seem to have been seriously considered by the British Government. There were several fairly good reasons why it should not have been. At that time the British Government had not had as much experience as it has had to-day of trying to deal with extreme nationalism after having refused concessions to moderate nationalism. To treat with Arabi after having rebuffed Sherif was too much like straining out a gnat and swallowing a camel. Furthermore, British official and public opinion had a deep and abiding mistrust of anything savouring of a military dictatorship. A feeling of loyalty and obligation to the Khedive was, rightly, a factor of considerable weight in dictating opposition to Arabi. But perhaps the most potent factor was the inability of the British Government to realize that, in a country governed by other than democratic methods, violence is the only way in which a government can be opposed. Arabi was advancing demands which in England could have been voiced in a peaceful and legitimate manner but which in Egypt could only be advanced by violence. Consequently, violence cannot necessarily be regarded as a sign of moral obliquity and political incapacity, particularly when, as in the case of the Arabi rebellion, violence was, generally speaking, restricted to the minimum necessary for the attainment of the ends in view.

After the collapse of the rebellion there was a considerable reaction in England from the martial enthusiasm which had accompanied the despatch of Wolseley's expeditionary force. The slaughter of Egyptian peasantry at Tel-al-Kebir and the pathetic incompetence of the American-trained[10] Egyptian Army proved something of an anti-climax after the horrific tales of massacre and revolt with which the British public had been regaled. It was generally felt that a foe who had been conquered so easily could not have been such a menace after all. In fact, the British public was experiencing an emotional 'hang-over' which communicated itself to the British Government.

This reaction was probably one reason for the fact that the settlement arrived at was not one adapted to the needs of the situation. This situation was not dissimilar to that which had existed after the French evacuation of Egypt nearly 100 years before. There was no actual or potential indigenous authority in Egypt. Khedival absolutism had been destroyed by the deposition of Ismail. Constitutionalism had been destroyed by the joint note. The Dual Control had been destroyed by Arabi, who in his turn had been destroyed by Sir Garnet Wolseley. The dislocation and the expense of war had made the Law of Liquidation anachronistic. Egypt had had a surfeit of international politics. What she needed was a few years of honest and efficient administration on the one hand, and the gradual development of representative institutions on the other. There is no doubt that Great Britain, with her imperial experience, would have been able to provide Egypt with the first, although there might have

127

been some legitimate doubt about her willingness to encourage the second.

But the matter was never put to the test. The prerequisites of an efficient administration were, first, the removal of the Court and Royal Family with all their limitless capacity for intrigue and corruption, and, secondly, the clearing away of the Capitulations, the mixed courts, the Dual Control, the Railway Board, and all the other international impedimenta which had been imposed on Egypt as a result of the Ottoman connexion and of Ismail's extravagance.

There were obvious difficulties about the abolition of the Khedivate. Anglo-French and, latterly, British policy in Egypt had been built round support of the Khedive against his domestic enemies. British armed intervention in Egypt had had as its avowed object the re-establishment of his authority. In the circumstances the abolition of the Khedivate would have been an act of bad faith. At the same time there is no doubt that its retention was politically deplorable in that it identified British rule from the beginning with a corrupt, oppressive, and incompetent social system.

After the collapse of the rebellion the Khedive called upon the conservative and experienced Riaz Pasha to form a Government. The main immediate interest of the Khedive and the new Government was to revenge themselves on Arabi and his associates. But although Great Britain had handed over the rebels to the Egyptian Government for trial, she demanded the right to decide on their fate. Lord Dufferin, the British Ambassador at Constantinople, who had come to Egypt in order to make recommendations to the British Government regarding Egypt's political future, found that his first task was to settle the fate of Arabi. He decided that it would be both impolitic and harsh to execute Arabi or any of his associates, against whom no specific crime of violence could be proved; it was therefore arranged that Arabi and his principal associates should plead guilty to rebellion and be sentenced to exile for life. There is little doubt that Dufferin's decision was both just and politic.

But it would have been better if Arabi had not been handed over to the Egyptian Government in the first place. The thwarting of that Govenment's well-known and, by Oriental standards, legitimate desire to have Arabi executed had a most deleterious effect on the prestige which it was painfully trying to recreate. Riaz Pasha resigned in protest, and was succeeded by Sherif Pasha.

In the realm of internationalism a good start was made by the abolition of the Dual Control. The Battle of Tel-al-Kebir had hardly been fought before France had made it clear that she expected the Dual Control to be re-established. The British Government returned a firm refusal, whereupon the French Government announced that it would 'resume its liberty of action in Egypt'. In practice, this 'liberty of action' amounted to an unrelenting and unreasoning hostility to Great Britain in Egypt which was persisted in by every method short of war for a period of over twenty years.

Having provoked France's enmity over Egypt it would, apart from any other consideration, have seemed obvious good sense to disarm France's potentiality for interference there. But the British Government, having obtained, or at all events sought, an international mandate for intervention, was reluctant to break away from internationalism in arranging for the future administration of Egypt. The maintenance of the integrity of the Ottoman Empire had come to be regarded by the powers as a necessary condition for the maintenance of peace in Europe. Any attempt by any one power to infringe that integrity was almost certain to bring all the other powers into concerted opposition. At the Conference in Constantinople which had preceded the British intervention in Egypt the Powers had mutually agreed 'not to seek in any arrangement which might be made in consequence of any concerted action for the regulation of the affairs of Egypt, any territorial advantages, nor any concession of any exclusive privileges, nor any commercial advantages other than those which any other nation might equally obtain'. Great Britain could not afford to incur the enmity of Europe in order to provide for the good government of Egypt. So the Capitulatory privileges, the abolition of which would have radically altered Egypt's status as a province of the Ottoman Empire, were retained, together with the burden of the annual tribute of £350,000 payable to Constantinople.

The other set of international limitations on Egypt's sovereignty, which had nothing to do with her status as a province of the Ottoman Empire, consisted of the mixed courts, the Law of Liquidation, and the Caisse de la Dette. It was not unreasonably expected by the powers that Great Britain should assume responsibility for the observance of the Law of Liquidation, since in the eyes of the powers the main object of intervention in Egypt had been to enforce that observance. The abolition of the mixed courts and the Caisse de la Dette were in a different category. Abolition would have involved no change in Egypt's status *vis-à-vis* Turkey, and no repudiation of any international agreement. The Caisse de la Dette existed in order to ensure the implementation of the Law of Liquidation; the value of the mixed courts, in so far as the powers were concerned, was to ensure that Egypt observed its financial and capitulatory obligations to European subjects. If Great Britain, having accepted on behalf of Egypt the obligations imposed by the Capitulations and the Law of Liquidation, had decreed the abolition of the mixed courts and the Caisse de la Dette, the powers could not reasonably have objected, provided that Great Britain made it clear that her responsibility would continue at least until the foreign debt had been liquidated. But instead of emphasizing the permanence of her occupation, which was desirable in order to ensure the fulfilment of every obligation which Great Britain had assumed in Egypt, the British Government, from the time of Tel-al-Kebir onward, continually stressed the temporary nature of that occupation. For example, in October 1882 Lord Dufferin was informed by Lord Granville that 'Her Majesty's Government contemplated shortly commencing the withdrawal of

British troops from Egypt'.[11] In January 1883 Lord Granville, in a circular to the powers, stated: 'Her Majesty's
Government are desirous of withdrawing it [the British
force] as soon as the state of the country and the organization
of proper means for the maintenance of the Khedive's
authority will permit of it.' As in the then state of Egypt, it
was impossible to contemplate any speedy attainment of a
state of affairs in which Egypt would be able or willing to
observe her international obligations without the guiding
hand of a foreign occupation, and since Great Britain
apparently contemplated a withdrawal before that stage
had been reached, it is not surprising that the Powers were
unwilling to concede the removal of guarantees which, in
default of a foreign occupation, were even more necessary
than they had been at the time of their inception.[12]

(It may of course be objected that a long-term plan for a
British controlled administration was not incompatible with
the speedy withdrawal of British troops. But the Dual
Control had collapsed precisely because it had no military
force behind it. There is no doubt that any European-
controlled administration, and particularly any European-
controlled administration pledged to the observance of
Egypt's obligations to her foreign creditors, would have
speedily collapsed without the existence of force in the background. The withdrawal of British troops would have
been tantamount to the withdrawal of any effective British
control.)

It is not difficult to understand the British Government's
point of view. Great Britain's main interest in foreign policy
was the maintenance of the balance of power in Europe.
From that point of view, the Egyptian entanglement into
which she had drifted was an unmitigated nuisance, since
it deprived her of that detachment from European affairs
on which her traditional foreign policy was based. The
British Government was already regretting the intervention
into which it had been jockeyed by its own irresolution and
by M. Gambetta's precipitancy. Great Britain wished to

divest herself of her Egyptian responsibilities as soon as she decently could.

With regard to domestic administration, the following is an extract from the instructions given by the British Government to Lord Dufferin when despatching him on his mission to make recommendations for the future administration of Egypt:

The success of the military operations undertaken by Her Majesty's Government has placed them in a position of authority and of corresponding responsibility in regard to the future government of the country. The Government, while desiring that the British occupation should last for as short a time as possible, feel bound not to withdraw from the task imposed on them until the administration of affairs has been reconstituted on a basis which will afford satisfactory guarantees for the maintenance of peace, order, and prosperity in Egypt, for the stability of the Khedive's authority, for the judicious development of self-government, and for the fulfilment of obligations towards foreign powers.

Assuming the desirability of an early withdrawal from Egypt, Great Britain's position was not dissimilar to that which had faced her after the Treaty of Amiens, except that the Turks were not, as they had been in 1802, sharing the occupation of the country with Great Britain. For some reason, Lord Dufferin, in his recommendations to the British Government, did not appear seriously to consider the possibility of a Turkish reoccupation. Instead, he attempted to adjust an essentially long-term process to the requirements of a short-term policy.

Lord Dufferin made the best of a bad job. The first essential was to provide for the restoration of public order and security. He recommended the re-forming of the Egyptian Army (which had been formally disbanded after the defeat of the rebellion) under British officers seconded from the British Army, and the establishment of a mobile gendarmerie under British·guidance for the policing of the rural districts. The next step was to provide a successor to the Dual Control which would ensure the proper super-intendence of Egypt's finances. Lord Dufferin recommended the appointment of a British financial adviser (Sir Auckland Colvin was the first incumbent of this post),[13] who would succeed to the powers and privileges previously conferred on the two Anglo-French Controllers. He also recommended the appointment of a British adviser and British inspectors in the Ministry of Public Works who would, by developing the irrigation and other resources of the country, devote themselves to securing an increase in the country's pro-ductivity sufficient to enable the service of the debt to be provided for without the necessity for the previous oppressive and destructive incidence of taxation.

On the political side Lord Dufferin recognized the im-mediate necessity for the continuance of the personal rule of the Khedive, exercised through his Ministers, but provided for a gradual progress towards constitutional government by the setting up of three representative bodies: (i) a Legislative Council consisting of thirty members, of whom fourteen were to be nominated by the Khedive and sixteen elected by indirect suffrage; (ii) a General Assembly consisting of the members of the Legislative Council plus the Council of Ministers plus forty-six provincial Notables; (iii) a Provincial Council in each province, elected by indirect suffrage to advise the *mudirs* in matters of general administration.

Lord Dufferin was, of course, not unaware of the contra-dictions inherent in the task which he had been set. In his recommendations, he more than once stressed the necessity of making haste slowly in the matter of withdrawal. Within the limits of his instructions it was impossible to recommend what the situation really needed—a complete reconstruction of the administrative system with a proportion of able Europeans administering, as well as laying down, policy. Failing this, it was obviously wise to maintain the framework of the old authoritarian system, within which a team of British advisers and inspectors would have the power to limit folly, even if they would not have the power to implement wisdom. An administration needs stability and experience before it can safely expose itself to the winds of democratic criticism. Democratic institutions operating on a weak and inefficient executive discredit democracy by creating chaos.

The necessity for despotism in Egypt lay not merely in the certain weakness of the executive. It lay in the no less certain irresponsibility of any representative legislature. Such a legislature in the post-Arabi period would not have enabled the will of the people to be reflected in the acts of the Government. It would, given sufficient scope, have prevented the Government from governing at all as the result of unwillingness or inability to distinguish between executive and legislative authority. In a country where oppressive tyranny had dried up the very sources of spontaneous public opinion, the only correct way of developing representative institutions was to start at the bottom from village, district, and provincial councils and assemblies. Only by building on these foundations, and with the help of a progressive system of education, would it have been possible to develop representative institutions to the point of being able to act as a check on governmental abuse and a spur to governmental reform.

Thus Great Britain, in her dual task of satisfying Egypt's creditors and rehabilitating Egypt's people (the attainment of the second being an indispensable condition of the fulfilment of the first), was burdened with a number of artificially created obstacles which can be summed up under the general headings of 'pashadom' and 'internationalism'. With pashadom she inherited an inefficient and corrupt system of administration and an unproductive, oppressive and unjust social order. With internationalism she inherited limitations of sovereignty so far-reaching as seriously to embarrass the business of administration particularly when, as was the case, these limitations were continually and deliberately exploited by another great power for the express purpose of causing such embarrassment.

On top of these inherited obstacles, additional troubles fell thick and fast. First, there was the financial situation which had become desperate as a result of the direct and indirect costs of the rebellion.[14] Secondly, revolt had broken out in the Sudan. Thirdly, there was an epidemic of cholera in Egypt. It was with these immediate problems that Sir Evelyn Baring had to contend when he returned to Egypt in September 1883 as British Agent and Consul-General in succession to Sir Edward Malet.

NOTES ON CHAPTER FIVE

1. The Shari'a Law is a body of precepts, based on the Quran and Hadith, applied to civil and criminal cases as well as to cases involving personal status. Ideally Islam recognizes no distinction between civil and religious principles, and the community of Islam is subject in all its activities to the law of Islam as revealed by the Prophet. In practice in Egypt, the application of the Shari'a Law has, since the time of Mohamed Ali, been restricted to cases involving the personal status of Moslems, which are still tried by the Shari'a Courts. The Code of the National Tribunals, both civil and criminal, is based on the *Code Napoléon*.

2. Capitulatory privileges were consistently abused by certain foreigners in connexion with drug-smuggling, the drink trade, prostitution, and gambling houses. Virtual immunity from domiciliary search and the leniency of many consular courts meant that these and kindred activities could often be carried on by foreigners with comparative immunity and at a considerable profit.

3. Sir Beauchamp Seymour, afterwards Lord Alcester.

4. Fifty is the lowest of many estimates, some of which put the number of Europeans murdered at over 200. There have been various theories about who was responsible for the massacre. Wilfred Blunt ascribes the responsibility to the Khedive, who wished to hasten European intervention by demonstrating that the Government was incapable of protecting the lives of foreigners. Other writers have blamed Arabi. The probable truth is that the massacre was the spontaneous result of the anti-European and anti-Christian propaganda being disseminated by the extreme nationalists and by the *'ulema*. Omar Pasha Lutfi, the Governor of Alexandria, appears to have been most negligent, and the civilian police completely useless, many of them having joined in the massacre. Order was eventually restored by the Egyptian regular forces sent to Alexandria at Arabi's orders. Among those wounded in the massacre was Sir Charles Cookson, the Acting British Consul-General.

5. By this time a total of twenty-six foreign warships were lying off Alexandria flying the flags of Great Britain, France, Italy, Austria, Russia, U.S.A., Spain, Greece and Turkey.

6. The ships of the line were *Alexandra, Superb, Sultan, Temeraire, Inflexible, Monarch, Invincible, Penelope*. The torpedo boat was *Hecla*. The gunboats were *Condor, Bittern, Beaver, Cygnet* and *Decoy*.

7. Opinions are conflicting about Taufiq's character and behaviour from the time of his accession to the British occupation. Malet regarded him as having behaved loyally and straightforwardly towards the Anglo-French. Blunt considered him as a thorough-paced intriguer negotiating with and deceiving both sides. The probable truth is that Taufiq was inspired by a quite natural determination to keep his throne at all costs. He wanted to be certain of not committing himself to the losing side. At the same time he probably wanted to avert foreign intervention if possible, as this could only result in his being more of a puppet than ever. He supported the Consuls-General and the Dual Control in their opposition to Arabi until they had been compelled, for the second time, to advise him to refuse to accept Sami's resignation. He then, outwardly at all events, threw in his lot with Arabi, and refused to accept the protection of the British fleet. In this refusal he was almost certainly actuated by the knowledge that acceptance of such protection would have finally lost him what little 'face' he had left in Egypt. He therefore remained the titular head of the state right up to and during the bombardment, with Arabi nominally acting under his orders. (Incidentally, by doing this, he made the bombardment an act of war against Egypt.) In thus submitting himself to Arabi, Taufiq avoided being deposed and, probably, murdered, and left himself with a chance of retaining the throne whatever happened. In view of the vacillations of European policy towards Egypt, it is not surprising that Taufiq found it necessary to reinsure himself with Arabi, for the sake not only of his throne, but of his skin. All things considered, there seems very little to censure in his behaviour, even though there is not much to admire.

8. The two strategic keys to the Delta are Kafr-al-Dawar, commanding the road from Alexandria, and Tel-al-Kebir, situated at the point where the Wadi Tumulat joins the cultivated area. Arabi's withdrawal to Kafr-al-Dawar was strategically sound, since a small force stationed there would have a good chance of holding the isthmus against an assault from the direction of Alexandria, thus denying access to the Delta from the north-west. But Arabi left the access from the east, from the Suez Canal, wide open, as the result of a misplaced faith in de Lesseps's megalomaniac assurances. Sir Garnet Wolseley, finding the front, or western, door guarded, went round to the back, or east, door, and walked in.

9. This was the first occasion on which Taufiq publicly and formally dissociated himself from Arabi. The 'rebellion' only became such as from that date. The significance of the announcement is that Taufiq had at last satisfied himself that the British were determined to crush Arabi.

10. General Stone, an American ex-officer of the Confederate Army, was still Chief of Staff of the Egyptian Army at the time of the Arabi rebellion. The other Egyptian staff officers had left at the time of Ismail's deposition. General Stone seems to have had little or no influence on the course of events.

11. The establishment of British troops in Egypt was fixed at 12,000, and it was provided that the Egyptian Government would pay a monthly sum of £48,000 to cover the cost of maintaining this force. During 1883 the establishment was reduced to 7,000.

12. Just as most European foreigners believed that Great Britain had deliberately manoeuvred to bring about her unilateral intervention, so they believed that Great Britain had no intention of withdrawing her troops from Egypt until compelled to do so. Although events were to justify the foreign critics in this latter respect, it seems probable that the British Government were perfectly sincere in their original intention to liquidate their Egyptian responsibilities as soon as possible. The Drummond-Wolff Convention (see

136

Chapter VII) is surely adequate proof of this sincerity. It is to be noted that the British Government did not advance strategic reasons for keeping a garrison in Egypt until after the 1914–18 War had persuaded them of the need for a permanent garrison for the protection of the Suez Canal. The strategic necessity for the maintenance of a British garrison in Egypt is not even referred to in Cromer's *Modern Egypt*, nor was it referred to in any official pronouncement prior to 1914. In fact, the strategic aspect only became important after the collapse of the Ottoman Empire had laid the Middle East open to a 'free for all' among the great powers. Up to 1914 it is probable that the British Government's real as well as stated reason for keeping a garrison in Egypt was the justified belief that the withdrawal of the garrison would defeat the primary objects of the Occupation—the financial and political stability of Egypt. Egypt's political stability was a *sine qua non* of Egypt's 'neutralization', which, so long as the Ottoman Empire was in being, remained a consistent feature of British foreign policy.

13. He returned almost immediately to India, and was succeeded by Sir Edgar Vincent who occupied the post until 1889.

14. Among the indirect costs were (*a*) the cost of the British Army of Occupation amounting to over £500,000 per annum, and (*b*) the cost of the indemnities for the massacre and fire in Alexandria, which were assessed at over £4,000,000.

CHAPTER SIX

THE SUDAN

THE southern frontier of Egypt had never been precisely defined until the Sudan Convention of 1889. Under the Pharaohs, the Ptolemies, and the Romans, the Egyptian frontier had at times been pushed as far south as Senaar and the borders of Abyssinia. The Coptic Church had been firmly established in Dongola and Senaar during the fifth and sixth centuries, and Abyssinia had been Christianized by Coptic missionaries. After the Moslem conquest the frontier receded and the twin barriers of the Cataracts and the desert combined to form Egypt's southern border. The Christian civilizations of Dongola and Senaar collapsed and the country reverted to savagery. The valley of the Upper Nile and its tributaries became known to the Arabs as the Sudan—the country of the black people.

Arab penetration of the Sudan came, in the first instance, not from the north, but from the east. Arab traders from the Persian Gulf, Oman, Hadramut and the Yemen founded settlements, which grew into principalities, along the East African coast from Suakin in the north to Dar-es-Salaam in the south. Originally, the main object of the Arab trade was ivory. But the African jungle was soon found to contain a more precious commodity—slaves. The domestic economy of the Arab world was to a large extent based on slavery, and since the era of Arab conquest had ended, the supply of European slaves had dwindled. There was consequently a ready market for the new 'black ivory'. Arab trading in Africa became synonymous with slave trading, and the Arab caravans which left the coastal ports for the interior were nothing but organized slave hunts, conducted with merciless and expert barbarity.[1]

It was not until the time of Mohamed Ali that the East Coast monopoly of the Sudan trade was challenged from the north. There was a great domestic market in Egypt for slaves. Moreover, Mohamed Ali regarded the Sudan as a likely recruiting ground for his armies, and a source of valuable potential exports, such as gold-dust, ivory, ostrich feathers and the like. The Sudan was also said to be rich in cattle. In 1820 Mohamed Ali sent an expedition into the Sudan under the command of his son Ismail, who established Egyptian authority in the Sudan as far south as Senaar and as far west as al Obeid.[2] In 1842 the Sultan recognized Mohamed Ali's viceroyalty over the Sudan. Egyptian control of the Sudan was relaxed after the death of Mohamed Ali, and in 1856 Said, after a visit there, seriously considered its abandonment. It would have been a good thing for Egypt if it had been abandoned at that time. The only economic activity in the Sudan was carried on by the slave-traders, who constituted the only real authority in the country and who provided such revenue as the Egyptian Government derived from it. The Egyptian Government thus had neither the means nor the will to suppress the slave trade. Many of the Egyptian officials were in fact slave-traders themselves, and many others received illicit profits from the slave trade. To an Egyptian official the only compensation for a period of service in the Sudan was the possibility of making a fortune as a result of oppression and fraud.

Ismail had large ideas about the Sudan. He garrisoned it with Egyptian troops after a serious mutiny of black troops at Tokar in 1865. In 1866 he obtained from the Sultan possession of the ports of Suakin and Massawa on the Red Sea. The occupation of Massawa brought Egypt into conflict with Abyssinia as a result of Egyptian attempts to expand into the interior. In 1874 the Egyptians occupied Keren, and in 1875 the port of Zeila, thus cutting off Abyssinia from access to the sea. In the same year an Egyptian force under

Colonel Arendroop, a Danish officer in the Egyptian service, advanced into Abyssinia and was routed with heavy casualties. Another Egyptian force, under Ratib Pasha, was sent to Massawa to avenge the defeat inflicted on Arendroop, but itself met with defeat when it attempted to invade Abyssinia. The Egyptians then withdrew from the interior, but continued to hold the ports of Massawa, Zeila, and Berbera.

Meanwhile, in the southern and western Sudan, the Egyptians were busy establishing their authority over Bahr-al-Ghazal, and Darfur, Bahr-al-Ghazal being occupied in 1868 and Darfur in 1875. But Ismail had designs more far-reaching than the mere establishment of garrisons and the planting of flags which was all that 'occupation' amounted to. He conceived the ambition of including in his dominions the whole course of the White Nile up to its sources. In order to reconcile Great Britain to his project, he publicized his intention of putting down the slave trade in the Sudan and, in 1869, appointed Sir Samuel Baker, the British explorer, as Governor of the new Province of Equatoria, stretching up the Nile southwards from Gondokoro to its undefined sources among the Great Lakes. Baker's instructions from Ismail were 'to extend Egyptian annexation as far as the Equator, to suppress the slave trade, to introduce a system of regular commerce, to open to navigation the Great Lakes of the Equator, and to establish a chain of military stations and depots at intervals of three days' march throughout Central Africa, with Gondokoro as the base of operations'.

Baker arrived at Gondokoro in 1871 and proclaimed all the territory between Gondokoro and the Great Lakes as being part of the Khedive's dominions. Posts were established at intervals along the river to apprehend slave-traders, who were in consequence driven away from the Nile route, by which slaves had been previously brought down to Omdurman for the market, to the caravan routes through Kordofan and Darfur. (By this time Egyptian competition forced the East Coast slave-traders to seek their merchandise in the lands east and south of the Great Lakes.) In 1873 Baker left the Sudan and was succeeded as Governor of Equatoria by Charles Gordon, who arrived at Gondokoro in February 1874, accompanied by Colonel Chaille-Long, an American in the Khedive's service, as his Chief of Staff. Gordon carried on Baker's fight against the slavers, while Chaille-Long undertook a perilous and too-little-known journey of exploration to the Great Lakes. In 1876 Gordon applied for and obtained from Ismail the appointment of Governor-General of the Sudan in order the more effectively to prosecute his campaign against slavery. Having cleared the Upper Nile route of slavers, the next step was to abolish domestic slavery among the Arabs of the Northern Sudan and so deprive the slave trade of one of its best markets. For so long as there continued to be a profitable market for slaves there would continue to be a slave trade, whatever preventative measures were taken against it. It was impossible to abolish the slave trade without first abolishing slavery and it was, in fact, hypocritical to try and do so. He who wills the end wills the means. The fact that Ismail, whose power in Egypt was absolute, continued to countenance domestic slavery (to say nothing of his flagrant abuse of the *corvée*) is conclusive evidence of his insincerity in trying to abolish the slave trade.

In 1879 Gordon resigned from his post as Governor-General of the Sudan in protest against the deposition of Ismail. During his stay in the Sudan he appears to have been able to do little permanently to reform the Egyptian administration, which was oppressive in those limited areas in which it was able to impose its authority, and completely ineffective everywhere else. He does seem seriously to have crippled the slave trade, and the resentment arising from this was one of the main reasons why the Mahdi was able to recruit the local magnates to the support of his rebellion, which started two years after Gordon's departure. (It must be borne in mind that the Moslems of the Sudan, who predominated in the north, were on the whole beneficiaries of the slave trade. It was the pagans of the south who were the victims.)

By the time Gordon left the Sudan the area under nominal Egyptian administration was rather larger than that comprised by the Anglo-Egyptian Sudan today, and included in addition Massawa, which is now part of Eritrea, Berbera and Zeila, which are now in British Somaliland, Tadjoura, which is now part of French Somaliland, and the provinces of Harrar and Bogos, which are now part of Ethiopia. In many of the Sudanese provinces, Europeans had been installed as governors in an effort seriously to combat the slave trade and introduce efficient methods of administration. Slatin Bey, an Austrian, was Governor of Darfur; Emin Pasha (whose real name was Schnitzler), a Prussian, had succeeded Gordon as Governor of Equatoria; Lupton Bey, an Englishman who had been in the Merchant Service, was Governor of Bahr-al-Ghazal.

Gordon was replaced as Governor-General by an Egyptian, Raouf Pasha, who in 1874 had expelled the Sultan of Harrar and annexed the province on behalf of the Khedive. In July 1881, Mohamed Ahmed, a native of Dongola, proclaimed himself to be the Mahdi[3] and raised the standard of revolt on Aba Island, about 150 miles south of Khartum. If the revolt had been decisively dealt with at the outset, it is probable that there would have been no further trouble. But the situation in Egypt at the end of 1881 was not such as to encourage the prospect of a successful military operation in the Sudan. No decisive action was taken to check the progress of the revolt. Malcontent slave-traders, together with more legitimate sufferers from Egyptian misrule, encouraged by the Mahdi's early successes, flocked to his standard. Raouf Pasha was recalled and replaced by Abdel Qader Pasha. By this time the province of Kordofan was in the hands of the Mahdists, but the revolt had not yet spread eastwards and northwards of Kordofan in the direction of the Blue Nile and Khartum. A well-equipped and well-led force could still have crushed it.

This was the situation in October 1882 when Great Britain, after the Battle of Tel-al-Kebir, had, to all intents and purposes, taken over the direction of Egyptian policy.

We have related how the British Government was already anxious to divest itself, as far as possible, of the responsibilities which it had undertaken in Egypt as the result of British armed intervention. It was certainly unwilling to add the Sudan to these responsibilities. Lord Granville was in a difficult position. It seemed premature to insist upon, or even to advise, the abandonment of the Sudan when the rebellion was confined to a single province, and could have been crushed by a comparatively small force if efficiently equipped and led. But it was quite certain that the Egyptians were unable to provide such a force, and the British Government was not willing to do so. The British Government sent a British officer, Colonel Stewart,[4] to the Sudan to report on the situation there. Apart from that, it appears to have done nothing until 7 May 1883, nearly nine months after Tel-al-Kebir, when Mr. Cartwright, the Acting British Consul-General,[5] was instructed 'that Her Majesty's Government are in no way responsible for the operations in the Sudan which have been initiated on the authority of the Egyptian Government'. This attitude could not be long maintained. The Egyptian Government was to all intents and purposes subject to the authority of the British as a result of the British Government's own act, and, having assumed responsibility for affairs in Egypt, the British became equally responsible for affairs in the Sudan, which was an integral part of Egypt. By disclaiming responsibility, Lord Granville ensured disaster.

The operations referred to by Lord Granville were, briefly, as follows. In November 1882 Abdel Qader Pasha had called for reinforcements and had been sent 10,000 Egyptian troops, fugitive-survivors of Tel-al-Kebir, mostly unarmed, and many of them in chains. These troops were sent to Berber via Suakin. In January 1883 Colonel Hicks, a retired British Indian Army Officer, was appointed by the Khedive as Chief of Staff to the Egyptian Army in the Sudan, with a staff of seven European officers. (These appointments were made without reference to the British Government, since none of the British officers concerned was on the Active List.) In February 1883 the Khedive gave instructions for the cessation of all offensive activity in the Sudan pending Hicks's arrival. At the beginning of March Hicks and his staff arrived in Khartum. Later in the same month Abdel Qader Pasha, who had been both Governor-General and Commander-in-Chief, was replaced by Aal-ad-Din Pasha as Governor-General and by Suleiman Pasha Niazi as Commander-in-Chief.

Hicks immediately set to work to organize the pitiful forces at his disposal. He was hampered at every turn by the passivity of the British Government, by the impotence, financial and otherwise, of the Egyptian Government, by the worthlessness of the Egyptian troops, by the obstructiveness of Suleiman Pasha. It is a wonder that he did not throw up his appointment. However, he persevered, and at length prevailed on the Egyptian Government to rusticate Suleiman Pasha to the Governorship of the Eastern Sudan and to appoint him as Commander-in-Chief in his place. At about the same time, Lord Granville, learning that Hicks was in the habit of communicating with the Egyptian Government through the British Consul-General, again warned Malet that the British Government was prepared to accept no responsibility for the conduct of affairs in the Sudan. Malet appears to have accepted this without protest and, in congratulating Hicks on his appointment as Commander-in-Chief, warned him that he could expect no help of any kind from the British Government. In these depressing circumstances, Hicks made his final preparations for an advance into Kordofan.

In September Hicks set off with a rabble of 10,000 men up the west bank of the White Nile to seek out and destroy the Mahdist forces in Kordofan. At Dueim he left the Nile and set out westwards in the direction of al-Obeid. That was the last that was heard of him in Cairo until late in November, when news trickled through that the whole force had been attacked near al-Obeid and annihilated almost to a man. Hicks himself and all his European officers had been killed. Those troops who were not killed had been captured and sold into slavery. Only one or two escaped to tell the melancholy tale. There was no force left even remotely capable of taking the offensive against the Mahdi who, from that time until his death, was virtually master of the Sudan.

Between the time of Hicks's departure from Khartum and the arrival in Cairo of the news of his destruction, Sir Evelyn Baring had replaced Sir Edward Malet as British Agent and Consul-General. If he had taken over a couple of months earlier, the Hicks disaster might have been avoided. Before ever the news reached Cairo, Baring had impressed on the British Government the necessity of assuming the direction of events in the Sudan and of advising the Egyptian Government to abandon it. Consequently, in September the British Government officially recommended to the Egyptian Government the abandonment of all territory south of Wadi Halfa or Aswan. This advice was obviously sensible. Egypt had no force, and no immediate possibility of raising a force, capable of holding the Sudan against the victorious rebels. The British Government had categorically refused to provide such a force. The long and vulnerable lines of communications made it impracticable to hold the country even as far as Khartum. The most that could reasonably be expected was the successful evacuation, while the river route still remained open, of the various garrisons scattered about the country. If immediate and energetic action had been taken, most of these garrisons might have been evacuated without serious loss of life. But the Egyptian Government, like many bodies which, having lost the substance, retain the shadow of power, were much concerned with the question of prestige. The abandonment of the Sudan, coming on top of all the other humiliations which Egypt had been forced to swallow, was undoubtedly a bitter pill. Furthermore, the Egyptian Government might legitimately have felt aggrieved that

Great Britain, having forcibly established herself in Egypt, was not prepared to defend Egypt.

Much valuable time was wasted. Sherif Pasha, the Prime Minister, in reply to the British Government's advice, told Baring that he proposed (a) to invite the Sultan to send 10,000 troops to the Eastern Sudan, where rebellion had broken out under the leadership of Osman Digna, a follower of the Mahdi, and (b) to hold the Nile Valley with Egyptian troops as far as Khartum. The British Government replied that they had no objection to the despatch of Turkish troops to the Eastern Sudan provided that such an expedition was financed by the Porte (this was equivalent to a veto on Turkish intervention), but that they insisted on the withdrawal of Egyptian troops to Wadi Halfa. This reply was accompanied by a private note to Baring which specified, for the first time, the real relations between the Egyptian Government and the British representative. The note stated: 'It is essential that in important questions affecting the administration and safety of Egypt the advice of the British Government should be followed for as long as the present occupation continues. Ministers and Governors must carry out this advice or forfeit their posts. The appointment of English Ministers would be most objectionable, but it will no doubt be possible to find Egyptians who will execute the Khedive's orders under British advice. The Cabinet will give you full support.' The British Government had at last realized the full implications of the British occupation of Egypt.

Sherif Pasha decided to resign office rather than accept the British advice. It proved unnecessary to proceed to the extreme of appointing British Ministers. Nubar Pasha, who had lately returned to Egypt after some years of the exile to which he had been consigned by Ismail, was prevailed upon to form a Ministry pledged to the abandonment of the whole of the Sudan down to Wadi Halfa, with the exception of Suakin. This started the ten years of intermittent, and occasionally acrimonious, partnership between Baring and

Nubar which was to do so much to shape the course of events under the British occupation. The decision to hold Suakin had already been acquiesced in by the British Government, since it was desirable to retain a *pied-à-terre* for the eventual reconquest of the Sudan. As has been related, rebellion broke out in the Eastern Sudan in August 1883. The Egyptian garrisons in Tokar and Trinkitat were beleaguered. In September an attempt to relieve these places by landing an Egyptian force from Suakin at Trinkitat had failed.[6] In November Suakin itself was attacked. It was necessary to reinforce it if it was to be held. Neither the British nor the Egyptians were anxious for Turkish intervention, and indeed it is improbable that the Turks would have intervened without being given a share of the administration of Egypt in return. So a scratch force of 4,000 Egyptian troops was raised under the command of General Valentine Baker, who had been appointed Chief of the Egyptian Gendarmerie. Baker set off in December[7] with orders to hold Suakin and relieve Trinkitat, but only to attempt to relieve Tokar and Sinkat if he could be certain of success. Unfortunately, Baker exceeded his instructions. His ill-armed and ill-disciplined rabble set out from Trinkitat to the relief of Tokar and was attacked, routed, and almost annihilated by Osman Digna's forces at al-Teb, between Trinkitat and Tokar. This defeat made further intervention necessary in order to hold Suakin. In February 1884 a British and Indian force of 4,000 men under the command of General Graham landed at Trinkitat with the mission of holding Suakin and Trinkitat at all costs, and of relieving Tokar if possible. (Sinkat had already fallen.) Graham was too late to save Tokar, which fell the day after his force landed, but he avenged Baker's defeat by a victory on the same battlefield. It was, however, only a *succès d'estime*, for immediately afterwards his force re-embarked at Trinkitat and transferred to Suakin. From Suakin another short advance was made into the interior and another victory won at Tamai, which relieved the immediate danger to Suakin.

At the end of May most of Graham's force re-embarked at Suakin, the rest remaining to garrison the town, together with a naval detachment from the East India Squadron. The whole episode was a highly unsatisfactory one from the point of view of Anglo-Egyptian interests. All that had been accomplished was the successful defence of Suakin. This could have been achieved by the despatch of a British force a quarter the size of Graham's without the necessity for sending Baker's disastrous expedition at all.

Meanwhile, the British Government, as a result of its previous denial of responsibility, was drifting into even heavier entanglements on the Nile Valley front. In January 1884 General Gordon was sent to Egypt with the mission of organizing the evacuation of Khartum, and such other garrisons as could be evacuated without detriment to the main objective. Communications were still open between Cairo and Khartum, and Gordon departed on his mission at the end of January, having, at his own request, been appointed Governor-General of the Sudan in order to facilitate his task.

The story of the Gordon Mission and the controversies surrounding it have been so extensively written about that it is unnecessary here to give more than a brief outline of the development of events. Baring was opposed to Gordon's mission from the first. He thought it unwise to send an Englishman at all and, if an Englishman had to be sent, thought Gordon unsuitable for the task of organizing an evacuation. It was only after Lord Granville, egged on by the British Press, had 'put a little pressure' on Baring that he agreed to accept Gordon.

From the time of his arrival in Khartum, Gordon showed a natural and creditable reluctance to effect a precipitate evacuation of the capital, which would have left the isolated garrisons to their fate and would have left the Mahdi in undisputed possession of the whole of the Sudan. He had, before his departure from Cairo, been authorized to try to make arrangements for organizing the hereditary local chieftains to carry on the fight against the Mahdi after the departure of the Egyptian forces.[8] On arrival in Khartum, he immediately saw that the chances of being able to do this were hopeless. He then suggested that a certain Zobeir, a slave-trader then living in Cairo, should be made Governor-General of the Sudan and given a subsidy with which to organize local resistance against the Mahdi.[9] Overcoming his repugnance to Zobeir's past, Gordon took the view (a) that the defeat of the Mahdi was essential for the protection of Egypt; (b) that, since Egyptian evacuation had been decided on, it was necessary to organize local resistance to the Mahdi; (c) that Zobeir was the only person available with the qualities and prestige necessary to organize such resistance; (d) that with financial help there was a chance that Zobeir might be able to overcome the Mahdi and set up a stable administration in the Sudan; and (e) that in spite of Zobeir's past the prospect of a Sudan ruled by Zobeir was preferable for Egyptians, British, and Sudanese alike to the prospect of the Sudan ruled by the Mahdi. Baring was impressed by Gordon's arguments, and recommended to the British Government the acceptance of Gordon's plan. But the British Government, which had been driven by the Press and by public opinion to send Gordon to Khartum, was now driven by these same agencies, which professed to be shocked by Zobeir's slave-dealing past, to refuse to implement the recommendations made by Gordon from Khartum.

By this time the rebellion had spread to the country north of Khartum, and it was becoming doubtful whether Gordon, unaided, would be able to fulfil the primary object of his mission by evacuating the Khartum garrison. Baring, with the concurrence of General Graham himself, of Sir Frederick Stephenson, the British Commander-in-Chief in Egypt, and of Sir Evelyn Wood, the Sirdar (Commander-in-Chief) of the Egyptian Army, recommended that Graham's force, then in the eastern Sudan, should be instructed to open a route between Suakin and Berber and so relieve the developing pressure on Khartum from the north. The British

Government rejected this recommendation on the ground of the undoubted difficulty and danger of using British troops in such an arduous operation in the heat of summer.

As from the beginning of April, regular communication between Cairo and Khartum was no longer possible. The British Government began to realize the necessity for sending a force to relieve Gordon. But it did not appreciate the urgency of doing so at once if it were to be done at all. In the event the relief expedition, commanded by Sir Garnet Wolseley, and proceeding, by Wolseley's advice, up the Nile Valley, did not leave Wadi Halfa until the beginning of October 1884.

Once the expedition had started, it made fairly good progress, reaching Korti on Christmas Day, 1884. At this point it divided into two columns, one cutting across the desert with a view to rejoining the Nile higher up at Metemmeh, the other proceeding by river up the long loop between Korti and Metemmeh. The desert column, numbering 1,800 men, left Korti on 30 December. On 17 January a successful action was fought at Abu Klea, between Korti and Metemmeh, and on 21 January the Nile was reached at Gubat, near Metemmeh. Here they met four steamers which had been sent by Gordon from Khartum to meet the relief expedition. On 24 January[10] two of the steamers started back for Khartum with British reinforcements on board. But it was just too late. When the steamers came within sight of Khartum the town was already in the hands of the Mahdists. It had fallen on 26 January and Gordon had been murdered by the victors on the same day.

When the news reached England, the Press and public opinion, which had caused Gordon to be sent to Khartum, and which had caused the rejection of the Zobeir proposal, went on the rampage. Howls of execration went up from newspapers of every shade of political opinion. The Voice of the People was seconded by the august chiding of the Queen. It seemed politically desirable to make some posthumous amends for what was universally regarded as the dastardly betrayal of Gordon. Political desirability was reinforced by the military advice of Wolseley, who recommended that the relief expedition be expanded into a campaign for the reconquest of the Sudan as far south as Khartum. On 9 February, Lord Hartington, the Secretary for War, in a despatch to Wolseley, stated: 'Your military policy is to be based on the necessity . . . that the power of the Mahdi at Khartum must be overthrown.' Wolseley, with the approval of the British Government, issued a proclamation to the people of the Sudan announcing that his mission was 'to destroy the power of the Mahdi at Khartum'. General Earle, the commander of the river column which had left Korti at the end of December, was instructed to press on to Abu Hamad. General Graham, with a British force of 13,000 men, was sent to Suakin with instructions 'to destroy utterly the power of Osman Digna, to arrange for the military occupation of the Hadendowa[11] territory, and to facilitate the construction of the Suakin-Berber Railway'.

In pursuance of these instructions, General Earle's column continued its advance towards Abu Hamad, and encountered and defeated the enemy in a skirmish at Kirbekan on 10 February in which General Earle was killed. On 24 February when the column was only thirty miles from Abu Hamad, Wolseley ordered it to fall back on Merowe. In the middle of March Graham's force landed at Suakin and advanced into the interior as far as Tamai on the road to Sinkat.[12]

By the beginning of April British public opinion had begun to cool down on the subject of Gordon. It was no longer electorally necessary to avenge his death. Moreover, affairs on the North-West Frontier of India were boiling up towards one of their periodical crises. So the forward policy in the Sudan was reversed overnight and evacuation again decided on. On 15 April orders were sent to Graham to cease preparations for the construction of the railway. On 24 April the Government announced in Parliament that it did not intend to proceed with offensive operations in the Sudan.

Having again decided on evacuation, the British Government refused recommendations from Wolseley and Baring that Dongola should be held, and in May issued instructions for a withdrawal to Wadi Halfa. In June the Liberal Government fell. Almost simultaneously with the demise of the Liberal Government, Mohamed Ahmed, the Mahdi, died in the full flush of victory, and was succeeded by Abdullah-al-Ta'aishi, known to history as the Khalifa,[13] a tyrannical and bloodthirsty rascal whose subsequent record of misrule in the Sudan has few parallels in history.[14]

The Conservative Government which succeeded to power in England confirmed the policy of evacuation to Wadi Halfa. In July Dongola was abandoned. It soon became apparent that the Khalifa was intent on invading Egypt proper. For the next few years it proved necessary to continue active operations for the defence of the Nile Valley below Wadi Halfa. In December 1885 the Khalifa's forces were defeated at Ginnis, between Dongola and Wadi Halfa. By May 1886 an Egyptian garrison was established at Wadi Halfa and a British garrison at Aswan. In April 1887 another attempt by the Khalifa to advance beyond Wadi Halfa was defeated at Sarras. In August 1889 a third and final attempt, led by Wad-al-Nejumi, a brave and chivalrous lieutenant of the Khalifa, who achieved the honourable fame always accorded by England to brave and chivalrous enemies, was defeated at Toski between Wadi Halfa and Aswan.

Meanwhile, active operations had been proceeding in the Eastern Sudan to secure the continued possession of the Red Sea littoral. In February 1889 Osman Digna's forces were routed in a pitched battle, Tokar was recaptured, and the menace of further offensive operations by Osman Digna removed, although Osman Digna himself remained alive and at large.

Apart from the Red Sea littoral, the whole of the Sudan south of Wadi Halfa fell into the hands of the Khalifa.[15] Within a few months of Gordon's death all the remaining

Egyptian garrisons in the Sudan had either surrendered or been annihilated, with the exception of those on the Abyssinian frontier, which were, as the result of British diplomatic influence in Abyssinia, safely evacuated with the help of the Abyssinian Government. The garrison of Dara, the capital of Darfur, under the command of Slatin Bey,[16] the Austrian Governor, had surrendered early in 1884, soon after Gordon's arrival at Khartum. At the end of April 1884 Lupton, in Bahr-al-Ghazal, deserted by his troops, had surrendered.[17] Emin Pasha in Equatoria, assisted by his comparative inaccessibility, continued to hold out in spite of the desertion of most of his troops and in spite of the news of Gordon's death and the abandonment of the Sudan. He remained at his post until 1889, when he was relieved, somewhat against his will, by an expedition organized and led by the explorer Stanley. The Senaar garrison made a most gallant defence under its successive Egyptian commanders, Hassan Sadiq, who was killed, and Nur Bey, who succeeded him, and was not finally overwhelmed until August 1885. Kassala, after an equally gallant defence, had capitulated at the end of July. The Harrar garrison was evacuated by the Abyssinians and the provinces of Harrar and Bogos annexed by Abyssinia. The ports of Berbera and Zeila were annexed by Great Britain to form the new colony of British Somaliland. Tadjoura was annexed by France and joined to the port of Obok to form the colony of Djibuti. Massawa was occupied by Italy and formed the nucleus of the colony of Eritrea.

The scramble for Africa which developed among the European powers during the 'nineties made it unlikely that the Sudan would remain long under the rule of an African tyranny. In 1885 Great Britain and Germany had signed a convention[18] in which Germany recognized the whole of the White Nile Valley as a sphere of British influence. France protested against the convention on the ground that the Sudan was under Turkish suzerainty. In 1894 Great Britain signed a convention with Belgium ceding to her a strip of territory between the thirtieth degree of longitude and the west bank of the Upper Nile, known as the Lado Enclave.[19] A few months later France signed a convention with Belgium by which Belgium ceded to France a route from the west through the Lado Enclave to the banks of the Nile. Great Britain thereupon warned France that the Egyptian Sudan included the whole of the White Nile from source to mouth. Towards the end of 1894 it came to the notice of the British Government that France was negotiating with Abyssinia in connexion with an expedition which was about to set out from the French possessions on the west coast, across Central Africa to the Nile, there to be joined by a Franco-Abyssinian force. The aim of this expedition was to link up the French colonies on the west coast with the French colony of Djibuti on the east coast and to claim the whole of the intervening territory as being under the French flag. In January 1895 the Italians, who, like their Egyptian predecessors, had been attempting to expand the colony of Massawa at the expense of the Abyssinians, were defeated by the Abyssinians at Adowa. Italy, who had occupied Massawa by favour of the British Government, appealed to Great Britain for a diversion which would prevent them from being flung into the sea by the victorious Abyssinians.

The French expedition made the reconquest of the Sudan desirable in order to prevent the French from exerting pressure on the British in Egypt as a result of their presence in the Sudan. The Italian request provided a convenient excuse for an advance into the Sudan. The Egyptian Treasury, after years of careful nursing by Cromer, was in a position to finance a campaign in the Sudan. The Egyptian Army, after ten years of British training, had been converted into an adequate fighting instrument. So, in March 1896, the British Government decided on the invasion of Dongola. The Caisse de la Dette, to whom, under the terms of the London Convention of 1886[20] application had to be made for any extraordinary expenditure, was asked to provide £500,000 out of its accumulated reserve. This request was granted by four votes to two, the dissentients being the

French and Russian representatives on the Caisse. The money was duly handed over. But the French and Russian representatives appealed to the mixed courts against their colleagues. They won their suit. The money had to be refunded, and a sum of £800,000 was advanced by the British Treasury for the expenses of the expedition.

Sir Herbert Kitchener, the Sirdar or Commander-in-Chief of the Egyptian Army, was placed in command of the expedition, which at the beginning was entirely an Egyptian Army affair, except for a force of 2,500 Indian troops landed at Suakin as a diversion. In May 1896 the expedition set out from Wadi Halfa. Contact was soon made with the enemy, and on June 7 the Battle of Firket was fought and won. On 13 September Dongola was occupied.

It was then decided to proceed to the reconquest of the rest of the Sudan. Work was started on the construction of a railway across the desert from Wadi Halfa to Abu Hamad in order to by-pass the Dongola Reach, where the cataracts made it difficult to ensure a regular flow of supplies. By August 1897 the railway had progressed sufficiently to enable the occupation of Abu Hamad. In the same month Berber was occupied. After this point had been reached, resistance was expected to develop on a serious scale, and Kitchener asked for reinforcements from the British Army. A brigade of four infantry battalions was sent immediately, to be followed shortly afterwards by a second infantry brigade, a cavalry regiment and a battery of artillery. With this British force, together with 22,000 Egyptian troops, the advance was resumed in March 1898. The Battle of Atbara was fought and won on 8 April. On 2 September the campaign was brought to a victorious conclusion at Omdurman on the west bank of the Nile opposite Khartum, when the Khalifa's main force of about 50,000 men was utterly defeated. The reconquest of the Sudan was virtually accomplished, although the Khalifa himself, with a small body of followers, remained in the field for over a year before being surrounded and killed in battle.

The Battle of Omdurman was thus as decisive in the reconquest of the Sudan as the defeat of Hicks had been fifteen years earlier in the loss of the Sudan. The whole campaign had cost £2,354,000, of which £1,200,000 had been spent on railways, £155,000 on gunboats, and £966,000 on other expenditure. Of the total of £2,354,000, £800,000 was provided by the British Government[21] and £1,554,000 by the Egyptian Treasury. Egypt had thus contributed the lion's share of both money and men. But the decisive factor was British leadership and organization, without which the campaign could not, at that time, have been successfully fought.

Meanwhile, in July the French expedition from the West Coast, led by Captain Marchand had, after an arduous march across Central Africa, reached Fashoda on the Upper Nile, expecting to join hands with the expedition from Abyssinia. But the Abyssinian expedition miscarried. Instead there arrived a message from Kitchener announcing the victory of Omdurman and his intention of visiting Fashoda. Immediately on the heels of the messenger, Kitchener himself arrived, escorted by four gunboats and three battalions of infantry. A first-class international crisis ensued. The British Government was prepared to go to war with France for the Upper Nile Valley. France shrank from the consequences of her diplomatic actions. Marchand was ordered to withdraw. The crisis was over.

In view of their attitude over Fashoda, it was hardly likely that the British Government would be prepared to extend to the Sudan the same apparatus of international control as existed in Egypt. Apart from imperialist considerations, institutions such as the Capitulations and the mixed courts would have been grotesquely unsuitable to a primitive country such as the Sudan was. A return to Egyptian rule would have been equally unsatisfactory even if, as in the case of Egypt itself, Egyptian rule had been made subject to British advice and inspection. But it was impracticable to detach the Sudan wholly from Egypt. It had been reconquered in the name of the Khedive, with a force largely composed of Egyptian troops and with money mostly supplied by the Egyptian Treasury. The Sudan Convention (see Appendix I) signed on behalf of the British and Egyptian Governments on 19 January 1899 recognized both the necessity for immediate separation from Egypt and the desirability of ultimate reunion with Egypt. It established in the Sudan a régime unique in international relations, to which the term 'condominium' was applied. The twenty-second parallel, passing through Wadi Halfa, was defined as the northern boundary of the Sudan; the southern boundary was left undefined. The British and Egyptian flags were to fly side by side over all public buildings. The country was to be ruled by a Governor-General, who was to be appointed by the Khedive on the recommendation of the British Government, and in whom supreme military and civil authority was to be vested. The jurisdiction of the mixed courts was specifically excluded from the Sudan. No foreign consuls were to be appointed to the Sudan without the consent of the British Government. To sugar the pill, it was provided that no special privileges were to be accorded to the subjects of any one or more powers. Great Britain was in fact to rule the Sudan in trust for Egypt. To enable her to do so, she had cleared away those international obstacles which had proved so detrimental to good government in Egypt, and which would have made good government in the Sudan next to impossible.

NOTES ON CHAPTER SIX

1. The most revolting feature of the trade was the wholesale castration of youths to meet the large demand for eunuchs in the harems. A large proportion of youths so treated died from the operation.

2. Ismail was murdered at Shendi, but the expedition was a success.

3. Literally 'one who guides in the right way'. Mohamed Ahmed was the most notable of a large number of Mahdis who have appeared in the Moslem world from time to time. Mahdism is a popular but unorthodox belief among backward Sunni Moslem communities. The Mahdi is one who has been sent by God to complete the work of the Prophet and to establish the religion of Islam all over the world. A great many superstitions have congregated round

Mahdism, including a curious one that the true Mahdi will have very long hands. The belief itself is supposed to be justified by one of the Hadith (traditions based on the supposed sayings of the Prophet), but is not accepted by orthodox Sunni teachers. Consequently, the influence of Mahdism has always been local, and organized through the medium of a *tariqa* or sect of devout followers who build up an esoteric cult around the personality of the leader. Each Mahdi therefore became the source of a cult similar to that of the various Dervish *turuq*. Members of the *tariqa* remained Sunni Moslems, although their practices were usually frowned on by the Sunni Moslem world lying outside the influence of the cult. Mahdism has some points of similarity with the Shiah belief in the 'hidden Imam', but there is never any question of a Mahdi being credited with divine power. According to the Mahdist tradition, the true Mahdi should not proclaim himself to be the Mahdi; he should be spontaneously recognized as such. This does not seem to have happened in the case of Mohamed Ahmed.

4. Colonel Stewart eventually went to Khartum with Gordon after having spent several months in the Sudan prior to Gordon's arrival. During the Siege of Khartum he attempted, under Gordon's orders, to take a river steamer down the Nile to Egypt, and was ambushed and killed by the Mahdists.

5. At this time both Malet and Cookson were in England on sick leave.

6. This force was accompanied by Captain Moncrieff, R.N., British Consul at Suakin, who was killed.

7. Among those who joined Baker's expedition as a volunteer was Morice Bey, an Englishman who was Chief of the Egyptian Coastguard Service and an ex-naval officer. Just before setting out he had written to a friend: 'I have eaten Egypt's salt for seven years, and I cannot now desert her in her hour of need.'

8. Gordon was accompanied to the Sudan by the Sultan of Darfur, who, however, soon turned back. The idea had been to use his influence in Darfur to combat the Mahdi.

9. Some idea of using Zobeir seems to have been present in Gordon's mind before he left Cairo. While in Cairo he had met Zobeir by chance—a meeting which proved embarrassing to both of them, since Gordon, during his previous administration of the Sudan, had had a son of Zobeir's executed. But Gordon was favourably impressed by the father, and there is no doubt that his later proposal regarding Zobeir was inspired by this meeting.

10. The reason for the three days' delay at Gubat has never been satisfactorily explained. Nor has the fact that the two steamers returned to Khartum reinforced by only twenty British troops. If the steamers had been immediately turned round with an adequate British force on board it seems possible that Gordon might have been saved.

11. The Hadendowa territory consisted of the hinterland round Suakin inhabited by the Hadendowa tribe immortalized by Kipling in his poem 'Fuzzy-Wuzzy'.

12. On this expedition a reconnaisance balloon was used; this is the first recorded use of aircraft in British military operations.

13. Khalifa means 'successor'.

14. During the thirteen years of the Khalifa's rule the population of the Sudan was reduced from about 6,000,000 to about 2,000,000.

15. Perhaps it would be more correct to say that it was not in the hands of Egypt. The Khalifa never established anything like effective control over a large part of the Sudan. Darfur was soon in revolt, and by 1890 the Khalifa

had withdrawn his forces from that province. The same thing happened in Bahr-al-Ghazal. Emin Pasha held out for some years in Equatoria, and part of that province was, with the consent of the British Government, temporarily occupied by the Government of the Belgian Congo. Other outlying parts of the Sudan were occupied by other foreign powers, as has been related in the text.

16. Slatin escaped from the Khalifa's prison in 1894, and after the reoccupation became Inspector-General of the Sudan and a much-respected figure in British official circles. He acquired British nationality and was unnecessarily humiliated by having it revoked during the 1914–18 War as a result of his Austrian parentage.

17. Lupton died in captivity in Omdurman.

18. This was the convention by which Germany acquired Heligoland and Great Britain Zanzibar.

19. It was subsequently provided that the Lado Enclave was to be returned to the Sudan on the death of King Leopold. This was duly done, and it is now part of the Anglo-Egyptian Sudan.

20. See Chapter VII. The London Convention was an amendment of the Law of Liquidation.

21. The original grant of £800,000 was made as a loan at 2¼ per cent. It was finally treated as a free contribution to the expenses of the expedition. The railway became the property of the Sudan Government.

CHAPTER SEVEN

CROMER

THE story of Lord Cromer's régime in Egypt is best told, not as a record of events, but as a description of administrative achievement. Consequently, the chronology of his régime will be briefly outlined at the beginning to provide a background for the main picture.

Sir Evelyn Baring (as he then was) arrived in Egypt in October 1883 to take over from Sir Edward Malet as British Agent and Consul-General. For the first four years of his term of office the financial state of Egypt, together with the events in the Sudan described in the last chapter, engaged the major part of his attention.

We have already described (in Chapter V) the limitations which Great Britain inherited on taking over responsibility for the administration and rehabilitation of Egypt. The most immediately serious of these limitations was the financial servitude imposed by the Law of Liquidation and guarded by the Caisse de la Dette and the mixed courts.

The financial burden imposed by the Law of Liquidation would have been a severe one under the most favourable circumstances. A combination of unfavourable circumstances made it an impossible one. First, the collection of revenue had been seriously interrupted by the rebellion. Secondly, actual expenditure and outstanding claims had greatly increased as a result of (a) Arabi's expansion of the army, (b) the Sudan campaigns, (c) the cost of the British Army of Occupation, and (d) the cost of the indemnities awarded in compensation for damages resulting from the Alexandria massacre and fire. In addition to all this, there had been, in 1883, a severe cholera epidemic and a low Nile. Egypt was once again on the verge of bankruptcy. And this time Great Britain had made herself responsible for Egypt's solvency. The Liberal Government's reaction to this was to send Lord Northbrook to report on the financial situation of Egypt. He arrived in Egypt in September 1884 and stayed for six weeks. His recommendations to the British Government need not concern us here, as they were not accepted. But one act of his brought about an important revision of the Law of Liquidation. In order that the Egyptian Treasury might be provided with its urgent and immediate financial requirements, Lord Northbrook advised the Egyptian Government to defy the Law of Liquidation by paying into the Treasury a part of the general revenue earmarked for the service of the Debt. The Egyptian Government acted on this advice, and the Caisse immediately sued the Government in the Mixed Courts. The British Government called an international conference in London to discuss ways and means of averting Egyptian bankruptcy. As a result of this conference, a convention was agreed to (March 1885) which had the effect of relieving the Egyptian Treasury from its most immediate embarrassments at the price of adding a German and a Russian Commissioner to the Caisse. The main provisions of the Convention were as follows:

(a) An internationally guaranteed loan for £9,000,000, bearing interest at 3 per cent., was floated and subscribed in order to finance the payment of the Alexandria indemnities and other urgent disbursements, including a grant of £1,000,000 for the rehabilitation of irrigation in Egypt.

(b) An agreement by the powers that their nationals in Egypt should be subject to house tax, stamp tax, and licence tax.

(c) A two-year moratorium on the interest payable on the Preference and Unified Debts. (Since the interest was collected directly by the Caisse, the moratorium took the form of a loan equal to two years' interest payable in 1887.)

(*d*) The suspension of the Sinking Fund for a similar period of two years.

(*e*) An increase in the 'standard' revenue from £4,897,888 to £5,237,000.

(*f*) Any surplus revenue left after providing for the 'standard' revenue and the Debt service to be divided fifty-fifty between the Caisse and the Treasury instead of being devoted 100 per cent. to the liquidation of the Debt.

(*g*) Any deficit in the 'standard' revenue to be met by the Caisse out of its reserves.

(*h*) The Caisse to have the power to allot sums from its reserves for essential expenditure by the Egyptian Treasury. (The Caisse to be arbiter of what was and what was not essential expenditure.)

(*i*) The Caisse to have the power to grant loans to the Egyptian Government out of its reserves.

(*j*) The international boards administering the railways, Alexandria Harbour, the telegraphs and the Domains and Daira lands to be continued.

The London Convention was a modification, but by no means an abandonment, of the principles behind the Law of Liquidation. Egypt's finances were still in international leading strings. The concessions made were the minimum necessary to avoid bankruptcy. The powers had no intention of giving Great Britain *carte blanche*, and they were determined to see that the foreign creditors should derive the first benefit from any prosperity which Great Britain might bring to Egypt.

In so far as the powers were genuinely concerned with the interests of the bond-holders, it is possible that their cautious attitude was dictated by Great Britain's expressed intention of evacuating Egypt as soon as practicable. But in the case of at least one power, the motive for intransigence was not primarily concern for the bond-holders, but a jealous determination to obstruct Great Britain's supposed designs in Egypt. Consequently, it is probable that any expression by the British of their determination to stay in Egypt would have augmented rather than alleviated French intransigence.

As has been related, the Liberal Government in England fell in the spring of 1885, a few weeks after the signature of the London Convention. The Conservative Government which succeeded showed itself no less anxious than its predecessor to put a term to British administrative responsibilities in Egypt. In August 1885 Sir Henry Drummond Wolff was sent by Lord Salisbury to Constantinople to invite the Sultan's co-operation in the settlement of the Egyptian question, which would make it possible for Great Britain to withdraw her troops from Egypt. As a result, a Turkish Commissioner, Mukhtar Pasha, was appointed by the Sultan to proceed with Drummond Wolff to Cairo to study the Egyptian question on the spot. After eighteen months of such study, a convention was signed in Constantinople between Great Britain and Turkey which provided: (a) that the British Government would withdraw their troops from Egypt within three years unless by the end of that time there appeared to be any danger to be apprehended for Egypt internally or externally; (b) that if at any time subsequent to the evacuation law and order was disturbed, or if the Khedivate refused to execute its duties towards its Sovereign Court (i.e. the Sultan), or refused to execute its international obligations, both the British and Ottoman Governments would have the right to occupy the country with troops; and (c) that if the Sultan did not avail himself of the right of occupation in these circumstances, the British Government was empowered to take military action on its own account.

This convention was subject to ratification by the Sultan. The Sultan was prevailed upon by France and Russia to postpone ratification. The British Government ultimately lost patience and Drummond Wolff was instructed to leave Constantinople. The Convention was in fact never ratified. The British Government never again invited Turkish co-operation in Egyptian affairs. The Drummond Wolff mission had come about as a result of the British Government's fear lest a common resentment over Egypt might drive Turkey, France, and Russia together into an anti-British bloc in the Eastern Mediterranean. By preventing the ratification of the convention, France and Russia overreached themselves. By enabling the British Government to demonstrate its reasonableness, they demonstrated their own unreasonableness. In the event, the only permanent result of the Drummond Wolff Mission was the continued but *fainéant* presence of a Turkish Commissioner in Egypt.

Of more importance than the Drummond Wolff Mission was the fact that, during 1886-7, Egypt's financial position improved sufficiently as to enable the interest and sinking fund payments on the debt to be resumed on the due date, and the two years' arrears paid off. The danger of bankruptcy and the consequent discredit of the British administration of Egypt had been averted. Finance ceased to be a nightmare and was relegated to the status of a mere anxiety.

In 1888 Nubar Pasha fell from power and was replaced by Riaz Pasha as Prime Minister. He had held office for five years during the most critical period of the British occupation. He had played his cards with great dexterity. In return for conceding Great Britain a free hand in the Ministries of Finance and War, and by the welcome which he had accorded to British assistance in the Ministry of Public Works, he had been enabled to retain almost untrammelled control of the rest of the Administration, including the Ministries of the Interior and of Justice. This meant that such matters as legal procedure and the organization of public security were beyond the reach of any effective reform.

A hierarchy of national courts, on the French model, had been established on Lord Dufferin's recommendation. A British Procureur-Général, Sir Benson Maxwell, had been appointed, but neither he nor his successor, Sir Raymond West, stayed long. Nubar Pasha was determined to prevent any overt British encroachment into the routine of the courts, and for a time he was able to have his way.

Similarly, in the Ministry of the Interior, Nubar succeeded in bringing about the resignation of Mr. Clifford Lloyd, a British Under-Secretary to the Interior, who tried to divorce the rural police force from the control of the provincial mudirs and to bring it under British control. As a result of Nubar's insistence, the police force became completely ineffective, and to preserve some semblance of public order Nubar was compelled to have recourse to special courts, known as 'commissions of brigandage', which became notorious for their tyranny and injustice. Once the immediate and overriding financial preoccupations were over, it was clear that the British could not allow this state of affairs to continue. Friction developed between Nubar and Cromer. His fall finally came about as the result of his attempt to make an Egyptian Head of the Gendarmerie after the death of Valentine Baker in 1888. Cromer withdrew his countenance from Nubar. The Khedive disliked him, anyway, and he was unpopular in the country as being a foreigner and a Christian. His successor, Riaz Pasha, was a Turco-Egyptian of the old school whose dislike of foreign influence was modified by his respect for strong government. By his talent for administration, which was far superior to Nubar's, he succeeded in staving off the onset of reform, but in 1891 he resigned rather than acquiesce in the appointment of a British Judicial Adviser. His successor was Mustafa Pasha Fahmy, who, with two brief intervals, was to continue as Prime Minister until Cromer's retirement in 1907.

In 1892 the Khedive died suddenly, and was succeeded by his eighteen-year-old[1] son, Abbas Hilmi. With his accession began another phase of resistance to British control. In 1893 an attempt by the new Khedive to form a Ministry without British advice brought him into sharp conflict with the British Representative. Abbas perforce accepted a face-saving compromise which resulted in Riaz Pasha becoming Prime Minister in place of Mustafa Fahmy, but from then on the co-operative relations which had existed between the Palace and the British Agency ceased. In 1894 an ill-advised attempt by the Khedive to seduce the Egyptian Army from its obedience to its British officers[2] led to Riaz' resignation and his replacement by Nubar Pasha. Nubar's hat was still in the ring, and neither age nor disappointment had diminished his political adroitness. He continued the fight for administrative autonomy from the point at which he had been compelled to relinquish it six years previously, and succeeded in obtaining abolition of direct British control of the provincial police in return for the appointment of a British Adviser to the Ministry of the Interior. He thus succeeded in obtaining a partial return to the policy of 'British heads and Egyptian hands', which was gradually being superseded by the imposition of a comprehensive system of British control over the whole administration. After less than a year in office, however, he was compelled by ill-health to retire finally from public life, and Mustafa Fahmy returned to office as Prime Minister in his place. From then on, until Cromer's retirement, the Egyptian Government proved to be a willing, if not always efficient, instrument for the execution of British policy in Egypt. Henceforward opposition was to come from the new nationalist movement which was beginning to arise from the ashes of the Arabi rebellion, and from the new Khedive and his entourage.

The next ten years were marked by steady administrative progress which was hindered neither by the slowly rising tide of nationalism nor by the cautious hostility of the Khedive. The Sudan was reconquered. The Aswan Dam was constructed. Increased productivity provided increasing revenue while at the same time enabling remissions of taxation. This decade of achievement was crowned in 1904 by the signature of the Anglo-French Agreement, thus bringing to an end the persistent hostility with which France had regarded British rule in Egypt. This Agreement signalized a reorientation of the European system of alliances which had come about as a result of the growing rivalry at sea between Great Britain and Germany. The megalomania of

166

Kaiser Wilhelm II succeeded in accomplishing what no British nor French statesman had ever been able to accomplish—an alliance between Great Britain and France. In so far as it affected Egypt, the Anglo-French Agreement provided for a French recognition of the British position in Egypt in return for British recognition of France's special position in Morocco, which France was at that time about to occupy in order to round off her position in North Africa. In the Agreement the British Government declared that it had no intention of altering the political status of Egypt; the French Government declared that it would not obstruct the British in Egypt by asking that a limit of time should be fixed for the British occupation.

More immediately important were the financial alleviations resulting from the Agreement. The internationalization of Egypt's finances was brought to an end. The Caisse de la Dette was relegated to the status of a debt-collecting office. The Egyptian Government was given full control of all its revenue other than that required for the service of the Debt.[3] The reserves which had been accumulating in the hands of the Caisse since the signature of the London Convention were handed over to the Egyptian Government.[4]

The Agreement did not provide for any change in the Capitulations or in the constitution of the mixed courts, but the political circumstances leading up to the Agreement did to a large extent cause France to cease using these institutions primarily as a means of embarrassing the British Administration in Egypt.

The financial alleviations deriving from the Anglo-French Agreement coincided with the political difficulties which were beginning to arise as a result of the resurgence of Egyptian nationalism. The long subservience of successive Egyptian Governments under Mustafa Pasha Fahmy had driven the whole of the rising generation of Egyptian nationalists into uncompromising opposition both to the Egyptian Government and to the British. At the same time the mutual hostility existing between the Khedive and Cromer had destroyed the old friendly relations which had existed between the Palace and the British during the reign of Taufiq, and had led the Khedive to flirt with the nationalists. But the nationalists hated and feared the Khedivate at least as much as they hated and feared the British. Abbas showed much ostentatious condescension to Mustafa Kamal, the nationalist leader, but such an alliance was too unnatural to form the basis of any joint action.

Cromer, who was beginning to see the necessity for creating some measure of popular support for the British connexion, was instrumental in forming the Hizb-al-Umma,[5] a moderate nationalist party which saw the practical advantages of accepting and trying to modify the *status quo* as an alternative to intransigent opposition to something which could not be got rid of. Cromer no doubt hoped on the one hand that prospects of office and advancement would attract the more moderate of the nationalists to acquiescence in the British connexion, and on the other hand that the Khedive and the extreme nationalists would neutralize each other by their mutual jealousies. These hopes were not fulfilled. In the first place, there was nothing in Cromer's stern paternal policy to attract even the most moderate nationalist. In the second place, an incident occurred in 1906 which not only destroyed any possibility which might previously have existed of nationalist co-operation with Great Britain, but which severely shook the faith which the average Egyptian had learnt to repose in the justice of British administration.

In the summer of 1906 a party of British officers was pigeon-shooting near the village of Denshawai in the Delta. A misunderstanding arose with the villagers (none of the British officers of the party spoke Arabic), there was a fracas, and a British officer was killed. The British Press reacted with its usual irresponsible hysteria. British official opinion in Egypt, which had been aggravated by the continual Press attacks[6] in the nationalist newspapers, decided that the Egyptians needed a lesson. The logic of imparting the lesson to a number of ignorant villagers was not discussed. A Special Court, consisting of British and Egyptian members, under the nominal presidency of an Egyptian, but under the actual direction of a British judge,[7] was set up to try the alleged culprits. Three death sentences and several sentences of flogging and imprisonment were imposed and executed. It was the biggest blunder and the worst crime which Great Britain has ever committed in Egypt. The name of Denshawai is still remembered and spoken whenever it is desired to arouse anti-British feeling in Egypt. At the time it was eagerly seized upon by the nationalists as a means of discrediting the British Administration in the eyes of the *fellahin*, whose goodwill had previously represented Great Britain's greatest political asset in Egypt.

The imposition and execution of the Denshawai sentences was a measure of the extent to which a dictatorial régime can lose touch with the people whom it is governing. The British official hierarchy had during the previous ten years surrounded itself with a protective covering of subservient Egyptian opinion which effectively insulated it from any knowledge of what the Egyptian people were really saying, feeling, and thinking. Fifteen years earlier the execution of the Denshawai sentences would have been inconceivable, not only because of their injustice, but because the effect on Egyptian opinion would have been appreciated. By 1906 British officials in Egypt had become more responsive to the views and prejudices of their colleagues than they were to the well-being of the people whom they were supposed to be governing. At best they were beginning to regard the administration of Egypt as an intellectual or technical problem with only a very exiguous relation to its impact on those administrated. At worst they regarded it as an occupation which enabled them to lead comfortable and care-free lives, immersed behind files in the mornings, and disporting themselves exclusively among their compatriots in the afternoons.

Cromer himself was not the sympathetic administrator he

had been. He now enjoyed dictatorial power in Egypt. To the British Government, as well as to the Egyptian Government, his word was law. 'Power corrupts; absolute power corrupts absolutely.' There has never been a human exception to this aphorism. Cromer was absent in England during the Denshawai incident, and was not directly responsible for what was done. But he must have been kept informed. But he probably did not regard it as important.[8] He too had become effectively insulated from the people of the country he had served so well.

In 1907, the year after Denshawai, Lord Cromer retired from the position which he had held for twenty-four years. He drove to the station for the last time through silent streets. Denshawai cast a gloomy shadow over his departure.

The twenty-four years of Cromer's term of office were years of impressive administrative achievement. The most important part of this achievement was the reform of the finances, since without this no other reform would have been possible.

Egyptian finances under the British occupation were administered in fact by a British Financial Adviser, who was the senior British official in the service of the Egyptian Government. He had the right to be present at meetings of the Council of Ministers. He was responsible for framing the Budget, for ensuring Egypt's continued solvency, and for meeting Egypt's obligations under the London Convention. Sir Auckland Colvin was the first Financial Adviser; he was succeeded in 1883 by Sir Edgar Vincent, who was followed in due course by Sir Elwin Palmer (1889–98), Sir Eldon Gorst (1898–1904), and Sir Vincent Corbett (1904–7).

Cromer himself was first and foremost a financier, and his methods provided just the antidote needed by Egypt after the extravagances of Ismail. He considered that his first task was to lighten the burden which Ismail had placed on Egypt sufficiently to allow free play to the natural energies of the people and the phenomenal fertility of the soil of

Egypt. He believed that Egypt could not but become prosperous if the evils of oppression and extortion were removed from her. In his first five years of office he kept public expenditure down to a minimum, with the significant exception of the £1,000,000 for irrigation development, which was earmarked for that purpose out of the Guaranteed Loan. When there was a surplus he saw that it was devoted to reduction of taxation rather than to schemes of development. He has been criticized for his parsimony in the realm of social services, such as education. But Cromer deliberately preferred low taxation to social services. Or rather he believed that low taxation would in due course render the revenue sufficiently buoyant as to provide the money for social services. For Cromer, in spite of being a somewhat dictatorial administrator, was a *laissez-faire* economist. He believed that the function of government was that of a policeman rather than that of a nursemaid, that people should neither unduly interfere nor unduly be interfered with.

The main results of Cromer's financial policy were summarized as follows by Cromer himself:[9]

. . . Direct taxation has been reduced by little less than £E.2,000,000[10] a year. In the domain of indirect taxation, the Salt Tax, the collection of which was attended with great hardship to the poorest classes of the population, the *octroi* duties, the bridge and lock dues on the Nile, and the tax both on river boats and on sea-fishing boats have been wholly abolished. The Registration dues on the sale of land have been reduced from 5 per cent. to 2 per cent. The light dues have been greatly diminished in amount. So also has the tax on ferries. The Customs Duties on coal, liquid fuel, charcoal, firewood, timber for building purposes, petroleum, livestock and dead meat have been reduced from 8 per cent. to 4 per cent. The inland fishery industry has been relieved from the vexatious and onerous restrictions which were formerly imposed on it. The Postal, Telegraph and Railway rates have been largely reduced. The only increase in taxation has been in the tobacco duty, which has been raised from 14 piastres to 20 piastres per kilo.[11] There cannot be a doubt that the whole Egyptian population is very lightly taxed. The taxation is, however, still unequally distributed. The urban population do not bear their fair share of the public burdens.[12] In this, as in so many other matters, the Capitulations bar the way to reform.

In spite of these large reductions in taxation, the revenue has grown from £E.8,935,000 in 1883 to £E.15,337,000 in 1906, an increase of no less than £E.6,402,000.

The expenditure has of course increased with the growing revenue, but it has been carefully controlled. In 1883 it amounted to £E.8,554,000, and in 1906 to £E.12,393,000, an increase of £E.3,839,000.

The following three facts will perhaps bring clearly home to the mind of the reader the general nature of the results obtained by the financial administration of Egypt since the British occupation in 1882.

In the first place I have to record that, up to 1888, either a deficit was annually incurred, or else financial equilibrium was preserved with the utmost difficulty. Then the tide turned. During the eighteen years from 1889 to 1906, both inclusive, the aggregate surplus realised by the Egyptian Treasury amounted to more than 27½ millions sterling.

The second fact which I have to record is no less striking. During the twenty years preceding 31 December 1906, extraordinary expenditure to the extent of £19,303,000 was incurred on railways, canals and public buildings. Of this large sum only £3,610,000 was borrowed. The remainder was provided out of revenue. Moreover, on 31 December 1906, a Reserve Fund of £3,050,000 stood to the credit of the Commissioners of the Debt. The Reserve Fund of the Egyptian Government amounted on the same date to £11,055,000, of which only £2,353,000 had at that date been engaged for capital expenditure. Both of these funds, amounting in the aggregate to £14,105,000, were provided out of revenue.

In the third place I wish to draw attention to the facts and figures relating to the indebtedness of Egypt. In 1883 the Capital of the Debt, which was then held exclusively by the public, amounted to £96,547,000, and the charge on account of interest and Sinking Fund to £4,268,000. Since then the Guaranteed Loan, which amounted to £9,424,000, has been issued; £4,882,000 has been borrowed for the execution of public works, and for the commutation of pensions and for allocations to the Khedivial family. The conversion operation of 1890[13] added £3,904,000 to the nominal capital of the Debt. In all £18,210,000 has been added to the capital of the Debt. On the other hand the Daira Loan, which in 1883 amounted to £9,009,000, has been entirely paid off.[14] The Domains Loan, which in 1883 amounted to £8,255,000, has been reduced to £1,316,000. The Guaranteed Loan has been reduced to £7,765,000, a reduction of £1,659,000 from the original amount. On December 28 the outstanding capital of the Debt in the hands of the public amounted to £87,416,000. The charge on account of interest and sinking fund borne by the taxpayers was £3,368,000. There has therefore in twenty-three years been a reduction of £9,041,000 in the capital of the Debt, and of £900,000 in the charge on account of interest and sinking fund.[15]

In 1883 nearly half the revenue was devoted to debt-redemption; in 1906 this proportion had been reduced to little less than a quarter. During the same period the annual revenue available to the Egyptian Treasury rose from £4,500,000 to about £11,500,000 sterling, in spite of the remissions in taxation. This increased revenue was derived (a) from duties on imports, the total value of which rose from £6,500,000 sterling in 1882 to £26,000,000 sterling in 1907; (b) from additional land tax deriving from the increase of the cultivated area from 4,800,000 *feddans* in 1882 to about 5,300,000 *feddans* in 1906 (the increase in crop area, due to perennial irrigation, was even more remarkable— 4,800,000 *feddans* in 1877 and 7,500,000 *feddans* in 1906); (c) from greater regularity and precision in the collection of taxes; (d) from the increased tobacco duties, combined with a prohibition of the growing of tobacco in Egypt.

Taking into account the capital sums spent on development which resulted in greater productivity per unit of manpower, some increase in the incidence of taxation per head would not have been unduly oppressive. But in point of fact the incidence of taxation remained the same at about £1·3 per head of the population, which rose from 6,800,000 in 1883 to about 11,250,000 in 1906. Thus the increased productivity resulting from capital development and the improved services financed out of revenue represented a clear dividend to the Egyptian people. (Whether this dividend was fairly distributed among the Egyptian people is a point which will be discussed in a later chapter.)

Let us now examine the nature of this dividend as it was distributed by the various spending departments. The most important of the spending departments was the Ministry of Public Works, and the most important activity of the Ministry of Public Works was irrigation, on the efficient administration of which the whole life of the country depended.

Since the time of Mohamed Ali, control of irrigation had steadily deteriorated. 'Every year some false step was taken in spite of the engineer. Every year the *corvée* lost ground in its out-turn of work; drains were abandoned or became useless, and canals became less of artificial and more of natural channels wholly influenced by the rise and fall of the Nile.'[16] It was clear that the rehabilitation of Egypt's finances was to a large extent dependent on the rehabilitation of Egypt's irrigation system. In 1883 a British Indian irrigation expert, Sir Colin Scott-Moncrieff,[17] was appointed Under-Secretary to the Ministry of Public Works, with a small staff of British Indian experts under him acting as advisers and inspectors.

One of the first things to be done was to find a substitute for the *corvée*. (The *corvée* was the term applied to the age-old system whereby forced labour was recruited every year at low Nile for clearing out the silt which had become deposited in the canals.) At the time when Scott-Moncrieff took over, it was estimated that this annual clearing necessitated the labour of one-eighth of the population for ninety days of the year. It was obvious that this labour could only be recruited and, once recruited, made to work by compulsion. The method of compulsion used from time immemorial was the *courbash*, or raw hide whip. Lord Dufferin, during the course

174

of his Mission, had caused a decree to be promulgated forbidding the use of the *courbash* for administrative purposes, i.e. for the collection of taxes or for the recruiting and stimulation of the *corvée*. This ban on flogging, while not invariably obeyed, made it impossible to work the *corvée* system at all. Even when the men were recruited they would not work. The substitution of the *corvée* by paid labour had become, not only a desirable reform, but an administrative necessity.

It was found that intelligent engineering enabled a considerable reduction in the amount of labour required, but after this had been taken into account it was estimated that an annual sum of £450,000 would be necessary to get the hired labour required to replace the *corvée*. The fact that the consent of the signatory powers to the London Convention was necessary to secure an increase in the 'standard' revenue to cover this amount, and the fact that this consent was only obtained with great difficulty, and at the expense of entirely irrelevant concessions in other matters, is an illustration of the difficulties and abuses of 'internationalism' as applied to Egyptian finances.

Apart from efficient maintenance, a considerable capital expenditure on the irrigation system was necessary if Egypt's revenue were to achieve the buoyancy required to enable her to sustain the burden of her foreign debt. A sum of £1,000,000 was allocated for the purpose out of the Guaranteed Loan of 1885. This sum was mainly devoted to the reconstruction of the Delta Barrage.[18] The Barrage, situated some fifteen miles north of Cairo at the apex of the Delta, had been built by French engineers during the last years of Mohamed Ali's reign in order to raise the level of the low Nile sufficiently to meet the requirements of summer crops in the Delta. But the maintenance of the Barrage had been so neglected that it no longer fulfilled its intended function. It had been intended to feed the Delta lands by means of three main canals leading off from the Nile at the Barrage. Of these, one, the Menufia, had been dug, but had become silted up; a second, the Behera, had been dug, but never used owing to the insufficiency of water; the third, the Taufiqia, had never even been dug. The Barrage itself had become incapable of holding enough water appreciably to raise the level of the low Nile. The Egyptian engineers had, in fact, abandoned all hope of using the Barrage, and were considering plans for providing summer water for the Delta by means of an expensive system of steam pumps. In face of considerable opposition from these engineers, who regarded the Barrage as a picturesque survival of past extravagances, Scott-Moncrieff and his assistants succeeded in restoring the Barrage to its proper function of providing summer water for the Delta.[19]

The next step was to extend perennial irrigation to the Upper Egypt lands, which were still dependent on basin irrigation supplemented by artesian wells. To do this, it was necessary to provide a sufficient head of water as to fill the irrigation canals at low Nile.[20] An ambitious scheme was worked out for the construction of a dam at Aswan and for supplementary barrages at Asyut and Zifta. But the usual financial difficulties barred the way. Money for capital expenditure could only be obtained out of the accumulated reserves which the Caisse was building up from its 50 per cent. share of the 'surplus' revenue collected by the Egyptian Treasury. The Caisse, under the terms of the London Convention, had the power to make either grants or loans to the Egyptian Government out of these reserves, but this power was in effect dependent on the consent of the signatory powers to the London Convention. There was no prospect of getting this consent for the financing of the Aswan Dam except at the expense of ruinous concessions in other directions. An arrangement was therefore made with the contractors by which the cost was to be paid by instalments out of revenue. Work on the Dam and barrages was started in 1896 and completed in 1903 at a cost of £2,000,000. Simultaneously, an area of 500,000 *feddans* in Upper Egypt was converted to perennial irrigation.

The execution of these two large schemes—the rehabilitation of the Delta Barrage and the construction of the Aswan Dam—only represented a part of the work taken in hand by the British irrigation engineers. The everyday work consisted of a gradual process of rescuing the irrigation system from the caprices of Nature and of bringing it under the control of man; of seeing that the water made available by the big schemes was distributed to the best advantage, and removed from the land by drainage when it had served its purpose.

The fruits of the work done were seen in the figures of increased population and increased crop and cultivable areas which have already been quoted, and in the facts that the yield of the cotton crop and that of the sugar crop trebled over a period of ten years. It was this solid achievement which made Egypt's financial recovery possible. As a result of the improved productivity brought about by the application of sound engineering, honest administration, and tenacity of purpose to the Egyptian irrigation system, Egypt was not only relieved from the thraldom which her creditors had imposed on her, but was able to devote ever-increasing sums to the health, educational, and other services which were so badly needed. It is sometimes assumed that Egypt's financial recovery was brought about by financial jugglery in Cairo. It was not. It came about as the result of a fruitful partnership between the British irrigation engineer and the Egyptian *fellah*. The expenditure was modest in relation to what was achieved. In later years, when the financial restrictions imposed by the London Convention had been removed, and when money was plentiful, much more was spent, and much less was done.

British reforms in the irrigation service met with little or no obstruction either from Egyptian official circles or from public opinion, and indeed owed a great deal to the co-operation of both. Egyptians and British were alike agreed on the necessity for improvements in the irrigation system. Egyptians had confidence in the Englishmen employed, and realized that they had not the technical competence to do themselves what was being done for them. They were willing to learn. No political passions were aroused. The beneficial results of British control were apparent to peasant and pasha alike. The pasha was in fact benefited as much as and, in the long run, more than the peasant. There was a general appreciation that Egypt was getting good value for money spent. This appreciation did not come automatically. It was bestowed—one might almost say extorted—as a result of the qualities of the British officials employed. Attempted reforms in other branches of the administration met with considerable obstruction, but in irrigation the need was so urgent, and the benefits so manifest, that criticism was silenced and obstruction waived.

Another service in which great reforms were quickly and effectively instituted was the Army, and for the same reasons. All Egyptians capable of influencing the future of events wanted an efficient Army, and realized that British assistance was necessary in order to make the Army efficient. (If they had not realized it before the abandonment of the Sudan, events in the Sudan soon forced this realization upon them.) The Egyptian Army officer class—the followers of Arabi—who were the only people who might have objected, were utterly discredited, anyway. Political considerations apart, it would have been fantastic to have reinstated them in any positions of military responsibility. Whatever of good there is to be said of the Arabi rebellion, it cannot be said that its leaders were either brave or efficient soldiers.

The *fellah* soldier had never had a chance. He had always been miserably paid, brutally treated, and since the death of Ibrahim Pasha disgracefully led. The black troops from the Sudan, whom Mohamed Ali had first introduced into the Army, had always shown courage, but had never been subjected to that firm but just discipline which is essential to convert a rabble into a fighting force. The Albanian and Circassian elements, which had been declining steadily since the days of Mohamed Ali, had been almost eliminated under

178

Arabi. Although their military record was better than that of either the Egyptians or the Sudanese, it was not considered desirable to resume their employment under the British occupation. Therefore, upon the recommendation of Lord Dufferin, a start was made with the building-up of a new Egyptian Army[21] composed of *fellahin* conscripts and Sudanese volunteers, commanded, as to the higher ranks, by officers seconded from the British Army. Sir Evelyn Wood was appointed Sirdar (Commander-in-Chief), and was succeeded in due course by Lord Grenfell, Lord Kitchener, and Sir Reginald Wingate. Good results were obtained from apparently unpromising material in a surprisingly short space of time. As early as 1889 the Egyptian soldiers gave proof of their mettle at Toski. The campaign for the reconquest of the Sudan, starting seven years later, showed finally that the Egyptian *fellah* was capable of becoming an adequate soldier if properly armed, properly fed, and well-officered. No similar proof was needed about the Sudanese.

The reforms which were attempted in the Ministries of the Interior and of Justice met with much more opposition, and were consequently much less effective. Both Ministries were tackled early in the occupation. Mr. Clifford Lloyd, a British administrator from Ireland, was already in Egypt with the mission of 'superintending internal reforms' when Baring arrived in October. 1883. Baring caused him to be appointed Under-Secretary for the Interior. He came into almost immediate collision with the Prime Minister, Nubar Pasha, who had spent a chequered career of public life in that dubious borderland which separates diplomacy from intrigue, and who was determined that the British occupation should be treated as a partnership between the British and himself for the purpose of governing Egypt. He had come into office at the price of acquiescence in the abandonment of the Sudan, and he was quite prepared to leave the liquidation of that question entirely to the British. Similarly, he was prepared to leave the British to deal with the financial nightmare and all its international ramifications. In return he was determined to have his own way at the Ministry of the Interior, the portfolio of which was usually held by the Prime Minister, and at the Ministry of Justice, in the affairs of which he regarded himself as an expert.

From the British point of view there was a great deal to be said for placating Nubar. He was co-operative in what were regarded as the most important matters—finance, the Sudan, and public works. He was *persona non grata* with the French, and could thus be relied upon not to intrigue with them. He had a genuine appreciation of the necessity for some measure of European control. As a cosmopolitan Armenian,[22] who had been a leading figure in Egyptian affairs for the previous twenty-five years, he not only served as a bridge between the Occidental and the Oriental mind but was also more conversant than anybody else with the intricate details of Egyptian administration. Last but not least, he was a very intelligent and charming man, who spoke French like a Parisian, and who had years of experience in dealing with European diplomats and statesmen.

Clifford Lloyd caused a decree to be issued which in effect and intention transferred the control of the provincial police from the *mudirs* to a European Inspector-General.[23] Nubar Pasha had no objection to the issue of such a decree. But he did object to Clifford Lloyd's atttempt to implement it. The dispute between the two men developed until it was a question of getting rid of either one or the other. It was the spring of 1884. Gordon was in Khartum; the Treasury was on the verge of bankruptcy. It would have been almost impossible to have found a suitable Egyptian to replace Nubar at such a juncture. The control of the provincial police was not worth a first-class political crisis. Nubar had gauged the position accurately and knew that he was safe in standing firm against Clifford Lloyd. He did so, and Clifford Lloyd resigned. His decree remained on the Statute Book, and everything went on much as before.

For the time being Nubar had won, and reform at the

Ministry of the Interior was postponed until a later date. Four years later, in 1888, Nubar was less successful. In that year Valentine Baker, the Head of the Egyptian Gendarmerie, died, and Nubar tried to insist on an Egyptian being appointed to succeed him. But by that time the position of affairs was less propitious for him. The Sudan question had been liquidated; the worst of the financial crisis was over. The occupation had established itself. Riaz Pasha had made his peace with the British and was ready to step into Nubar's shoes. So this time it was Nubar who resigned.

Riaz Pasha was no more disposed than Nubar had been to welcome any British interference with the detailed administration of the country, and it was not until 1894 that any effective measure of control was introduced into the Ministry of the Interior. Nubar Pasha was again Prime Minister in what proved to be his last term of office. He was still chafing at the British police inspectorate, which had been introduced by Lord Dufferin, and a compromise was arranged by which the police reverted to Egyptian control in return for the appointment of a British adviser to the Ministry of the Interior.

The presence of a British adviser facilitated reforms in a great many directions.[24] Prisons, sanitation, and kindred services began to be brought nearer to European standards of humanity and efficiency. At the cost of leaving the main citadel—the authority of the provincial *mudirs*—unviolated, successful assaults were made on those outworks which were less influentially defended and where, as in the case of irrigation, the beneficial results of British interference were immediately apparent. As a result, the technical services were gradually Europeanized; the administrative services were left much as they were.

The Ministry of the Interior was, and is, the greatest fount of patronage in Egypt, and is also the Department of State with which the ordinary citizen is most intimately concerned. The authorities who were in fact the rulers of the people, the *mudirs*, the *mamurs* and the *umdas*, were all appointed by the Minister of the Interior. The officials of the Ministry could, and to a large extent did, control the bestowal of the benefits as a result of reforms in other departments of state. Any attempt seriously to reform Egyptian administration was bound to be limited in scope, unless full control were established over the Ministry of the Interior, both at the centre and in the provinces. The Nubar-Clifford dispute was crucial. Control of the provincial police was clearly only the first of a number of far-reaching reforms which Clifford Lloyd intended making at the Ministry of the Interior. The result of these reforms would have been to bring the district administration of Egypt under British control, and would have made Egypt, to all intents and purposes, a British colony. Clifford Lloyd was, in fact, trying to introduce by the back door a régime which had already been implicitly rejected by the British Government. His failure to do so ensured that Great Britain's impact on Egypt would never be more than skin-deep.

British control ultimately became more fully established at the Ministry of Justice than at the Ministry of the Interior. But here, too, Nubar Pasha won the first round.

The area of jurisdiction effectively controlled by the Ministry of Justice was a comparatively limited one. The consular courts were entirely outside its jurisdiction. The mixed courts were nominally subject to it, but actually quite independent of it. The Shari'a courts, which concerned themselves with matters of personal status as between Moslems, were administered by the Grand Qadi, who was appointed by Constantinople. Most of the religious minorities had their own religious courts. There remained criminal cases in which the accused was an Egyptian national, and civil cases in which both parties were Egyptian and where no question of foreign interest[25] was involved.

In 1883, the national courts, which had been instituted some years earlier on the French model, were reorganized, and a British Procureur-Général (Sir Benson Maxwell) appointed. He did not stay long in Egypt, and was replaced by Sir Raymond West, who made a determined attempt to transfer from theory to practice the spirit of the reforms which the reorganized courts were intended to signalize. In so doing he fell foul of Nubar Pasha, the creator of the mixed courts, who regarded the administration of justice as his *forte*. He was at least as determined to make his co-operation with the British dependent on non-interference at the Ministry of Justice as he was in his dispute with Clifford Lloyd at the Interior. He had his way and Sir Raymond West departed. The national tribunals continued in being, but such was the incompetence and venality of the judges that they soon ceased, even nominally, to be the effective source of criminal justice. Nubar, alarmed at the increase of crime in the provinces, appointed 'commissions of brigand-age', under the presidency of the *mudirs*, to deal out summary justice in crimes of violence. These commissions soon degenerated into appalling instruments of arbitrary oppression reminiscent of the worst days of Ismail. Scandals connected with them were partly responsible for Nubar's fall in 1888. It was apparent that closer control of the administration of justice would have to be instituted by the British if British rule in Egypt were not to be utterly discredited. In 1891 a British Judicial Adviser was appointed, in spite of bitter opposition from Riaz Pasha, who resigned from his post as Prime Minister in consequence. (The three principal survivors of the preoccupation period—Sherif, Nubar, and Riaz—had thus all in their turn collided with and been ousted by the British: Sherif over the abandonment of the Sudan, Nubar over the control of the Gendarmerie, and Riaz over the control of the administration of justice.) Henceforward, with the exception of two brief intervals, when Nubar and Riaz each returned to power for a few months, Cromer had to rely on the collaboration of a Prime Minister[26] who had attained his position as a result of subservience to the British, who, unlike Nubar, had no strong views of his own, who, unlike Riaz, had no great administrative ability, and who, unlike Sherif, had no following in the country. The results were not, on the whole, beneficial either to Great Britain or to Egypt.

From the time of Sir John Scott's appointment as Judicial Adviser, a determined effort was made to bring the national tribunals to a level which would enable them to eschew tyranny and at the same time act as an effective deterrent to crime. The attempt was only partially successful. The two main difficulties were, first, the difficulty of securing an adequate number of judges who were qualified professionally, morally, and temperamentally for their appointments. This was a question of time and education. The second difficulty was more serious. It proved impossible to instil even into the normally law-abiding Egyptian any respect for the law as such. There was not then, and to a large extent there is not to-day, any general feeling in favour of co-operating with the law in the suppression of crime. There was not then, and there certainly is not to-day, any feeling in favour of voluntarily giving evidence in a court of law, or of giving truthful evidence if one is compelled to give any evidence at all. This difficulty is also no doubt a question of time and education. But a lot of both is required. And if the law is to be respected the law itself must first of all become respectable.

A Commission of Judicial Control was appointed to supervise the work of the various courts. A few British judges were appointed. The standard of the Egyptian judges gradually improved. A tradition of decent professional conduct grew up on the Bench and among the Bar. The worst abuses disappeared. But the British reformer was never quite happy in the Egyptian courts of law. He felt, with some reason, that the French legal system was ill-adapted to the needs of a comparatively primitive community. He felt that the procedure was not understood and therefore not supported by the ordinary law-abiding citizen. It was too far removed from the traditional system of personal justice to act either as a deterrent to evildoers or as an encouragement to welldoers. It bred a multiplicity of little lawyers who interposed an effective barrier between justice and the citizen. It was a medium through which it seemed quite impossible to 'put across' the British conception of justice. This was a grave misfortune, for at least half of good administration consists in the inculcation of standards. It was the lower criminal courts which, in the eyes of the British reformer, suffered most from the imposition of the French system. The British mind likes to regard justice, and especially criminal justice, as being related to some accepted standard of conduct recognized equally by the judges, by the accused and by the public. The French mind, and the French system, is more intent on the accurate interpretation of a written code which is held to cover every conceivable contingency.

A major disability under which the administration of justice lay was the system of Capitulations. This system, as it had been developed in Egypt, not only gave foreigners immunity from the Egyptian criminal law, but also prevented any law affecting foreigners from being promulgated without the consent of the Capitulatory powers. In 1887 a small improvement was made in this ludicrous state of affairs, when the powers agreed to delegate to the General Assembly of the mixed courts authority to approve legislation dealing with minor administrative matters. (In 1911 the powers of the General Assembly were considerably broadened in the matter of approving legislation, but it was still debarred from approving any law affecting taxation.) Any important new law, or any law involving taxation, remained dependent for its implementation on the consent of the powers, which consent was usually obtained, if at all, only as the result of a long process of bargaining often indistinguishable from blackmail.

At the beginning of the occupation it was found that European nationals were exempt from several direct taxes borne by Egyptians, including stamp tax, professional tax, and house tax. In spite of the manifest injustice of this discrimination, it took a long course of international bargaining before the necessary unanimous consent of the powers had been obtained in order to enable the application of these taxes to foreigners. (The professional tax had eventually to be withdrawn altogether as a condition of French agreement to financial arrangements connected with the abolition of the *corvée*.)

Towards the end of his career in Egypt, Cromer propounded a scheme for the creation of a Legislative Council consisting of thirty-six members of mixed nationalities, some nominated and some elected, which would have authority to amend, reject, or approve all legislation. The object of this scheme was to evolve a system of law applicable to all the inhabitants of the country without distinction of nationality, and to give all the inhabitants of the country representation in the framing of laws. The scheme obviously involved the disappearance of the Capitulations. It never came to fruition. Such a scheme would have stood no chance of acceptance by the powers before the signature of the Anglo-French Agreement of 1904, and it is to be presumed that Cromer, who had an acute sense of what was, and what was not, politically possible, delayed propounding the scheme until the Agreement had been signed. It would probably have met with a good deal of opposition in any case if it had ever reached the stage of formal submission to the powers, who had got into the habit of regarding the Capitulations as a means, not of protecting the legitimate rights of their nationals residing in Egypt, but as a means of extorting minor concessions from Great Britain in matters which were often wholly unconnected with Egypt, and who would probably have been unwilling, at that time, to relinquish such a useful diplomatic instrument.

The British were able to do no more than very slightly to mitigate the evils arising from internationalism in the administration of justice. By the end of Cromer's term of office the financial restrictions on Egypt's autonomy had almost disappeared; the legislative and juridical restrictions were almost unimpaired.

The immunity from Egyptian criminal law enjoyed by European foreigners, and the extent to which this immunity was abused by many consular courts, not only placed a large and influential section of the community beyond the reach of the Law, but brought the administration of the law into disrepute, by preventing it from fulfilling its function of punishing and deterring criminals. Furthermore, the perpetuation of foreign privilege, and the frequent abuse of this privilege, made it even more difficult than it otherwise would have been to eliminate indigenous abuses based on unjustifiable privileges. To the Egyptian mind it seemed natural that people in a position to enforce their claim to privileges should do so, and the attitude of the powers towards the Capitulations seemed to justify the pashas in their attitude towards their indigenous social problems.

The limitations imposed on reform in the Ministries of the Interior and of Justice arose inevitably out of the limitations of authority accepted by Great Britain at the outset of the occupation. They cannot reasonably be ascribed to any failure on the part of the administrators. The only real administrative failure of the Cromer régime was in education.

Administration can only be judged by its results. The administration of the Ministry of Public Works was good because the results were demonstrably good. That the reorganization of the Army was well-accomplished was apparent from a comparison of the behaviour of Egyptian troops at Tel-al-Kebir and at Omdurman. That the administration of Egypt's finances was efficient is proved by a comparison between the Egyptian Budgets of 1883 and 1906. That such reforms as were carried out in the Ministries of Justice and the Interior constituted an improvement on the precedent state of affairs was beyond dispute, and was not seriously disputed. By the same criterion of results, both short- and long-term, the administration of education[27] was deplorable. It was not merely that so little was done; the little that was done was ill-done.

On assuming responsibility for the administration of

Egypt the British had two choices before them with regard to education. They could either have regarded education as a principal means of bringing about the rehabilitation of the country, or they could have regarded it as something which the Egyptians could be left to run themselves subject to the reform of any glaring abuses. Under the first method it would have been treated in the same way as finance or public works; under the second method it would have been treated in the same way as the subjects dealt with by the Ministries of the Interior and of Justice. Various reasons combined to rule out the first method of approach. Financial stringency made it difficult to allot the money which would have been necessary if education were to be regarded as a major item in the administrative programme. The supposedly temporary duration of the occupation militated against the adoption of an essentially long-term process of rehabilitation. And last, but not least, the whole British administrative tradition was opposed to treating education as an instrument of policy. The first method having been discarded for these cogent reasons, it is unfortunate that the second method was not logically applied. Instead, a disastrous compromise was made. On the one hand, there was a half-hearted recognition of the desirability of using education as a means of moral and technical progress. On the other hand, there was a reluctance either to spend the money or to devise the means for doing this. The result was that the existing system of education was first left to muddle along as best it could and then, when money became more plentiful, developed in a way which bore no relation to the moral or material needs of the country.

It is hardly necessary to state that the existing system was chaotic. There were the religious schools, ranging from the village *kuttabs* (mosque schools) to the al-Azhar University, the sole object of which was to teach pupils to read and write as a preliminary to acquiring a knowledge of the Quran and of Islamic theology. There were the Government schools, which had been developed by Ismail on the French model.

These consisted of a top-heavy and unco-ordinated structure in which secondary education, imparted mostly in French, was inconsequently inserted between a totally inadequate foundation of primary and an almost non-existent super-structure of higher education. And, finally, there were the foreign schools, mostly run by missions, which provided a limited amount of both primary and secondary education, in accordance with no recognized curriculum and subject to no form of control.

The system adopted under the British occupation was, roughly, to develop primary education through the *kuttabs*, and to 'marry' the *kuttabs* to the secular Government secondary schools, which were allowed to develop on much the same lines as those on which they had started. There was little efficient provision for higher education; the first secular university in Egypt did not come into being until 1909. Technical education was likewise neglected.

The basic fault of the system, apart from the derisory sums of money allotted to it, was that far too much import-ance was attached to secondary education, compared with primary education, on the one hand, and with higher and technical education, on the other. Far too great a proportion of the population continued to receive no education at all, owing to the shortage of primary schools, and of those who did receive a primary education far too large a proportion received a secondary education. Conversely, of those who received a secondary education, only those who could afford to study abroad were able to obtain efficient higher or advanced technical education.

The main results of this lop-sidedness were: (*a*) a lack of that popular interest in education which can only exist when there is a sufficient proportion of literacy among the masses of the population to enable them to appreciate the advantages of education; (*b*) a general apathy towards reform of any kind, due in part to the continued high proportion of illiteracy; and (*c*) a supply, far exceeding any possible demand, of young men with a secondary education which unfitted them for manual work, but which left them unprovided with any qualifications for other than routine clerical work.

These results had a devastating effect on the future course of events in Egypt. Widespread illiteracy made the masses both responsive to organized agitation and at the same time apathetic to any real grievance unless this was called to their notice by means of organized agitation; economic frustration led to the creation of a hard core of middle-class discontent and disillusion which periodically boiled over into organized agitation and violence. The comparative lack of Egyptians with higher and technical qualifications retarded the achievement of, without decreasing the desire for, national independence, and impaired the achievements of national independence when this at length was gained. Government education in Egypt was to a large extent instrumental in fostering that unrest which derives, not from the demerits of the Government, but from the deficiencies of the malcontents.

In spite of the failure over education, the Cromer régime was, administratively, a success. The finances were restored. The irrigation service was rehabilitated and improved. The incidence of taxation was lowered. Those twin instruments of oppression, the *courbash* and the *corvée*, were totally abolished in theory, and all but abolished in fact. The Army was made into an efficient fighting force. The Sudan was recovered. The administration of justice was, to some extent, purified. The police were made more efficient and less tyrannical. All this had been accomplished in less than a quarter of a century under the limiting conditions imposed by the maintenance of the Khedival façade, by the London Convention, by the Capitulations, and by the mixed courts.

Politically the Cromer régime was less successful in overcoming the difficulties inherent in the circumstances of the occupation. Wolseley's army had crushed a popular insurrection, and had restored an inefficient and discredited régime. Rightly or wrongly, this régime was used as the instrument of British administration, which thus became identified at the beginning with tyranny, corruption, and incompetence. The efficiency and honesty of most of the British advisers and inspectors succeeded to a large extent in mitigating the bad effect of this initial association, but did not succeed in arousing enthusiasm for a régime which, whatever its virtues, neither inherited nor attempted to create any tradition of popular loyalty or affection.

The necessity for honouring the terms of the London Convention imposed in the early years of the occupation a policy of administrative parsimony which is incompatible with popularity. The benefits which accrued from the occupation came too gradually and too indirectly to be effective for the purposes of political propaganda. The resultant lack of enthusiasm was, as Cromer himself recognized, inevitable. But he hoped that such material advantages as the occupation brought would on the one hand create an educated public opinion prepared to co-operate with the British in the business of government, and on the other hand prevent the apathy of the masses from degenerating into hostility. This hope was doomed to disappointment. The calamitous effect of Denshawai on Egyptian public opinion has already been noted. But the importance of Denshawai from this point of view was in its effect on the *fellahin*. Educated nationalist opinion had set hard against the British connexion, and it was already becoming apparent that the task of finding responsible and representative Egyptians to co-operate with the British in the business of government was going to become more and more difficult. It was, of course, inevitable that a nationalist movement should have arisen. It was probably inevitable that a section of such a movement should be violently and intransigently anti-British. It was nevertheless unfortunate that there should have been so few points of contact between the British and the nationalists, and doubly unfortunate that such points of contact as there were should have tended to diminish rather than to increase as time went on. For this it seems that what might be called the strategy of the British administration was to blame.

Every administration, and indeed every organization, has both its tactic and its strategy. In the course of its current activities it forms an attitude towards its future activities. It becomes set in a certain direction, it acquires a certain method of approach. The British administration in Egypt started by confining its activities to the giving of advice which was acted upon by the Egyptian organs of government. The British advisers were the heads and the Egyptian officials the hands. Inevitably the British advisers began to experience a sense of frustration when they saw that their administrative blueprints, although for the most part conscientiously followed, suffered in the course of being transferred from paper to reality as a result of lack of expertness on the part of the executants. Consequently, as the British advisers became established, and as the financial position began to improve, a tendency crept in to appoint British hands as well as British heads. Egyptian officials were displaced or found their prospects of promotion blocked as the result of Englishmen being appointed over their heads. The ability of some of the new British officials did not inspire the same reluctant but spontaneous respect which had been commanded by the handful of highly qualified and highly paid British administrators at the beginning of the occupation. The anglicization of the administration did not, in Cromer's day, advance as far as it was to do later, but the tendency was there. In 1885 there were perhaps 100 senior European civilian officials in Egyptian government service. In 1906 there were over 1,000. There was, as yet, no question of favouring an Englishman because he was an Englishman. The Englishmen who were appointed were still appointed because no Egyptians could be found to do the job equally well. But the resentment created more than offset the additional efficiency achieved. The British administration was rowing against the rising tide of nationalism. The British oarsmen may have been better than the Egyptian oarsmen, but it is doubtful whether the speed of the boat was thereby increased. Potential Egyptian administrators were converted into bitter anti-British nationalists because of the lack of any legitimate scope for their talents.

There would have been far less resentment if the British administration had started with British Ministers and with an Englishman in every key post, and from that beginning, embarked on a policy of cautiously and gradually replacing Englishmen by Egyptians. The British would then have been rowing with instead of against the tide of nationalism. It was the gradual intensification of British control which acted as fuel to the flames of nationalism. A gradual relaxation would have had the opposite effect. But in view of the exiguity of British control at the outset, any relaxation would have been incompatible with the continuance of British control at all. All the trouble arose from the fact that the initial arrangements were made on the assumption of a short-term occupation.

In his last years in Egypt, Cromer displayed a certain aura of infallibility, a certain assumption of rectitude, and a certain contempt for Egyptian opinion. But essentially the trouble was not of his making. During the whole of his term of office in Egypt, he was continually being faced with the choice between administrative efficiency and political expediency. He may be said to have leaned a little too heavily to the side of administrative efficiency, and in so doing contributed to the ultimate defeat of the administrative ends which he had so clearly in view. But, when all is said, he made infinitely fewer mistakes and achieved infinitely more solid results than any other British administrator of his generation.

NOTES ON CHAPTER SEVEN

1. Actually Abbas Hilmi was not yet eighteen at his accession. In order to avoid the political complications of a regency, his age was taken according to the Moslem or lunar year, which made him just eighteen.

2. Abbas publicly expressed his dissatisfaction with the training of the Egyptian Army during a tour of inspection in Upper Egypt. Kitchener, then Sirdar, promptly sent in his resignation. Abbas was compelled by Cromer to

issue an Order of the Day expressing his satisfaction with everything he had seen during his tour of inspection.

3. The annual service of the Debt, amounting to £3,600,000, was henceforward secured on the revenue from the land tax, instead of from the miscellaneous sources provided for in the Law of Liquidation. The sum required was paid by the Treasury to the Caisse. The only important limitation on Egypt's financial autonomy was a provision that the Preferred Debt should not be converted until 1910 and the Unified Debt until 1915.

4. These reserves amounted to £5,500,000 sterling.

5. The People's Party.

6. During Cromer's régime there were no restrictions on the freedom of the Press other than those provided by the Common Law. Cromer believed that freedom of the Press and freedom of speech were valuable safety-valves for the expression of feelings which otherwise might be expressed more dangerously.

7. Sir Walter Bond.

8. He admitted later in his book, *Abbas II*, published in 1915, that the Denshawai sentences had been unnecessarily severe.

9. Cromer's *Modern Egypt* (Macmillan). First edition Vol. II, Part vi, Ch. LIII, pp. 447-450.

10. £E. signifies Egyptian pound, or 100 piastres. It was 'pegged' to the English pound, which was equivalent to 97½ piastres. The £E. was therefore equivalent to about £1 0s. 6d.

11. The effect of the increase in the tobacco duty was greater than is apparent from these figures, for the increase in duty was accompanied by a prohibition of tobacco growing in Egypt.

12. This state of affairs has now been more than remedied.

13. This consisted of the conversion of the Preferred Debt from 5 per cent. to 3½ per cent.

14. From the proceeds of the sale of the Daira Lands to the public.

15. After 1904 the service of the Debt ceased to be a serious burden on the Egyptian Treasury. Forty years later Egypt was Great Britain's creditor to the tune of some £400,000,000, as a result of military expenditure in Egypt during the Second German War.

16. Extract from report by Colonel Ross quoted in Cromer's *Modern Egypt*.

17. He was succeeded in 1892 by Sir Walter Garstin.

18. Or, more properly barrages, since there is a barrage across each of the two arms of the Nile at the point of their intersection.

19. The provision of summer water for the Delta was important on account of cotton cultivation.

20. The principal irrigation canals of Upper Egypt are the Ibrahimieh, leading off from the west bank of the Nile at Assiut and running as far as Giza; the Yusufia, leading off from the west bank of the Nile at Deirut and running to the Fayum; and the Fuadieh, running off from the east bank of the Nile at Nag Hamadi (where a barrage has been constructed) as far as Abnub, opposite Assiut. The Yusufia is a very ancient canal, probably dug originally in Roman times; the Ibrahimieh was dug during Ismail's reign for the purpose of irrigating the sugar crops on the royal estates in Middle Egypt; the Fuadieh was dug only recently.

21. The Egyptian Army was formally disbanded by Khedival decree immediately after the suppression of the Arabi rebellion.

22. Nubar's father had been an Armenian moneylender in Constantinople. To the end of his life Nubar knew hardly any Arabic. He acted as Ismail's principal agent in his various negotiations with the Porte and with the European powers. Among his most important negotiations were those in connexion with the Suez Canal and the mixed courts. He also negotiated the *firman* by which Ismail was given the title of Khedive and the right of succession by primogeniture for his heirs. Opinions are divided as to the fidelity or otherwise of his services to Ismail and to Egypt. He certainly spent money with a very liberal hand. How much public money found its way into his own pocket is a matter for conjecture. In the Anglican Cathedral in Cairo there is a tablet in memory of Nubar Pasha with the inscription, 'Justice is the foundation of Empires'.

23. In fact, it was not merely the control of the provincial police that was in dispute. Clifford Lloyd had his way about that, at all events on paper. The real point at issue was the extent to which British control was to be applied in the day-to-day administration of Egypt.

24. One bad effect which the presence of the British adviser had was a tendency to over-centralization which at the present day is carried to fantastic lengths at the Ministry of the Interior.

25. The mixed courts claimed, and were allowed, jurisdiction in cases where 'mixed interests', i.e. matters affecting foreigners, were involved, even though the principal parties to the case were of Egyptian nationality.

26. Mustafa Pasha Fahmy.

27. Education was administered by the Department of Public Instruction under the Ministry of the Interior until 1906, when the Department was elevated into a Ministry with a British adviser.

CHAPTER EIGHT

GORST AND KITCHENER

TOWARDS the end of his long term of office, Lord Cromer had become convinced, and had succeeded in convincing the British Government, that the process of handing back the administration of Egypt to Egyptian hands would have to be spread over a large number of years if the standard of administration was to be maintained at anything like the level achieved. He recognized, nevertheless, that there must be some progress, however gradual, in this direction, and that the time had come to pay some attention to the political as well as to the purely administrative aspect of affairs in Egypt. Unfortunately, there appeared to be no very promising methods of approach available. Since the accession of Abbas Hilmi, Cromer's relations with the Palace had been almost consistently acrimonious, and the original occupation policy of restoring the power of the Khedive had been pushed into the background. The Legislative Council, Legislative Assembly, and provincial councils called into being by Lord Dufferin had received little encouragement, and played no part in shaping the policy of the Administration. The nationalist movement, which had grown up to a large extent independently of these attempts to organize public opinion, was becoming increasingly hostile and increasingly vocal. The Government had little interest, either with the Palace, or with the various councils and assemblies, or with the nationalist movement, and its members were regarded as little more than British nominees, chosen for their subservience and actuated by self-interest.

Cromer had made various attempts to minimize the

dangerous isolation which was growing up between the Administration and public opinion. He had had some success in fostering the formation of the Hizb-al-Umma,[1] a moderate counterpart of the Hizb-al-Watani[2] which had been formed by Mustafa Kamal, the young leader of the nationalist movement. He had also attempted to form friendly relations with Mohamed Abdu, the leader of the Islamic Modernist movement. Mohamed Abdu had been exiled after the Arabi rebellion, but had been subsequently allowed to return to Egypt, and had been appointed Rector of al-Azhar, where he had initiated a number of long-overdue reforms. Although Cromer apparently believed that he had succeeded in convincing Mohamed Abdu of the desirability of the British occupation, there is no doubt that he over-estimated the extent both of Mohamed Abdu's acquiescence and of his influence.

But Great Britain's greatest political asset in Egypt was the fact that the *fellahin* were, on the whole, well-disposed towards the British occupation. While the limitations of British control had prevented them from being rescued entirely from the tyranny of pashadom or from the oppressions of the moneylender, they had derived certain solid and recognizable benefits from the occupation, and it would have been difficult to induce in them any very violent feelings of antipathy towards the British. It was Denshawai, or, rather, the propagandist use made of Denshawai, that created the possibility of organizing anti-British public opinion on a large and country-wide scale. The fact that Denshawai also struck a blow at the influence of the Hizb-al-Umma, the 'collaborationist' wing of the nationalists, was a small thing beside the effect it had on the reputation which Great Britain was beginning to build up for herself as the protector of the *fellahin*.

Lord Cromer retired in the year following the election to power of a Liberal Government in England for the first time for over ten years, and governmental feeling in England combined with events in Egypt to dictate a change in British policy. Lord Cromer was succeeded as British Agent and

Consul-General by Sir Eldon Gorst,[3] who had had a long experience of Egyptian affairs, having been successively Financial Secretary, Adviser to the Interior, and Financial Adviser. His views as to the necessity for a new political approach coincided with those of the British Government. The main lines of the policy on which he embarked may be summarized as follows:

(a) The improvement of relations between the British Agent and the Khedive. The strained relations which had existed between Abbas and Cromer could not have continued indefinitely. It was necessary either to depose the Khedive or to secure his co-operation. Gorst's attempt at co-operation was obviously sensible and reasonable, even though it involved the resignation of Mahmud Pasha Fahmy, who had been Prime Minister for the previous thirteen years, and who was too deeply committed to Cromer's anti-Khedive attitude to make an acceptable partner in the new policy of attempted co-operation.

(b) The 're-Egyptianization' of the Administration. Reference has already been made to the increasing tendency towards the replacement of Egyptians by Englishmen in the higher ranks of the Administration which had been so marked a feature of the last years of the Cromer régime. The criterion has ceased to be 'Can an Egyptian do the job adequately?' and had become 'Cannot an Englishman be found to do the job better?' It was already becoming apparent that the quest for maximum administrative efficiency would defeat its own object by creating political friction, the effects of which would more than nullify any additional administrative efficiency achieved. There is a point beyond which it is neither wise nor safe to increase administrative efficiency in opposition to public opinion, since, in the long run, administrative efficiency depends on the co-operation of public opinion. Here again Gorst's policy was not only politically expedient, but administratively sound. The British advisers, in appointing their British subordinates, were losing sight of the end in their preoccupation with the means.

(c) The enlargement of the powers of the Legislative Council, the General Assembly, and the provincial councils created by Lord Dufferin. Cromer had not encouraged the development of these bodies, which had under his régime enjoyed little more than a nominal existence. The result was that there was no legitimate channel of consultation or criticism between the Government and the governed. It would, of course, be absurd to pretend that the councils and assemblies created by Lord Dufferin were in any sense representative of the Egyptian masses. They were composed exclusively of landlords and notables who certainly had less interest in the welfare of the people than had the British administrators. But it was becoming urgently necessary to provide for some means of constitutional consultation and criticism, if only for the purpose of lowering the political temperature, which was becoming superheated. Gorst therefore arranged: (i) That the provincial councils should be regularly elected, with each *markaz* having its own representative; that they should meet more frequently; that they should be consulted as of right by the *mudirs* in administrative matters affecting the province; and they should be given certain definite powers over primary education and over the appointment of *ghaffirs* (watchmen). (ii) That the meetings of the Legislative Council and General Assembly should be held in public (the name of Legislative Assembly was changed to General Assembly); that members of the Government should attend important debates and answer questions put to them.

The enlargement of the powers of the provincial councils was overdue, and the results were not unencouraging. The enlargement of the powers of the Legislative Council and General Assembly, however laudable in intention, was not justified by results. The Government was neither sufficiently experienced nor sufficiently popular to be able to stand up to the criticisms of an elected assembly. The members of the Council were neither sufficiently educated nor sufficiently public-spirited to be able to distinguish legislative and executive functions or between criticism and obstruction. They used their enlarged powers, not to put the Government in touch with public opinion, but to try to prevent the Government from governing at all.

Gorst's policy has been unfavourably criticized by almost every British writer on the subject.[4] It has been pointed out, with some truth, that a policy of 're-Egyptianizing' the administration, carried out simultaneously with a policy of exposing the Administration to organized and detailed criticism, was basically unsound. It has been objected, with equal truth, that the encouragement of the dictatorial tendencies of the Khedive was incompatible with the enlargement of the powers of the elected bodies. But at the same time something had to be done to lower the political temperature. A rigid adherence to sound administrative principles would have defeated its own object. It was above all necessary to divide and distract the three converging forces—the Palace, the Notables, and the middle-class nationalists—who were threatening to unite against the British occupation. The only alternatives to such a policy were, on the one hand, violent and probably bloody repression, and, on the other hand, a speedy evacuation.

When this has been said, it must be acknowledged that the short-term results of Gorst's policy were disappointing. The Khedive, who appeared to regard Gorst's conciliatory attitude as a sign of weakness in face of the growing nationalist opposition, judged that the time was ripe to strengthen his own position by trying to play the British and the nationalists off one against the other. As a result, he came to be regarded with equal distrust by both. The nationalists were by no means appeased by such relaxation of British control as was affected, and clamoured for more.

The British officials, and more particularly the British and other foreign commercial communities, did not take kindly to the actual and contemplated relaxations of British control. The British officials felt a natural objection to a policy which could not but be detrimental to their own personal prospects of advancement, but they were also distressed at the administrative deterioration which they felt was inherent in the new policy. The foreign commercial communities had come to regard the British occupiers as a convenient police force for the safeguarding of their exceptional and largely unjustifiable privileges, and naturally objected to any weakening of this safeguard.

The political situation took a turn for the worse after the premature death, in February 1908, of Mustafa Kamal, the gifted young leader of the Hizb-al-Watani. Mustafa Kamal had always refused to use Moslem fanaticism as a recruiting agent for the nationalist movement. Himself a Europeanized agnostic,[5] he would have no truck with the *'ulema*, and refused to countenance any anti-Christian agitation. His successor, Mohamed Farid, was less able and less scrupulous. He fell under the influence of Moslem fanaticism in general and under that of a certain Shaykh-Shawish Abdul Aziz, who became Editor of the nationalist newspaper *Al-Liwa*, in particular. The fact that the Prime Minister, Butros Pasha Ghali (who had succeeded Mustafa Fahmy) was not only a Copt, but had been President of the Special Court set up to try the Denshawai case, and had, as Foreign Minister, signed the Sudan Convention of 1899, made him a broad mark for increasingly scurrilous attacks in the nationalist Press. The Press Law of 1881, which enabled the Government summarily to suppress newspapers for offences against public security (meaning, as usual in this connexion, for opposition to the Government), was reinvoked for the first time since the occupation, but its application was hampered by the Capitulations, since an offending newspaper had only to assume a façade of foreign ownership in order to render itself to all intents and purposes free of the Press, or indeed almost any other, Law.

In February 1910 the obstruction from the Legislative Council reached its height in clamorous opposition to an agreement made by the Government with the Suez Canal Company, which provided for an extension of the Canal

Company's Concession for a further period of forty years after the expiry of the original concession in 1968, against a lump sum payment to the Egyptian Government of £E.4,000,000 plus a share in the annual profits. No attempt was made to debate the agreement on its merits. The opportunity was merely taken to denounce the Prime Minister as a traitor. The man who had betrayed Egypt to the British over the Sudan and over Denshawai was now alleged to have betrayed Egypt to the Canal Company. The Government decided to refer the agreement to the General Assembly. As might have been expected, and as perhaps was expected, the General Assembly repudiated the agreement with only one dissentient voice. On the following day, on 10 February 1910, Boutros Pasha Ghali, who had for weeks been the object of a constant barrage of abuse from the nationalist Press, was assassinated by a young fanatic.[6]

A disquieting feature of the nationalist agitation which had culminated so tragically was the prominent part played by secondary school students—youths of from fourteen to eighteen—who at about this time formed the habit, which they have not yet discarded, of seizing every opportunity to neglect their studies and indulge in political demonstrations. Student agitation has been so marked a feature of Egyptian political life for the last forty years that it is worth while dwelling for a moment on its origins. It has already been related how education in Egypt was developed in such a way as to provide a surplus of secondary school graduates with no higher or other qualifications.[7] Apart from a limited number of openings in commerce and the professions, the only prospect of secure employment for these people was in Government service. It thus became an economic necessity for the student class to blackmail the Government into providing employment for an ever-increasing number of young men who would otherwise become unemployable. Political agitation was the form of blackmail employed. The Government, instead of dealing with the problem radically by taking steps to equate supply to effective demand, took the easier course of turning the lower ranks of Government service into a gigantic system of outdoor relief. By so doing they prevented student agitation from developing into a menace at the expense of clogging the channels of routine administration with a vast army of underworked, incompetent, and underpaid clerks, who, most of them, not only performed no useful function whatever, but by their very presence, obstructed the performance of useful work by other people.

This process had already started in Cromer's time, and Cromer had secured the appointment of a promising young nationalist lawyer, Saad Zaghlul,[8] a son-in-law of Mustafa Fahmy, as head of the newly-formed Ministry of Education, in the hope that he would be able to discipline the students. He was unable to do so for the simple reason that the students had already learnt that the exploitation of their nuisance value was the best means of securing their economic future.

The murder of Boutros Pasha Ghali shocked both the Notables and the middle-class nationalists into a belated sense of reality. They realized how incapable they would be of controlling the mob violence they had done so much to incite. They saw the danger of letting political agitation undermine the foundations of public security. They realized that the immediate attainment of their political aims was incompatible with the maintenance of public security, and consequently with the preservation of their own property or employment. They began to appreciate that religious fanaticism could not be turned on and off like a tap to suit the political exigencies of the moment. The pashas became frightened of the middle-class nationalists; the middle-class nationalists became frightened of the mob.

Owing to this reaction of feeling, there was extraordinarily little open opposition to the régime of repression instituted by the British in co-operation with the new Government under Mohamed Pasha Said,[9] who had been Minister of the Interior in the Ghali Government and who succeeded Ghali as Prime Minister. Ghali's murderer was caught, tried, and executed without any untoward incident occurring. The revived Press Law was given the widest possible application. Shaykh Shawish was imprisoned for sedition. The powers were persuaded to delegate to the General Assembly of the Mixed Courts authority to approve, by a two-thirds majority, the application to foreigners of any new legislation not involving taxation. This to a great extent untied the Government's hands with regard to such new legislation as appeared desirable from time to time in the interest of public security.

Whether the intention of Gorst's policy had been to divide the internal forces which in 1907 had appeared to be coalescing against Great Britain must remain uncertain. One can only record the fact that, in effect, his policy turned out to be a classic example of 'divide and rule'. The historian must take his choice between Machiavellianism and muddling through. But Gorst's British critics had not given him sufficient credit for the fact that when Lord Kitchener succeeded to the post of British Agent and Consul-General on Gorst's death in July 1911, the internal situation in Egypt was a good deal less menacing than it had been when Gorst succeeded Cromer in 1907.

One of the greatest problems of imperial administration is to find officials who can at the same time avoid subservience and act loyally towards their superiors. In the early days of the occupation these extremes were avoided mainly because the British officials were few in number, and had a share in formulating the policy which they carried out. By the time of Cromer's departure the British official machine had become unwieldy and inflexible, governed by prejudice rather than by reason, by self-interest rather than by any instinct for the common weal. It verged on sabotage in its opposition to Gorst; it approached servility in its furtherance of the not always well-conceived plans of his successor.

Lord Kitchener was essentially a soldier and a man of action who had an abiding contempt for politicians. He came to Egypt with an immense prestige. He had a considerable knowledge of and a great affection for the common people of the country, and was determined to play the benevolent despot. Circumstances were propitious for the assumption of such a role. The events of the past four years had demonstrated, not only in England, but to a certain extent also in Egypt, the desirability of a strong government. The British officials were enthusiastically in favour of a return to autocracy. There was plenty of money in the Egyptian Treasury. The incipient alliance between the Khedive, the Notables, and the nationalists had been broken up. If Egypt had had a surfeit of administration under Cromer, it had had a surfeit of politics under Gorst, and the time was ripe for a swing of the pendulum away from politics and back to administration. (It may perhaps sound odd to refer to administration and politics as if the two were incompatible, since in a well-ordered western democracy the two have become synonymous. It remains true, however, that in a politically backward country political development can only take place at the expense of administrative efficiency.

The first major problem with which Kitchener had to deal arose from the outbreak of war in Libya, on Egypt's western border, between Turkey and Italy. Egypt was still legally a part of the Ottoman Empire and, consequently, a belligerent in international law. Moslem feeling had been greatly stirred by Italy's unprovoked attack, and many Egyptians were in favour of giving assistance to Turkey. Kitchener imposed a policy of strict neutrality on Egypt without forfeiting the goodwill of the Turks, the Italians, or the Egyptians themselves. It was an impressive display of his authority and prestige.

For all his dislike of politicians, Kitchener was unable entirely to ignore politics. By a strange irony, it was Kitchener who first provided Zaghlul with a platform for the exercise of his considerable demagogic talents. The enlargement of the powers of the Legislative Council and the General Assembly had demonstrated that one of these two bodies was redundant. By the Organic Law of 1913 they were replaced by a body called the Legislative Assembly, composed of seven nominated and sixty-six elected members. The new body was invested with much the same powers as had accrued in a somewhat haphazard way to its predecessors; it was given power to veto proposals for increases in direct taxation; its members could interrogate Ministers and call for information in much the same way as Members of the House of Commons; legislation had to be explained and justified to the Assembly before it could become law (although the Assembly had not the power to veto legislation except in respect of direct taxation).

Thus, in this one respect, Kitchener followed and even elaborated the policy initiated by Gorst. But relations with the Khedive[10] and the policy regarding the employment of Englishmen in the Administration reverted to the *status quo ante* Gorst. The policy of fostering democratic institutions in Egypt, to which Great Britain now appeared to have committed herself, was quite incompatible with a policy of strengthening the power of the Khedive, which was the only basis on which co-operation with Abbas could have been founded. And in any case such co-operation would almost certainly have been impossible to anyone of Kitchener's temperament. The wisdom of reversing Gorst's policy of 're-Egyptianization' was more questionable. It was true that grievous defects and deficiencies existed in various departments of the Administration, particularly in the Interior,[11] and public security had suffered as the result of the withdrawal of British inspectors from the provinces. It was true that a defective system of public education was proving itself incapable of providing a sufficient number of qualified Egyptian recruits for the higher posts in the public service. At the same time, it was a grim reflection on British methods of administration that, after twenty-eight years of rehabilitation, it should still be considered necessary to replace Egyptians by Englishmen instead of being well advanced on the reverse process. Not only this, but the quality of the British recruits was no longer what it had been. In the senior posts Kitchener was apt to put a higher value on the quality of obedience to his wishes than he was on other and rarer qualities. In the more junior posts favouritism and nepotism were beginning to creep in. Room was beginning to be found for 'old So-and-So'. In the process of attempting to Westernize Oriental administration, British officialdom was becoming to a certain extent affected by Orientalism. The effects of the resultant deterioration were to become apparent during the war years.

Meanwhile the work of material progress went forward, particularly in the sphere of irrigation, which in Egypt is the basis of nearly all material progress. The Aswan Dam, completed in 1903, was heightened, thus increasing the potential area of perennial irrigation. Between 1899 and 1913 the cultivated area increased by 100,000 *feddans* and the crop area by 750,000 *feddans*. The population rose from 9,700,000 in 1897 to 11,287,000 in 1907 and to 12,294,000 in 1914. The annual value of exports increased from £18,000,000 in 1904 to £24,000,000 in 1914, and imports from £14,000,000 to £21,000,000 during the same period.

The development of perennial irrigation created a number of grave problems, not all of which were satisfactorily solved. The application of water to the land all the year round made it necessary to dig deep ditches to drain the water off from the subsoil. In the Delta the landfall was insufficient to drain the water off by gravity, and the subsoil water level rose by nearly 3 metres in twenty years, until in 1908 the mean level of subsoil water in the Delta was only 1 metre below the surface. The land was becoming waterlogged. The cotton crop yield fell from $5\frac{1}{4}$ *kantars* per *feddan* in 1895 to just over 3 *kantars* per *feddan* in 1909.[12] The soil, deprived of the silt deposit which had previously revivified the basin lands, and exhausted by the continual succession of summer and winter crops made possible by the new abundance of water, became more and more dependent on artificial fertilizers imported from abroad. Perennial irrigation meant that the soil had continually to be squeezed of water on the one hand and fed with nitrogen on the other. A system of mechanical pumping stations was started in the northern Delta to assist in the draining of the subsoil water into the sea.[13] Increased exports of cotton[14] made it possible to pay for the necessary imports of artificial fertilizers.

Other ills arising from perennial irrigation were less easily repaired. The perpetual presence of water on the land turned Egypt into a soggy, muddy country. The majority of the rural population became infected with bilharzia, a hookworm infesting the Nile mud, which enters the pores of the skin and has a most deleterious effect on physical and mental energy. Malaria and other diseases deriving from damp also became prevalent. Hashish smoking[15] intensified the bilharzia-induced debility which it was intended to alleviate. It almost seemed as if progress had merely substituted non-mortal endemic diseases for mortal epidemic ones, and that Egypt was, in consequence, exchanging a small and hardy population for a large and feeble one.

No such doubts as these worried Kitchener. He did not like to have doubters about him. When Sir Paul Harvey, the Financial Adviser, expressed doubts as to the wisdom of some of Kitchener's expenditure on public works, he was replaced as Financial Adviser by a gentleman who had been Kitchener's A.D.C.[16] and whose financial qualifications were not immediately apparent. But he provided the money for the agricultural schemes which Kitchener had at heart. These schemes were not always wisely conceived, and suffered from the disadvantage of being imposed from above rather than being recommended from below. If politics were becoming more democratic, administration was becoming more dictatorial. Both suffered in consequence.

Kitchener's reforms, which were intended to benefit the agricultural population, did not always have their intended effect. The new Legislative Assembly, which was designed to give agriculturalists a larger voice in the affairs of the country, became under Zaghlul's leadership the forum and sounding-board of urban nationalism. The Five-*feddan* Law, which was intended to protect smallholders by providing that holdings of 5 *feddans* or less could neither be pledged as security for, nor seized in payment of, a debt, meant in practice that the small landowner found it even more difficult than before to get credit at other than exorbitant rates. For example, the Five-*feddan* Law crippled the activities of the Agricultural Bank, which had been started in 1902 with the object of advancing money to small agriculturalists at low rates of interest against adequate security.[17]

But in spite of certain miscalculations, administrative concentration on the improvement of agriculture provided a salutary antidote to the political confusion caused by the impact of a popular Assembly on an inexperienced and *fainéant* Executive. In a rough-and-ready way, Kitchener did manage to steer a middle course between administration and politics, and to provide a safety-valve for political activity without serious detriment to essential administrative requirements. It is, nevertheless, possible to discern, in the developments which took place during Kitchener's term of office, the seeds of the troubles which were to burst forth so violently in 1919. The Egyptian Government became more and more subservient to the British and less and less representative of any section of Egyptian public opinion. The British official community coagulated to form an aloof and unsympathetic bureaucracy with no points of social contact with any class of Egyptian society. The nationalists, who had reverted to legal methods as a result of the repression following on the murder of Butros Pasha Ghali, used the Legislative Assembly mercilessly to harass the Government. The Legislative Assembly became not, as was intended, a consultative body, but an organized Opposition to the Government. This Opposition consisted mainly of a new school of 'constitutional' nationalists, led by Zaghlul, which was at first primarily anti-Khedive rather than anti-British. Abbas had, in fact, unwittingly performed a useful function for the British by splitting Egyptian nationalism into two groups, one of which, the Hizb-al-Watani, was suspected from time to time of 'under-the-counter' dealings with the Khedive, and the other, the 'constitutionalists', which was quite prepared, for the time being, to ally itself with the British in opposition to the Khedive. In this way Abbas's presence on the throne delayed a head-on collision between the nationalists and the British. The influence of the Hizb-al-Watani declined steadily after the creation of the Legislative Assembly, which served as a training ground for the new and formidable Egyptian nationalism which was to emerge, fully fledged, at the end of 1918 under the leadership of Zaghlul.

Kitchener left Egypt for England on leave in the summer of 1914. At about the same time, Khedive Abbas left for his usual summer visit to Constantinople. Thus the two principal actors on the Egyptian stage were absent when the outbreak of war sent the curtain up for the next act. Neither of them was ever to return to Egypt.

NOTES ON CHAPTER EIGHT

1. The Hizb-al-Umma did not in fact come into formal existence until October, 1907, six months after Cromer's final departure from Egypt.

2. National Party.

3. Gorst was recommended to the British Government by Cromer as his successor.

4. Exceptions are George Young in *Egypt* and Sir Ronald Storrs in *Orientations.*

5. Through the influence of a Frenchwoman, Mme. Juliette Adam, Mustafa Kamal had at an early age become secretary to a French politician, and his political apprenticeship was served in France. This may help to account for his anti-British proclivities.

6. Ibrahim Nassif al Wardani, a young Moslem Egyptian. He belonged to a secret terrorist society called Tadaman, one of the members of which was Shafiq Mansur, a leading member of the gang responsible for the terrorist murders of the post-war years.

7. Apart from al-Azhar there was no University in Egypt until 1926, when the Fuad-al-Awwal University was inaugurated.

8. Saad Zaghlul remained Minister of Education until after the murder of Ghali Pasha, when he became Minister of Justice in the new Government formed by Mohamed Pasha Said. In this capacity he fell foul of the Khedive, and was dismissed from office. He is said to have developed a grievance against the British for not having supported him on that occasion. In 1912 his father-in-law, Mustafa Pasha Fahmy, asked Kitchener to arrange for his appointment

as Intendant of the Egyptian Educational Mission in Paris. Kitchener refused this favour, and by so doing probably altered the course of Egyptian history. In 1913 Zaghlul was elected to the newly-created Legislative Assembly, and became its President. Between that time and the prorogation of the Assembly on the outbreak of war he established himself as the most eloquent and the most persistent of the Government's critics. Saad Zaghlul was, like Arabi, of *fellah* extraction. He had been a lawyer by profession. He entered politics as a result of his marriage to a daughter of Mustafa Pasha Fahmy. He was thought highly of by Cromer, who made a eulogistic reference to him in his farewell speech prophesying that he would 'go far'.

9. Mohamed Pasha Said remained Prime Minister until the beginning of 1914, when he quarrelled with the Khedive. For some reason, Kitchener did not support him, although he had been reasonably co-operative with the British, and he was dismissed. He was succeeded by Hussein Pasha Rushdi, who was to remain Prime Minister throughout the war years.

10. Kitchener's first serious clash with the Khedive was in 1913, when Abbas attempted to sell to an Italian syndicate the Mariut Railway, a line which he had had constructed from Alexandria along the coast towards the Libyan frontier. (Libya had been taken from Turkey by the Italians in 1911.) Abbas's offer to the syndicate included permission to extend the line to Sollum, on the Libyan frontier. Kitchener intervened and secured the cancellation of the option. At about the same time Kitchener removed from the Khedive's personal control the Awqaf funds (funds bequeathed and donated for religious purposes) and created a Ministry to manage them. The control of these funds by the Khedive's entourage had led to grave abuses, and large sums of money had been misappropriated. Kitchener's action was generally acknowledged to be salutary.

11. One of Gorst's first acts, in pursuance of the policy of 're-Egyptianization' had been to appoint as Adviser to the Interior a certain Mr. Chitty, who was well-known to be sympathetic to Egyptian nationalism. Mr. Chitty set to work to cut out, as far as possible, British intervention in routine matters of administration. This undoubtedly led to a deterioration in administrative efficiency.

12. It had risen to 12½ by 1912.

13. The scheme was delayed by the war and was only finally completed in the nineteen-thirties. By that time much of what had previously been the most fertile land in Egypt had greatly deteriorated. The position has now (1953) improved and the problem of drainage in the Delta, if not entirely solved, is well in hand.

14. Between 1885 and 1890 the average annual value of cotton exports had been just under £9,000,000. Between 1910 and 1914 it was just over £29,000,000.

15. The main reason for taking hashish is to counteract the sexual lassitude induced in males by bilharzia. The long-term effect of hashish is, of course, to aggravate the trouble, thus setting up a vicious spiral which can only be broken, not by putting down hashish smuggling, but by eliminating bilharzia.

16. Lord Edward Cecil, who published an entertaining book of Egyptian reminiscences entitled *The Leisure of an Egyptian Official*.

17. The Agricultural Bank, in fact, failed in its main object, which was to replace the village moneylender as a source of credit for small landowners. When its successor, the Credit Agricole d'Egypte, was founded in 1931, it was exempted from the provisions of the Five-*feddan* Law.

CHAPTER NINE

THE PROTECTORATE

THE first few days of war passed quietly in Egypt. On 5 August 1914, the day after Great Britain had declared war on Germany, the Egyptian Government, under pressure from the British Agency, issued a proclamation pointing out that the British occupation rendered Egypt liable to attack from the enemies of the British Government, forbidding all financial and commercial dealings with the nationals of Great Britain's enemies, and urging Egyptians to lend all possible aid to Great Britain. In after years the Prime Minister, Hussein Pasha Rushdi, was bitterly assailed by Egyptian nationalists for having issued this proclamation without having extracted some *quid pro quo* from the British in return. But at the time the proclamation was received quietly in Egypt. In fact, Egypt had assumed the only relationship with Great Britain compatible with the realities of the situation.

At the time of the proclamation, most educated Egyptian opinion was far more concerned with the economic than with the political implications of the war. It was realized that, with a major war in Europe, the disposal of the cotton crop and the continued import of essential commodities could only be secured with the assistance of Great Britain. It was not a moment for exploiting nuisance value. At the same time, Rushdi Pasha would have been well advised to have armed himself against his domestic opponents by holding out for some reciprocal pledge from the British Government. The opportunity was lost, and the issue of the proclamation widened still further the gap between the Government and the nationalists.

The uncertainty about the disposal of the cotton crop,

which was about to be picked, caused the beginnings of a financial panic. Competent steps were taken to deal with the situation. A short moratorium was declared; the notes of the National Bank of Egypt were declared legal tender;[1] the collection of the coming instalment of the land tax was postponed. By November arrangements had been made for the Egyptian Government to buy cotton on the open market on behalf of the British Government, and the worst of the crisis was over. Simultaneously far-sighted steps were taken to restrict the cotton acreage in order to increase the acreage devoted to food crops.

Meanwhile, on 18 October, a decree had been issued proroguing the Legislative Assembly, which was due to meet in November, *sine die*. This measure was also quietly accepted by Egyptian opinion and even by the members of the Assembly themselves. This quiescence is only explicable when it is born in mind that the leadership of Egyptian nationalism had now passed irrevocably to the 'constitutionalists', who were more anti-Khedive than anti-British, and who were particularly anxious not to embarrass the British in view of Abbas's known inclination towards Turkey, whose entry into the war against Great Britain was realized to be only a matter of time.

The outbreak of war found Abbas in Constantinople. Neither the British, nor the Prime Minister (who was acting as Regent), nor the nationalists desired his return. It is not quite clear to what extent Abbas desired it himself. After his failure to capture Egyptian nationalism, he had turned towards intrigue with the Porte, which, he realized, had been committed by Enver and his associates to entry into the war, at the appropriate moment, on the side of the Central Powers.

The growing certainty of Turkish hostility created a difficulty for the British Government. Egypt was still legally a province of the Ottoman Empire, and the Khedive was subject to the suzerainty of the Sultan. Thus, in the expected event of Turkey entering into the war on the side of Germany,

Egypt would become legally at war with Great Britain. A legal sanction would then exist for the commission of hostile acts by Egyptians against the British occupation, and the acts of the Egyptian Government, in so far as they were designed to assist Great Britain, would become illegal. The resultant situation would clearly have been Gilbertian. But it appears in the light of after-knowledge that the British Government exaggerated the practical difficulties likely to arise from such a situation. One reason, and perhaps the main reason, for this exaggeration lay in the quite disproportionate importance that was attached by British administrators in Egypt, in India, and elsewhere to the pan-Islamic propaganda being disseminated by the Ottoman Government. It was considered that the declaration of a *jihad*, or holy war,[2] which was expected to accompany an Ottoman declaration of war on the Allies, would not only place a severe strain on the loyalty of Moslems in countries subject to the *de jure* or *de facto* rule of the Allies, but would provide a positive incentive for active resistance to Allied rule. As far as Egypt was concerned, the physical proximity of Turkish-controlled territory[3] and Turkish armies accentuated the potential danger to be apprehended from a declaration of a *jihad*, and, quite apart from any question of a *jihad*, necessitated the presence of greatly increased British forces in Egypt to defend the Suez Canal. The fact of hostilities between Great Britain and Germany made the invasion of Egypt a theoretical but remote possibility. The immediate prospect of hostilities with Turkey brought the prospect of invasion very much nearer.

War between Great Britain and Turkey was actually declared on 6 November 1914. Four days earlier, Sir John Maxwell, the British Military Commander in Egypt, had declared a state of martial law. This declaration was followed by a military proclamation which announced that Great Britain would take upon herself the whole burden of the defence of Egypt, and that she would not call for any active participation in the war from the people of Egypt. This proclamation was made at the request of the Prime Minister, Rushdi Pasha, who had protested bitterly against the imposition of martial law and had threatened to resign. But it is doubtful whether the protests of Rushdi Pasha would have prevailed had not the British authorities been over-impressed with the importance and extent of pro-Islamic feeling and the necessity for conciliating it.

The same anxiety is apparent from the political decision taken with regard to the future status of Egypt. It is not the British habit to pay very much regard to logic in the solution of political problems. Unfortunately, in this instance, the British tradition was discarded and the illogicality of leaving Egypt as a province of the Ottoman Empire, while at the same time associating her with the British war effort, was allowed to obscure the fact that any change in Egypt's political status was beset with serious practical disadvantages. Assuming, as it was assumed, that the maintenance of the *status quo* was impracticable, there were two clear-cut alternatives. One was to tighten the bond between Egypt and Great Britain by incorporating Egypt into the British Empire; the other was to loosen the bond and declare Egypt independent. But the first alternative seemed incompatible with the nature of Great Britain's self-imposed mission in Egypt, and the second alternative was incompatible with the effective prosecution of the war. As in the case of the Sudan fifteen years previously, an *ad hoc* solution was recommended and finally adopted.

The British Agency's recommendation was that a protectorate should be declared over Egypt. The status of a protectorate had never been clearly defined, but it was understood and accepted that the assumption of a protectorate by a great power over a small one was only valid if the small power had requested such a step to be taken. No such request was made by the Egyptian Government or by any other Egyptian body. The declaration of the Protectorate on 19 December 1914 was a unilateral act by Great Britain. As far as the status of Egypt in international law was concerned, Great Britain had merely evaded one illegality by slipping into another. But there were more practical disadvantages than this in Egypt's new status. While adding nothing to the efficacy of British control over Egypt (which was assured, not by Egypt's legal status, but by the presence of British armed forces), the terms of the Protectorate on the one hand humiliated Egyptian nationalist feelings and on the other hand aroused vague but disturbing hopes for the future which might be embarrassing to implement, but which would certainly be difficult to deny. The Arabic word for protectorate—*himaya*—was in itself humiliating, since it was the word habitually used to describe the status of local Christian minorities under the protection of some European power. The provision by which the Egyptian Ministry of Foreign Affairs was abolished and its attributions transferred to H.B.M.'s Representative was likewise humiliating. The humiliations might have been forgotten in the course of time. But the prospects which were held out in presumable compensation for the humiliations would never be forgotten. These prospects were conveyed in the following two passages from the declaration:

His Majesty's Government have repeatedly placed on record that the system of Treaties, known as the Capitulations, by which Your Highness' Government is bound, are no longer in harmony with the development of the country; but, in the opinion of His Majesty's Government, the revision of those Treaties may most conveniently be postponed until the end of the present war.

In the field of internal administration, I am bound to remind Your Highness that, in consonance with the tradition of the British policy, it has been the aim of His Majesty's Government, while working through and in the closest association with the constituted Egyptian Authorities, to secure individual liberty, to promote the spread of education, to further the development of the natural resources of the country, and, in such measure as the degree of public enlightenment may permit, to associate the governed in the task of Government. Not only is it the intention of His Majesty's Government to remain true to such a policy, but they are convinced that a clearer definition of Great Britain's position in the country will accelerate progress towards self-government.

It is undoubtedly true that there were strong reasons against annexation. There was the possibility of international difficulties;[4] it would probably have been necessary to find Englishmen of sufficient calibre to form a Ministry in Egypt at a time when men of such calibre were urgently needed for duties more directly connected with the war effort. There was the argument put forward by the acting British Agent, Mr. (afterwards Sir Milne) Cheetham, to the effect that, since the war was bound to cause a certain amount of administrative dislocation, it was preferable that the British should not assume more responsibility for administration than they already possessed. The various unpopular measures of control necessitated by the war would probably be accepted more readily as coming from an indigenous rather than a specifically British Administration. And, lurking in the background, was the pan-Islamic bogyman which, at that time, infused an air of compromise and apology into every manifestation of British policy in the Moslem world.

But, assuming annexation to be inadvisable, the Protectorate in no respect constituted an improvement on the existing state of affairs. Nobody had been conciliated. Many who might have accepted annexation, and who had accepted the existing state of affairs, were irritated. Not one jot nor one tittle was added to the realities of British control. Egypt's international status remained as anomalous as before. Since the Protectorate was, by international usage, invalid, it could not be said legally to invalidate Ottoman suzerainty. Similarly, it could have no effect on the Capitulations. In so far as the existing state of affairs was changed, it was changed for the worse.

The Protectorate was declared on 19 December. On the following day it was formally announced that Khedive Abbas Hilmi II had been deposed and that his uncle, Prince

Hussein Kamal, had been made ruler of Egypt with the title of Sultan.[5] Abbas, if he had been allowed to return to Egypt, would have been an intolerable nuisance under wartime conditions, both to Great Britain and to Egypt, and the decision to depose him was undoubtedly justified. His successor, a son of Ismail, was an elderly man, a large landowner of exemplary life, and much respected. During his short reign (he died in 1917) he did what was expected of him, and played his allotted role of a dignified and venerable figurehead.

The exigencies of martial law did not at first have any serious effect on everyday life in Egypt. General Maxwell had served in Egypt before the war, knew the country well, and was in close accord with the civil administration, both Egyptian and British. But as the importance of Egypt as an operational base increased, so the military machine became more complex, more impersonal, more widely delegated, more ruthless, and inevitably more inefficient. The inefficiency of military administration in a base area is proverbial. It is also inevitable, in time of war. In any sort of civilian administration, whether it be a department of government, a business house, or a factory, the responsible officials have not, generally speaking, been appointed to positions of responsibility until they have proved, by their work in more junior posts, their fitness for such responsibility. The same applies to a military administration in peacetime or in a small colonial war fought by regular troops. But in a world war, fought by a civilian conscript army, the best and most experienced soldiers are needed for the organization and direction of operations. The base areas are for the most part administered by men who are occupying posts of responsibility for which they have not been trained, and for which, in many cases, they are not fitted. They have to try to learn their jobs in the process of doing them, and inevitably mistakes are made even by good men. Complex administrations have to be devised overnight, and staffed with whoever happens to be available, at a time when most of the best men have already found their niches in the war machine. Unaccustomed responsibility breeds arrogance, overwork causes irritation, and opportunity too often leads to corruption.

The imposition of martial law meant in effect that the British Army became the supreme legislative and executive authority in Egypt. At first these powers were sparingly used. But as time went on genuine military necessities, combined with the autocratic tendencies of a military régime, extended the incidence of martial law over nearly every aspect of Egyptian life. Unfortunately, this extension was not accompanied by any constructive liaison between the military administration and British civilian officials.

The progressive deterioration in the quality of British officials in Egypt has already been noted. This deterioration became more marked during the war as many of the best men departed for jobs, in the fighting line and elsewhere, which appeared to be more directly connected with the war effort. The most important of these departures was, of course, that of Lord Kitchener, who had been appointed Secretary of State for War in the British Government. After an interregnum of about six months, during which the direction of the British Agency was in the hands of Sir Milne Cheetham, Sir Henry MacMahon, a distinguished Indian civil servant, came to Egypt as High Commissioner. (The post of British Agent and Consul-General had been elevated into that of High Commissioner as a result of the Protectorate.) Sir Henry MacMahon had had no previous experience of Egypt and, although a man with a fine administrative record, was not in a position to impress the Egyptians with a world-wide reputation in the same way as Kitchener had been. In the press and turmoil of war he was unable either to get a grip of the complex problems of Egyptian administration or to impress his personality upon those responsible for Egyptian administration.

British officials were torn between their patriotic desire to meet the demands of the military as expeditiously and as fully as possible and between their duty to maintain a just and efficient administration in Egypt. They received little assistance from their Egyptian colleagues, who for the most part cared little for good administration, and who, since they could blame martial law for any act of oppression, whether or not necessitated by military demands, had no particular objection to doing what the Army required of them in the way of material requisitions, recruitment of labour, and so on. In fact, martial law became a convenient excuse for either sabotaging or ignoring all the administrative barriers which British officials had for the past thirty years been trying to erect between the common people of Egypt and the tyranny of an irresponsible executive. Harassed on the one side by the exigencies of the military, and frustrated on the other side by the insouciance of Egyptian Ministers and senior officials, the British civilian officials in Egypt almost ceased to perform any useful function at all, except to transmit the requirements of the British Army to the various Egyptian executive authorities.[6]

The position of the British officials was made more difficult than it otherwise would have been because, in spite of the Protectorate, they still had no clearly defined positions of authority. If, as in India or the British colonies, they had constituted the civil power, they could more easily have harmonized military requirements with the interests of the population. It would no doubt have been possible, even in the existing circumstances, for them to have acted as efficient intermediaries between the British Army and the Egyptian Ministers without detriment either to military requirements or to civilian interests. It was in fact done in the early days of martial law. But British civilian officialdom was soon swamped by the military invasion.

By the end of 1914 one British Territorial division, two Indian divisions, and the first units of the Australian Imperial Forces had arrived in Egypt. In December 1914 active operations started in Sinai and on the Suez Canal as the result of a Turco-German raid on the Canal from Palestine.

Early in 1915 Egypt was made the base for the Mediterranean Expeditionary Force which was being prepared for the Gallipoli campaign. By the summer of 1915 military operations were in full swing on the Gallipoli Peninsula and thousands of wounded were being evacuated to Egypt. Towards the end of 1915 an Egyptian Expeditionary Force was formed for the invasion of Palestine. This new force was placed under the command of General Sir Archibald Murray, who set up his headquarters at Ismailia. By the beginning of 1916 there were thirteen divisions of troops and no fewer than three General Headquarters in Egypt: G.H.Q., Mediterranean Expeditionary Force, at Alexandria under Sir Ian Hamilton, G.H.Q., Egyptian Expeditionary Force, at Ismailia under General Sir Archibald Murray, and G.H.Q., British Troops in Egypt, in Cairo under General Sir John Maxwell. The Gallipoli evacuation and the squeezing out of Maxwell, who relinquished his command after it had been reduced to a base area, reduced the number of G.H.Q. to one and the number of divisions to nine by the end of March 1916.

Although the pledge absolving Egypt from any active participation in the war had been broken a few days after it had been given by the despatch of Egyptian Army artillery to assist in the defence of the Suez Canal, it remained true that the demands of the military on the civil population had not been considerable for the first year of the war. Hospital accommodation for the Gallipoli casualties had been required and had been generously given. A considerable number of buildings had been requisitioned to house the ever-increasing number of military administrative offices. A number of military regulations controlling drink, prostitution, etc., had been issued and implemented. Enemy aliens and suspected enemy sympathizers had been rounded up and interned. A censorship had been established which was later to become a byword for tyrannical incompetence. But military exigencies had not demanded, and General Maxwell had had the good sense to refrain from, the imposition of any considerable interference with the normal life of the average Egyptian.

But towards the end of 1915 the formation of the Egyptian Expeditionary Force and the preparations for the invasion of Palestine caused a sudden, drastic, and permanent increase in military demands on the civil population in respect of labour, transport, animals, and fodder. In December 1915 land was requisitioned and labour recruited for doubling the railway line between Ismailia and Zagazig. A few weeks later an Egyptian Labour Corps and a Camel Transport Corps were formed to assist in the construction of a system of light railways in Sinai. These Corps were formed by voluntary recruitment, and at the outset the rates of pay offered were sufficiently attractive to enable the recruiting to be genuinely voluntary. Serious difficulties over voluntary recruitment only began to arise when the Egyptian Expeditionary Force moved forwards across Sinai into Palestine. This meant that recruits had to move farther and farther away from their homes into what was, to them, an unknown and unattractive country. Traditional memories of the campaigns of Ibrahim Pasha equated foreign service with almost certain death. A number of Egyptian operational casualties were in fact incurred. Recruiting began to fall off at the same time as lengthening lines 'of communication began to call for more and more recruits.

At this stage the British could either have openly revoked their pledge and persuaded the Egyptian Government to provide the necessary recruits by means of conscription (which already existed in Egypt) or have adopted the more Oriental alternative of retaining the fiction of voluntary service and introducing the fact of compulsory recruitment. Unfortunately, the Oriental alternative was drifted into. The British Army required so many recruits. The Egyptian Government was asked to provide them by voluntary recruitment. The *mudir* of each province was instructed to provide so many 'volunteers'. The *mudir* instructed the *mamur* of each *markaz* that so many 'volunteers' must be furnished.

The *mamur* threatened each *umda* with dire penalties unless he produced his allotted quota of 'volunteers'. In this way the required number of 'volunteers' was obtained. The officials concerned did not mind, as they were in a position to make a private profit by selling immunity from recruitment. All the old abuses began to creep in again. Requisitioning of animals was carried out as arbitrarily and oppressively as the recruitment of labour. Payments made by the Army were not ungenerous, but they were often delayed, and did not always find their way into the hands of the right people. In any case, payment of the full market price and a little more cannot compensate the *fellah* for the loss of his camel or donkey, which is essential to him for his livelihood. The British civilian official, the only person who had both the ability and the will to preserve the *fellah* from injustice, was overwhelmed and could do little more than passively watch the destruction of most of what British officials had been able to build up over a period of thirty years. Fortunes were made by the few at the expense of the many. Contractors flourished with even more than their previous Ismailian luxuriance. The military departments administering security, censorship, and intelligence added to the burdens of war by irresponsible, inconsequent, uninformed and tyrannical incursions into civil administration and politics. Relations between the British military and civil authorities degenerated into a state of endemic feud. The military machine had become so vast and unco-ordinated that the most fatuous orders were issued as if by some process of spontaneous generation. A collection for Red Cross funds was somehow converted into a forced levy on a predominantly Moslem population. An order was issued, and to some extent implemented, for the disarmament of the civil population in a country where the average villager keeps a gun in the same way and for the same purpose as the average British rural householder keeps a dog. As the war receded from Egypt the disabilities arising from the war seemed to increase. This was partly because of the genuine demands of the long line of communications between Egypt and Palestine, but partly because the subordinate formations which remained to administer martial law in Egypt were becoming progressively more incompetent and more autocratic.

In the last year of the war a further cause of discontent arose. The wise restrictions on the cotton acreage which had been instituted at the end of 1914 were afterwards rescinded as a result of clamour from the big landowners who objected to restrictions on the cultivation of their most profitable crop. (The price of cotton rose during the war from $12 a *kantar* in 1914 to $39 a *kantar* in 1917, by which time about 30 per cent. of the irrigated area was under cotton.) The result was that by the end of 1917 a serious shortage in foodstuffs had developed. This shortage was accentuated by military requisitions, and prices rocketed. The poorer townsmen could no longer afford to purchase their minimum requirements. Tardy Government action over cost-of-living allowances led to considerable hardship and consequent bitterness among the urban manual and clerical workers.

Thus in the closing stages of the war a situation had been created in which both the rural and the urban masses were suffering considerable hardship and injustice under a British Protectorate as the result of a war in which their British protectors had specifically exempted them from active participation, and in which they had, in any case, very little interest. The situation had not been brought about deliberately by the British; some of the abuses were even unconnected with the war and had resulted from the selfish and sometimes dishonest exploitation of the war by Egyptian officials and landowners. But it was only to be expected that the beneficiaries would encourage the victims to believe that the British were responsible for all their troubles, even had the British, by their declaration of the Protectorate, not themselves accepted responsibility for the administration of Egypt. In any case, in view of the nature of Great Britain's connexion with Egypt, such a responsibility was inescapable, irrespective of Egypt's nominal status. It is clear that the

Protectorate status had been chosen by Great Britain without a clear realization of British responsibility for the maintenance of good administration under the stress and strain of a war which had come to Egypt as a result of the British connexion. If this responsibility had been realized it would have been immediately apparent that the Protectorate was not an adequate instrument for its discharge. What had happened was that the pendulum had swung back from administration to politics; the Protectorate was designed to alleviate political at the expense of creating administrative problems. But in the long run, the Protectorate exacerbated the political problems it was intended to alleviate.

As early as the spring of 1917 it had become necessary for the Residency to give some consideration to the political complications of the Protectorate. The health of Sultan Hussein was known to be frail, and in the event of his demise the problem of Egypt's political status would again come up for review. The possibility of annexation was again mooted, and was in fact advocated by the High Commissioner, Sir Reginald Wingate (who had succeeded Sir Henry MacMahon in 1916). From the British point of view, the course of the war had greatly enhanced the importance of Egypt as a link in the imperial system. The expected dissolution of the Ottoman Empire would, it was believed, start a 'free for all' among the Powers for the control of the Ottoman heritage in Asia. Great Britain, who had borne the whole burden of the war against Turkey, was not disposed to let the strategic control of these territories, on which the security of communications with India and her Far Eastern possessions depended, slip from between her fingers into the hands of some presently allied but potentially rival power. Although Egypt's importance in relation to the rest of this territory was grossly overrated by the British Government (the Foreign Office was still not only bemused by the pan-Islamic bogyman, but imagined, for some extraordinary reason, that the leadership of pan-Islam would, on the collapse of the Ottoman Empire, devolve upon Egypt, and thus invest Egypt with the leadership of the Moslem world in general and the Arab world in particular), there was no doubt that the control of Egypt would be a decisive factor in the control of the Ottoman Empire's Asiatic heritage. This consideration obviously enhanced the desirability of annexation. And indeed, if continued administrative control of Egypt was deemed to be an imperial necessity, there was everything to be said for making that control as efficient and as effective as possible. The Protectorate was essentially a temporary expedient which could either be expanded into annexation or gradually dissolved into independence.

But the declaration of the Protectorate had been accompanied by a definite statement of the British intention to accelerate progress towards self-government. Although self-government is not necessarily the same thing as independence, progress towards self-government is incompatible with a tightening of administrative control, and is only compatible with an eventual willingness to abandon administrative control entirely. Therefore Great Britain had the choice either of going back on the declaration of the Protectorate or of proceeding with the policy of gradual emancipation laid down in the declaration. But while Great Britain did not want to relax her hold on Egypt, she was unwilling to antagonize those Egyptians, who had collaborated with her by adopting the first alternative, which would have been regarded as a breach of faith even by 'moderate' Egyptian opinion. It was therefore decided to maintain the Protectorate and to trust to the future to find some means of reconciling Egyptian nationalist aspirations with the supposed requirements of imperial strategy. Consequently, when Sultan Hussein died in October 1917, his brother Ahmed Fuad succeeded him as Sultan and the Protectorate remained in being.

Soon after Ahmed Fuad's accession, the Prime Minister, with one eye on the temporarily acquiescent nationalists and the other eye on the new Sultan, who was already showing signs of his autocratic proclivities, began to display a not unnatural anxiety to strengthen his prestige by securing from the British as large an instalment as possible of the Capitulatory reforms and constitutional advances foreshadowed in the declaration of the Protectorate. It was obvious that his position would become extremely difficult if the war should end without his having been able to secure substantial concessions in these respects. The policy on which the British Government had embarked imposed on them the necessity of bolstering up the political credit of a 'collaborationist' Government by every means compatible with the maintenance of effective British control. But it was necessary to act with reasonable despatch. It was to be expected that the end of active hostilities would immediately be followed by a spate of political agitation, and it was essential, from the British point of view, that the Egyptian Government should be able to demonstrate that collaboration with the British during the war years had been suitably rewarded by, at all events, the partial implementation of the promises implied in the declaration of the Protectorate.

A Commission had been appointed in March 1917 to make recommendations for the future of the Capitulations. In December 1917 a Special Commission was set up to examine the whole question of the Capitulations and constitutional reform. In spite of the urgency of the matter, very little progress seems to have been made on either of these commissions, which were both dominated by the personality of Sir William Brunyate, the Judicial Adviser. Such progress as was made public did not contribute materially to the ends in view. First, the possibility of a satisfactory revision of the Capitulations was gravely jeopardized by a leakage of information which made it clear that Sir William Brunyate was urging on the Commission a plan which involved the abolition of the consular courts, the unification of the mixed courts with the national courts, and the substitution of an Anglicized mode of procedure for the existing adaptation of the *Code Napoléon*. Such protests as the last of these proposals might have evoked from the Egyptian nationalists were completely drowned by the protests of the foreign communities in general and the mixed courts Bar in particular. Brunyate's proposals were seen as a perfidious plot to rob European foreigners of their privileges and European lawyers of their livelihood at one fell swoop.

Brunyate's proposals for constitutional reform had an even more unfavourable reception. Some time after the appointment of the Special Commission, Brunyate had been asked by the Prime Minister to draft a note on constitutional reform to act as a basis of discussion for the Commission. The Judicial Adviser, in preparing his note, appeared to ignore the fact that the whole object of the Commission was to devise ways and means of constitutional advance which, while preserving the essentials of the British connexion, would be sufficiently acceptable to Egyptian public opinion to enable the Government to stand up to nationalist criticism. The note proposed a two-chamber legislature, the upper house of which was to be composed of the Egyptian Ministers, the British advisers and representatives of the foreign communities. This upper chamber, composed largely of foreigners, was to have a preponderating voice over the lower chamber, which was to be entirely Egyptian, in initiating, approving, amending and vetoing legislation. Brunyate's proposal was, in fact, similar to that outlined by Cromer in 1905. Whatever its theoretical merits in 1905, it had, in 1918, no appeal whatever to any section of Egyptian opinion. It was not within the realm of things which are politically possible. It could not conceivably have formed the basis of any useful discussion on constitutional reform. Its only possible use was the one to which Rushdi Pasha eventually put it—a peg on which to hang a threat of his own resignation.

It was not long before Rushdi Pasha was to need such a peg. Brunyate's note was presented to him at the beginning of November 1918. On 11 November the Armistice with Germany was signed and the war was over. On 13 November

Saad Zaghlul presented himself at the Residency at the head of a delegation which claimed to represent the people of Egypt, and which demanded complete independence for Egypt. For some time Zaghlul had been in close touch with a group which consisted of several members of the defunct Legislative Assembly, of Ismail Sidqi, an ex-Minister in the Rushdi Government, who had resigned in 1915, and of Mohamed Mahmud, a Balliol-educated man who had been a provincial *mudir*. It was from this group that the delegation to the Residency was formed, and it was from this delegation that the Wafd,[7] which was for many years synonymous with Egyptian nationalism, derived its name. Sir Reginald Wingate appears to have been taken by surprise at the comprehensiveness of the delegation's demands and, instead of pointing out that Egypt's political future could only be discussed with representatives of the Egyptian Government, told Zaghlul that his demands would have to be submitted to London before a reply could be given. This reply by the High Commissioner naturally increased the difficulties in which the Egyptian Government found themselves. The end of the war had overtaken them without their being able to point to a single concession obtained by them from the British Government in return for their co-operation during the war, and it now appeared that the High Commissioner was not even prepared to give them that support in face of their domestic opponents to which, not unreasonably, they felt themselves to be entitled. Zaghlul, in the course of a few minutes' truculence, had been able to gain more from the British than the Government had been able to do after four years' co-operation in the British war effort.

Zaghlul quickly followed up his advantage by a request to the High Commissioner to be allowed to proceed to London with his delegation to discuss their demands with the British Government. The High Commissioner recommended to the British Government that this request should be granted. He may have been actuated by a desire to disembarrass the Egyptian Government of Zaghlul and his followers by sending them out of the country. But it is difficult to see how the British Government could have received such a delegation, which, so far from being sponsored by the Egyptian Government, was bitterly opposed to it. One is driven to the conclusion that the High Commissioner made his recommendation without a full appreciation of its implications. The British Government brusquely rejected his recommendation, and for the next few months the difficulties of the situation were increased by the fact that the British Government paid very little attention to the views expressed by their representative in Cairo.

Immediately the refusal of Zaghlul's request had been made public, Rushdi Pasha endeavoured to repair his damaged prestige by a proposal that he and his colleague, Adly Pasha Yeghen, should proceed to London to negotiate with the British Government on Egypt's political future. The High Commissioner immediately forwarded this proposal to London with a recommendation that it should be accepted. This time he undoubtedly had right and wisdom on his side. The one hope of averting a serious crisis was to strengthen the hands of the Rushdi Government sufficiently to enable them to deal with Zaghlul and his followers. The psychological effect of an invitation to London would have been most valuable from the point of view of prestige, particularly after the refusal meted out to Zaghlul. But, however appropriate the moment might be from the point of view of the Egyptian Government, it was most inappropriate from the point of view of the British Government. The Armistice had only been signed a few days previously and ministers, under-secretaries, and most of the senior officials of the Foreign Office were fully occupied on other and more urgent tasks than that of attending to Egyptian politics. So the High Commissioner's recommendation was once more rejected in terms which made it clear that the consideration of Egypt's political future was very low down on the list of Foreign Office priorities. This reply completed Rushdi's discomfiture and exhausted his patience. He had already allowed the contents of Brunyate's note to be made public in order to demonstrate to Egyptian opinion his disapproval of it (since the contents of the note had already leaked out, as official secrets in Egypt always do, he was forced to do this in order to dispel any suggestion that he was prepared to acquiesce in it), and he now presented to the Sultan his resignation. Adly Pasha Yeghen followed his example.

Meanwhile, Zaghlul had been busy trying to establish the Wafd's claim to represent Egypt. Local committees were formed up and down the country. Signatures were collected on manifestoes, and demonstrations were held in support of Zaghlul's claim to speak for the Egyptian people. It was in fact clear that the Wafd did represent the dominant trend in Egyptian opinion and that the Egyptian Government did not. Unfortunately, there was no constitutional means by which the Wafd could bring the pressure of public opinion to bear. In the same way as in the time of Arabi, legitimate grievances could only be ventilated by means of agitation leading imperceptibly but inevitably towards violence. But although the country lacked the constitutional machinery by which an unpopular government could be replaced by a popular one, the Government lacked the authority for imposing its own will on a reluctant public opinion. Indigenous autocracy had been destroyed, and had been replaced neither by indigenous democracy nor by an effective foreign autocracy.

The situation was infinitely more dangerous than it had been in 1907; British officialdom was far less efficient than it had been then and far less in touch with what was going on; the masses, both in the towns and villages, were thoroughly disaffected; Abbas was no longer there to divide and distract the forces of nationalism; the administrative justification for Great Britain's continued presence in Egypt had been largely vitiated by the incompetence and confusion of the war years. The immediate task before the High Commissioner was to bring about a lowering of the political temperature as a preliminary to an attempt to form an

Egyptian Government which would on the one hand be reasonably representative of Egyptian nationalism and on the other hand be ready to accept a modified protectorate as a basis for future relations with Great Britain. It was evident that this task would not be an easy one.

Faced with the resignations of Rushdi and Adly, the High Commissioner succeeded in getting the British Government's agreement to Rushdi's proceeding to London within a matter of weeks. But the psychological moment had now passed; Rushdi realized that no concessions which he would be able to obtain in London would have the faintest chance of appeasing nationalist sentiment in Egypt unless he could associate Zaghlul in his discussions with the British Government. The High Commissioner therefore recommended that Zaghlul should be allowed to accompany Rushdi to London. The British Government would have done well, on this occasion, to have listened to his advice. But the Foreign Office, which appeared at that time to regard any opposition to British plans in Egypt as amounting to incipient rebellion, again refused to have anything to do with Zaghlul. Thereupon, on 1 March 1919, Rushdi, who, together with Adly, had been induced to withdraw his previous resignation, once more resigned, and his Government with him. At this point the High Commissioner was recalled to London for consultation.

There appears to have been little realization, either in London or at the Residency, that matters in Egypt had reached a very critical stage. There was no appreciation of the extent to which the masses had become responsive to organized anti-British propaganda. There was no realization of the fact that the benefits of British administration had been almost forgotten, since these benefits had for the previous four years been almost non-existent. There was, above all, no understanding of the fact that the political classes, and not only the nationalists, regarded the Protectorate as purely an administrative measure made necessary by the war. It had been accepted quietly so long as the war went on, but the moment the war was over no party was prepared to admit its continuance without radical revision. There was a general feeling, also, that Egypt's co-operation during the war gave her the right to participate in the discussions then taking place in Paris on the post-war disposal of the Ottoman Empire. The fact that Egypt had not been invited to participate in these discussions created a widespread suspicion that Great Britain was determined to regard Egypt as part of the spoils of the Ottoman Empire accruing to her as a prize of victory. Since this was the apparent reward of the Rushdi Government for their co-operation with the British and for the moderation of their political demands, it is not surprising that the nationalists eschewed both co-operation and moderation.

A few days after the High Commissioner's departure, the political crisis came to a head. Zaghlul, who was anxious to prevent the formation of a new government as the first step in a campaign designed to paralyse all administrative activity, addressed a petition to Sultan Fuad which was intended to deter him, by intimidation, from any attempt to form a new government. Sir Milne Cheetham, who again found himself Acting High Commissioner at a moment of crisis, judged that it had become necessary at this point forcibly to restrain Zaghlul. After having obtained the permission of the Foreign Secretary, who was obviously more amenable to suggestions of coercion than of conciliation, Sir Milne arranged for General Watson, Acting General Officer Commanding British Troops in Egypt, to deliver a final warning to Zaghlul and eleven other members of the Wafd, reminding them that martial law was in force, and ordering them to abstain from conduct calculated to bring about a state of disorder. This warning was ignored, and two days later Zaghlul himself, Hamid al Bassal, a previous member of the Legislative Assembly, Ismail Sidqi, and Mohamed Mahmud were arrested and deported to Malta.

Having regard to the policy of the British Government at that time, which was definitely opposed to any important modification of the Protectorate in favour of Egypt, the arrest of Zaghlul and his associates was inevitable sooner or later. That being so, it was apparently wise to make the arrests before and not after disturbances had started. But the Residency had not kept itself accurately informed of the situation. They seemed to have imagined that a display of firmness was all that was necessary to allay nationalist agitation and create that atmosphere of calmness in which political concessions within the framework of the Protectorate could be leisurely and amicably discussed with a moderate Egyptian Government. The strength and ramifications of the nationalist movement, the popular support which it commanded, and the organization which it had built up were appreciated neither in Cairo nor in London. It may be doubted whether the British Government, by agreeing to the arrest of Zaghlul and his associates, would have taken the first step in an anti-nationalist policy if they had realized that such a policy could only be implemented at the point of the bayonet. Accurate, comprehensive, and objective information would have spared the British Government their subsequent choice between humiliation and bloody repression.

Lack of such information meant that the consequences of Zaghlul's arrest had not been foreseen nor guarded against. On 9 March, the day after the arrests, the students deserted their studies and demonstrated in the streets; by 12 March there was a state of insurrection all over Lower Egypt; railway track was being torn up, telegraph and telephone wires cut, buildings set on fire, and movable property destroyed. In Tanta British troops were compelled to open fire. By 15 March the disturbances had spread to Upper Egypt; on 18 March, eight British soldiers were murdered in a railway carriage at Deirut Station in circumstances of revolting barbarity.

On 17 March a capable and energetic soldier, General Bulfin, arrived in Cairo to take command of British troops in Egypt. He immediately despatched a number of small mobile columns into the provinces, and by the end of the month organized violence had almost ceased.

Meanwhile, Mr. Lloyd George, the British Prime Minister, alarmed at the news from Egypt and dissatisfied with the calibre of British representation at the Residency, had summarily superseded Sir Reginald Wingate by appointing General Sir Edmund Allenby as 'Special High Commissioner' in his place.[8] General Allenby arrived in Egypt on 25 March with a mission 'to exercise supreme authority in all matters military and civil, to take all such measures as he considers necessary and expedient to restore law and order, and to administrate in all matters as required by the necessity of maintaining the King's Protectorate over Egypt on a secure and equitable basis'.

The new High Commissioner soon arrived at a true estimate of the situation. It was desirable to secure the acquiescence of the Egyptian people in the continued British occupation of Egypt. The influence of nationalism was such that this acquiescence could not be secured except at the expense of considerable concessions to nationalist sentiment. These concessions could only be discussed with the acknowledged leaders of nationalism. But it was desirable at the same time to avoid giving the impression of a surrender to violence, particularly as there was no physical need for such a surrender. The immediate situation was now well in hand, and General Bulfin's columns were having little difficulty in restoring order. It would have been wise to have allowed General Bulfin to complete his task and, since there was no government in office, to have placed the country under a military administration for a few weeks before beginning to treat with the nationalists. Instead the policy of coercion was abandoned as precipitately as it had been adopted. On 31 March, less than a week after his arrival, the new High Commissioner issued a proclamation in which he stated that 'the time has come when responsible Egyptians, with the interests of their country at heart' should submit to him a statement showing what steps they considered necessary to

235

restore tranquillity. This proclamation was followed, as it was bound to be followed, by another proclamation, issued on 7 April, which announced that Zaghlul and his three associates would be released from internment in Malta and allowed to proceed wherever they wished.

It is difficult to avoid the conclusion that the timing of these releases was as ill-considered as the decision to make the arrests had been. Granted that their eventual release was desirable, it would seem that the appearance of a surrender to violence could, and should, have been avoided. By the end of March the situation was sufficiently in hand to ensure that a short period of military administration would not have met with any serious resistance. At the end of such a period the releases would have been welcomed as a voluntary concession, instead of being regarded as a triumph for successful agitation.

For good or ill, however, it was decided that the change of policy which had become necessary should be made suddenly rather than gradually. The immediate effects of this decision were not encouraging. After a day or two of rejoicing and the reinstallation of Rushdi Pasha as Prime Minister, demonstrations again broke out. A strike of Government officials, which had started in a small way on 3 April, became general in all Government offices. Rushdi Pasha again resigned on 21 April, after twelve days in office. It was now clearly incumbent on the High Commissioner to set the machinery of administration going again. This he did with some success. He got the Government officials back to their desks by proclaiming that all those who were not at work by the following day would be treated as having resigned from the service; he got the students back to their studies by threatening to close the schools for an indefinite period. He persuaded Mohamed Pasha Said, who had been Prime Minister before the war, and who enjoyed considerable prestige in Egypt, to form a Government.

Meanwhile, Zaghlul and his associates had gone from Malta to Paris to lay their case before the statesmen assembled

236

at the Peace Conference. On their arrival in Paris they were met with the news that the United States had given formal recognition to the British Protectorate over Egypt. Zaghlul, who had taken President Wilson's Fourteen Points seriously, was taken aback by this example of transatlantic *Realpolitik*. His discomfiture communicated itself to his followers in Egypt, and produced a lowering of the political temperature which coincided with Mohamed Said's assumption of office.

The stage now seemed set for the peaceful pursuance of the policy inaugurated by General Allenby when he had ordered the release of the Malta detainees. In ordering these releases, the High Commissioner had, in fact, committed the British Government to negotiations for the abolition of the Protectorate and for the grant of political concessions to Egypt compatible with nationalist aspirations. But the British Government did not yet appreciate the implications of this change of policy. Lord Curzon, speaking in the House of Lords on Egypt at this time, said: 'I cannot declare too emphatically that His Majesty's Government have no intention of ignoring or abandoning the obligations and responsibilities which they incurred when the task of governing Egypt was laid on their shoulders. These obligations have been confirmed by the declaration of our Protectorate over the country.' Almost simultaneously it was announced that a Mission headed by Lord Milner would shortly be proceeding to Egypt in order to examine and make recommendations for the future relations between Great Britain and Egypt.

On receipt of this news in Egypt, the nationalists immediately got busy organizing public opinion in preparation for the arrival of the Mission. The appointment of the Mission was announced in May, but by the end of the summer there was still no sign of its arrival in Egypt. By that time the political activity excited by the announcement of the Mission had reached such a pitch that Mohamed Said judged it advisable to ask for its indefinite postponement. The High

Commissioner found himself unable to agree with him, and Mohamed Said resigned on 19 November. He was replaced as Prime Minister by Wahba Pasha, a comparative nonentity. Simultaneously, the High Commissioner issued the following statement in connexion with the Mission, which was now ready to leave England:

> The policy of Great Britain in Egypt is to preserve autonomy in that country under British protection, and to develop a system of self-government under an Egyptian ruler.
>
> The object of Great Britain is to defend Egypt against all external danger and the interference of any foreign Power, and at the same time to establish a constitutional system in which, under British guidance, as far as may be necessary, the Sultan and his Ministers and elected representatives of the people may in their several spheres and in an increasing degree, co-operate in the management of Egyptian affairs.
>
> His Majesty's Government has decided to send to Egypt a Mission which has as its task to work out the details of a Constitution to carry out this object; and, in consultation with the Sultan, his Ministers and the representatives of the people of Egypt to undertake the preliminary work which is requisite before the future form of government can be settled.
>
> It is not the function of the Mission to impose a constitution on Egypt. Its duty is to explore the ground; to discuss in consultation with authorities on the spot the reforms that are necessary and to propose, it is hoped in complete agreement with the Sultan and his Ministers, a scheme of government which can subsequently be put into force.

If this statement was intended to be conciliatory it failed in its object. For behind the fine words there lurked the hard truth contained in the first sentence: 'The policy of Great Britain in Egypt is to preserve autonomy . . . under British protection.' It was intended to maintain the Protectorate. The effect of the statement was consequently to create a political atmosphere which made negotiation impossible. Neither the British Government nor, apparently, the Residency realized that the nationalists would not be conciliated within the framework of the Protectorate, and that the only alternative to conciliating the nationalists was to fight them.

The Milner Mission arrived in Egypt on 7 December 1919. Its terms of reference were as follows:

> To enquire into the causes of the late disorders, and to report on the existing situation in the country, and on the form of Constitution which, under the Protectorate, will be best calculated to promote its peace and prosperity, the progressive development of self-governing institutions, and the protection of foreign interests.

During the weeks preceding the arrival of the Mission, the Committee of Independence, the executive organ of the nationalist movement which had been set up after the deportation of Zaghlul and his associates, had been busy organizing a comprehensive boycott of the Mission. The completeness of this boycott provided the Mission with eloquent testimony of the strength of the nationalist movement. No Egyptian outside the Palace or the Government would have anything to do with the Mission. The will of Zaghlul, operating through the Committee of Independence, was obeyed throughout Egypt. Presumably impressed with this demonstration, the Mission, three weeks after its arrival in Egypt, issued the following statement, which admitted, by implication, its willingness to recommend to the British Government the abandonment of the Protectorate:

> The Mission has been sent by the British Government with the approval of Parliament to reconcile the aspirations of the Egyptian people with the special interest which Great Britain has in Egypt and with the maintenance of the legitimate rights of all foreign residents in the country.

This statement, although it did mitigate hostility, did not put an end to the boycott, and the Mission sailed for England in March 1920 without ever having been able to get in touch with non-official Egyptian opinion.

Just before the arrival of the Mission in Egypt, nationalist sentiment had begun to manifest itself in a new and alarming form. Zaghlul and the Committee of Independence had not been directly guilty of violence, although their campaign of propaganda had indirectly resulted in violence. But in every popular movement there is a terrorist fraction, and Egyptian nationalism was no exception to the general rule. Butros Ghali had been murdered in 1910, and there had been attempts on the lives of the Sultan and the Prime Minister in 1915. Towards the end of 1919 terrorism broke out again, this time against the British. On 22 November a British officer was murdered; on 23 November four British soldiers were fired at and wounded; on 2 December two British soldiers were fired at and wounded; on 26 December two British soldiers were wounded; in January 1920 a bomb was thrown at Sirry Pasha, a member of the Cabinet; in February a bomb was thrown at Shafiq Pasha, the Minister of Agriculture. There was no reason to believe that the Committee of Independence as a whole had any connexion with this terrorist activity; there is some reason to believe that some members of the Committee were in communication with the terrorists. The pattern is a familiar one; a nationalist movement struggling for independence always collects undesirable allies whom it can neither denounce nor acknowledge. At the same time, genuinely deploring terrorism and realizing that their propagandist activities inevitably beget terrorism, nationalist leaders are faced with the alternatives of abandoning nationalist propaganda or conniving at murder. They run the risk, on the one hand, of being identified with and, on the other hand, of being destroyed by terrorism.

The Milner Mission left Egypt convinced of the necessity for an accommodation with nationalism, but without having been able to get in touch with the nationalists. Zaghlul was still in Paris. Having failed to make any impression at all among the representatives of the powers, Zaghlul had the choice between returning to Egypt to continue his political campaign and of proceeding to London to get in touch with the Milner Mission. He was probably the only person in

Egyptian public life who could have approached the Mission without being denounced as a traitor. Persuaded by Adly Pasha, he decided to approach the Mission, which welcomed his initiative. Unofficial negotiations were started with Zaghlul and his 'delegation'. There seemed every prospect of a settlement which would put Egypt on the high road to sovereign independence. But Zaghlul had become the prisoner of his own propaganda. His rapid rise to power had made enemies for him in Egypt who would not have been slow to use his own arguments against him should he come to any accommodation with the British. He must have been aware of the practical advantages of a settlement with Great Britain, and he was certainly made aware that such a settlement was obtainable on far more favourable terms than would have been considered possible a year previously. But he was not a big enough man to abandon demogogy in favour of practical statesmanship. He realized that his personal ascendancy in Egypt was based on his powers as an agitator, and he was unwilling to risk losing that ascendancy by stepping down into the humdrum area of political give-and-take. That being so, the negotiations were doomed from the start. Zaghlul was merely using the Mission as a means of covering up the failure of his visit to Paris.

The story of the Milner-Zaghlul negotiations followed a pattern which was to become drearily familiar in the subsequent course of Anglo-Egyptian relations. During the course of the negotiations Zaghlul announced that he would be unable finally to agree to any proposals without consulting public opinion in Egypt. A Memorandum was accordingly drawn up embodying the heads of the terms on which the British Government would be prepared to negotiate a Treaty. Four members of Zaghlul's 'delegation' then returned to Egypt with the Memorandum, ostensibly with a view to 'trying it out' on nationalist opinion. Nationalist opinion in Egypt had been largely created and was entirely directed by Zaghlul. Anything of which Zaghlul had expressed his approval would have been accepted by nationalist opinion. But Zaghlul carefully refrained from expressing any such approval for the Memorandum. He must have known that a noncommittal attitude on his part would ensure its rejection in Egypt. So it turned out. The four members of Zaghlul's 'delegation' returned to England, and Zaghlul, who apparently hoped for further concessions, informed the Mission that, while the proposals were generally speaking acceptable, further modifications would be necessary if the assent of the Egyptian people were to be secured. Lord Milner wisely refused to be drawn and negotiations were broken off in November 1920.

The main points embodied in the Memorandum were as follows:

(i) Recognition of the sovereign independence of Egypt as a constitutional monarchy with representative institutions.

(ii) An alliance between Great Britain and Egypt by which Great Britain would undertake to assist Egypt in defending the integrity of her soil and by which Egypt would undertake to render all assistance in her power in the event of Great Britain being engaged in war, even if Egypt's territory were not threatened.

(iii) Egypt to confer on Great Britain the right to maintain a military force on Egyptian soil for the protection of Imperial communications. The presence of this force was not to constitute a military occupation of Egypt.

(iv) Egypt to appoint a British Financial Adviser to exercise the powers previously exercised by the Caisse de la Dette, and a British Judicial Adviser to be kept fully informed on all matters connected with the administration of the law in so far as it affected foreigners.

(v) Egypt to transfer to Great Britain the Capitulatory rights previously possessed by foreign Powers provided that Great Britain secured the consent of the Powers in question to such a transfer.

(vi) Egypt to have the right to terminate the services of

foreign officials within two years of the signature of a
Treaty on payment of compensation at rates to be determined in the Treaty.

This Memorandum was to form the starting-point for all
subsequent Anglo-Egyptian negotiations for a treaty. The
public acknowledgement[9] by Great Britain of her willingness to go so far was a political triumph for Zaghlul. Tactic-
ally, his refusal to support the proposals in the Memorandum
as the basis for a treaty was probably sound. He had committed Great Britain to a set of proposals from which it would
be difficult for her later to recede, while he had not committed Egypt in any way. On the assumption that Egypt's
best interests lay in the quickest possible severance of her
special connexion with Great Britain, Zaghlul had done well
for Egypt. But on any objective view this was a large assumption. Zaghlul's decision to continue the political struggle
with Great Britain meant that the energies of Egyptian
nationalism would have to be devoted for an indefinite
period to political agitation rather than to that administrative achievement which Egypt needed so badly. He had
created the possibility of setting Egyptian nationalism to
constructive work in circumstances which would have left
the internal administration of Egypt almost entirely in
Egyptian hands. There existed among his followers much
ability, much energy, much enthusiasm, and much idealism
which could, at that time, have been creatively used for the
benefit of the people of Egypt. He preferred to continue the
struggle and to keep the minds of his followers concentrated
on opposition to the forces of government. It is difficult not
to believe that, in taking this decision, he was actuated by
considerations of personal prestige rather than by any
objective appreciation of the interests of his country. He was
an agitator, not an administrator. It was not in him to control an administrative machine; he was not fitted for the task
of beating political swords into administrative ploughshares.
    Later attempts to secure a treaty were frustrated by

domestic jealousies. But Zaghlul at this time could have snapped his fingers at his personal and political rivals. For the last time for fifteen years Egypt was sufficiently united as to give its (unofficially) accredited representative a free hand. Zaghlul chose to continue the struggle with British imperialism. By his choice he destroyed Egyptian nationalism as a regenerative force, and plunged Egypt into the welter of political intrigues which have inhibited all fruitful public activity for the last thirty years.

The publication of the Milner-Zaghlul Memorandum made the abolition of the Protectorate inevitable. It could be abolished in one of two ways: either as the result of a treaty between Great Britain and Egypt or by means of a unilateral act on the part of Great Britain. Zaghlul had rejected the way of a treaty, and it seemed certain that he would be in a position to sabotage any attempt by anyone else to negotiate a treaty. But there were obvious disadvantages attaching to any unilateral act by Great Britain. Neither Zaghlul nor anybody else would be committed to recognizing it, and Zaghlul would be almost certain to oppose it. There was therefore much to be said for trying to negotiate a treaty without Zaghlul in the hope that Zaghlul would lose his grip of public opinion sufficiently to enable such a treaty to find acceptance in Egypt. The British Government therefore, in forwarding the Milner Report to the High Commissioner in January 1921, requested him to ask the Sultan to send an Egyptian delegation to London to negotiate the terms of a treaty. Lord Allenby replied that it would be impossible to form a delegation without a specific announcement of the British Government's intention that the Protectorate should be replaced by a treaty of alliance. Consequently, in February 1921 the British Government authorized the High Commissioner to inform the Sultan that, although the recommendations of the Milner Report had not been accepted *in toto*, the British Government was prepared to accept the abolition of the Protectorate as the basis of treaty negotiations.[10]

There followed a confused process of wrangling over the composition of the Delegation. On 14 March a new Cabinet was formed, with Adly Pasha as Prime Minister. Zaghlul, who hated Adly as being his nearest rival in Egypt and as being a man of infinitely greater personal integrity and ability than himself, published a manifesto insisting that any treaty negotiations must be preceded by the abolition of the Protectorate and the termination of martial law.[11] The publication of this manifesto was followed by the return of Zaghlul in person from Paris, whither he had gone after the breakdown of the negotiations in London. He arrived at Alexandria on 5 April, and his triumphant reception must have proved a disappointment to anyone who imagined that Zaghlul had in any way lost his hold over the people of the country. Adly, who realized that it would in all probability be useless to attempt negotiating a treaty without including Zaghlul in the delegation, made considerable efforts to conciliate him. But Zaghlul had chosen his course and kept to it. At the end of April, Adly abandoned his conciliatory efforts and on 10 May announced the composition of the delegation, which was headed by himself and included, *inter alia*, Rushdi, the wartime Prime Minister, and Sidqi, who had by this time quarrelled with Zaghlul. Zaghlul, whose political animosity to the Government was sharpened by personal jealousy of Adly, flung himself with zest into the business of agitation. This agitation inevitably led to some rioting, and it must have been with some misgiving that Adly left for London at the end of May with the rest of his Delegation.

It was quite clear that negotiations were doomed in advance unless the British were prepared to take some steps to restrict the activities of Zaghlul and his associates. It was also clear that these activities would have to be restricted sooner or later in any case, since they were incompatible either with the successful conclusion of a treaty or with the implementation of a unilateral termination of the Protectorate by Great Britain on certain defined conditions. Since a treaty was the preferable of the two alternatives, it might have been wiser to have taken action against Zaghlul in May, when rioting in Cairo and Alexandria provided a plausible excuse for doing so. But the British authorities, presumably still banking on the chance of Zaghlul losing his popularity,[12] left him at liberty, and by so doing discredited Adly without placating the nationalists.

Adly could have secured from the British Government terms at least as favourable as those outlined in the Milner-Zaghlul Memorandum. Zaghlul was determined to prevent the conclusion of a treaty negotiated by Adly on these or any terms. The possibility of a favourable treaty negotiated by Adly was abhorrent to him. In adopting the attitude he did, he was not so much neglectful of the interests of his country as genuinely unaware that these interests were a relevant factor in the situation, except for propaganda purposes. It was not his business to advance his country's interests; it was his country's business to advance his interests. It is difficult to escape the conclusion that this was the light in which Zaghlul regarded the identification which he had achieved between his own personality and Egypt's national aspirations. The idea of service to his country was one which was genuinely incomprehensible to him. In this respect he was no worse than his rival politicians. The tragedy of Egyptian nationalism was that he was no better.[13]

The negotiations between Adly Pasha and Lord Curzon broke down in November 1921, ostensibly owing to British insistence on maintaining a garrison in Egypt, but actually because Zaghlul could, and would, have sabotaged any treaty negotiated by Adly, however favourable to Egyptian interests. Adly returned to Egypt in December and immediately resigned. Sarwat Pasha, who had acted as deputy Prime Minister throughout the summer, agreed to take office as Prime Minister on condition that Great Britain recognized Egypt as an independent sovereign state and agreed to the reconstitution of the Egyptian Ministry of Foreign Affairs. The British Government accepted these conditions, and Sarwat became Prime Minister on 15 December 1921.

There was now only one course left open to the British Government—a unilateral announcement abolishing the Protectorate and instituting a régime compatible with the undertaking given to Sarwat. The removal of Zaghlul was an essential preliminary of such action. On 19 December he was prohibited, under martial law, from indulging in any political activity. On his refusing to obey this order, he was arrested[14] and exiled first to Aden and then to the Seychelles. The way was now clear for the formal abolition of the Protectorate and for the institution of an independent régime on terms which would safeguard Great Britain's international obligations and strategic interests in Egypt.

Lord Allenby and his advisers seem to have had a clearer picture of the situation than the Foreign Office. They appreciated that the breakdown of the treaty negotiations and the exile of Zaghlul must be followed by giving in another form the concessions which Great Britain had been prepared to give in a treaty. The Foreign Office, on the other hand, appeared to imagine that the Milner-Zaghlul Memorandum, followed by the Curzon-Adly negotiations and the undertaking to Sarwat, committed them to nothing, and that, in default of a treaty, the administration of Egypt could proceed as before. They further appeared to imagine that this could be accomplished without the removal of Zaghlul. (His arrest and deportation appear to have taken place on the High Commissioner's initiative.)

Having removed Zaghlul, the High Commissioner had great difficulty in persuading the British Government to accept the inevitable consequence of all that had gone before. After an acrimonious exchange of telegrams, in one of which Lord Allenby offered his resignation, the High Commissioner left for England, accompanied by two of his staff,[15] to explain the situation personally to the Cabinet (3 February 1922).

This delay had its natural consequences. Violence once again boiled over. The terrorist wing of the nationalist movement became active, and in the month of February,

247

during the High Commissioner's absence in England, there were four separate murderous attacks on Englishmen in Cairo, three of which were fatal. On the last day of February Lord Allenby returned to Egypt. He had been able to convert the Cabinet to a belated appreciation of the realities of the situation, and had succeeded in extracting from them a Declaration which put a formal end to the Protectorate and made of Egypt an independent sovereign state for the first time for nearly 2000 years. The text of the Declaration, which was published in Egypt on 28 February 1922, the day of the High Commissioner's return, was as follows:

Whereas His Majesty's Government, in accordance with their declared intentions, desire forthwith to recognize Egypt as an independent sovereign State; and whereas the relations between His Majesty's Government and Egypt are of vital importance to the British Empire; the following principles are hereby declared:

1. The British Protectorate over Egypt is terminated and Egypt is declared to be an independent sovereign State.
2. As soon as the Government of His Highness shall pass an Act of Indemnity with application to all inhabitants of Egypt, Martial Law, as proclaimed on 2 November 1914, shall be withdrawn.
3. The following matters are absolutely reserved to the discretion of His Majesty's Government until such time as it may be possible by free discussion and friendly accommodation on both sides to conclude agreements in regard thereto between His Majesty's Government of Egypt:

 (a) The security of the communications of the British Empire in Egypt.
 (b) The defence of Egypt against all foreign aggression or interference, direct or indirect.
 (c) The protection of foreign interests in Egypt and the protection of minorities.
 (d) The Sudan.

 Pending the conclusion of such agreements the *status quo* in these matters shall remain intact.

Thus the policy of conciliation inaugurated by the Milner Mission was brought to its logical conclusion. In essence, Egypt was conceded what she had been offered, and what Zaghlul had rejected, in the Milner-Zaghlul Memorandum. In spite of the limitations of the four 'reserved points', the Egyptians themselves and not the British were henceforward to be the real rulers of Egypt.

NOTES ON CHAPTER NINE

1. A feature of peacetime economic life in Egypt had been the flow of gold into the country during the autumn to finance the purchase of the cotton crop, and the drain of gold from the country during the rest of the year to pay for imports. (Usually the drain was less than the flow due to Egypt's favourable trade balance.) The flow of gold stopped as a result of the war, and it became necessary to finance the purchase of the cotton crop by means of paper money. This paper money was at first issued against gold held on Egyptian account in London, but in 1916 the increasing note issue made necessary by British military expenditure and the rise in prices, combined with the impossibility of purchasing enough gold, caused Egypt to abandon the gold standard, which had already been abandoned by Great Britain, and to use British Treasury bills instead of gold as backing for the note issue. (The British Government bought the Egyptian Government's existing gold holding.) In this way Egypt adopted the sterling standard, which she has been on ever since, except for a temporary reversion to gold in company with Great Britain between 1925 and 1931. The effect of this financial link-up with Great Britain was to maintain a fixed rate of exchange between Great Britain and Egypt and to some extent to subordinate Egypt to Great Britain's financial policies, even after British control had been relaxed. The close commercial relations between Great Britain and Egypt, which were quite independent of any political connexions and which derived from Lancashire's need for good quality cotton on the one hand and from Egypt's need for manufactured goods on the other, made the maintenance of a fixed relation between the two currencies desirable after the automatic working of the gold standard had disappeared, and there has never been any great political feeling in Egypt about Egypt's theoretical financial subservience to Great Britain. Egypt left the sterling group in 1947, mainly for political reasons, but this gesture, while subjecting Egypt to some minor inconvenience, has had no effect on the fixed relation between the pound sterling and the Egyptian pound (£1 sterling equals 97½ Egyptian piastres).

2. According to Moslem tradition, a *jihad* proclaimed by the Khalifa (at that time the Sultan of Turkey) against the infidel is bound to be supported by all true Moslems.

3. Apart from the danger from Palestine, there was some danger to be apprehended from the Senussi, a Moslem religious sect inhabiting the Libyan oases, nominally under Italian rule, but actually in revolt against the Italians and at that time fanatically anti-European. In the winter of 1915–16 Senussi forces, incited by the Turks, invaded Egypt and captured the frontier post of Sollum. Sollum was recaptured in the spring of 1916, but it was necessary to keep a small British force on the western frontier of Egypt for most of the four years of the war against Turkey.

4. In the Anglo-French Agreement of 1904 Great Britain had bound herself not to make any change in the political status of Egypt. Presumably the Protectorate, like the illegitimate baby, might be excused on the ground that, unlike annexation, it was only a small change.

5. Before the declaration of the Protectorate, it would have been legally impossible to have deposed Abbas Hilmi except by a *firman* from the Sultan of Turkey. Abbas Hilmi's deposition shared the doubtful legality of the Protectorate.

6. The distinction must be borne in mind between the British officials of the Residency, who were on the High Commissioner's staff and employed and paid by the British Government, and the far more numerous officials in the service of the Egyptian Government. These officials, at all events until 1923, were in the difficult position of being nominally subject to the Egyptian Government while to all practical ends they were subject to the authority of the British representative. The Egyptian anxiety to get rid of British officials after 1923 was principally motivated by the feeling that such officials were servants of the British Government first, and servants of the Egyptian Government second.

7. *Wafd* is the Arabic word for 'delegation'.

8. Afterwards Lord Allenby. As conqueror of Palestine in the First German War he enjoyed at the time of his appointment as High Commissioner a reputation analogous to that of Kitchener twelve years earlier.

9. The Memorandum had not been intended for publication. But Zaghlul had published it as soon as it had been drawn up.

10. The Report of the Milner Mission was to the effect that the Protectorate should be abolished and replaced by a treaty on the lines set out in the Milner-Zaghlul Memorandum. Lord Milner, the Head of the Mission, had been in Egypt as Financial Secretary and subsequently as Financial Adviser during Cromer's time. He was by no means a liberal-minded man and his conversion to a liberal view of Egyptian nationalism is significant.

11. The termination of martial law had to be preceded by an Act of Indemnity giving immunity from subsequent legal proceedings to all persons in Egypt who had been concerned in the administration of martial law. Apart from this, Zaghlul's insistence on the abolition of martial law was clearly motivated by his desire to have as much freedom as possible for agitation.

12. Zaghlul's popularity was, of course, a measure of the very efficient countrywide political organization consisting of the Committees of Independence which had been built up by Zaghlul and his associates over the past eighteen months. These Committees of Independence were the basis of the Wafd political party, which was formed in 1923 and which was easily the best organized and most powerful political party in Egypt, in spite of the fact that its history was one of continual secessions by its ablest members.

13. This is admittedly a controversial view of Zaghlul, and one which will probably not command much acceptance to-day. But it is difficult to point to any occasion, whether in power or in opposition, when he showed the slightest constructive interest in the welfare of the Egyptian people or any enthusiasm for the reform of the Egyptian Administration.

14. Zaghlul, triumphant to the end, is said to have lightened the pockets of the British officers responsible for guarding him at Suez by beating them every night at poker. Up to the time of the Stack murder, Zaghlul's personal relations with the Englishmen with whom he came into contact were invariably cordial, and the political battles were conducted without personal animosity. Zaghlul was never personally an Anglophobe, as Mustafa Kamal had been.

15. Sir Gilbert Clayton and Mr. (later Sir Maurice) Amos.

CHAPTER TEN

AN ASSESSMENT OF THE BRITISH OCCUPATION

GREAT BRITAIN occupied Egypt in 1882 in order to prevent the government of Egypt from falling into the hands of Arabi and his associates. This was done in order to forestall the probable eventual intervention by the European powers in support of the bondholders, which would have been provoked by an Arabi Government, and which might have endangered the security of British communications with India. Great Britain's desire was not primarily to occupy, but to neutralize Egypt. This could only be done by placating the bond-holders and by protecting their interests. The experience of the Dual Control showed that this could only be done by a military occupation accompanied by a drastic reform of the administration. Great Britain set herself to provide both one and the other. Various considerations, which have already been discussed, prevented her from effecting any more than superficial reforms of the administration. In so far as certain services were actually performed by Englishmen, as in the Ministries of Finance and Public Works, they were positively well done; in so far as they were merely supervised by Englishmen, as in the Ministries of the Interior and of Justice, they were negatively well done in that certain of the grosser abuses fell temporarily into desuetude. But there was no radical change of outlook or method. British administration was merely added as a superstructure to the existing fabric of government. Weaknesses in the fabric were patched and buttressed, but the rotten foundations remained, and eventually proved more inadequate than ever under the additional weight which they had to support.

The two great and interrelated achievements of British administration—finance and irrigation—have already been discussed in detail. The irrigation achievement allowed the revenue to be raised sufficiently to enable Egypt to meet both her foreign debt and the expenses of domestic administration without recourse to harsh taxation; the financial achievement ensured the proper collection and administration of this increased revenue. The twin achievements laid the foundations of Egypt's present material prosperity. But the fact that they were not paralleled in other fields of administration meant that the increased material prosperity only benefited a comparatively small number of people. Although British irrigation engineers caused water to flow into all the fields of Egypt, the resultant flow of wealth was not so widely nor so evenly distributed. The rich were confirmed in their riches, the poor in their poverty. The lot of the poor was certainly alleviated in several important respects. They were no longer beaten, they were no longer forced to work for nothing. But the general level of health, enlightenment, and material well-being did not rise proportionately with the increase in wealth. This was due, not to the demands of the foreign debt, the burden of which steadily decreased relatively and absolutely as the years went by, but to the fact that the social structure of Egypt diverted increases of wealth into the hands of the few as surely as the irrigation system of Egypt diverted water into the canals.

British administration in Egypt may be likened to the rehabilitation of a fertile estate which has been brought to bankruptcy by a long course of inefficient management. The object of British administration was to restore the solvency of the estate by increasing productivity on the one hand and by controlling expenditure on the other. Its object was not to associate the workers in the profits of the estate; nor was it to improve the lot of the workers except in so far as such improvement contributed to increased productivity. Viewed as the rehabilitation and management of an estate, British administration in Egypt was triumphantly successful, at all events on a short-term basis. It is unfair to judge it as an experiment in imperial rule, since such an experiment was not attempted.

The task of rehabilitation may be said to have been accomplished when Lord Cromer completed his long term of office in 1907. His successor's task was to hand back the estate to the owners, under proper safeguards for continued good management. This task was complicated, first, by the difficulty of deciding who the owners were, and, secondly, by the lack of any smoothly working administrative machine which would continue to work efficiently in Egyptian hands. Great Britain had originally refused to undertake fundamental reforms on the ground of the temporary nature of her occupation. The consequences of this refusal gradually came to be used as an excuse for making the occupation permanent. It was, in fact, infinitely more difficult to terminate a 'temporary' occupation than it would have been to terminate a 'permanent' occupation of the colonial type.

It is difficult to determine the exact point at which strategic considerations began to dictate the course of British policy in Egypt. As long as the Ottoman Empire was in being, Great Britain's strategic interests were secured by the 'neutralization' of Egypt and the Levant. But in the event of the dissolution of the Ottoman Empire it was necessary for Great Britain that she should not find her communications with India menaced by a French occupation of the Levant unaccompanied by a British occupation of Egypt. From about the beginning of the twentieth century the prospect of Ottoman dissolution began to throw its shadow over British policy in Egypt. By the time Kitchener succeeded Gorst, the British Government seems to have become convinced of the necessity of consolidating and extending British control in Egypt. At the outbreak of war they shrank, as we have seen, from actual annexation, but there can be little doubt that the declaration of the Protectorate was intended as the first bite at a cherry which they intended to swallow at a later date. The war, which

precipitated the fall of the Ottoman Empire and the consequent great power scramble for south-west Asia, confirmed,
in the eyes of the British Government, the necessity for the
continued occupation and control of Egypt.

But the British Government did not realize that continued
British control of Egypt could only be justified, if at all, in
the eyes of the world and in the eyes of the British and
Egyptian peoples, by a progressive improvement in standards
of administration. Imperialism is not merely the negative
protection of interests. The basis of imperialism is the
positive imposition of a *pax*, which implies the imposition of
certain standards of security and justice in all places where
imperial troops are stationed for strategic purposes. The only
moral justification for imperialism is the *pax* which accompanies the legions. Great Britain in Egypt tried to secure the
presence of the legions without being prepared to enforce
the *pax*. She tried to placate Egyptian nationalism by
relinquishing administrative, in exchange for retaining
strategic, control. She did not placate the nationalists, whose
appetite was whetted by the concessions they had secured
and, by relinquishing the responsibilities while retaining the
privileges of occupation, destroyed the moral basis on which
her position in Egypt rested. The 1922 Declaration was of a
piece with that transient phase of British imperialism which
sought to equate the doctrine of 'self-determination' with
the realities of imperial survival. It was a compromise
between two rival sets of interests. The common people of
Egypt got the worst of both worlds. On the one hand, they
lost that protection from arbitrary oppression which the
British occupation had, until 1922, to a greater or less extent
provided. On the other hand, the presence of British troops
underwrote a régime of 'law and order' which, in practice,
meant a prohibition of revolutionary social changes.

The development of events leading up to the declaration
had a broad inevitability springing from the original
circumstances of the occupation. The indigenous autocracy
of the Khedive, although formally upheld, had been in

practice discredited; the popular forces of nationalism had been crushed. No attempt was made to create a comprehensive British autocracy or to evolve an indigenous democracy. The result was the evolution of an oligarchy of rich landlords and middle-class careerists on whom descended the mantle of nationalism, divested of its popular attributes.

When, after the 1922 Declaration, Egypt assumed responsibility for the direction of her internal affairs, the British occupation had lasted for almost exactly forty years. At the beginning of that period Egypt had been bankrupt; at the end she was prosperous in so far as the state finances were in a flourishing condition. Her population had increased from just under 7,000,000 to about 12,000,000. The average annual value of her imports had quadrupled and that of her exports trebled. But the economic and social standards of the mass of her people remained about the same. The proportion of urban to rural inhabitants had increased, but Egypt remained predominantly an agricultural country. The division of landownership between big landowners and smallholders remained about the same. (In 1913 12,558 landlords, each with more than 50 *feddans*, owned 2,420,558 *feddans*, or nearly half the cultivated area of Egypt, while 1,411,158 peasants, each owning less than 5 *feddans*, only owned 1,418,959 *feddans* between them.) Apart from the splitting up of the great Khedival estates, the average size of the large properties had tended to increase as a result of land purchase, while the average size of the small properties had tended to decrease as a result of the Moslem Law of Inheritance and of the increased population. The middle-sized properties—those of over 5 and under 50 *feddans*—tended either to become absorbed into the larger estates by purchase or else to be parcelled and reparcelled out into smaller properties. There had been no appreciable rise in the general standard of living, since increased population and a rise in the cost of living had absorbed the increase in the national income derived from increased productivity.

The increased productivity and the increased population

derived primarily from the change-over to perennial from flood irrigation. This process, which had started under Mohamed Ali, was energetically taken up by the British irrigation engineers. The reconstruction of the Delta barrages and the construction of the Aswan Dam and its satellite barrages were motivated by the determination to convert as much as possible of the land of Egypt to perennial irrigation with a view both to increasing the total crop area and to enabling the increased cultivation of the lucrative summer crops, such as cotton and sugar, for which the climate of Egypt was eminently suited.

It is on the benefits and advantages of perennial irrigation that Great Britain's contribution to Egypt must primarily be judged. The development of perennial irrigation represents Great Britain's most important, most enduring, and most far-reaching work in Egypt. It is the only field, administrative, political, or cultural, in which the influence of the British occupation can be said fundamentally and permanently to have affected the development of Egyptian life.

It is doubtful whether either Mohamed Ali's French engineers or the British engineers who followed them realized the far-reaching consequences that were to spring from perennial irrigation. They only saw increased efficiency, increased productivity, increased wealth. They saw the possibility of growing two crops where one had grown before, of buying the machines and techniques of Europe in exchange for the summer export crops. They saw the possibility of increasing the revenue, while at the same time lightening the burden of taxation. There were other things which they did not see. They did not see that the perennial fructifying presence of water on the land set a veil between the land and the cleansing power of the sun, which dried out the basin lands during the season of low Nile. They did not see that the continual cropping made possible by perennial water would exhaust the soil and make its continued fertility dependent on the application of ever-increasing quantities of artificial fertilizers. They did not at first appreciate the magnitude of the problem presented by the necessity of draining the perennial water from the subsoil after it had done its fructifying work. They did not see the ravages of the bilharzia snail, which the perennial water brought to nearly every village household in Egypt. They did not foresee the debilitating effect of a change from a usually dry climate into a perennially damp one. Perennial irrigation has not been an unmixed blessing for Egypt. Good administration, working with the increased revenue made possible by perennial irrigation, might have mitigated its attendant evils. As it was, Egypt was saddled with social and technical problems with which she was unable to deal, arising from, or accentuated by, perennial irrigation. The drainage problem has been largely, if belatedly, solved. But the sapping of physical and mental energy caused by bilharzia still constitutes one of Egypt's gravest social problems. There are severe periodical outbreaks of malaria which take heavy toll of an undernourished and debilitated population. The exhaustion of the soil is held at bay by liberal doses of artificial fertilizer, but may become a desperate problem in the course of the present century. Meanwhile, the teeming increase in the population has overtaken both increased irrigated area and increased productivity. Something of the fertilizing influence of the perennial water seems to have communicated itself to the loins of the population. A large landless class of labourers has sprung up, some of whom have emigrated to the towns, others of whom have remained in the villages dependent on sporadic employment at harvest time and on public works. The presence of this surplus labour kept wages down and land rents up.

It is difficult to escape the conclusion that what might be termed the book-keeping approach to the rehabilitation of Egypt resulted in increasing wealth for the few, accompanied by increasing misery for the many. In spite of superficial reforms, old inequalities became consolidated. Pashadom, on the point of being overwhelmed by nationalism at the time of the Arabi rebellion, was reinstated and endowed with sufficient wealth with which to corrupt nationalism and turn it from a popular movement into the plaything of party politicians.

Inevitably, Great Britain in Egypt became identified with all those forces of reaction and oppression which it had been the aim of the earlier British administrators to eliminate. Inevitably the maintenance of law and order resolved itself into a protection of the privileges of pashadom. And inevitably pashadom, not content with the economic advantages which it had gained as a result of the British connexion, began to covet the political prestige of nationalism and to dispute the leadership of nationalism with Zaghlul and his middle-class followers.

The 1914–18 War had the same disturbing effect on the social hierarchy of Egypt as it had on the social hierarchy of Great Britain. Egypt, too, had its *nouveaux riches* who, together with the wealthier and more successful members of the professional and merchant classes, began to 'gate-crash' the hitherto exclusive preserves of the Turkish-descended landowning aristocracy. The result was to broaden the bases of both pashadom and nationalism and to create (*a*) a nationalist political front comprising the agricultural, professional and business magnates which, although racked with internal dissensions arising from personal jealousies among its members, was united in its desire for national independence, and (*b*) an economic front consisting of the same magnates, who, whatever their personal jealousies and political differences, were united in their determination to retain possession of the grossly disproportionate share of the national wealth which they had managed to appropriate for themselves.

This was the position with which Great Britain was faced in 1919. She was confronted with a powerful combination of entrenched privilege which was politically nationalist and socially reactionary. This alliance between nationalism and reaction was a formidable one, since it was impossible either to play reaction off against nationalism, as had been done in

1882, or vice versa. Great Britain, having broken up 'subversive' nationalism, was now confronted with a nationalism purged of its subversiveness in alliance with reaction purged of its 'collaborationism'.

In the early days of the occupation, Great Britain had had the support of the magnates because she protected them from the nationalists, and of the common people because she protected them from Egypt's foreign creditors. By crushing 'subversive' nationalism and by rehabilitating Egypt's finances, Great Britain deprived herself of both these sources of support. Looked at from another angle, she had also successfully accomplished the mission which had brought her to Egypt. But the strategic importance of Egypt to the British Empire, which had been largely created as the result of international events occurring during the course of the British occupation, forbade Great Britain to leave, or even to relax her hold upon, Egypt. She was thus compelled to fight the nationalist front which her policy had unwittingly created. The unilateral Declaration of 1922 solved nothing; it merely narrowed and concentrated the issue to the four 'reserved points'. The tension was relaxed, not by the Declaration, but by the emergence of the Palace as a domestic opposition to the nationalists, diverting nationalist energies from the anti-British offensive in the same way as Abbas Hilmi had done a dozen years earlier. The struggle for power, under the new Constitution, between the nationalists and the Palace will form the theme of the following two chapters.

CHAPTER ELEVEN

THE CONSTITUTION

THE Declaration was, as has been stated, the logical outcome of the Milner Mission's attempt to negotiate a treaty with Zaghlul. Zaghlul had refused a treaty and had been able to prevent Adly from concluding one. The Declaration, accompanied as it was by the deportation of Zaghlul, was designed to give moderate nationalism the opportunity of establishing itself sufficiently to enable the relationship with Great Britain as laid down in the Declaration to be confirmed in the provisions of a freely negotiated Treaty.

The immediate results of the Declaration were not unencouraging. On 1 March 1922 Sarwat Pasha formed a new Government. On 15 March Sultan Ahmed Fuad was proclaimed King of Egypt with the title of Fuad I. On the same day the Residency formally handed over the control of Egypt's foreign affairs to the Egyptian Prime Minister. These events, although arousing little public enthusiasm, were opposed by little public protest. That was the most which could have been expected.

The most important task before the new Government was to make arrangements for the drafting of a Constitution for the new Egyptian state. One of its first acts was to set up a Commission for this purpose. The definition of the powers of the monarch was obviously a vital factor in the framing of the Constitution. Since the declaration of the Protectorate and the deposition of Abbas Hilmi the influence of the Palace had been negligible. With the abolition of the Protectorate, the old rivalry between the nationalists and the Palace again asserted itself. The partial, and enforced, quiescence of the

Wafd mitigated but did not resolve the acerbity of the renewed conflict. The new King was not prepared to accept the role of a constitutional monarch without a struggle. He was determined not only to reign, but to rule. But he was intelligent enough to realize that his determination would only be achieved as the result of a long course of intrigue.

Irritated by Sarwat's attempts to limit the power of the Crown under the new Constitution, Fuad sought an early opportunity to embroil the new Prime Minister with the Residency, and at the same time to ingratiate himself with the nationalists. He insisted that he should be described in the Constitution as King of Egypt and the Sudan. This was in direct contravention of one of the four 'reserved points' and could not be persisted in against British objections. But it was a shrewd move on the part of the King, for on this particular issue he was certain to have the support of everybody in Egypt except those who had the actual responsibility for the conduct of affairs. Even Adly Pasha, who, with an eye to the future, was busy forming a political party, the Liberal Constitutionalists, for the elections which would follow the promulgation of a Constitution, told Sarwat that he and his followers were not prepared to support him against the Palace in this matter. Sarwat thereupon resigned (November 1922) and was replaced as Prime Minister by Taufiq Pasha Nessim, a supporter of the Palace.

But the King had achieved nothing permanent by getting rid of Sarwat. The Residency was not prepared to budge over the question of the Sudan, and was, moreover, getting impatient at the delay in promulgating a Constitution. In early February 1923 the High Commissioner insisted that Nessim be replaced by a Prime Minister who would, without further delay, prepare a Constitution which would, on the one hand, respect the existing status of the Sudan and, on the other hand, conform with the nationalist demand for representative government. The obvious choice was Adly, but he, with an eye on the future elections, refused to take office unless the British agreed to the abolition of martial law. The Residency took the view that such abolition was impossible so long as the Wafd remained intent on their determination to oppose any *modus vivendi* with the British. The King, who now realized that he would have to do the best he could with the sort of Constitution on which the British insisted, took British advice and called on Yehia Pasha, an ex-Cabinet Minister with no party affiliations, to form a Government. Yehia Pasha accepted and the new Ministry took office in March.

Adly's stipulation about martial law was simply a pretext to avoid taking office. Owing to the attitude of the Wafd, the continuance of martial law, at least until the Constitution was promulgated, was as necessary for the Egyptian Government as for the British. The Wafd had been campaigning against the Declaration ever since it had been announced and during the course of 1922 several British officers and officials had been the victims of murderous attacks. The Wafd had injudiciously associated itself with the terrorists by the publication of a manifesto which was a clear incitement to violence against both the Government and the British. As a result of this manifesto, several Wafdist leaders had been arrested, and the Wafd itself seemed to be becoming more and more committed to subversive activity.

The business of the Yehia Government was to implement the Declaration of Independence by promulgating a Constitution, by preparing for elections, and by making arrangements with the Residency for the future of British officials and for the abolition of martial law. A Constitution acceptable both to the nationalists and to the British was promulgated on 20 April 1923, less than five weeks after Yehia Pasha had assumed office. On 5 July an Act of Indemnity was promulgated and martial law abolished. An electoral law was promulgated and first-stage elections[1] fixed for the end of September. Finally, in October a law was promulgaged embodying the agreement which had been reached with the Residency regarding future conditions of service and terms of pensions and compensation for European officials in the Egyptian service.[2]

In all these activities the Yehia Government was considerably less hampered by the opposition of the Wafd than its predecessors had been. This was partly because Yehia Pasha himself could not be suspected of using his term of office to consolidate his future political career, but mainly because the British had apparently resigned themselves to the ultimate necessity of co-operating with the Wafd as the only alternative to a Palace dictatorship. This realization was signalized by the release of Zaghlul from his internment at Gibraltar (whither he had been transferred, for health reasons, from the Seychelles) on 24 March, ten days after Yehia Pasha's assumption of office, and by the simultaneous release of six Wafdist leaders from detention in Egypt. For their part, the Wafd, having made their protest against the Declaration, and having secured the release of their leaders and the promulgation of a Constitution in accordance with their desires (in so far as relations between Parliament and Palace were concerned), decided to desist from any action which might postpone the abolition of martial law or the holding of elections, and to concentrate their energies on the obtention of power at the elections.[3] Their political opponents were unable, and the British apparently unwilling, to put any obstacle in the way of the Wafd's constitutional ambitions. The Palace was at pains to avoid any appearance of hostility to the Wafd.

Zaghlul returned to Egypt in September, in time for the elections. The two stages of the elections took about four months to complete. Polling was conducted without serious disturbance, and when the final results were published in January 1924 the Wafd was found to have secured 190 out of 214 seats in the Chamber of Deputies. This result was a triumph both for the personality of Zaghlul and for the organization which the Wafd had built up. In the electoral campaign Zaghlul and his followers had shown little hostility to the British and had concentrated their fire on the Wafd's principal domestic opponents, the Liberal Constitutionalists, led by Adly Pasha.

As soon as the result of the elections was known, Zaghlul was called upon by the King to form a Ministry. There appeared to be some ground for hope that, with an overwhelming majority behind him, he would be prepared to abandon demagogy and to devote himself to administration on the one hand and to the regularization of Egypt's relations with Great Britain on the other.

The British were well-disposed, the more so since the Labour Party, which had frequently and sometimes inopportunely expressed its sympathy with Egyptian nationalism, had just come into office. The Liberal Constitutionalists had been decisively defeated at the elections. The Palace had still to find a way of exercising its influence within the framework of the Constitution. Zaghlul had what was to prove a last opportunity of making a constructive use of the prestige which he had built up for himself in the eyes of the Egyptian people.

Such hopes as may have been formed were to prove illusory. If Zaghlul had had a larger vision or a greater flair for statesmanship, he might have realized that the surest way of completing Egypt's independence would be to convince Great Britain of Egypt's ability to conduct her affairs in a responsible manner. He would certainly have realized that the tactics which had hitherto brought him success in opposition could not, with similar success, be pursued unchanged now that he was at the head of the Government of a sovereign state. But Zaghlul had neither the talent nor the taste for administration. He was not interested in the results of independence, which was to him not a means to an end, but an end in itself. He was incapable of seeing Egyptian politics except in terms of struggle. He remained the prisoner of his past activities and utterances. He was eventually to learn wisdom, but by that time it was too late, both for himself and for Egypt.

To a man who thinks of politics solely in terms of 'struggle', it is inevitable that any concession should appear as a sign of weakness. The action of the British Government in pardoning 150 persons convicted of various crimes of violence under martial law, which was no doubt intended as a gesture of conciliation towards Zaghlul, confirmed Zaghlul in his intention of attacking the four 'reserved points' in the Declaration of Independence.

The British Government, immediately upon Zaghlul's accession to office, expressed its willingness to negotiate a treaty with Egypt. This willingness was expressed in a telegram from Mr. Ramsay MacDonald, the British Prime Minister, which was read out at the opening of the first Egyptian Parliament on 15 March 1924. This willingness is only explicable on the ground of the British Government's belief that Zaghlul would be prepared to negotiate a treaty on the lines of, and with the reservations laid down in, the Declaration of Independence. The illusory nature of this belief was immediately made apparent in the Speech from the Throne, when Mr. MacDonald's telegram was acknowledged in the following words: 'My Government is prepared to enter into negotiations, free from all restrictions, with His Majesty's Government, so as to realize our national aspirations with regard to Egypt and the Sudan.'

Zaghlul's attitude as Prime Minister was thus made clear from the beginning. Given a free choice between an agreement and a fight with Great Britain, he had chosen a fight. But he did not realize that the principal weapon in such a fight—namely, popular agitation—was one which would undermine the authority of and finally destroy his own Administration. It is unwise to foment domestic agitation and try to govern a country at the same time.

Lord Allenby, in his insistence on the Declaration of Independence, had forced upon the British Government a statesmanlike way of escape from a situation which had become impossible. His policy had succeeded in that a Constitution had been promulgated, and in that Zaghlul had tacitly accepted the situation by participating in the elections and by accepting office. The transition had been accomplished in a comparatively orderly manner, without serious violence and without the exercise of any drastic pressure by Great Britain. There seemed no immediate necessity for the British Government to take any initiative in the matter of a treaty. Whether the Residency misread the mind of Zaghlul or whether they regarded a treaty as an essential means of stabilizing Anglo-Egyptian relations is uncertain. At all events, the Residency lost no time in pressing on the British Government the desirability of inviting Zaghlul to negotiate, even though conversations with Zaghlul had made it apparent that he would insist on concessions going far beyond the Declaration. Specifically, the Residency recommended that the British Government be prepared to concede withdrawal of British troops from Cairo and Alexandria and relinquishment of the right and duty of protecting foreigners, in return for a military alliance which would safeguard British interests in Egypt.[4]

The recommended concessions were not in themselves unreasonable. But it was fairly obvious that expressed willingness to make such concessions would merely be regarded by Zaghlul as a starting-point for demanding further concessions. Although the British Government had not committed itself to the Residency's recommendations, these recommendations must have been known to Zaghlul, and the result was what might have been expected. When Zaghlul, at the British Government's invitation, arrived in London in September for conversations with Mr. Mac-Donald (who was Foreign Secretary as well as Prime Minister) he immediately demanded the complete evacuation of British troops from Egypt and the removal of all remaining vestiges of British control. He was not prepared to discuss. He apparently imagined that he would be permitted to dictate. Under the circumstances, negotiations were out of the question, and Zaghlul was back in Cairo before the end of October.

Meanwhile, the Wafd, presumably deterred by their Governmental responsibilities from provoking trouble in

Egypt, had turned their subversive energies on the Sudan. In July there was rioting in Omdurman, and in August a mutiny of Egyptian troops at Atbara. These events were accompanied by protests from the Council of Ministers and from the Senate against alleged British attempts to create a 'separatist' party in the Sudan, and against a British declaration of policy that the Government had 'no intention of abandoning the Sudan in any sense whatever'.

On his return to Cairo Zaghlul threw aside such moderation as he had previously shown. Almost immediately he proceeded to embroil himself with the Palace, and even went to the length of threatening to organize demonstrations against the Throne. A few days later he refused to renew the contract of the British Judicial Adviser.[5]

The pursuance of Zaghlul's aims necessitated a connivance in subversive propaganda and incitement to violence which would have been irresponsible in an opposition leader and which was criminal in a Prime Minister. It is probable that Zaghlul was genuinely shocked by the assassination of Sir Lee Stack, the Governor-General of the Sudan and the Sirdar of the Egyptian Army, which took place in Cairo on 19 November. But a sane man is held to be responsible for the foreseeable consequences of his actions. Zaghlul was unable to control, and must have known that he would be unable to control, the forces of subversion and terrorism which he had neglected to suppress and which he had, in some sort, encouraged. A man who brandishes a loaded pistol in public is blameworthy if it goes off by accident and kills somebody. Absence of deliberate intent can only reduce the charge from murder to manslaughter.

Lord Allenby's reaction to the crime was, not unnaturally, one of furious indignation. Sir Lee Stack was a personal friend, a trusted colleague, and at the time of his assassination a guest at the Residency. Moreover, Lord Allenby was justifiably angry with Zaghlul for the way in which he had responded to his invariable patience, sympathy, and courtesy. But indignation is a bad counsellor.

The terms of the ultimatum which Lord Allenby presented to the Egyptian Government, without awaiting the approval of the Foreign Office, were such as to alienate those Egyptians who might have been prepared to break with Zaghlul and try to guide Egyptian nationalism on to a less sterile path than the one which Zaghlul had persistently been following. The assassination, deplorable as it was, did provide the opportunity for discrediting Zaghlul in the eyes of his fellow countrymen without attacking Egyptian nationalism in itself and without creating the impression that Great Britain was making of the assassination an excuse to re-establish part of the *status quo ante* the Declaration of Independence. This opportunity was not taken.

The text of the ultimatum, which was presented personally by Allenby to Zaghlul in the Egyptian Chamber of Deputies, was as follows:

The Governor-General of the Sudan and Sirdar of the Egyptian Army, who was also a distinguished officer of the British Army, has been brutally murdered in Cairo. His Majesty's Government consider that this murder, which holds up Egypt as at present governed to the contempt of civilized peoples, is the natural outcome of a campaign of hostility to British rights and British subjects in Egypt and the Sudan, founded upon a heedless ingratitude for benefits conferred by Great Britain, not discouraged by Your Excellency's Government and fomented by organizations in close touch with that Government. Your Excellency was warned by His Majesty's Government little more than a month ago of the consequences of failing to stop this campaign, more particularly as far as it concerned the Sudan. It has not been stopped. The Egyptian Government have now allowed the Governor-General of the Sudan to be murdered, and have proved that they are incapable or unwilling to protect foreign lives. His Majesty's Government therefore require that the Egyptian Government shall:

(i) Present ample apology for the crime.
(ii) Prosecute enquiry into the authorship of the crime with the utmost energy and without respect of persons, and bring the criminals, whoever they are, and whatever their age, to condign punishment.

(iii) Henceforth forbid and vigorously suppress all popular political demonstrations.

(iv) Pay forthwith to His Majesty's Government a fine of £500,000.

(v) Order within twenty-four hours the withdrawal from the Sudan of all Egyptian officers, and the purely Egyptian units of the Sudan Army, with such resulting changes as shall be hereafter specified.

(vi) Notify the competent Department that the Sudan Government will increase the area to be irrigated at Gezira from 300,000 *feddans* to an unlimited figure as need may arise.

(vii) Withdraw all opposition in the respects hereafter specified to the wishes of His Majesty's Government concerning the protection of foreign interests in Egypt.

Failing immediate compliance with these demands, His Majesty's Government will at once take appropriate action to safeguard their interests in Egypt and the Sudan.

The details 'hereafter specified' in respect of the Sudan and of foreign interests were set out in a second communication, which may be summarized as follows:

(*a*) The purely Sudanese element in the Egyptian Army to be formed into a Sudan Defence Force under British command and responsible to the Sudan Government only.

(*b*) The terms of retirement of foreign officials laid down by the Yehia Government were to be adjusted in accordance with the wishes of His Majesty's Government.

(*c*) The offices of Financial Adviser and Judicial Adviser, as well as the Head of the European Department of the Ministry of the Interior were to be retained with status and functions intact.[6]

The terms of the ultimatum, as presented, were open to criticism on several grounds. The demand for the suppression of 'all popular political demonstrations' was too loose and vague to appear appropriately in such a document and, taken at its face value, was incompatible with constitutional government. The demand for a fine might more appropriately have been expressed as a demand for compensation of the victim's family. But the most serious error was the wording of the paragraph dealing with the Gezira irrigation. Egypt's principal legitimate and only vital interest in the Sudan derives from the fact that control of the Sudan involves control of Egypt's water supplies. British control of the Sudan could only be tolerable to Egypt provided that this vital interest were fully safeguarded and provided that Egypt were allowed a full and free voice in the discussion of any scheme for the control or exploitation of Nile waters in the Sudan. The wording of the Gezira paragraph in the ultimatum not only deprived Egypt of this voice, but conveyed the implication that the British Government was prepared to use the control of Nile water as a means of bringing Egypt to heel as and when this might become necessary. After the anger and confusion had subsided, it was, of course, realized by all responsible Egyptians that the British Government had no intention of doing any such thing. The only outcome of the threat was an Anglo-Egyptian Nile Water Commission, which in due course arrived at an agreement satisfactory to both parties. But the memory of the threat rankled. It was a gift to unscrupulous propagandists, and it cast a shadow over Anglo-Egyptian relations for many years to come. Of all the sanctions with which we might have threatened Egypt, this was the one, above all others, which should have been left alone.

The Egyptian Government, in reply to the ultimatum, accepted the first, second and fourth demands and rejected the others.[7] But the time for negotiation was past. Zaghlul was to be left in no doubt that the resources of Allenby's goodwill were exhausted. Instructions were given to the Sudan Government for the immediate and forcible implementation of the fifth and sixth demands, and the Tobacco Customs at Alexandria were seized as a pledge for the execution of the seventh. Lord Allenby further suggested to the British Government that diplomatic relations with

Egypt should be severed and that hostages should be taken and shot in the event of any further assassinations. These suggestions, which were not accepted in London, are an indication of the state of mind prevailing at the Residency. Indignation rather than judgement was still in the ascendancy. The suggestion for the severance of diplomatic relations was meaningless; that for the shooting of hostages barbarous. After making full allowance for the emotional stresses under which the High Commissioner was labouring, it is clear that the confidence of the Foreign Office must have been severely shaken in the Residency's powers of good judgement.

However, the immediate results appeared to justify the High Commissioner's policy. Zaghlul, who had remained unimpressed by Allenby's conciliatoriness, was thoroughly frightened by his anger. If he had stood firm on the ground of his reply to the ultimatum, in which he had agreed unreservedly to apology, indemnity, and punishment, but rejected the other demands, he would have had Egyptian, and to some extent British and world, public opinion behind him. But his courage deserted him, and with it his political acumen. Three days after the assassination he handed his resignation and that of his Ministry to the King.

Adly Pasha and the Liberal Constitutionalists were unprepared to take office in the circumstances obtaining, and Zaghlul was replaced by Ziwar Pasha, a Turkish-Egyptian of the old school, who formed a Ministry of nonentities who were quite prepared to make up for their own impotence by sheltering behind the ample resources of the British High Commissioner.

An agreement was soon reached with the new Ministry regarding the status of the Financial and Judicial Advisers and on the conditions of retirement of foreign officials. The Tobacco Customs were evacuated. The immediate crisis was over. Zaghlul was for the time being utterly discredited, and his party was in disorder. A new Government had been formed. British authority stood higher than at any time since the end of the war. Any resentment which might have been felt at the severity of the British demands was temporarily eclipsed by the fear of British reprisals. But on a longer view, the situation was far from satisfactory from the British point of view. The only permanent alternative to the Wafd appeared to be a Palace autocracy, sustained by a greater or less degree of British support, and inevitably productive of serious internal disorders as soon as the Wafd had had time to regroup its scattered forces. It was by British influence that a democratic Constitution had been imposed on the Palace, and the whole trend of British policy in Egypt from 1907 onwards had been to encourage the development of Egypt on democratic lines. It would have been difficult for the British Government to react to the excesses of Zaghlul by conniving at the destruction of the Constitution and at a return to an autocracy whose excesses had been the principal cause of the original British intervention in Egypt. Such a policy would not only have committed the British Government to a much deeper embroilment in Egyptian affairs than they were prepared to contemplate, but would have sharpened all those antagonisms which it was necessary to appease if Anglo-Egyptian relations were ever to develop on fruitful lines.

The encouragement of a 'middle' party between the Wafd and the Palace, which would be able to stand up to the Wafd without the necessity either of an alliance with the Palace or of reliance on British support, became the principal immediate objective of British policy in Egypt. Ziwar Pasha was encouraged by the Residency to broaden the base of his Ministry by the inclusion of some members of the Liberal Constitutional party. But neither Adly nor Sarwat nor Mahmud were prepared to take part in the delicate task of fighting the Wafd with the one hand while resisting the dictation of the Palace and the Residency with the other. There was, however, one man in the Liberal party who felt himself equal to the task. Ismail Sidqi had been a member of the Rushdi Government at the outbreak of war. He had resigned in 1915 and had been one of the original group which had made up the Wafd. Subsequently he had quarrelled with Zaghlul and had joined Adly. But he was no party man and was not disposed to remain sitting on the fence with Adly waiting to see how things would turn out. He agreed to join the Ziwar Ministry as Minister of the Interior, and from the time of his appointment became the real head of the Government. He determined that. the Chamber of Deputies with its large Wafd majority, would have to be dissolved before the Wafd had recovered from its confusion and returned to the offensive. He started to purge the provincial administrations of Zaghlul's Wafdist appointees, and to appoint supporters of his own in their place, in order to ensure favourable 'supervision' of the new elections.

Parliament was dissolved on 24 December, and immediate arrangements made for the holding of new elections. The King, who now judged it safe publicly to express his opposition to the Wafd, placed himself behind the formation of a new party, the Ittihad. The Wafd returned to the fray. Sidqi devoted his efforts to trying to rig the elections against the Wafd by reminding his provincial appointees that their continued employment was dependent on a Wafdist defeat. His efforts were almost brought to naught by the spinelessness of the Liberals, who, presented with a matchless opportunity for electoral success, revealed themselves as the boulevardiers they were by confining their electoral activities to the political clubs and *salons* of Cairo and Alexandria. Had it not been for the Ittihad, the ineptitude of the Liberals would have enabled the Wafd to gain a clear majority, in spite of Sidqi's efforts. As it was, the Wafd obtained just under half the total seats, the other half being distributed between the Liberals, the Ittihadists and a number of Independents.[8] The election of Zaghlul as President of the Chamber made Ziwar's position impossible, and he immediately offered his resignation and that of his Ministry. The Palace (and the Residency) had two choices open. If

273

Ziwar's resignation were accepted, the only possible alternative Government would be one dominated by the Wafd. If it were refused, it would be necessary to dissolve Parliament in order to enable the Ministry to carry on. The latter course was chosen and the newly-elected Parliament dissolved on 26 March 1925. The attempt to establish a 'middle' party, or coalition of parties, had failed. The Constitution was in suspense, and the King and Sidqi were, in effect, rival candidates for the autocratic government of the country.

In June 1925 Lord Allenby relinquished his post as High Commissioner and returned to England. He had been High Commissioner for just over six years. He had taken up the post at an extremely critical time. By a judicious blend of concession and firmness, he had restored order rapidly and without serious bloodshed. He had imposed on a reluctant Foreign Office a policy which recognized the realities of the political situation in Egypt. Despite the autocratic tendencies of the Palace and the intransigent opposition of the Wafd, he secured the peaceful implementation of the Declaration of Independence, and had watched over the inauguration of constitutional life in Egypt. He had held firmly to his course, in spite of the disapproval of the Foreign Office, and in spite of the vigorous and not always discriminating criticism and opposition of British official and commercial circles in Egypt. And events, on the whole, justified his confidence in his policy. But after the first elections and the rise of Zaghlul to power, he seems to have lost his touch. He miscalculated the effect on Zaghlul's mind of his evident anxiety for treaty negotiations. Zaghlul, thinking solely in terms of political struggle, was genuinely unable to appreciate Allenby's desire for an amicable settlement of Anglo-Egyptian differences. The injudicious violence of Allenby's reaction to the assassination of Sir Lee Stack has already been commented on.

But Allenby's greatest achievement in Egypt was the affection for himself and the respect for Great Britain which he inspired in all classes of Egyptians. There was nothing small or mean about him. His anger with Zaghlul after the Sirdar's assassination was of a piece with his previous sympathy with him. Both the sympathy and the anger were feelings which the average Egyptian could appreciate. At a time when British good faith was being freely impugned by the politicians and people of the Middle East, Allenby's massive integrity and straightforwardness shone forth with a brightness which neither nationalist resentments nor British mistakes could dim.

There was an interval of some four months between the departure of Allenby in June and the arrival of Lord Lloyd, [9] his successor, in October. During most of this time both Ziwar and Sidqi were absent in Europe, the former on holiday, the latter negotiating with the Italian Government over the definition of the boundary between Egypt and Libya. The King took the opportunity to set on foot an intrigue which resulted in the resignation of Sidqi and the other Liberal Ministers from the Government. This caused the Liberals and all those who viewed with alarm the prospect of a Palace dictatorship to come to terms with the Wafd, and to look to the Wafd as the potential saviours of the country from royal autocracy. The Wafd, emboldened by returning popularity and prestige and more at home in opposition than in power, started an agitation for the re-assembly of Parliament in October in accordance with the Constitution. After an attempt by opposition senators and deputies to meet in the Houses of Parliament had been foiled by police, an unofficial Assembly was convened at the Continental Hotel, which elected Zaghlul as its President.

This was the situation which confronted Lord Lloyd, the new High Commissioner, on his arrival in Egypt. One of his first acts was to persuade King Fuad to agree to the posting of Nashaat Pasha, the Chief of the Royal Cabinet and the hand behind the political intrigues of the Palace, to a diplomatic post abroad. He then made an unsuccessful attempt to detach the Liberals from the Wafd and to induce some of their number to serve in Ziwar's Ministry. In view

275

of the Liberal refusal, the removal of Nashaat only temporarily alleviated a situation from which the only issue seemed to be another general election, a return to a constitutional régime, and a Wafdist Government. The rift between the Palace and the Government on the one side and the Wafd on the other was by this time so wide that Ziwar was determined to prevent the Wafd from returning to power as the result of new elections. Realizing that elections could not be long postponed, he promulgated a new electoral law, which had been drawn up by Sidqi a few months previously, when he had still been a member of the Government. The purpose of the new law was to make it easier for the provincial authorities to influence the elections in favour of the Government. The implementation of this law could not fail to exacerbate the already bitter relations between Government and Opposition. The Wafd announced its intention of boycotting any election conducted under the new law, and the High Commissioner (who had advised against the promulgation of the law) advised Ziwar to withdraw it. Thereupon Ziwar abandoned the struggle and resigned himself to the inevitability of a Wafdist victory.

The prospect of such a victory made it necessary for the British Government to decide on the attitude to be adopted towards Zaghlul after the elections in the event of the Wafd being returned to power. Would the British Government be prepared to acquiesce in Zaghlul's return to the Premiership, bearing in mind the circumstances in which he had previously quitted it? Eventually they accepted the High Commissioner's view that Zaghlul's assumption of the Premiership should be discouraged. The principal reason for Lord Lloyd's view appeared to be the general impression which existed among both British and Egyptian Government officials that Lord Allenby had at the time of the formation of the Ziwar Ministry intimated that the British Government would not countenance Zaghlul's return to power at a later date. This assurance had been called for by many Egyptian officials who were called upon to replace Zaghlul's nominees and who, in the event of Zaghlul's return to power, would be likely to suffer from the petty vindictiveness· which was one of Zaghlul's less attractive characteristics.

The elections, which were completed just before the end of May, gave the Wafd 144 seats out of 201. The British attitude about Zaghlul's assumption of the Premiership soon became known to the newly-elected Wafd deputies, and this, combined with the arrival of H.M.S. *Resolution* at Alexandria, was sufficient for them to induce their leader to decline office. Adly Pasha, fortified by promises of support from the Residency, from the Palace, and even from Zaghlul himself, was prevailed upon to preside over a coalition Ministry consisting of three Liberals and seven Wafdists. Zaghlul was elected President of the Chamber. It soon appeared that experience, or advancing years, had taught him moderation and discretion. He seemed to have lost his jealousy of Adly. He used his authority with the Wafdist deputies to avoid attacks on the Government, on the Palace, or on the British. The Egyptian political prospect looked fairer than it had done for some time.

But it was not long before the forces of intrigue and personal ambition began to make themselves felt. The Royalist newspapers, reflecting the King's irritation at his enforced impotence, began to taunt Zaghlul for his sub-servience to the British. Sidqi, in his capacity as Chairman of the Parliamentary Finance Committee, asked awkward questions about Palace expenditure. Adly and Zaghlul began to quarrel about the continual interference of Wafdist deputies in the machinery of administration. The unaccus-tomed exercise of moderation caused the Wafdist deputies to become restive. Zaghlul continued to hold the key to the situation. He could hold his supporters, and himself, in check so long as he wished to do so. He had a powerful reason for wishing to do so, since the probable alternative to the existing régime was a reversion to Palace rule in circum-stances which would most likely ensure British support for the Palace.

In spite of this imposed restraint, and largely as a result of the weakness and lack of cohesion of the Liberals (whose leaders, Adly, Sarwat, Sidqi and Mahmud, were at least as antagonistic to each other as they were to Zaghlul), the Wafdist deputies began to exercise an increasing influence on the policy of the Government. In April 1927, after nearly a year in office, Adly, weary of the continual necessity of dealing with pressure exercised on him from three different directions—the Palace, the Residency, and the Wafd—resigned, and was replaced by Sarwat Pasha.

At the beginning of the year, when Adly was still in office, Lord Lloyd had made representations to the Egyptian Government regarding the retention of British officials in the Egyptian service. Under the agreement of 1923, it had been provided that those British officials who wished to do so should be allowed to remain in the Egyptian service until 1927. No provision had been made for the retention of British officials after that date.[10] By the end of 1926 it had become apparent that the Wafdist majority was determined to get rid of most, if not all, British officials as soon as the time limit laid down in the 1923 agreement had expired, and to replace them by Egyptians, and in some cases by non-British Europeans. Lord Lloyd took the view that the continued service of a certain minimum of British officials was necessary in order to enable Great Britain to discharge her responsibility for the protection of foreign lives and property in accordance with one of the four 'reserved points' of the Declaration of Independence. With the somewhat dubious concurrence of Whitehall, he succeeded in inducing the Egyptian Government to agree to the retention of certain British officials and also to ensure that any Government posts filled by non-Egyptians should be filled by British nationals except with the specific consent of the British Government.

In the summer of 1927, after Sarwat had taken office, the Residency again intervened with the Egyptian Government, this time in connexion with the status and powers of senior

British officers in the Egyptian Army. The Egyptian Government, under pressure from the Wafd, had been showing a tendency to by-pass the British Inspector-General and to place the day-to-day control of the Army entirely in the hands of the Minister of War, who was a Wafdist. Lord Lloyd took the view that the maintenance of effective British control over the Egyptian Army was an essential condition of the efficient discharge of the responsibilities which Great Britain had reserved to herself in Egypt. Furthermore, he considered that the Wafdist manœuvres had for their object the subjection of the Army to the political control of the Wafd. Again with some difficulty, he secured Whitehall's consent to his intervention, and again he was successful in gaining his point with the Egyptian Government without a political crisis.

It was by this time becoming apparent that the delicacy of the British position in Egypt was being enhanced by a growing divergence of view between the Residency and the Foreign Office, Lord Lloyd, who was a natural autocrat, had little sympathy with Egyptian nationalism, and such sympathy as he may have had at the outset did not survive his term of office in Egypt. This lack of sympathy naturally caused him to attach more importance to the reservations contained in the 1922 Declaration than to the progress towards complete independence so clearly foreshadowed in the Declaration. In practice, this led him to resist and oppose any development which tended to weaken such British control as still remained in Egypt on the ground that such weakening was incompatible with the maintenance of British responsibilities for the protection of foreign interests as reserved in the 1922 Declaration.

In these circumstances it was to be expected that Lord Lloyd would find himself in disagreement with the action of the Foreign Office in opening discussions with Sarwat on the subject of a treaty when the Egyptian Prime Minister accompanied King Fuad on a State visit to London in August 1927. It was also to be expected that the Foreign

Office, which was more anxious to arrive at a permanent and agreed settlement with Egypt than it was to perpetuate the essentially *ad interim* situation created by the 1922 Declaration, should have discounted his objections.

But in the circumstances obtaining, the desirability or otherwise of a treaty was irrelevant, since it was inconceivable that any treaty negotiated by Sarwat would receive the ratification of the Egyptian Parliament. Whatever concessions Sarwat might succeed in extracting from the British Government, the Wafdist majority would never allow a non-Wafdist Premier to enjoy the prestige of a successfully negotiated treaty. Any faint possibility that the Wafd might have been prepared to consider on its merits any treaty negotiated by Sarwat disappeared with the death of Zaghlul Pasha towards the end of August. Nahas Pasha, his successor in the Wafd leadership, was no more than the mouthpiece of the party, unable and unwilling either to restrain his followers or to direct their energies into constructive channels.

As it happened, the draft treaty negotiated between Austen Chamberlain and Sarwat did not involve any important retreat on Great Britain's part from the 'reserved points', except that it was agreed that the garrisoning of Egypt by British troops should be reviewed ten years after the signature of the Treaty and that, in the event of a disagreement then, the matter should be referred to the Council of the League of Nations. The Sudan was left outside the scope of the discussions. The Financial and Judicial Advisers were to continue their functions as before, and Great Britain was to continue to be responsible for the protection of foreign interests, pending the modification of the Capitulations.

But the content of the draft treaty was unimportant. Nobody who was not in control of the Egyptian parliamentary majority had the faintest chance of getting a treaty ratified, whatever its content. The alternative course of dissolving parliament and overriding the Constitution would have been acceptable neither to Sarwat, who was the principal author of the Constitution, nor to the British Government, which had insisted on the democratic nature of the Constitution, nor to the King, who disliked Sarwat. The only result of the Sarwat-Chamberlain negotiations was the resignation of Sarwat and his Ministry in March 1928, after a long course of futile bargaining with the Opposition, and the accession to office of a Wafdist Ministry with Nahas Pasha as Prime Minister.

Once again the Liberal 'moderates' had failed to find a middle way between demagogy and autocracy. Among their number were the only four able statesmen Egypt possessed— Adly, Sidqi, Sarwat and Mahmud. Each of them was infinitely more able than anyone whom the Wafd could have produced after the death of Zaghlul. But they were all antagonistic to and jealous of each other, and without the peculiar gifts necessary for the creation and maintenance of a party machine. Turkish in blood (except for Mahmud, who was a pure Egyptian), European in culture and autocratic in temperament, in their hearts they despised the Egyptians, and could not bring themselves to compete with provincial lawyers for the allegiance of nationalist carpet-baggers. Each of them, in his turn, was to find himself at the head of affairs, and none of them, when at the head of affairs, could count on the support of any of the other three. Lacking the prestige of the Palace and the solidarity of the Wafd, they failed time and again to secure themselves from the intrigues of one and from the attacks of the other. By the beginning of 1928 Adly and Sarwat had had their chances. Those of Mahmud and Sidqi were still to come. The autocratic régimes of Mahmud and Sidqi were in sharp contrast to the pliability of those of Adly and Sarwat. But fundamentally all four suffered from the same weaknesses.

The new Wafdist Ministry was short-lived. Soon after coming into power, Nahas was compelled, by pressure from the Residency, to abandon a proposal for an amendment of the law relating to public assemblies, which would, in the

High Commissioner's estimate, have proved a menace to public order and to the safety of the foreign communities. The proposal, which meant in effect that the police were deprived of all power of effective intervention at public meetings, was an extremely irresponsible one to have been put forward by any government, and it was almost certainly intended to facilitate organized agitation against both the Palace and the Residency. Even Zaghlul, at his most irresponsible period in the summer of 1924, had opposed a similar proposal when put foward by a private Member.

A few weeks later it became apparent that Nahas was as indiscreet in his private, as he was irresponsible in his public, life. Early in 1927, when Vice-President of the Chamber he, with two other deputies, had entered into an agreement with the mother of Prince Sayf-al-Din, a lunatic half-brother of the King, to transfer the guardianship of her son's estate from the King's hands to her own. In return for securing the transfer, Nahas and his two confederates were to receive a fee of £130,000. When Nahas was Prime Minister, the document embodying the agreement fell into the hands of the Palace. It was a golden opportunity for the King. Having made a private bargain with Mahmud Pasha, the only Liberal in the Nahas Ministry, who thereupon resigned office, His Majesty had the document published in the Press, summarily dismissed Nahas, and called upon Mahmud Pasha to form a Ministry. Two days later Parliament was adjourned for a month. For the second time in four years a Wafdist Ministry had ended in confusion and disgrace.

A month later the King, acting on the advice of his new Ministry, dissolved Parliament. For the second time in four years the Constitution was virtually suspended.

Given the past behaviour of the Wafd and the known views of the High Commissioner, it was hardly to be supposed that these developments were unwelcome at the Residency. Mahmud Pasha was an able administrator and had sufficient independence of mind as to make it improbable that he would be content with the role of a Palace nominee. He had been educated at Balliol and had an understanding and liking for British life and methods. He had been in Government service in early life, but had had to resign as a result of a disagreement with the Khedive in which he had felt aggrieved at not having received the support of Lord Kitchener. He was one of the original members of the Wafd and had shared Zaghlul's exile at Malta in 1919. But, like every other able statesman in Egypt, he had soon quarrelled with Zaghlul. He joined Adly's Liberal Party, but personal rivalries and jealousies had inhibited any fruitful co-operation with the abler of his colleagues and he had become, in all but name, an Independent.

Fortified by the discomfiture of the Wafd, by the support of the Residency, and by the temporary benevolence of the Palace, Mahmud Pasha's Ministry proceeded to govern Egypt with the nearest approach to efficiency that had been seen for many years. Public security was improved and the provincial administration purged once more of its political appointees. Agreements were arrived at with Great Britain over the administration of Nile waters in the Sudan,[11] over Egypt's share of the Ottoman Debt, and over certain financial legacies of the 1914–18 War. But the British Government, or, to be exact, certain permanent officials of the Foreign Office, were by no means satisfied with the state of affairs in Egypt. They were unhappy about the suspension of the Constitution, and seemed to imagine that the High Commissioner had had some share in bringing this about. They were anxious to see Anglo-Egyptian relations legitimatized by a treaty, and were not at all in sympathy with Lord Lloyd's view that the reserved points were sacrosanct. They did not share the High Commissioner's concern for British business interests in Egypt, and were only concerned with British strategic interests, which they considered would be more adequately safeguarded by a friendly and independent Egypt than by a resentful Egypt in leading-strings. Debarred by the 1922 Declaration from doing anything constructive in Egypt, they were unwilling to perpetuate an artificial situation by the continual exercise of an undefined but effective power of veto. They contemplated with aversion the possibly onerous commitments which the pursuance of Lord Lloyd's policy might at any time involve.

This underlying disagreement between the Foreign Office and the Residency remained dormant for as long as the Conservative Government, which had appointed Lord Lloyd, remained in power. But when the Labour Government came into office after the 1929 General Election, Mr. Henderson, who had succeeded Mr. Austen Chamberlain as Foreign Secretary, lost no time, and certainly expended no courtesy,[12] in getting rid of Lord Lloyd on the somewhat curious ground (as he explained in the House of Commons) that his views on Egyptian policy had been in opposition to those of his Conservative predecessor at the Foreign Office. This statement was not then or later contradicted by Mr. Chamberlain, but the truth of the matter probably was that Mr. Henderson, not unwillingly, perhaps, had assented to the wishes of his permanent officials.

As early as June 1929, before ever Lord Lloyd had resigned, and apparently without Lord Lloyd's knowledge, treaty discussions had already started between Foreign Office officials and Mahmud Pasha, who was on holiday in England at the time.

The terms of the draft treaty negotiated by Mahmud Pasha represented a very considerable advance on the Sarwat draft as far as Egypt was concerned. British troops were to be withdrawn from Cairo and Alexandria and concentrated in the Canal Zone. The Sudan was reserved for subsequent discussion; the British Government relinquished their responsibility for the protection of foreign interests,[13] and promised to use their good offices with the powers with a view to the abolition of the Capitulations. But the British Government insisted that they would only be prepared to recognize a treaty which had been ratified by a freely elected Egyptian Parliament.

Mahmud Pasha returned to Egypt in August with the

draft treaty in his pocket. In September, Sir Percy Loraine,[14] Lord Lloyd's successor as High Commissioner, arrived in Egypt to find Mahmud Pasha busily engaged in negotiations with the various party leaders. The result of his negotiations was as might have been expected. The Ittihadists and the Liberals accepted the draft treaty. The Wafd rejected it. As in Sarwat's case, the contents of the treaty were irrelevant as far as the Wafd was concerned.

Faced with the opposition of the Wafd and with the British Government's insistence on elections, Mahmud Pasha resigned office.

The British Government's anxiety for the Egyptian Constitution was to have the paradoxical effect of securing its formal suppression. Mahmud Pasha's Ministry was replaced by a caretaker Government under Adly Pasha, which had the task of preparing for the elections to which the British Government attached so much importance. The Liberals boycotted the elections and a big Wafdist majority was returned. Nahas Pasha, who had by the events of the past few months been strangely converted into a British protégé, duly became Prime Minister, and before long took up the treaty negotiations at the point where Mahmud had left them. He found himself in a difficult position. On the one hand, he was estopped from accepting the draft treaty as it stood in view of his previous opposition to it. On the other hand, the British Government had made it clear to Mahmud Pasha that the draft Treaty represented the 'high-water mark' of concession. Neither side could recede from the position so recently and (in the case of Nahas) so publicly taken up. So, after a few weeks of futile skirmishing, negotiations were broken off, ostensibly on the ground of the British Government's refusal to accede to Nahas's demand for free Egyptian immigration into the Sudan.

Nahas Pasha was sorely in need of the prestige which a successfully negotiated treaty would have conferred on him. The Palace was implacably hostile to him. Of the remaining Liberal leaders (Sarwat was dead and Adly had retired from public life), Mahmud was as angry with Nahas as he was with the British, and Sidqi was already plotting his downfall. The stage was set for a head-on collision between the Palace and the Wafd. It was not long in coming, and it was provoked by the Wafd. In June 1930 the Government presented to the King for his approval a Bill providing that any Minister who violated the Constitution should be subject to heavy penalties. Innocent as such a Bill no doubt appeared to Mr. Henderson, it was in fact a direct and deliberate challenge to the Palace. The King, whose plans were laid, took up the challenge. He refused to sign the Bill. Nahas Pasha offered the resignation of his Ministry. The King accepted it and called upon Sidqi to form a Government. Sidqi moved to the centre of the stage as if to a cue. As soon as the new Ministry was formed, the King prorogued Parliament. Nahas attempted to fight. There was rioting in Cairo and Alexandria and some provincial towns. The British Government sent warships to Alexandria, Port Said, and Suez. Then the Foreign Office instructed the Residency to warn both Sidqi and Nahas that they would both be held responsible by the British Government for the safety of foreign lives and property.[15] Nahas thanked the British for their intervention. Sidqi protested against British interference, asserted his ability to keep order, and requested the departure of the warships. Since order was in fact restored within a few days, and since there was no damage to foreign lives or property, the Residency must have had some difficulty in deciding whether the thanks or the protest were the more embarrassing.

In October, the 1923 Constitution was abrogated, Parliament dissolved, and a new Constitution and Electoral Law promulgated by royal decree. The new Constitution decisively tilted the balance of power away from the legislature and towards the executive. The principal object of the new electoral law, which was similar to that which Ziwar had tried to introduce in 1925, was to keep the Wafd out of office.

The Labour Government's Egyptian policy, in the year following Lord Lloyd's resignation, had not been such as to afford their supporters any great satisfaction. They had aimed at a treaty with a friendly Egyptian Government and at the restoration of the 1923 Constitution. What had happened was that there had been two abortive attempts to negotiate a treaty, that the Constitution had been abrogated, and that a Prime Minister was in office whose first act had been to make a successful protest against British interference. The British Government had failed either accurately to predict or in any sense to control the course of events in Egypt. This was not because they had abandoned intervention in Egypt's affairs. They had merely substituted ineffective for effective intervention.

NOTES ON CHAPTER ELEVEN

1. Under the 1923 electoral law, elections were held in two stages, the first stage, in which the electors as a whole elected a college of electors, and the second stage, in which the college of electors elected the deputies.

2. By the terms of this Agreement European officials were given the choice between retiring on 1 April 1924 or of remaining in service until 1 April 1927. In either event, they were to be appropriately compensated according to their grade and length of service. The terms of compensation were revised in favour of the European officials under the terms of a revised agreement arrived at with Ziwar Pasha's Government in November 1924. No British Officials (except those provided for in the 1922 Declaration (see Chapter IX)) had the option of remaining after 1 April 1927, although the Egyptian Government could, of course, make arrangements to retain any who wished to stay. When the time came, Lord Lloyd made an agreement with the Egyptian Government for the continued service of a certain number of British officials in the police. The last remaining British officials were dismissed from Egyptian Government service at the end of 1951, soon after the denunciation of the Anglo-Egyptian Treaty.

3. The Wafd was formed into a political party for the purpose of contesting the elections. Its organization was based on the various Committees of Independence which had been formed up and down the country by Zaghlul and his associates in 1919.

4. This, in fact, was the basis of the treaty eventually negotiated in 1936.

5. After the 1922 Declaration British Financial and Judicial Advisers had been retained, on the insistence of the British Government, in order to safeguard Great Britain's financial and judicial responsibilities towards foreigners as provided for in the Capitulations.

6. The Head of the European Department was an Englishman, and was responsible for the control of the police and other executive officers in matters affecting foreigners.

7. The apology and the fine were tendered immediately. Eight persons were arrested and tried for the murder. Seven of them were found guilty and executed. Subsequently, seven members of the Wafd were charged with complicity in the crime. Of these seven, one was convicted and sentenced to death, and the other six were acquitted. Judge Kershaw, the British President of the Court which tried them, dissented from the judgements of his Egyptian colleagues in three of these acquittals, and subsequently resigned as a protest against what he described as 'a grave miscarriage of justice'.

8. The great influence exercised by many local magnates in the provinces has always led to the election of a large number of deputies to Egyptian Parliaments who are bound by no party ties.

9. Previously Governor of Bombay, and before that, a Conservative Member of Parliament.

10. See Note 2, above.

11. As an indirect result of the sixth paragraph of the ultimatum presented to the Egyptian Government after the assassination of Sir Lee Stack, a Nile Commission, with an Egyptian member, had been set up in 1925. Political disagreements regarding the status of the Sudan prevented the Report of this Commission from being accepted either by the British or by the Egyptian Governments, and consequently Egypt's rights in the control of Nile waters remained undefined. Mahmud Pasha's Government took up the matter with the Residency and, by divorcing the question from politics, an agreement was soon reached on the lines recommended by the Commission.

12. A full account of the circumstances of Lord Lloyd's resignation is given in Chapter XVIII of Lord Lloyd's book, *Egypt Since Cromer* (Vol. II).

13. This was a necessary consequence of the withdrawal of British troops from Cairo and Alexandria. The only object of their presence in these cities was for the protection of foreigners. The abolition of the Capitulations followed naturally from a British abandonment of any claim to protect foreign interests. By 1930 Egypt's ability to provide reasonable security for foreign residents was no longer in doubt. But, so long as Great Britain maintained her claim to protect them, the powers would insist on the maintenance of the Capitulations as a counterweight. Conversely, so long as the Capitulations remained in force, Great Britain had to protect foreign interests. It is fair to add that the persistence of this limitation on Egypt's sovereignty for fourteen years after the Declaration of Independence was due more to Egyptian domestic rivalries than to any foreign 'imperialism'.

14. Formerly British Ambassador at Ankara. He was the first career diplomat to be chosen for the post of British Representative in Egypt since the Occupation.

15. It is unusual for such a step to be taken except in the event of a civil war.

CHAPTER TWELVE

THE PALACE

IT was not likely that the theory and practice of constitutional monarchy would make a strong appeal to a descendant of Mohamed Ali and a son of Ismail.[1] Both Mohamed Ali and Ismail had regarded the Egyptian state as their own personal property. We have seen how, in the reign of Taufiq, there was an influential body of notables who wished to curb and define the powers of the monarch by means of a constitution. These constitutionalists, as a result of their more or less fortuitous alliance with the Arabi nationalists, lost their importance during the first years of the British occupation, during which time Taufiq, acting as the catspaw of British policy, exercised the prerogatives of an absolute ruler. But under Abbas Hilmi, who was less amenable than Taufiq had been to British guidance, indigenous opposition to the Palace had again made itself felt. The nationalists under Mustafa Kamal, like the nationalists under Arabi, were not constitutionalists. Arabi had been opposed to Taufiq, not because of his absolutism, but because of his foreign connexions. Mustafa Kamal, after a brief flirtation with Cromer, who was rigidly opposed to the Khedive, and who was prepared to sponsor moderate nationalism as a counterweight, was eventually won over to the side of the Khedive. The new opposition came from the rural magnates, whose desire for local power in their districts directly conflicted with the Khedive's despotic ambitions. These magnates were able to use the rift between the British Agency and the Palace to their advantage, and the Legislative Council and General Assembly created by Gorst gave them the opportunity for organized opposition to the Executive.

Since the powers wielded by these bodies were very limited, it was inevitable that this opposition should take the form of propaganda, incitement, and harassing tactics generally.

It was not long before leadership in the Legislative Council passed out of the hands of the magnates and into those of the lawyers. These lawyers started off as the nominees of the magnates, and ended as professional politicians, whose forensic successes and popular reputations made them independent of their former patrons. The Legislative Council became a training ground for the constitutional politicians of the future, and this fact partly explains the peculiar irresponsibility of future Egyptian Parliaments. For the Legislative Council never became a deliberative body, as was presumably intended; what it did become, as we have seen, was an organized attempt to prevent the government from governing.

After the war, the magnates, faced with the prospect of a constitution, had to choose between support for the Palace and co-operation with the professional politicians, who had grown up in the Legislative Council and who had by this time stolen the nationalist thunder to such an extent that they were regarded as being synonymous with Egyptian nationalism. Most of the magnates, haunted by legends of Ismail, chose the latter alternative in the hope of being able to reassert their domination over Zaghlul and the lawyers. In consequence of this alliance between the magnates and the lawyers, the Palace was forced to accept a 'democratic' Constitution.[2] The King thereupon set himself the task of detaching from the nationalists sufficient of the 'marginal' magnates and their hangers-on to enable him once more to assume a dominant role in the affairs of the State. As long as Zaghlul lived he made little permanent headway against the strong personality of the Wafdist leader and the efficient organization of the Wafdist party machine. But the very dominance of Zaghlul weakened the Constitution by preventing the emergence of a 'centre' party which would have served as a constitutional alternative to the Wafd. The death of Zaghlul in 1927, followed by that of Sarwat in 1928, left the Constitution without an able defender.

The Palace's first attempt to overthrow the Constitution, with the help of Mahmud Pasha, was frustrated by the British Government's insistence on elections as the condition of a treaty. The second attempt, in collaboration with Sidqi Pasha, was more successful. Neither the King nor Sidqi was particularly anxious for a treaty. Both of them preferred British troops in Cairo to a Wafdist majority in Parliament, and both shrewdly judged that Great Britain would not interfere with any régime in Egypt which was able to maintain law and order without their assistance.

For the next five years Egyptian politics were almost exclusively concerned with domestic matters, and it was not until Mussolini's Abyssinian adventure brought Europe to the verge of war that the struggle between the Palace and the Wafd became merged with the larger question of Egypt's future relationship with Great Britain.

Sidqi Pasha spent the winter of 1930–1 preparing for the first General Election under the new Constitution, which was to be held in the spring. The Liberals had joined the Wafdists in denouncing the new Constitution, both parties announced that they would boycott the election, and Mahmud was publicly reconciled with Nahas. As Sidqi had committed himself to elections, it was necessary to have lists of candidates for the elections. So he founded a new party called al-Shaab (the people), complete with newspaper and well-equipped central offices. At the same time he decided that it would be inappropriate for the parties who were boycotting the elections to do any electioneering. He therefore endeavoured to prevent Nahas and his followers from visiting the provinces. This prohibition produced some diverting incidents, including one which involved Nahas and Makram Ebeid, his principal henchman, spending the night in a railway siding in Upper Egypt.

The elections passed off without serious disorder and without a great deal of genuine voting. Satisfactory results were, however, produced and a Chamber consisting of Shaabists, Ittihadists and Independents was duly elected. The decencies having been preserved sufficiently as to satisfy the Residency, Sidqi Pasha, with a subservient Parliament on the one hand, and a still fairly benevolent Palace on the other, started on a course of autocratic and moderately efficient rule, under which the students were kept at their studies[3] and the opposition politicians confined to impotent grumbling. It had not, however, been part of the royal plan to destroy the 1923 Constitution in order to enable Sidqi to play the dictator. The King had been compelled to use the services of a strong man in order to get rid of the Wafd. It now remained to get rid of the strong man.

During these years of domestic rivalries, the British occupation had an unacknowledged but decisive effect on the course of events, since the presence of British troops prevented any serious recourse to violence. Since this was so, and since neither the King nor Sidqi could afford an appeal to popular sentiment, it followed that the rivalry between the Palace and the Government had to be carried on entirely through the medium of backstairs intrigue. The Government, although in many respects efficient, provided the Palace with numerous opportunities for a whispering campaign against it. Sidqi eventually fell in January 1933, after he had been in office for just over two years, a record for any Government since the 1922 Declaration. A villager of Badari in Upper Egypt complained that he had been tortured during the course of an investigation by the Parquet.[4] His complaint was taken up by the enemies of the Government, and received some prominence. The Minister of Justice attempted to hush the matter up. The scandal assumed major proportions. Sidqi, who had just suffered a mild paralytic stroke, took the opportunity to resign. He was replaced by Abdul Fattah Pasha Yehia, a far less able man than Sidqi, and a nominee of the Palace. While the new Ministry devoted itself almost entirely to ferreting out the numerous scandals which had marked the Sidqi régime, the

influence of the Palace, now mainly exercised by Ibrashi
Pasha, the Director of the Royal Estates, grew stronger and
stronger and was exercised more and more openly. The
resentment which was created by this was directed not so
much at the fact of Palace rule as at the way in which the
Palace used its growing power to pervert the course of
justice and to revive all the worst excesses of the bad old
days of Ismail.[5] If the Palace had been interested in good
administration and in the popular welfare, it is possible that
its growing power would have been welcomed by the mass
of the population, if not by the politicians. As it was, a
continued development of the royal despotism might well
have created a revolutionary situation and a swing-back
from autocracy to demagogy.

Sir Percy Loraine had by this time been replaced as High
Commissioner by Sir Miles Lampson.[6] In September 1934
the Residency made its first decisive intervention in
Egyptian politics for over four years, when it warned the
Palace and the Government of the danger of the situation,
and advised the curtailment of Ibrashi's powers. Nahas,
fearful of being accused by the Palace of having inspired
this British intervention, joined with the Palace in publicly
protesting against it. The intervention had its effect, however, and Ziwar Pasha, who had been made Prime Minister,
ten years earlier, after the assassination of Sir Lee Stack, was
appointed to the vacant post of Chief of the Royal Cabinet,
where he would be in a position to control Ibrashi. The
following month Yehia Pasha resigned and was replaced as
Prime Minister by Taufiq Nessim Pasha. During his previous
tenure of office in 1923, Nessim Pasha had been a King's
man, but subsequently he had opposed the 1930 Constitution, and his advent to power was generally recognized as
being the beginning of the end of Palace rule.

At the end of November the 1930 Constitution was
abrogated and Parliament dissolved. In January 1935 the
Wafd emerged from its political retirement and met in party
congress. In the same month the students of al-Azhar, which

had, during the Yehia régime, fallen deeply under the influence of the Palace, went on strike, demanding the dismissal of the Rector, Shaikh Ahmed Zawahiri, a Palace nominee, and the reinstatement of Shaikh Mustafa al Maraghi, who was known for his Wafdist sympathies. The reaction from Palace rule was gathering strength, and it was not long before the tide was definitely running in the other direction. In April 1935 Ibrashi resigned, and in May Shaikh Maraghi was reinstated as Rector of al-Azhar. In the same month Ziwar Pasha, having accomplished his task of getting rid of Ibrashi, also resigned. King Fuad, mindful of the role played by his Prime Minister, Nessim Pasha, in these events, and remembering that the Wafd had protested against the British intervention which had been the cause of all the trouble, now made a bold change of front and attempted to negotiate an alliance with the Wafd as a means of getting rid of Nessim and of combating further British interference. Nahas was shrewd enough to refuse the offer. He realized that he had only to swim with the tide to bring himself once more into power. And the tide was running away from the Palace.

By this time Italian preparations for the invasion of Abyssinia had become the principal preoccupation of European statesmen. As the summer wore on, Egyptian politicians began to realize that their country would occupy a key position in the event of a League of Nations war against Italy. They regarded the situation either with apprehension at a danger or with exhilaration at an opportunity, according to their various moods and temperaments. A desire to blackmail Great Britain was almost equally balanced by a desire to be protected by Great Britain. Meanwhile, Great Britain was making such precautionary dispositions as were necessary, with scant regard to Egyptian national susceptibilities. Arrangements were made to transfer the headquarters of the Mediterranean Fleet from Malta to Alexandria without consultation with the Egyptian Government, who were apparently first informed of the matter through the medium of an election speech delivered by Mr. Runciman on 18 October.[7]

It was becoming urgently necessary for Egyptian politicians to declare themselves. The Prime Minister had the support neither of the Palace nor of the Wafd. The question was whether the Liberals and Independents would support Nessim in an anti-Wafd coalition, or whether they would ally themselves with the Wafd, turn Nessim out, call for elections, and attempt to face the crisis as a united nation. Before the end of October Sidqi, who was personally incensed with Nessim for having abrogated the 1930 Constitution, gave a lead by calling for a united front of all political parties. A few days later Egyptian political opinion of all shades was incensed by a cabled extract from an article in the London *Times* which stated, *inter alia*, that 'British official circles would consider it a great tragedy should Egypt try to take advantage of the present situation to obtain commitments and undertakings'. On 7 November Sidqi's appeal for a united front was reinforced by Mahmud Pasha, who attacked Nessim Pasha for subservience to Great Britain and called for treaty negotiations with a view to defining the respective responsibilities of Great Britain and Egypt in the not unlikely event of war in the Mediterranean. The tragedy which British official circles deprecated so much appeared to have begun.

Sir Samuel Hoare, the British Foreign Secretary, then made a speech at the Guildhall during the course of which he took it upon himself to make some deprecating remarks about the 1923 Constitution, combined with some advice to Egypt about the future conduct of her internal affairs. Whether these references to Egypt were motivated by tactless ignorance or by some Machiavellian design is uncertain. The immediate results of the speech were an outbreak of anti-British rioting in Alexandria, the issue of a joint statement by Nahas, Mahmud, Sidqi and Yehia in which Nessim was again denounced for subservience to Great Britain, and a petition to the King, signed by the same four politicians, calling for the restoration of the 1923 Constitution, which had been suddenly and unexpectedly sanctified by the strictures of Sir Samuel Hoare. But Sir Samuel had not finished with Egypt yet. In another speech made on 5 December he stressed that the British Government was much too occupied with the international crisis to consider any question of a treaty with Egypt. This second speech was no less instantaneous in its effects. Nahas, Mahmud, Sidqi, and Yehia, who now styled themselves the 'United Front', called upon the High Commissioner and impressed upon him the desirability of opening treaty negotiations. This *démarche* was accompanied by a statement that a United Front government (that is to say a government including Nahas, Mahmud, Sidqi, and Yehia as its leading members) would be prepared to conclude a treaty on the lines of the draft treaty negotiated between Mr. Henderson and Nahas Pasha in 1930. In the meantime, Sir Samuel Hoare had been compelled to resign from office as a result of the abortive Hoare-Laval Pact, and the Foreign Office was free to take advantage of the initiative which had been offered by the Egyptian 'United Front'. The British Government announced that they were prepared to fix an early date for opening negotiations on the lines indicated by the Egyptian opposition leaders. Nessim Pasha, who was being pursued by a particularly vindictive form of personal attack,[8] thereupon resigned office. Nahas Pasha was invited to form a coalition government, but refused to do so, thereby effectually disposing of any suggestion that his adherence to the United Front had been dictated by other than opportunist motives. An interim Government was therefore formed (January 1936) by Ali Pasha Maher, and preparations started for the holding of elections. Ali Maher was regarded as being an adherent of the Palace; for a time it appeared as if the centrifugal tendencies always present in Egyptian politics were about to assert themselves, to destroy the United Front and bring about a condition of political stalemate which could only be resolved either by British intervention or by a head-on collision between the Palace and the Wafd. But the danger was averted and an all-party Egyptian treaty delegation was announced on 13 February. Negotiations started in Cairo at the beginning of March between the Egyptian Delegation and the British Delegation led by the High Commissioner, Sir Miles Lampson. The British Government had already made it clear that they accepted the 1930 draft treaty as the basis of negotiations, but that they would require some modifications in the military clauses of that draft.

The negotiations made slow progress, and on 7 April were adjourned for Easter. There were strong undercurrents in Egyptian political life working in opposition to the conclusion of a treaty. The Palace was by tradition Italophil; King Fuad had spent most of his early years in Italy, where his father, Ismail, had been in exile. The conclusion of a treaty with Great Britain in the then state of her strained relations with Italy was repugnant to those public men who had been brought up in the Palace tradition. Apart from this, Nahas was anxious, for reasons of prestige, to spin out the negotiations until after the elections in May, which he expected would return him to power as Prime Minister.

Such was the situation when, in the middle of April, King Fuad, who had been gravely ill for some time, died, leaving as his heir and successor his only son, Faruq, who was a minor. Almost immediately after the King's death the elections were held, and the Wafd was returned with a large majority. Ali Maher resigned and Nahas became Prime Minister of an entirely Wafdist Cabinet. Nahas was now master of the situation. The long struggle between the Palace and the Wafd was temporarily resolved in favour of the latter, owing to the fact that the Regency Council was appointed by the Government. With a large majority at his back and the Palace under his control, Nahas could do what he liked.

Another factor, too, was operating in favour of a treaty. It had by this time become apparent that there was no immediate danger of war between Great Britain and Italy, and that Mussolini was going to become firmly established in his East African empire. This factor both diminished the immediate danger and increased the ultimate advantage, from Egypt's point of view, of a firm understanding with Great Britain. On a long view, the only alternative to an alliance with England was domination by Mussolini's Italy. For once Egyptian politicians were brought hard up against the realities of the international situation. They had to choose between Great Britain and Italy, and there was no question of hedging on the choice. Gently but inexorably, the position was brought home to the Egyptian negotiators. With the example of Abyssinia in front of them, and with the influence of the Italophil Palace temporarily in abeyance, there could only be one choice.

NOTES TO CHAPTER TWELVE

1. The following is a family tree showing the principal descendants of Mohamed Ali:

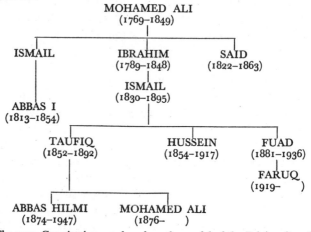

2. The 1923 Constitution was based on the model of the Belgian Constitution. There was a Chamber of Deputies elected in two stages by adult male suffrage, and an elected Senate. No major Government decisions were legal until ratified both by the Senate and the Chamber of Deputies. The principal difference between the 1923 and the 1930 Constitutions was that the Senate

under the 1930 Constitution was partly nominated and had greater powers in comparison with the Chamber than was the case under the 1923 Constitution.

3. The part played in Egyptian politics by the students has already been commented on. The Wafd, when in opposition, invariably used students for political demonstrations, and it became the habit of political parties to compete with each other for the support of the student bodies. Politicians in power not unnaturally found it difficult to rein enthusiasm which they had excited when in opposition. The effect of student politics both on education and on public order was disastrous. Political action was not confined to the secular students; the theological students of al-Azhar frequently indulged in political demonstrations.

4. The Parquet is a sort of Public Prosecutor's office which is attached to every *markaz* or district. It is independent of the police and under the control of the Minister of Justice. The investigation of a crime and the preparation of a charge, which in England would be entrusted to the police, is in Egypt (and in France) handed over to the Parquet after the preliminary investigation, or *procès-verbale*.

5. Ibrashi's principal preoccupation was the augmentation of the royal estates. Land was sold to the King for nominal sums in return for titles and decorations, water was diverted from certain lands in order to force their owners to sell. During the course of his reign, and particularly during the latter part of it, King Fuad amassed a very large fortune by methods which caused a good deal of resentment.

6. Previously British Minister in China. Now Lord Killearn.

7. General Elections in Great Britain, which were held at this time, resulted in the 'National' Government again being returned to power. Sir Samuel Hoare again became Foreign Secretary, until he was replaced soon after the elections by Mr. Eden, who was Foreign Secretary at the time of the signing of the Treaty.

8. It was alleged, on the evidence of a *mésalliance* which he had contracted, that he was insane and incapable of managing his private affairs.

CHAPTER THIRTEEN

THE 1936 TREATY

THE provisions of the 1936 Treaty (see Appendix III) can be summarized under the three headings: (*a*) Military, (*b*) Sudan, and (*c*) Capitulations.

Military. The British military occupation of Egypt was replaced by a military alliance of twenty years' duration, under which Great Britain was conceded the right, subject to certain limitations and conditions, of maintaining armed forces on Egyptian territory both in peace and in war. The peacetime strength of the British Army in Egypt was limited to 10,000 men, to be stationed within an area defined in the Treaty, consisting of a strip of land on either side of the Suez Canal. The Royal Air Force was given the freedom of the skies over Egypt, and the right to construct and maintain a number of aerodromes in the Canal Zone; the Royal Navy was conceded the use of Alexandria Harbour for a period of eight years. The Egyptian Government agreed to provide barracks for British troops in the Canal Zone, and to build certain specified roads to facilitate the deployment of British troops from the Canal Zone in the event of war. In such an event, the Egyptian Government agreed to provide 'all the facilities and assistance in her power, including the use of ports, aerodromes and means of communication'. In return, the British Government undertook to defend Egypt from invasion and to provide equipment and technical assistance for the Egyptian armed forces.

Sudan. The Anglo-Egyptian Convention of 1899 was confirmed, and both parties affirmed that 'the primary aim of their administration in the Sudan must be the welfare of the Sudanese'. Egyptian as well as British troops were to be placed at the disposal of the Governor-General for the defence of the Sudan,[1] and Egyptian immigration to the Sudan was to be unlimited except 'for reasons of public order and health'.[2]

Capitulations. The British Government agreed to use its influence for the speedy abolition of the Capitulations in Egypt so as to provide for 'the disappearance of any restrictions on Egyptian sovereignty in the matter of the application of Egyptian legislation (including financial legislation) to foreigners', and for the establishment of a transitional régime 'for a reasonable and not unduly prolonged period . . . during which the Mixed Tribunals will remain and will, in addition to their present judicial jurisdiction, exercise the jurisdiction at present exercised by the Consular Courts'.[3] Great Britain was unable, of her own motion, to terminate either the Capitulations treaties or the régime of the mixed courts, but, as the result of consultations with the interested powers, was able to give satisfactory assurances to the Egyptian Government that no obstacle would be raised by the other powers against the abolition of the Capitulations and the mixed courts, in the event of the signature of a treaty between Egypt and Great Britain. Since Great Britain, as the result of the projected treaty, would no longer be responsible for the protection of foreign interests in Egypt, and since Great Britain would also be pledged to defend Egypt from foreign invasion, the powers had in fact no option but to acquiesce in the abandonment of privileges which could only be maintained either by the fact of British occupation or by the threat of European intervention.

The duration of the Treaty was for twenty years, but it was provided that, with the consent of both parties, negotiations for revision could be entered into at any time after the expiry of ten years after the signature of the Treaty. If at the end of twenty years the parties were unable to agree on the necessity or otherwise of the continued presence of British forces in Egypt, the question was to be referred to the League of Nations for a decision.

The Treaty was well received in Egypt. Two days after its signature and publication (26 August 1936) British troops were cheered in the streets of Alexandria, an event for which there was probably no precedent in Anglo-Egyptian relations. The Prime Minister, Nahas Pasha, received an ovation on his return to Egypt from London. The Treaty was ratified in the Egyptian Parliament by 202 votes to 11 (and in the British Houses of Parliament without a division). These events were indicative not so much of popular enthusiasm as of the temporary political ascendancy of Nahas Pasha. Domestic events in Egypt during the previous twelve months had secured Nahas Pasha against accusations of treason; for the time being, nobody had either the power or the will to organize opposition to the Government. There was therefore no counterblast to the enthusiasm for the Treaty organized by the Wafd.[4]

On the merits of the case, both parties to the Treaty had solid reasons for satisfaction. Great Britain had secured her strategic requirements and the maintenance, to all intents and purposes, of the *status quo* in the Sudan. Egypt had secured a guarantee of the full sovereign rights which had previously been denied to her by reason of the Capitulations and of Great Britain's retention of the right of protecting foreign interests. It was nevertheless true that Egypt had secured nothing which she could not have secured at any time during the previous ten years had domestic circumstances been propitious, and a good deal less than had been claimed for her by nationalist politicians from Zaghlul onwards. Of the four points reserved in the 1922 Declaration, one—the protection of foreigners and minorities[5]—had been conceded by Great Britain, but the other three—Imperial communications, the Sudan, and the defence of Egypt—had been conceded by Egypt to Great Britain. The international situation in Europe and the domestic situation in Egypt combined for the time being to stifle criticism, but it was clear that the Treaty would not in Egypt be regarded indefinitely as a final and satisfactory settlement of accounts with Great Britain.

However, for the time being all was jubilation and self-congratulation. In accordance with the terms of the Treaty, Great Britain sponsored, and secured the success of, Egypt's application for membership of the League of Nations. In January 1937 Egypt invited the Capitulatory powers to a Conference at Montreux in order to discuss the abolition of the Capitulations as provided for in the Treaty. The Conference opened in April. All went smoothly. The Capitulatory privileges which had hamstrung Egyptian administration for so long were abolished by a stroke of the pen, and foreign residents in Egypt descended overnight from a position of enviable, sought-after, and tax-free privilege to the status of aliens. This status was tempered by the following modifications:

(a) The Egyptian Government undertook that legislation applied to foreigners would not be inconsistent with the principles generally adopted in modern legislation, and would not be discriminatory against foreigners or foreign companies.

(b) It was agreed that for a transitional period of twelve years the mixed courts would both continue to adjudicate in 'mixed interest' cases[6] and take over the jurisdiction of the consular courts in criminal cases affecting foreigners. It was further agreed that for the same period the consular courts should continue to adjudicate on matters of personal status affecting their own nationals. At the end of the transitional period of twelve years it was provided that the judicial powers of the mixed courts and consular courts should pass in their entirety to the Egyptian national courts.

The Montreux Convention, which embodied these agreements, came into effect on 1 October 1937, and marked the end of the long period of international control with which Egypt had been burdened.

The military alliance with Great Britain and the recognition of the condominium in the Sudan was the price which

Egypt had to pay for the sovereignty conferred on her by the Montreux Conference. Egypt conceded to Great Britain that which she could not for the moment obtain in return for an advantage which she could only secure through British influence. Times had changed during the fifty-five years of the British occupation of Egypt and, in 1937, there was no European power which had both the power and the will to oppose whatever disposition Great Britain might choose to make for the future of Egypt. The 1936 Treaty, like any other treaty, was based on the reality of power. Great Britain was able, by reason of her armed forces and of her strategic position in the Middle East,[7] to continue to occupy Egypt and the Sudan in spite of Egypt's wishes, to defend Egypt with or without her assistance, and to compel the powers to relinquish their Capitulatory privileges in Egypt. Great Britain's acknowledged ability to do these things, combined with the position of domestic affairs in Egypt and of international affairs in the eastern Mediterranean, induced the Egyptian Government of the day to acquiesce in the temporary unavailability of one half of the loaf to which they aspired in return for effective possession of the other half.

The 1936 Treaty was forced on Egypt in so far as it reflected the relative strength of the pressures which Great Britain and Egypt could bring to bear on each other. It was obvious that the Treaty would cease to be effective if and when the relation between these pressures altered in favour of Egypt. The effective duration of the Treaty—in so far as the military and Sudan clauses were concerned—was determined by this fact of power rather than by the twenty-year period laid down in the Treaty.

The 1936 Treaty marks the end of that epoch in Anglo-Egyptian relations which opened with the bombardment of Alexandria in 1882. By the 1922 Declaration Great Britain had handed the internal administration of Egypt over to the representatives of the people of Egypt. But she remained responsible for the protection of foreign interests in Egypt, and the British Army of Occupation continued in its old role as protector of foreign interests as well as carrying out its newer role of defending imperial communications. The turbulence of the years immediately preceding the Declaration, the inexperience of the Egyptian administration, and the weight of British official and foreign commercial opinion in Egypt would have made it impossible for Great Britain in 1922 to propose, or for the other European powers to accept, any arrangement which would have involved leaving foreign interests in Egypt without foreign legal and military protection. It therefore happened that the Residency, in the exercise of its function of guarantor and guardian of Capitu·latory privileges, continued after 1922 to exert a considerable, though gradually diminishing, influence in Egyptian domestic affairs. The extent of that influence was conditioned both by the personality of the British High Commissioner and by the degree of responsibility exercised by the Egyptian Government of the day. Thus, after the departure of Lord Lloyd and the temporary eclipse of the Wafd, the scope and frequency of British intervention rapidly declined. Nevertheless, the High Commissioner, with the British Army at his back, remained the real power in the country, without whose acquiescence no major step could be taken.

But this power was regarded by successive British Governments, not as a privilege to be maintained, but as a burden which they were anxious to lay down in exchange for suitable arrangements for securing British strategic interests in Egypt. We have described the various attempts which were made to negotiate a treaty during the nineteen-twenties. These attempts were motivated on the British side by a desire to escape from a troublesome commitment without relinquishing control of the Suez Canal or of the Sudan. There was no immediate danger of war, and therefore no immediate necessity to arrive at an understanding with Egypt. After the fall of the Wafd in 1930, Sidqi Pasha and his successors had no desire to stoke the fires of Egyptian nationalism by the discussion of controversial matters with Great Britain, and the British Government, for its part, was well content with a situation in which foreign interests were unmolested and the British occupation unchallenged. But Mussolini's East African adventure and the contemporaneous revival of Egyptian nationalism destroyed the precarious tranquillity which had becalmed Anglo-Egyptian relations for the previous five years. Great Britain was faced with the immediate possibility of having to use Egypt as a base for a large-scale war in the Mediterranean. From being potentially important, Egypt's strategic position became immediately vital. At the same time it became clear that Egypt could not again be used as she had been in the 1914–18 War. It was desirable, if possible, to secure Egypt's free consent to and co-operation with any campaign which might have to be fought on or from Egyptian territory.

The 1936 Treaty was concluded under the shade of Mussolini. Although the prospect of an immediate war over Abyssinia had receded by the time the Treaty was signed, the British attitude towards the Treaty was dominated by the necessity of providing herself with the means (a) of securing a base for attacking both Libya and Italian East Africa, and (b) of severing communications between Italy and Italian East Africa. For this purpose, it was essential not only to have military control of both Egypt and the Sudan, but to secure a friendly and co-operative population in both these countries. The importance of protecting foreign interests in Egypt dwindled into insignificance beside the attainment of these objectives, particularly as the previous thirteen years had provided reasonably sufficient evidence of Egyptian ability to maintain an adequate level of security and justice within her territory.

On the Egyptian side, Mussolini's prospective triumph in Abyssinia provided almost equally cogent reasons for a settlement with Great Britain. It was apparent that the only immediate alternative to a British occupation was an Italian one. It was also apparent that the British would not leave Egypt unless ejected by the Italians, and that the only way to get rid of the British was therefore to assist the Italians in

306

substituting themselves for the British. This would have subjected Egypt to war, with the alternative of Italian gratitude or British vengeance at the end of it. By a graceful acceptance of continued British protection, Egypt was able to secure both a limitation of the scope of military occupation and the termination of the last vestiges of international control.

As a result of the Treaty, the British position in Egypt was for the first time defined and regularized by an alliance concluded with Egypt. For this reason, the Treaty did, in a real sense, mark the end of the British occupation. The 1922 Declaration had been a unilateral act by Great Britain which had modified, without fundamentally changing, the relations between the conqueror and the conquered. The 1936 Treaty was a negotiated agreement to which Egypt was a free and consenting party.

We have seen how, from the beginning of the twentieth century onwards, strategic considerations gradually replaced the original reasons for which Great Britain had occupied Egypt in 1882. The period from 1922 to 1936 was, from Great Britain's point of view, by way of an experiment to demonstrate whether strategic control of a country was compatible with that country's administrative independence. Such a combination was, at that time, a new departure in Imperial policy, a leap in the dark, taken with reluctance, attended with misgivings, and qualified with reservations. Lord Lloyd was obviously sceptical of the success of the experiment, and did all he could to limit the scope of its application. But on the whole it worked. Egypt learnt to manage her own affairs to an extent which convinced Great Britain that the lives and property of foreign residents, on the one hand, and the strategic dispositions of British forces, on the other, would not adversely be affected by Egypt's assumption of full sovereign independence.

The significance of the period 1922–36 lies in the growth of confidence: the growth of Egyptian self-confidence by which she was enabled, in her negotiations with Great

Britain, to substitute constructive statesmanship for sterile agitation; the growth of British confidence in Egypt by which she was enabled to assume the preservation of internal security in Egypt without reserving to herself the option of interfering in Egypt's internal affairs; the growth of European confidence in Egypt by which the Capitulatory powers were enabled without protest to consent to the abandonment of their jealously-guarded Capitulatory privileges in Egypt; and, lastly, the growth of Egyptian confidence in Great Britain which enabled Egypt voluntarily, if temporarily, to abandon the concept of 'struggle' against Great Britain in favour of the concept of alliance with Great Britain.

This growth of confidence was almost entirely a product of the last seven years of the fourteen-year period between the 1922 Declaration and the 1936 Treaty. The conditions were created first by the death of Zaghlul in 1927 and then by the departure of Lord Lloyd in 1929. It is doubtful whether any policy other than that followed by Lord Lloyd would have succeeded during Zaghlul's life-time. Zaghlul was too wedded to the concept of 'struggle' to have abandoned the policy of hostility to Great Britain on which he had climbed to power and fame. After Zaghlul's death the rivalry between the Palace and the Wafd became more of an even contest, with the result that each vied with the other in courting the favour of Great Britain. The régime in Egypt from 1929 to 1935 was unpopular with Egyptian nationalists at the time, and has not been regarded by them with any enthusiasm in retrospect. But this régime, unwittingly, perhaps, performed a useful service for Egyptian nationalism. It kept Egypt quiet and justified Great Britain's new policy, adopted after Lord Lloyd's departure, of non-intervention in Egypt's internal affairs. Thus it came about that the struggle for internal power in Egypt, which in the nineteen-twenties had been a competition in resistance to Great Britain, became in the nineteen-thirties a competition in reasonableness towards Great Britain. From the point of view of idealist nationalism, this may have been unsatisfactory; from the point of view of practical nationalist achievement, it proved more immediately fruitful than the years of agitation.

NOTES ON CHAPTER THIRTEEN

1. Egyptian troops had been removed from the Sudan after the assassination of Sir Lee Stack in 1924 (see Chapter XI).

2. This question of free Egyptian immigration into the Sudan had been the ostensible cause of the breakdown of the Henderson-Nahas negotiations in 1930 (see Chapter XII).

3. That is to say, the trial of foreigners on criminal charges. Matters of personal status affecting foreigners were reserved to the consular courts during the transitional period.

4. The anniversary of the signature of the Treaty was for some years celebrated as a public holiday. A set of stamps was also issued to commemorate the signature of the Treaty.

5. The minorities to which this reservation was intended to apply consisted mainly of the Egyptian Copts and other Egyptian Christians.

6. 'Mixed interest' cases included both cases where a foreigner was one of the parties to a suit and cases where a matter affecting foreign interests was involved, although both parties to the suit might be Egyptians. It sometimes happened that Egyptian litigants would plead a 'mixed interest' in order to get a case tried by the mixed rather than by the national tribunals.

7. Henceforward the term Middle East, which came into general use during the Second German War, will be used in this book to include approximately those territories from Iran in the east to Egypt in the west and from Turkey in the north to the Sudan in the south.

CHAPTER FOURTEEN

THE SECOND GERMAN WAR

ALMOST exactly three years elapsed between the signature of the Treaty on 26 August 1936 and the outbreak of war between Great Britain and Germany on 3 September 1939. During these three years the most important immediate effect of the Treaty was derived from the fiscal freedom conferred on Egypt by the abolition of the Capitulations. Under the Capitulatory régime the direct taxation of foreigners was only possible as the result of the unanimous agreement of the Capitulatory powers to such taxation. In practice, the preliminary negotiations involved meant not only that no direct taxation was imposed on foreigners,[1] but also that no direct taxation was imposed on Egyptians either, since public opinion would not have tolerated a tax which Egyptians had to pay, but from which foreigners were immune. Consequently, Government revenue was confined to the proceeds of indirect taxation, of which Customs duties and dues formed easily the largest proportion. (Until 1934 Egypt's freedom even in this respect had been curtailed by the existence of a reciprocal Customs agreement with Great Britain.) The pattern of indirect taxation which had thus been imposed on Egypt was a very vicious one, since it made it impossible to correct by direct taxation the increasing disparity between riches and poverty which accompanied the progressive increase in Egypt's agricultural productivity. The fiscal freedom conferred by the Montreux Convention was soon taken advantage of by the introduction of taxes on personal incomes, and on commercial and professional profits. But technical inexperience in the assessment and collection of direct taxes, together with the resistance of the politically powerful agricultural landlords, led to widespread evasion, and the pattern of taxation imposed by the Capitulations has not, since their abolition, been successfully adapted in accordance either with Egypt's financial resources or with her social needs.[2]

The financial effect of Egypt's new freedom was thus less marked than it might have been. The social effects, although masked and retarded by the war, were in the long run far more important. Under the Capitulations the large population of Levantines—Italians, Greeks, Syrians, Jews, and so on—permanently resident in Egypt had no incentive to Egyptianize either themselves or their businesses. To be a foreigner was to be a privileged person; those who had no foreign nationality tried to acquire it. Egyptians who had no foreign connexions sought to obtain them. Foreign businesses employed their own compatriots in responsible positions, and the possibilities of responsible employment for Egyptians were largely confined to Government service. The levers of influence were in foreign hands; if a foreigner, or even an Egyptian, wanted anything done, or undone; if he wanted injustice corrected or justice diverted; if he wanted pressure brought to bear, he still looked automatically towards the Residency.[3] After 1937 all that was changed. Foreign nationality was no longer a privilege; it was a liability. Instead of Egyptians seeking for foreign connexions, it became necessary for foreigners to seek for Egyptian connexions. Foreigners permanently domiciled in Egypt came to realize the necessity for regarding themselves and for being regarded as Egyptians, and for assimilating themselves to the country of their adoption. For the first time since the age of the Pharaohs, Egyptian nationality ceased to be a badge of inferiority; and Egyptians, instead of courting foreigners, began to be courted by them. The reality, as well as the appearance of power, had shifted from the British to the Egyptians.

Meanwhile, the position of the British forces in Egypt remained to all intents and purposes in *statu quo ante* the 1936

311

Treaty. Withdrawal to the Canal Zone, as provided in the Treaty, was contingent on the construction of barracks in the Canal Zone by the Egyptian Government.[4] When war broke out in September 1939 British forces were still occupying Abbasiya, Qasr-al-Nil, Helmieh, Citadel, Mustafa, Heliopolis, Helwan, Abuqir and other camps and air stations in and around Cairo and Alexandria.

So long as the young King remained a minor, the old rivalry between the Wafd and the Palace necessarily remained in abeyance. When he became of age in 1937 and the Regency came to an end, political life in Egypt soon reverted to the old pattern. Immediately and inevitably, the Palace began to exert its attraction upon those elements and personalities in Egyptian public life who, for one reason and another, were dissatisfied with the Wafdist Government. At the time of the signature of the Treaty Nahas had been at the height of his power and influence. The terms of the Treaty had been agreed to by an all-party delegation which not only made ratification of the Treaty by an overwhelming majority certain, but also secured the Government against any subsequent accusation of treason. He was at the head of a party which had just won a decisive victory at the polls; the Palace was under his effective control; his party was united; there was no effective opposition; he was lauded as the architect of a Treaty by which Egypt's sovereign independence was recognized among the nations. Within fifteen months all was changed. The Treaty was no longer popular; the Party was split; the Palace had become the centre of active opposition to the Government. At the end of 1937 Nahas, faced with the hostility of the Palace, with disaffection within the Government, and disillusionment in the country, resigned office. The wave of nationalist and constitutional enthusiasm which had swept the Wafd into power in the spring of 1936 had exhausted itself; Nahas had succumbed to the operation of that centrifugal force which always operates so powerfully in the public life of a country where personalities are more important than policies and personal jealousies more powerful than party loyalties.

Nahas Pasha's successor as Prime Minister was the old Liberal-Constitutional statesman, Mohamed Mahmud, who took office at the head of a coalition Government consisting of Liberals, Saadists (a new party of dissident Wafdists under the leadership of Ahmed Pasha Maher), and Independents. The new Government confirmed its position at a General Election held in April 1938, when the Wafd was heavily defeated. In the same way as ten years previously, this 'constitutional' Government proved to be a halfway stage towards a return to Palace rule, now represented by Aly Pasha Maher, brother of Ahmed Maher and Chief of the Royal Cabinet. In August 1939, when it was apparent that a European war was all but inevitable, Mahmud Pasha, old and in failing health, resigned, and Aly Maher became Prime Minister of a Government of Saadists and Independents, from which the Liberals were excluded.

On the outbreak of war the new Government unhesitatingly fulfilled its Treaty obligations towards Great Britain. Martial law was declared and diplomatic relations broken off with Germany. The Prime Minister issued a statement associating Egypt with Great Britain's war effort.

Egypt's international position remained anomalous in that, although by the terms of the Treaty she was allied with Great Britain and had placed her resources at the disposal of Great Britain, she was not officially at war with Germany. Since she could not, in the circumstances, claim the privileges and immunities or undertake the functions of neutrality, the only practical difference between the existing state of affairs and a state of war was that the Egyptian armed forces were not committed to active hostilities against Germany. Although the point was for the time being academic, there was, inevitably, discussion and dissension, both publicly in the Press and privately in the Cabinet, about the pros and cons of a declaration of war. Essentially, the advantages and disadvantages could be quite simply stated. If Egypt declared war, her military contribution, over and above what she was already making, would not provide any important accretion of strength to the Allies, and could not in any case affect the ultimate issue. This was recognized by the British Government, which did not press Egypt for a declaration of war. If the Allies won, such a declaration would give Egypt a right to a seat at the Conference table by the side of the victors and a share in the spoils of victory. But if the Allies lost, such a declaration would expose Egypt to the vengeance of the enemy, whereas if Egypt made no such declaration she would be able to plead that she was a country held in military occupation by Great Britain against her will. Those who opposed a declaration of war pointed out that Egypt had everything to lose and nothing to gain by such a declaration, since any concessions which Egypt might be able to wring from Great Britain in the event of an Allied victory would not be dependent on whether or not Egypt declared war. Those who supported a declaration of war asserted that Egypt, by the 1936 Treaty, stood or fell with Great Britain in any event, whether she liked it or not and, unable to escape the consequences of an alliance with Great Britain in the event of an allied defeat, should make certain of realizing the full advantages of such an alliance in the event of an Allied victory.

Italy's entry into the war in the summer of 1940 sharpened the urgency of the problem at the same time as the German victories in Europe reinforced the arguments of those who were opposed to a declaration of war. In the event, Egypt broke off diplomatic relations with Italy as well as with Germany, but declared war on neither country, even after Egyptian territory had been invaded, first by Italian, and later by German, armies.

It is doubtful whether Egypt's decision, persisted in until the last few weeks of the war, had any effect on the course of hostilities. On the one hand, Italo-German restraint in the aerial bombardment of Egypt was dictated neither by respect for international law nor by the fear of an Egyptian declaration of war; on the other hand, the course of the war in the

Western Desert would not have been affected by such armed assistance as Egypt would have been able to provide.

Whether or not Egypt declared war on the Axis powers, it was clear that Egypt could only be defended and the British position in the Middle East secured by a more or less complete subordination of Egyptian policies to the British war machine. The threat of invasion, together with the situation created by the German victories in Europe, not unnaturally placed a great strain on Egyptian loyalty to the 1936 Treaty. The position was a delicate one. On the one hand, no Egyptian Government could afford to defy the British, who were in effective occupation of Egypt. On the other hand, with the war going as badly as it was for the Allies, and with the imminent possibility of exchanging a British for an Italian occupation, Egyptian politicians were pardonably reluctant to make themselves conspicuous for collaboration with Great Britain. Even the normal allurements of office were barely sufficient to counterbalance the difficulties and dangers of effecting a reconciliation between the necessities of the present and the possibilities of the future.

In these circumstances, a heavy responsibility rested on the shoulders of the young King Faruq and his advisers. In order to ensure the maintenance of the dynasty in Egypt, it was necessary, first, to retain popular support by avoiding an appearance of undue subservience to Great Britain; secondly, to avoid provoking British hostility by undue resistance to British wishes; and, thirdly, to avoid identification with British interests in the eyes of the Axis powers, who might at any time supplant Great Britain in Egypt. The performance of this delicate and difficult feat of tight-rope walking was complicated by the existence of the Wafdist opposition, which was still able to command a majority of votes in the Senate. Nahas Pasha, always more astute in opposition than in power, was looking for an opportunity to turn the changes and chances of war to political account.

In April 1940, some weeks before Italy entered the war, the Wafd had presented a memorandum to the British

Ambassador protesting against the Emergency Regulations, which had been promulgated at the British instance, and in particular against the control of cotton exports, which had also been introduced at the British request and which was exceedingly unpopular with the Egyptian landowners. The memorandum went on to ask for a guarantee that British forces would be evacuated from Egypt at the end of the war, that Egypt would participate in the Peace Conference, and that Great Britain would, at the end of the war, recognize Egypt's sovereignty over the Sudan. This memorandum, coming as it did from an opposition party, was rejected by the British Embassy, but its publication served to bring the Wafd into the limelight as the guardians of Egypt's national aspirations.

In June 1940, immediately after Italy's entry into the war, open disagreement between the Prime Minister and the British authorities made it necessary for the Palace either to come into direct collision with the British or to dismiss Aly Maher. Another Coalition Government was formed with the Independent Hassan Pasha Sabri as Prime Minister.

Egyptian willingness to co-operate with Great Britain naturally ebbed and flowed with the fortunes of war. The Battle of Britain, the German failure to invade Great Britain, Wavell's victories in the Western Desert, and the successful Abyssinian campaign all contributed to reduction of political tension in Egypt during the winter of 1940–1. In the spring of 1941 the effect of the German invasion of the Balkans was counterbalanced, as far as Egyptian official and public opinion was concerned, by the swift and successful British occupation of Syria and Iraq. Whatever might be the case in Europe, in the Middle East Great Britain was still able to protect her friends and to punish her enemies.

The German invasion of Russia in May 1941 may be taken as the starting-point of a train of circumstances in Egypt which led to the British *coup d'état* of February 1942. Militarily, it was obvious that a Russian defeat would jeopardize the whole British position in the Middle East, and would lead either to a British abandonment of the Middle East or to savage warfare in the Middle East. Ideologically, the fact of an Anglo-Russian alliance, together with the increasingly socialist sympathies of popular opinion in England and the 'left-wing' character of the nascent resistance movements in Europe, caused the Egyptian ruling class to regard the possibility of an Anglo-Russian victory as only slightly, if at all, less disturbing than the possibility of an Anglo-Russian defeat. Other things being equal, nearly all educated Egyptians would, up to May 1941, have pre-ferred a British to a German victory. For perhaps a year after May 1941 there was a section of Egyptian public opinion which regarded a German victory as the lesser of two evils.

The prevalence and growth of this feeling in Palace and Government circles almost automatically produced an equal and opposite reaction in the ranks of the Wafdist opposition. Nahas Pasha and the Wafd had little to hope for from an Axis victory. Nahas himself had been the principal architect of the 1936 Treaty; he had not overtly or covertly yielded to the temptation of intriguing with the Axis Powers either before or during the war. In the event of an Axis victory, the Wafd had no chance of outbidding the Palace for the favour of the Axis powers. Ideologically, Nahas had less difficulty than his opponents in subscribing to the war aims of the Allies; in practice, all of the Wafd's domestic battles had been fought in defence of the Constitution and free elections; in theory, the Wafd had always stood for demo-cratic government and the rights of the common man. On the long view, the survival of the constitutional principles for which the Wafd stood was compatible only with the defeat of the Axis; on a short view, the only possibility of an early return to power was by exploiting the widening rift between the coalition Government and the British authorities.

The equivocal attitude of the Egyptian Government was giving the British increasing cause for concern. The new threat developing from the north, the growing German strength in Libya, the increasing flow of British soldiers and arms to Egypt via the Red Sea, and the new war in the Far East which started in December 1941 with the Japanese attack on Pearl Harbour, all enhanced the vital importance of Egypt as a military base. A complete identity of view between the British and Egyptian authorities was, more than ever, an essential condition of the successful prosecution of the war in the Middle East. Reluctance openly to intervene in Egyptian internal affairs was overcome by what was regarded at the time as the overwhelming necessity of war. In January 1942 Lord Killearn, the British Ambassador, urgently requested King Faruq to dismiss Hussein Pasha Sirry (Prime Minister in succession to Hassan Pasha Sabry, who had died in office during 1941) and his Government, and to call upon Nahas Pasha to form a Government in his stead. This request was finally acceded to on 2 February in face of a British threat to depose King Faruq by force and install a Government of their own choosing. Sirry Pasha and his Government departed, and Nahas Pasha became Prime Minister at the head of a Wafdist Government.

The hesitation of the Palace in acceding to the British demand was only partly motivated by personal and political objections to Nahas Pasha. From the point of view both of internal prestige and of possible future relations with the Axis it was far less undesirable to have capitulated to force than to have voluntarily accepted British dictation. By resisting to the last moment, and then yielding, the young King successfully fulfilled the essential wartime requirements of Palace policy.

On a short view, Nahas had won a resounding victory over his political opponents; on a long view, his position was a good deal less favourable. Even on the assumption of an Allied victory, the circumstances of his taking office had presented his opponents with a deadly weapon to use against him as soon as British protection was withdrawn.

The British, for their part, had secured a Government in Egypt, the lives of whose members almost literally depended on an Allied victory, and which could therefore be relied on to co-operate whole-heartedly with the British war effort. It was not long before this co-operation was put to a severe test.

By the end of July 1942, the fortunes of the Allies were at their lowest ebb. In the Far East Hong-Kong, Singapore, the Dutch East Indies, and Malaya had fallen to the Japanese, and the British Navy had suffered the most grievous losses in capital ships. In Russia the Germans had overrun the Ukraine and were advancing into the Caucasus. In the Middle East, the British Army had been defeated in Libya, Tobruk had surrendered, and the Germans had advanced to within seventy miles of Alexandria. The British were making open preparations to evacuate Cairo and Alexandria. It is to the eternal credit of the Wafdist Government and the Egyptian people that they stood firm at this grim moment. Nahas and his colleagues had made their choice, and they stood to it like men.

It was not long before their confidence was signally vindicated. In October the victory of Alamein was won, and followed by a pursuit of the Germans by the British Eighth Army along the north coast of Africa to Tunisia. In Russia, the successful defence of Stalingrad, followed by a Russian counter-offensive and the withdrawal of the Germans from the Caucasus, extinguished the threat to Egypt from the north-east. The nutcrackers which had been closing on Egypt were broken. Contemporaneously with these allied victories in Russia and Libya, Anglo-American forces landed in Morocco and Algeria. It was apparent that the war was not only moving away from the Middle East, but that, with Russian resistance unbroken and Anglo-American strength mounting, the Allies were certain to win. Nahas Pasha had backed the right horse.

NOTES ON CHAPTER FOURTEEN

1. The only direct taxes imposed during the Capitulatory régime were the land tax, the house tax, and the *ghaffir* tax.

2. During the war, when material shortages occurred simultaneously with large British military expenditure, the lack of any effective machinery for direct

taxation greatly accentuated an inflationary situation. After the war this lack, combined with the inflationary effect of most of the indirect taxes imposed by the Government, has defeated the attempts of successive Egyptian governments to check the rising cost of living, and has prevented them from devoting other than derisory sums for social services.

3. After the 1936 Treaty the post of British High Commissioner was abolished and replaced by that of British Ambassador, and the Residency consequently became the British Embassy.

4. The provision of the Treaty by which the Egyptian Government was to provide barrack accommodation in the Canal Zone in exchange for the accommodation vacated by British troops in Cairo and Alexandria was severely and increasingly criticized in Egypt. In the event, barrack accommodation in the Canal Zone was provided by the British Government.

CHAPTER FIFTEEN

EGYPT AND THE ARAB LEAGUE

WITH the tide of war receding from the sands of the Middle East, men's minds naturally turned towards the future. Militarily, the events of 1939–42 had convinced the British Government, first, that strategic control of the Middle East would continue to be a vital element in British global strategy, and, secondly, that a base in Egypt was an all-but-essential condition of that strategic control. Politically, British diplomatic and administrative experience had convinced the British Government that this strategic object could only be achieved with the consent and, if possible, with the active co-operation of the people and governments of the Middle East.

With these ends in view, it became the object of Great Britain's Middle East policy to associate the British Government with the encouragement of political stability and with the promotion of economic development in the countries of the Middle East. These two aims were, of course, complementary, since the attainment of the one was an essential condition of the attainment of the other.

There were several specific obstacles and one general obstacle in the way of this attainment. Among the specific obstacles were Zionism, the political rearguard action which the French were fighting in the Levant States, and the territorial, dynastic, and personal rivalries which divided the numerous independent and semi-independent Arab states and principalities of the Middle East. The general obstacle was the difficulty of effectively influencing the countries of the Middle East without controlling them to an extent which would be politically impracticable.

The British Government proposed to try to overcome these difficulties by the encouragement of political, economic, and cultural co-operation and integration between the Arab states, and by the provision of economic assistance to various projects which would become feasible as the result of such co-operation and integration. It was reasonable to suppose that a league of Arab states acting together would have less fear of foreign domination, and less suspicion of foreign intentions than a collection of weak, disintegrated, and dis-contented states consumed with mutual rivalry and internal discord.

It was for many reasons inevitable that Egypt should be the leading partner in any effective league of Arab states. She was the wealthiest, most populous, most advanced technically, and generally the most powerful of the Arab states. Geographically and culturally, Egypt occupied the position of a bridge between Western Europe and the Arab world. Thus it was that the trend of British Middle East policy after the Battle of Alamein widened Egypt's political horizons until they included the whole of the Arab-speaking world, from the shores of the Atlantic to the waters of the Persian Gulf and from the edge of the Indian Ocean to the mountains of central Asia.

The two principal sponsors of Arab unity were Nahas Pasha, the Prime Minister of Egypt, and Nuri Pasha as-Said, the Prime Minister of Iraq. Both had obtained office as the result of British intervention,[1] and both were ambitious to enhance their positions in their own countries by building up a reputation for statesmanship in a wider field. It was fitting, therefore, that they should take the lead in initiating a policy which owed its inspiration to Great Britain,[2] and which would depend for its success on a widening of the horizons usually surveyed by Arab politicians.

In October 1944, after nearly two years of consultations, bargaining, and intrigue, and Arab Unity Conference, with delegates attending from all the Arab states, met in Alex-andria under the presidency of Nahas Pasha. While the idea of Arab unity was unexceptionable, there was in the minds of Arab rulers and governments a good deal of hesitancy about its practical application. In the first place there was a good deal of suspicion deriving from its British origin. In the second place, there was a good deal of jealousy about Egypt's assumption of leadership. In the third place, both Ibn Saud and the Syrian National Bloc suspected the motives of what appeared to be a British-inspired Wafdist-Hashemite combination. In the fourth place, the Lebanon, with its Christian majority, was not anxious to encourage a pan-Arab, which might in practice turn out to be a pan-Islamic movement. And so the Arab League, which emerged from the Alexandria Conference, was inaugurated with a good deal of mental reservation on the part of the signatories.

It is outside the scope of this book to trace the history or to try to assess the importance of the Arab League except in so far as it affected Anglo-Egyptian relations. The only important practical result of the Arab League, and the only important respect in which its existence affected Anglo-Egyptian relations, was the development of a common Arab policy towards Palestine, which culminated in May 1948 in a joint Arab invasion of the Jewish state of Israel.

Palestine was the one subject on which the rulers and governments of the Arab states were more or less united in opinion. Those who genuinely wished for Arab unity saw in Palestine the one immediately possible basis of common agreement on which to lay the foundations of such unity. Those who did not wish for Arab unity, but who realized the political necessity of making some gesture in favour of it, saw in Palestine the possibility of canalizing the activities of the Arab League into non-controversial channels. Willingness and ability to do anything about Palestine varied considerably, but in October 1944 the practical possibility of doing anything at all seemed sufficiently remote to justify unanimous agreement on a theoretical policy.

The Arab League, which had been envisaged by the British Government as the vehicle for the political integration and the economic rehabilitation of the Middle East, thus became nothing more than an Arab alliance against Zionism. Anti-Zionist zeal became the measure of Arab prestige; Arab rulers and governments became the creatures of their own propagandist utterances. During the next three years, the failure of the Arab states to agree upon any joint policy or to embark on any joint action over any matter other than Palestine inevitably resulted in Palestine assuming a disproportionate importance as being the linch-pin which held the Arab states together. The more they disagreed about other matters, the more necessary it became to preserve a façade of agreement about Palestine. For the preservation of a façade of Arab unity *vis-à-vis* the great powers was important to each of the Arab states, however little they might be disposed to construct a background of reality to that façade. Thus it happened that the interplay of rivalries within the framework of the Arab League took the form of competing for the patronage of the Arabs of Palestine, until what had been regarded by most of the participants as a familiar political game gradually assumed the lineaments of a reality which brought the Arab states into a war which none of them desired and for which none of them was prepared.

In spite of latent dissensions, the Arab League created sufficient of a stir in the world to make it an apparent factor to be reckoned with in post-war affairs.

One day after the signature of the Covenant of the Arab League, Nahas Pasha was dismissed from office in circumstances which will be related in the next chapter, and the Wafdist Government replaced by a Saadist Government, with Ahmed Pasha Maher as Prime Minister. The new Government did not intend that Nahas's removal should affect Egypt's claim to leadership of the Arab states, and King Faruq took the place of his ex-Prime Minister in the centre of the Arab stage.

The departure of Nahas from the scene marked, albeit almost imperceptibly, a change in the aims and objects of the Arab League as far as Egypt was concerned. Nahas Pasha had seen the Arab League primarily as an association of Arab politicians and Arab nationalist parties, as an instrument of propaganda and agitation for the promotion of Arab unity and Arab independence. After Nahas's departure, the emphasis shifted to the attainment and maintenance of the sovereign independence of each separate Arab state. Under the aegis of the heads of the Arab states, the Arab League tended to become a concert of Arabia mainly concerned with the maintenance of the *status quo*.

At the Alexandria Conference arrangements had been made for the formation of a permanent Arab League secretariat, with its headquarters in Cairo. An Egyptian, Abdel Rahman Azzam, was appointed Secretary-General. State visits were exchanged between King Faruq and Abdul Aziz Ibn Saud. Egypt and Saudi Arabia had for some time been estranged, and the principal object of these visits was to consolidate and publicize the resumption of amicable relations between the two countries. In the spring of 1946 King Faruq acted as host to the heads of the Arab states who assembled in Conference at Inshass, the King of Egypt's country residence. Interspersed with these state occasions were fairly regular meetings of the Prime Ministers and Foreign Ministers of the Arab states.

Meanwhile, the problem of Palestine was drifting towards its climax. The temporary settlement embodied in the British Government's 1939 White Paper had strictly limited Jewish immigration into Palestine, and had envisaged an ultimate situation in which both Arabs and Jews would acquiesce in the permanent existence of a semi-autonomous Jewish minority in a British-protected, predominantly Arab Palestine. It is possible that such a solution would have satisfied the Arabs of Palestine if it had been accompanied by more rapid steps towards Arab self-government in Palestine. But it was by no means acceptable to the Jews, who from 1939 onwards organized themselves to resist such a solution, and after the tide of war had receded from the

Middle East came out in open rebellion against the Mandatory Government.

By the middle of 1945 the situation in Palestine was as follows:

(*a*) The Arabs were demanding independence for an Arab Palestine, 'undivided and undiminished'.

(*b*) The Jews were demanding 'statehood' for a Jewish Palestine, 'undivided and undiminished'.

(*c*) The Arab claim was supported *in toto* by the Arab League, and the Jewish claim was supported in part by the U.S. Government.

The British Government dealt with the situation first by arranging for the appointment of an Anglo-American Commission to make recommendations for the future of Palestine, and then by handing over the problem to the United Nations. After the Committee appointed by the United Nations had issued a report recommending partition, the British Government announced their intention of withdrawing from Palestine. The date for the completion of the withdrawal was finally fixed for 15 May 1948. This decision was followed by a statement that no United Nations organization would be allowed to establish itself in Palestine until the British withdrawal had been completed. This was tantamount to a declaration that the Arabs and Jews would be left to fight it out between themselves.

During the three years between the end of the Second German War and the British withdrawal from Palestine, the Zionists had been fighting a guerrilla war against the British, and the Arab states had been awaiting an opportunity for effective intervention. The Arab League had been prevented from active intervention by the fact that such intervention would have brought them into conflict with the Mandatory power. When the Mandatory power announced its imminent withdrawal, the Arab League was faced with the necessity, or provided with the opportunity, of implementing its declarations and promises to the Arabs of

Palestine. Indeed it almost seemed as if the British Government were inviting them to do so.

The Zionists were well-organized and well-armed. The Palestine Arabs were ill-organized, ill-armed, and torn with internal dissensions. They could not, by any stretch of imagination, be considered capable of successfully resisting, let alone overcoming, the Zionists without the active intervention of the armed forces at the disposal of the Arab League. Of these forces, the most efficient and the most favourably placed for intervention was the Arab Legion, the British-trained national army of Transjordan. King Abdullah of Transjordan made no secret of his intention of annexing to his own dominions as much of Palestine as he could occupy; there was also little doubt that he was prepared to compromise with the Zionists to the extent of arranging a partition of Palestine with them. It was unlikely that the governments of Lebanon, Syria, Iraq, or Saudi Arabia would be able or willing to raise any effective opposition to this design. It therefore became incumbent on Egypt to make large-scale preparations for a campaign against Zionism in Palestine in order to prevent the disposal of Palestine from becoming a matter of private arrangement between Abdullah and the Zionists, a procedure which would have meant the destruction of the Arab League, the creation of a Jewish state, and a great accession of strength and prestige to Abdullah, who was not only personally unpopular with most of the Arab leaders, but who was regarded by them as a tool of the British. If Abdullah had been left to fight the battle of Palestine alone, it would, in most Arab eyes, have been a case of Great Britain leaving by the front door and returning by the back.

Militarily and psychologically, Egypt was ill-equipped for the war which had now become inevitable. There had never been much spontaneous enthusiasm in Egypt for the cause of the Palestine Arabs. Despite four years of Arab League propaganda, there was little feeling of kinship with Arabism —the average Egyptian never thought of or referred to himself as an Arab. There were practically no historical, cultural, racial, or other ties between Egypt and Palestine. To the inhabitants of Syria and Transjordan, Palestine was part of their own land; to an Egyptian, it was a country as foreign as America is to England. The Arab inhabitants of Palestine were bound to the inhabitants of Syria and Transjordan by a common history, by common habits of life, and by frequent intercourse across the artificial and newly-created frontiers which had been erected between them. There was no such common bond—except that of language—between the Palestine Arabs and the Egyptians of any class.

Militarily, the Egyptian Army was ill-trained and ill-equipped. It had had no experience of modern warfare. Its supply, transport, and servicing arrangements were hopelessly inadequate to the needs of a serious campaign. In spite of political pronouncements about Palestine, no active preparations were made until the last moment for a military invasion of Palestine. It seemed that the official view was either that something would turn up to prevent war or that, in the event of war, Zionist resistance would be negligible.

On 15 May, the date on which the British Mandate was terminated, the armies of Lebanon, Syria, Jordan, and Egypt, with detachments from Iraq and Saudi Arabia, marched forward to the liberation of Arab Palestine. On the same day the Jewish state of Israel was proclaimed, and recognized within a few hours by the U.S. Government. As the British were evacuating Palestine, the Israelis had taken possession of Haifa, Jerusalem, Jaffa and Tel Aviv, together with the coastal plain and the valley separating the hills of Samaria from the hills of Galilee. The liberation of Palestine therefore involved the ejection of the Israelis from all the main towns and most of the plain-land of Palestine. The Arab plan of campaign was somewhat was follows: Nothing much could be expected from the Syrian and Lebanese armies; their task was to contain as many Israeli troops as possible by attacks on Jewish settlements near the Syrian and Lebanese frontiers. The main plan was a converging advance on Tel Aviv by the Transjordan Arab Legion (to which were attached units of the Iraqi Army) from the east and the Egyptian Army from the south. This plan miscarried. The principal strength of the Arab Legion was diverted to an attack on Jerusalem, which succeeded in capturing the Old, but failed to capture the New, City. The Egyptian Army, advancing against negligible resistance up the coastal plain from Gaza, failed to contain enough Israeli forces to protect the left flank of that part of the Arab Legion which had debouched from the Judean mountains into the coastal plain. By the time of the first truce it was evident that the Zionists would only be defeated, if at all, as the result of a long and resolute campaign. It was also evident that the Arab League was neither militarily nor politically capable of sustaining such a campaign. Unfortunately, neither Arabs nor Israelis were disposed to a compromise which would have recognized the state of Israel and put an end to the fighting. Such a recognition would have been an intolerable humiliation for the Arab League after their promises of liberation to the Palestine Arabs, and the Israelis were by this time in no less of an uncompromising mood than the Arabs. They had taken the measure of the Arab forces; they were receiving substantial assistance from abroad, and realized that they could gain by fighting what the Arabs would never concede in negotiation. And so the fighting was resumed. The Arabs were now at a serious disadvantage. The truce, which had enabled the Israelis to mobilize their resources and improve their organization, had resulted in the weakening of such co-operation as there had been between the various Arab forces. The Egyptian and Transjordan forces each considered that the other had let them down; the Iraqi soldiers were discontented at being so far from home; Ibn Saud contented himself with the presence of a token Saudi force with the Egyptian Army; deserters from the Lebanese Army amounted to about half its front-line strength. After a battle at Latrun, when the Israelis were enabled, as a result of Egyptian inactivity, to put their whole forces in the field against the Arab Legion, Abdullah abandoned any further attempt at co-operation with the Egyptians, and concentrated his attention on the siege of the New City of Jerusalem. As a result, the Israelis were able to turn south and inflict a decisive defeat on the Egyptian Army, which cleared the way for an Israeli occupation of the Negev, exposed Egypt to an Israeli invasion, and pressed the Egyptian forces into a narrow strip of coast between Gaza and the Egyptian frontier. Only the presence of British forces on the Suez Canal and the despatch of a British force to Aqaba prevented an Israeli invasion of Egypt and Transjordan. The war subsided into a series of uneasy armed truces, after the Israelis had occupied Galilee and the Negev. The Arab League had suffered an unmitigated defeat. But within the compass of this defeat was a victory for Transjordan. Her army, although mauled, was un-defeated, and the other Arab states were in no position to dispute Abdullah's annexation of all that part of Palestine (consisting of Samaria and the hill country south of Jerusalem, as well as the Old City of Jerusalem itself) which remained in Arab hands.[3]

The Egyptian public had been kept officially in ignorance of the progress of the war, and the news of Egypt's defeat was only gradually broken to the people in much the same way as the news of the death of a parent is gradually broken to a small and sensitive child. Thus the news came to Egypt not as a sudden disaster, but as a gradual and not unfamiliar feeling of disappointment, attributable to the ingratitude of allies and the machinations of the great powers. But nobody in Egypt had really cared much about Palestine, and the principal reaction among educated people was that Egypt should henceforward confine her efforts to the pursuance of her more immediate national interests.

Egypt and the other Arab states remained officially at war with Israel. A peace treaty would have involved a formal acknowledgement of defeat. It was always possible that some turn in the international situation might achieve for the

Arabs what they had been unable to achieve for themselves. There was also the problem of the Palestine Arab refugees. Some 750,000 Palestine Arabs had either been driven or had fled from those parts of Palestine which had been occupied by the Israelis. The Israelis refused to consider repatriating more than a very small proportion of these refugees, and a peace treaty with Israel would have involved acquiescence in their expulsion. Such acquiescence would not only have been a sorry alternative to the liberation which had been promised; it would have imposed an obligation on the Arab states to resettle the refugees in their own territories. It was much easier and much less humiliating for everyone but the refugees themselves to hand over the problem to the United Nations and to demand their resettlement in the lands which the governments of the Arab states had promised and failed to obtain for them by force.

As far as the other Arab states were concerned, the refugees were regarded as unwanted but at the same time as legitimate children; for the Egyptians they were not only unwanted, but also illegitimate—the embarrassing fruit of an expensive, humiliating, and unenjoyable liaison. All parties in Egypt agreed tacitly to regard the Palestine adventure as something to be referred to as little and forgotten as quickly as possible.

But it was not possible entirely to forget it. Egypt now had a relatively powerful and potentially hostile state on her north-eastern frontier. She had just given a demonstration of her own military incompetence and unpreparedness. The measûre of her failure in her war against Israel was to some extent the measure of her shortcomings as a modern state. The Palestine war brought Egypt up against the realities, the responsibilities, and perils of sovereign independence, from which her connexion with Great Britain had hitherto protected her.

From the British point of view, the Palestine war destroyed any possibility of a Middle East strategy based on the co-operation of the Arab League. The Palestine war confirmed and perpetuated the Balkanization of the Middle East. The chickens hatched after the First German War had come home to roost. The attempt to build up some sort of successor to the Ottoman Empire in the Middle East had failed. This failure was primarily due to the failure of the Arab world either to absorb Zionism into or to eject it from its system. Instead, it remained as an irritant foreign body, sapping vitality, hindering growth, and hastening dissolution.

NOTES ON CHAPTER FIFTEEN

1. Nuri as-Said had become Prime Minister of Iraq after the British suppression of the Rashid Ali rebellion in the spring of 1941.

2. The germ of the Arab League is generally held to have been contained in a speech delivered by Mr. Eden, the British Foreign Secretary, early in 1943, in which he said that the British Government would welcome and encourage economic and political co-operation between the Arab states of the Middle East. Such co-operation was, as a matter of economic necessity, developed during the war under the auspices of the British-controlled Middle East Supply Centre. After the war the British Government established in Cairo a mission, separate from the British Embassy, entitled the British Middle East Office, which was intended to replace the Middle East Supply Centre as a quasi-permanent, peace-time diplomatic agency for maintaining liaison with the Arab Middle East as a whole.

3. A strip of coastal plain between Gaza and the Egyptian frontier, which was occupied by the Egyptian Army during the war, has remained in Egyptian possession, and continues (in 1953) to be administered by Egypt.

CHAPTER SIXTEEN

POST-WAR NATIONALISM

WHEN the Wafd returned to office in 1942, the Party remained true to its usual pattern of consolidation in opposition, followed by disintegration in power. The Wafd's previous period in office, from 1936 to 1938, had ended with the secession of Ahmed Maher and his followers to form the Saadist Party. During his wartime period of office Nahas Pasha lost the support of his principal lieutenant, Makram Pasha Ebeid, who, together with a few followers, resigned from the Government, left the Wafdist Party, and launched a campaign of bitter political and personal abuse against Nahas Pasha. The effect of this campaign on public opinion, combined with British reluctance to interfere on Nahas's behalf, enabled the King in October 1944 to dismiss Nahas and his Government from office. He was succeeded by Ahmed Maher, at the head of a mainly Saadist Government. This Government in January 1945 consolidated its position by winning a General Election which was boycotted by the Wafd.

The new Government, now that all possibility of Axis vengeance had departed, was eager to range itself on the side of the victorious Allied powers. War was declared on Germany and Japan in February 1945, and two days later Egypt signed the United Nations Charter. Egypt's declaration of war did not prove entirely bloodless. It cost the life of Ahmed Maher, the Prime Minister, who was assassinated by a fanatic, apparently in protest against Egypt's declaration of war. He was succeeded as Prime Minister and as leader of the Saadist Party by Fahmy Pasha Noqrashy.

In May 1945, when the war in Europe had ended, martial

law in Egypt was partially lifted; the Press censorship, arbitrary arrest and imprisonment, and the ban on public meetings were abolished. The lifting of these restrictions let loose a long-pent-up flood of nationalist sentiment in the Press and in the cafés. Egypt's passive role in the war had made it impossible for her nationals either to satisfy or to exhaust those feelings of militant patriotism which are inevitably stirred by the spectacle of a world at war.

In July 1945 Nahas Pasha, aiming to establish himself and the Wafd as the champions of Egyptian independence, sent a note to the British Ambassador which recapitulated the demands set out in the note addressed by him to the British Ambassador in April 1941. These demands were essentially complete evacuation of British forces from Egypt and union of the Sudan with Egypt. In the following month, Noqrashy Pasha, the Prime Minister, speaking in the Senate, made it clear that the Government wished to negotiate a new treaty which would provide for the departure of foreign troops from Egypt and for 'the unity of the Nile Valley'. In November 1945 these two demands were reiterated in the King's Speech at the opening of a new session of Parliament, when it was stated that conversations with Great Britain were already taking place.

The tone of official speeches remained courteous and conciliatory. But public feeling was being whipped up both by the opposition Press and by the Moslem Brotherhood, and student demonstrations, unknown for nearly ten years, began to parade through the streets of Cairo.

The Moslem Brotherhood had been formed in 1930 by a certain Hassan al Banna, and had existed obscurely for some years as a purely religious body. But with the leaders of the Wafd and other political parties becoming more and more middle-aged and more and more respectable, the Moslem Brotherhood tended to attract to itself all those ardent and violent young nationalists who, twenty years previously, would have been supporters of the Wafd. By 1945 the Brotherhood had developed into a considerable organization, part of which operated overtly and devoted itself to cultural, educational, social, and religious activities, and part of which constituted the nucleus of a political terrorist society.

It was obvious that Egyptian public and political opinion would become infected with the restiveness of the students unless the Government was able to obtain fairly rapidly from Great Britain some concession to nationalist demands. Unfortunately, the British Government showed a surprising insensitiveness to the desirability of making some generous gesture towards a Government which was doing its best to keep irresponsible nationalist fervour in check. There was no move to evacuate British troops or British Military Headquarters from Cairo, although there was no conceivable military reason for their remaining there. Everything went on as if the British military authorities intended to remain in Cairo for ever. It was difficult even for the least suspicious Egyptian to believe that this was due not to bad faith, but to the reluctance of mainly non-combatant and often only temporarily military administrative officers to exchange the amenities of Cairo for the Nissen huts and bell-tents of the Canal Zone. Behind the scenes a stubborn and unfortunately prolonged rearguard action was being fought on paper between the War Office and the Foreign Office; the former had dug itself well into the requisitioned buildings of their Cairo headquarters; the latter were rather half-heartedly endeavouring to eject them.

While this paper war was going on public opinion in Egypt was getting more and more impatient and less and less reasonable. There was a certain amount of rioting and some attacks on British troops. In December 1945 the Egyptian Government made its first formal demand for a revision of the 1936 Treaty. A note from the Egyptian to the British Government asked for a revision of their mutual relations on the ground that the Treaty had been concluded in the midst of an international crisis and had been accepted by Egypt only under the pressure of necessity. It stated that the military situation which the Treaty had been designed to meet had ended with the war, and that the time had come for a new arrangement. The note went on to say that 'the presence of foreign troops on our soil in peacetime, even if stationed in distant areas, is wounding to the national dignity'. It concluded by asking the British Government to fix an early date for formal negotiations, which should include the question of the future status of the Sudan, for a revision of the 1936 Treaty.

The British Government replied formally and rather coldly in a Note which concluded as follows:

It is the policy of His Majesty's Government to consolidate in a spirit of frankness and cordiality the close co-operation achieved by Egypt and the British Commonwealth during the war, to which Your Excellency's note bears testimony, and to place it on a footing of full and free partnership as between equals in defence of their mutual interests and with full respect for the independence and sovereignty of Egypt. Therefore, notwithstanding the provisions of Article 16 of the Treaty of 1936, His Majesty's Government declare themselves willing to undertake, with the Government of Egypt, a revision of the Treaty arrangements between them in the light of their mutual experience and with due regard to the Charter of the United Nations for ensuring international peace and security. Instructions will shortly be sent to His Majesty's Ambassador in Cairo[1] to hold preliminary conversations with the Egyptian Government to that end. His Majesty's Government take note that the Egyptian Government desire that the forthcoming discussions should include the question of the Sudan.

The publication of this noncommittal and temporizing reply was followed in Egypt by rioting, by the resignation from the Government of Makram Ebeid[2] and two other Ministers, and finally by the resignation of the Prime Minister and that of his Government.

The immediate cause of Noqrashy's resignation was the criticism aroused by vigorous police action against student demonstrators, as a result of which a number of students had been killed. The underlying cause was that Noqrashy

336

realized that he had no hope of securing a revision of the Treaty on terms which would be acceptable to Egyptian public opinion. Even if the British Government had been prepared to make important concessions to the Egyptian point of view (and there was no sign that they were prepared to do so), Noqrashy was neither sufficiently strong nor sufficiently popular to be able either to compel or to cajole Egyptian public opinion into the acceptance of any arrangement which he was likely to negotiate with Great Britain. He would have had to face the opposition of the Wafd, which was irreconcilably opposed to what it regarded as a minority Government led by a renegade Wafdist and holding power as the result of faked elections which had been boycotted by the Wafd. He would also have had to face the terrorism of the Moslem Brotherhood and the rioting of the students without the aid of the security regulations which had so recently been abolished and which it would have been politically impossible to reinstate.

It was clear that the Wafd would oppose any Treaty revision negotiated by any government other than a Wafdist government, and that they would refuse to be represented on any Treaty delegation formed by any government other than a Wafdist government. It was not quite clear whether it would carry its opposition to the extent of identifying itself with the revolutionary aims and terrorist practices of the Moslem Brotherhood. It was probable that it would not do so; the Wafd had lost much of the fire and enthusiasm of its earlier days and, in common with the other 'constitutional' political parties, had a vested interest in the maintenance of law and order. The Wafdists were at least as frightened as anybody else at the possibility of revolution, and, if it came to the point, would have been found on the same side of the barricades as their political rivals.

The choice before the Palace after Noqrashy's resignation was either to recall the Wafd to power or to entrust the Government to somebody capable of dealing with the consequences of not recalling the Wafd. In the circumstances, the choice of Ismail Pasha Sidqi was almost automatic.

Ismail Pasha Sidqi has never received his due either in Egypt or abroad. He was the last survivor of the 'old guard' of Egyptian nationalists who had formed the original Wafd. He had soon broken away from Zaghlul, and for over twenty years had played a genuinely independent role in Egyptian public life. A Turk by race, an autocrat by temperament, and a realist by instinct, he had nothing in common with the raucous demagogy of the Wafd. After his term of office as Prime Minister from 1930 to 1933, he had devoted himself mainly to big business, in which he amassed a large fortune. In politics he played the part of a detached elder statesman, observing, encouraging, criticizing. During the war he had been an outspoken critic of British policy in Egypt. Later he was to become an equally outspoken critic of Egyptian policy in Palestine, and was the only Egyptian who dared raise his voice in public against what most educated Egyptians privately realized to be disastrous folly.

The new Government, which consisted of Liberals and Independents, and in which Sidqi himself held the portfolios of the Interior and Finance as well as being Prime Minister, received a vote of confidence in the Chamber. The Saadists abstained from voting. Under the new Government, rioting continued, but with a difference. It suited Sidqi to have a certain amount of rioting, which served to demonstrate to the British Government the extent of nationalist feeling in Egypt. Under Noqrashy the Government was rapidly losing control of the situation; under Sidqi there was just as much rioting as, and no more than, suited Sidqi's purposes.

On 7 March 1946, less than three weeks after forming a Government, Sidqi was able to announce the names of the delegation appointed to negotiate the revision of the Treaty with Great Britain. Sidqi had tried, and failed, to secure Wafdist co-operation, but apart from this the delegation was a representative one. The Wafdist terms had been that Nahas should lead the delegation, that Wafdists should be in a majority on the delegation, and that elections should be held in the near future. After these terms had been refused by Sidqi, the Wafd publicly announced that it would not be bound by the result of the negotiations; this meant that they would do their best to sabotage any new or revised treaty, irrespective of its terms, which had not been negotiated by the Wafd.

The Wafdist boycott seriously prejudiced any chance there might have been of successful negotiations. Nevertheless, at the beginning of April the British Government named the British delegation, which was headed by Mr. Bevin, the Foreign Secretary, and which included Sir Ronald Campbell, the British Ambassador in Cairo, and Lord Stansgate, the Secretary of State for Air.[3]

On 7 May, two days before the discussions were due to start in Cairo, Mr. Attlee, the British Prime Minister, announced that the British Government had accepted the principle of a complete withdrawal of British forces from Egypt in peacetime in the event of a satisfactory agreement being arrived at over the question of treaty revision as a whole. This was confirmed in Cairo next day by Sidqi Pasha.

Mr. Attlee's announcement was hotly criticized in the House of Commons by the Conservative Opposition on the grounds both that it was a tactical mistake to open negotiations with a concession and that it would be strategically unwise to evacuate Egypt, anyway. If a gesture was intended, a visible and immediate evacuation of Cairo and Alexandria would probably have been more effective than a promised future evacuation of the whole of Egypt. The desirability of some move in this direction had, however, apparently been recognized by the British Government. On 4 July 1946 Cairo Citadel was handed over by British to Egyptian troops; at the end of July it was announced that Headquarters, British Troops, in Egypt and General Headquarters, Middle East, would be moved from Cairo to the Canal Zone by the end of the year. Arrangements were subsequently made that all British troops in Egypt should be withdrawn into the area laid down in the 1936 Treaty by 1 May 1947.

Meanwhile, treaty negotiations proceeded to the accompaniment of almost continual barracking from the Wafdist Press. But the British announcement about eventual evacuation from Egypt and the arrangements being made for evacuation from Cairo and Alexandria contributed to a lowering of tension, and in spite of the Wafdist Press the political atmosphere seemed relatively propitious for an agreement.

After Great Britain had conceded the principle of total evacuation in peacetime, there remained only two real difficulties in the way of a successful agreement. First, it had been made clear by Mr. Attlee that the acceptance of the principle of evacuation in peacetime was within the framework of an alliance with Egypt which would provide for the use of Egypt as a wartime base by Great Britain. The Egyptian delegation, which accepted the principle of such an alliance, wished the return of British forces to Egypt to be made conditional on the actual declaration of war in the Mediterranean or Middle East area, while the British wished to have Egypt available as a base as soon as war appeared imminent in any part of the world. This, of course, raised the further problem as to who should decide whether or not war was imminent.

The other difficulty seemed likely to prove even more intractable. The 1936 Treaty had left the status of the Sudan unaltered, had confirmed the validity of the 1899 Convention, and affirmed that the welfare of the Sudanese people was the paramount consideration in providing for the administration of the Sudan.

Since 1936 there had been considerable political activity in the Sudan. Two political parties had emerged: the Umma, which aimed at making the Sudan independent both of Great Britain and Egypt, and the Ashigga, which aimed at a union of the Sudan with Egypt. It was commonly believed in Egypt that the Umma was sponsored by the British; the

Ashigga was certainly sponsored by Egypt. The emergence of these two organized parties made it impossible to arrive at an agreement with Egypt about the Sudan over the heads of the Sudanese themselves. Egyptian insistence on an immediate change in the status of the Sudan would wreck the negotiations, without altering the reality which had been created by the political awakening of the Sudan.

Several members of the Treaty delegation, harassed by the opposition of the Wafd, and fearful of the possible consequences to themselves of being associated with an agreement which would be repudiated both by the Wafd and by the Moslem Brotherhood, were not particularly anxious to facilitate the negotiations. But Sidqi was confident of his ability to negotiate a satisfactory Treaty, to get it through Parliament, and to defy the extra-parliamentary opposition of the Wafd and the Moslem Brotherhood. There was in fact no insuperable difficulty about finding a formula to cover the conditions under which British troops would return to Egypt, and it might even have been possible to find a satisfactory formula to cover both Egyptian claims and British responsibilities in the Sudan. At the end of September Sidqi, determined to force the hands of the reluctant members of his delegation, resigned office. As he calculated, nobody else was prepared to form a government, and a few days later he returned to power with his position somewhat strengthened. He publicly announced that he was in favour of an alliance with Great Britain based on the complete evacuation of British forces from Egypt in peacetime, and declared his willingness to leave the question of the Sudan outside the Treaty, to be settled in separate negotiations. Immediately after making this announcement, Sidqi departed for London. While in London he reached agreement with Mr. Bevin on the draft of a Treaty. By the terms of the draft, the British Government agreed to the complete evacuation of Egypt by the end of 1949; the Sudan was covered by a protocol, of which the text was as follows:

The policy which the High Contracting Parties undertake to follow in the Sudan within the framework of unity between the Sudan and Egypt under the common Crown of Egypt, will have for its essential objective to secure the well-being of the Sudan . . . the development of self-government, and consequently the exercise of the right to choose the future status of the Sudan. Until the High Contracting Parties, in full common agreement, realize the latter objective, after consultation with the Sudanese, the Agreement of 1899 will continue and Article II of the Treaty of 1936 . . . will remain in force.

The question of the Sudan wrecked the draft Treaty. Whether by accident or design—probably the latter—it was rumoured in Cairo, immediately after Sidqi's return from London, that the British Government had accepted Egypt's demand for unity of the Sudan with Egypt under the Egyptian Crown. The persistence of this rumour was such that Mr. Attlee was obliged publicly and categorically to state that 'no change in the existing status and administration of the Sudan is contemplated, and no impairment of the right of the Sudanese ultimately to decide their own future'.[4] A fortnight later a reference to the Sudan was made in the King's Speech at the opening of the new session of Parliament, when it was stated that 'Egypt regarded the Sudan as a brother State, and one of Egypt's aims would be to develop their interests and prepare them for self-government as soon as possible.' This, of course, implied that responsibility for the Sudan's future would, by the terms of the draft Treaty, be transferred to Egypt.

As a result of the uncertainty caused in the Sudan by the prevalent rumours and by the reference to the Sudan in King Faruq's speech, the Governor-General of the Sudan, with the authority of the British Government, issued the following statement on 7 December:

The Sudan Protocol, in fact, provides that the Sudanese people shall—when they are ripe for self-government—be free to choose the future status of the Sudan. Nothing in the proposed Treaty can prejudice the right of the Sudanese to achieve their independence.

The next day Sidqi Pasha issued a statement to the effect that the Governor-General's statement was not in accordance with the recent London talks resulting in the Sidqi-Bevin draft Treaty. Immediately after issuing this statement Sidqi Pasha and his Government resigned office. The draft Treaty was dead. It only remained for Noqrashy Pasha, who succeeded Sidqi Pasha as Prime Minister, to bury it.

On 27 January 1947 it was announced simultaneously in London and in Cairo that negotiations between the two governments for a revision of the 1936 Treaty had been broken off. The statement issued by Noqrashy Pasha attributed the failure of the negotiations to the British refusal to agree (a) to immediate, complete and unconditional evacuation and (b) to the implementation of the unity of Egypt and the Sudan and the restitution to Egypt of her rights in the administration of the Sudan in order to facilitate the preparation of the Sudanese for self-government. The statement concluded by saying that the Egyptian Government would submit its case for Treaty revision to the Security Council of the United Nations. On the same day Mr. Bevin in the House of Commons stated that the only reason for the breakdown of the negotiations was a last-minute change of mind by the Egyptian Government on the construction to be placed on the Sudan Protocol.

What had really happened was that, during Sidqi's absence in London, personal jealousies and political fears had combined to ensure the repudiation of any arrangement, however favourable, which Sidqi might be able to make in London. Sidqi was therefore unable to secure the support either of the Palace or of his colleagues in the Treaty delegation for the compromise arrangement embodied in the Sudan Protocol. In order to avoid repudiation at home, therefore, he was compelled to subscribe to an interpretation of the Protocol which ensured its repudiation by Great Britain.

343

The assertions made by Noqrashy Pasha when announcing the breaking-off of negotiations could not be left unanswered, and Mr. Attlee, in the House of Commons, briefly traced the course of the negotiations, stating that by the beginning of December a draft Treaty had been drawn up, which the Egyptian Government had declared itself as being ready to sign, but that subsequently the Egyptian Government had demanded unacceptable assurances about the interpretation of the Sudan Protocol.

Mr. Bevin, in his announcement on 27 January, had made it clear that the British Government's previous acceptance of the principle of complete evacuation had been dependent on an agreement being reached over a revised Treaty, and, negotiations to this end having broken down, the British Government stood on the terms of the 1936 Treaty—that is to say, that British forces would remain in Egypt within the numbers and territorial and time limits laid down in that Treaty.

In July 1947 the Egyptian Government submitted a Note to the Security Council of the United Nations requesting the total and immediate evacuation of all British troops from Egypt and the termination of the existing administrative régime in the Sudan. The Note, which was extremely hostile in the tone adopted towards Great Britain, stated *inter alia* that British troops were maintained in Egyptian territory against the unanimous will of the Egyptian people, that the presence of foreign troops within the territory of a United Nations member in time of peace and without its consent constituted an offence to its dignity, a hindrance to its normal development and an infringement of the United Nations Charter. With regard to the Sudan, the note stated that in 1899 Great Britain had forced upon Egypt its participation in the administration of the Sudan, had subsequently assumed full authority there, and was, by instigating and encouraging an artificial separatist movement, adopting a policy designed to sever the Sudan from Egypt.

The note went on to say that the 1936 Treaty, by which

344

Great Britain justified her occupation of Egypt and her administration of the Sudan, was invalid as being incompatible with the United Nations Charter, and could not therefore be regarded as binding on Egypt. As direct negotiations with Great Britain for a revision of the Treaty had failed, Egypt took the view that Great Britain's insistence on the fulfilment of the 1936 Treaty constituted a dispute between the two countries, carrying with it a threat to peace, and was therefore submitting the dispute to the United Nations in accordance with the terms of the Charter.

At about the same time, Egypt, as a further gesture of disapproval towards Great Britain, abandoned her membership of the Sterling Bloc[5] during the course of financial negotiations for the repayment by Great Britain of sterling balances accumulated to Egypt's credit in London during the war years.[6]

Legally, the case against Great Britain which Egypt was about to submit to the United Nations depended on two points. First, was the 1936 Treaty freely negotiated, or had it been imposed on Egypt under duress? Secondly, was the 1936 Treaty, even if it had been freely negotiated, compatible with the United Nations Charter, or was it superseded by the United Nations Charter? The 1936 Treaty could only be said to have been negotiated under duress in the sense that Great Britain would, in view of the then international situation, certainly have continued to keep troops in Egypt even if a treaty had not been signed. Egypt had signed the Treaty in order to derive as much benefit as possible from a situation in which she was compelled to acquiesce, anyway.[7] But, in form, the Treaty had been freely negotiated and had at the time been greeted with great enthusiasm in Egypt. There was nothing in the United Nations Charter to justify the setting aside of such a freely negotiated agreement, since the presence of foreign troops in Egypt had not, in form, been imposed on Egypt, but had been specifically agreed to by the accredited representatives of Egypt subject to certain

345

defined conditions over a definite period of years. The same considerations applied to the Sudan.

Since one of U.N.O.'s principal functions was to insist on the sanctity of treaties in general, it was unlikely that the Security Council would sanction the tearing up of one particular treaty at the request of one of the parties to it, provided that that treaty had been freely negotiated and was being faithfully observed by the other party. The failure of Egypt's case was almost a foregone conclusion unless she could show either that the Treaty had been signed under duress or that Great Britain herself was failing to observe the provisions of the Treaty.

It is not likely that the Egyptian Government had any illusions about the weakness of their case from the legal point of view, and it is probable that they hoped to recruit international sympathy and to bring international pressure to bear on Great Britain. In other words, Egypt relied not on the legal but on the moral aspect of her case.

As far as the presence of British troops in Egypt was concerned, Egypt had a fairly good moral case. It was not easy morally to justify the presence of foreign troops in a friendly country against the wish of the Government of that country, even if their presence was authorized by a treaty, unless there was some obvious, immediate and pressing military need for their retention. In 1936 the military need had been obvious, immediate and pressing, but in 1947 the Axis had been defeated and the menace from Soviet Russia had not yet developed. There was no hostile nor potentially hostile power within 1,000 miles of Egypt's frontiers. It would no doubt have been inconvenient from the point of view of Britain's global strategy to withdraw her troops from Egypt except on the basis of an agreed arrangement as in the Sidqi-Bevin draft Treaty, but it would have been difficult to find a precedent for holding a reluctant ally to the letter of the terms of a Treaty concluded eleven years previously under circumstances which had been totally changed by the issue of a world war.

346

Egypt's moral case over the Sudan was considerably weaker, but not entirely non-existent. Before the Mahdi's rebellion the Sudan had been an integral part of Egypt. It had been temporarily lost to Egypt as a result of that rebellion, and had subsequently been reconquered in Egypt's name and largely at Egypt's expense. After the reconquest, the sole reason for not reincorporating the Sudan into Egypt was the British desire to avoid saddling the administration of the Sudan with the international restrictions with which Egypt was at that time burdened. When the last of these international restrictions was swept away at the Montreux Conference in 1937, the case for continuing the separation between Egypt and the Sudan was obviously weakened. But although it was weakened, it was not destroyed. The temporary and forcible separation of one part of a country from its motherland, if such separation be sufficiently prolonged, creates a situation in which it is neither practicable nor customary to restore it without consulting the wishes of the inhabitants of that part, who during the period of separation may have acquired new habits, new allegiances and new ambitions. But more important than the historical argument was the fact, patent to any disinterested observer, that the Sudan was being well-governed and progressing towards self-government under the existing dispensation, and the general belief that the Sudan would be neither well-governed nor make any progress towards self-government under Egyptian rule.

Noqrashy Pasha badly mismanaged the Egyptian case. In the first place, he did not, in his case before the Security Council, distinguish between Egyptian acceptance of the principle of a Treaty with Great Britain and their objection to certain provisions of the existing Treaty. He made it appear that Egypt was trying to repudiate an obligation rather than seeking a remedy for a grievance. In the second place, in regard to the Sudan, Noqrashy Pasha neither recognized the efficiency of British rule, which would have been confirmed by any commission of enquiry and which

347

was admitted privately by informed Egyptian opinion, nor appreciated the existence of a general disbelief, outside Egypt, in Egypt's capacity to achieve a similar level of efficiency.

In the circumstances, Egypt's wisest course before the Security Council would have been to concentrate on the demand for the withdrawal of British troops from Egypt, and to have reserved the question of the Sudan for further negotiations with Great Britain. Then she would have had a strong case, for Great Britain had already agreed on the principle of withdrawal, but had considered that agreement to be voided as a result of failure to agree over the future of the Sudan. It would not have been difficult for Noqrashy to have created the impression that the British Government was using the failure to agree over the Sudan as an excuse for retaining troops in Egypt after having already agreed to withdraw. But such a line was politically impossible for the Noqrashy Government. It would have laid them open to the accusation of abandoning the Sudan. Thus it was that the Egyptian case at the Security Council, as presented by Noqrashy Pasha, was addressed rather to Egyptian public opinion than to the members of the Security Council. Consequently, the members of the Security Council were not particularly impressed.

It is unnecessary to follow the complicated fortunes of the Egyptian case as presented at Lake Success. The only possible favourable result from Egypt's point of view would have been the creation of a climate of international opinion which would have compelled the British Government to make some concession to Egyptian demands as a preliminary to the reopening of negotiations. Any chance of creating such a climate was destroyed by the fact that Noqrashy regarded it as politically necessary to use the occasion for making a political speech for domestic consumption rather than for presenting a reasoned argument before world opinion. In the event, the Security Council, after calling on Egypt and Great Britain to resume negotiations for a revision of the 1936

Treaty, referred Egypt's case to the Assembly, where it slowly sank into oblivion beneath the cumbrous weight of United Nations routine procedure.

Noqrashy Pasha, having progressed down a blind alley as far as it was possible for him to go, was able to return to Egypt without having uttered a word which could reasonably have been objected to even by the most ardent Egyptian nationalist.

His return to Egypt at the end of August 1947 coincided with the beginning of a grim period in Egyptian history, during which Egypt was to experience pestilence, international isolation, military defeat, and grave internal disorders.

NOTES ON CHAPTER SIXTEEN

1. Sir Ronald Campbell.

2. Makram Pasha Ebeid, a Copt and an Oxford graduate, had for the previous fifteen years been regarded as Nahas's principal lieutenant and *eminence grise*. His attacks on Nahas after his resignation from the Nahas Government eventually resulted in his being arrested and sent to prison. When the Maher Government came in, Makram stepped straight out of a prison cell into the office of Minister of Finance, where he devoted most of his attention to exposing the financial scandals of the previous régime.

3. Lord Stansgate was the real leader of the delegation, as Mr. Bevin did not come to Cairo. Before being elevated to the Peerage, Lord Stansgate was Mr. Wedgwood Benn.

4. Neither the Egyptian nor the British Governments were quite honest over the Sudan Protocol. The Egyptian Government was anxious to conceal from the Egyptian public the fact that recognition of the King of Egypt as King of the Sudan did not involve any administrative changes in the Sudan, while the British Government was anxious to conceal from the Sudanese the fact that it had agreed to recognizing the King of Egypt as King of the Sudan.

5. The Sterling Bloc consists of a number of countries, either members of the British Commonwealth or having special relations with Great Britain who pool their foreign currency resources, contributing their foreign currency earnings to the pool and drawing their foreign currency requirements from it.

6. At the end of the war this sterling balance, which consisted of Treasury bills issued against Egyptian currency notes issued to cover the expenditure of the armed forces in Egypt, amounted to some £400,000,000. The terms on which this credit was released to Egypt and, in particular, the extent to which it was convertible into dollars were the subject of several financial agreements made annually with Egypt between 1945 and 1950 until, in 1951, final arrangements were agreed on for the liquidation of this credit over a period of years.

7. The Egyptian Government of the day had, in fact, seen the wisdom of the allegedly Chinese proverb: 'If rape is inevitable, lie down and enjoy it.' But this attitude, although enlightened, does make it difficult for the assaulted one to complain about it afterwards.

349

CHAPTER SEVENTEEN

THE MORNING AFTER

IMMEDIATELY after Noqrashy's return from Lake Success, a serious outbreak of cholera in the Nile Delta temporarily diverted the attention of both Government and people from the international scene. By the end of November, when the worst of the outbreak was over, the fiasco at Lake Success had been conveniently forgotten, and the stage had been set for a more ambitious demonstration of Egyptian nationalism.

As soon as the invasion of Palestine started on 15 May, the Egyptian Government declared a state of martial law, under which they assumed power of Press and mail censorship, requisitioning, sequestration of enemy property, arbitrary arrest, and imprisonment and trial by military courts. These powers were, on the whole, exercised with reasonable moderation, with the exception of the censorship, which was used, foolishly and indiscriminately, in an attempt to conceal from the Egyptian people the disastrous course of the war. But the news of defeat filtered through, together with tales of inefficiency, corruption, and cowardice in high places, of the misappropriation of war charities, of the stealing of military stores, of the neglect of the wounded. Martial law and the censorship prevented any open criticism, but the result of the revelations was to fill people with a sense of disgust, not with the Government only, but with the whole constitutional régime, and immensely to enhance the popular appeal and prestige of the Moslem Brotherhood.

The Moslem Brotherhood was the Egyptian representation of a phenomenon which recurs in almost exactly the same form in every country where drastic political and social changes are overdue. Such movements invariably become dominated, and perverted, by a mystique of surreptitious violence, which begins as a means to an end, and soon becomes an end in itself, practised indiscriminately, pointlessly, with great skill, self-sacrifice, and powers of organization. As has been related, the Moslem Brotherhood started as a religious movement and only gradually turned to politics. But by 1948 its principal activity was political terrorism and its ultimate aim revolution. It was believed to have been responsible for the murders of Ahmed Maher, the Saadist Prime Minister, of Amin Osman, the Wafdist ex-Minister of Finance, of Selim Zaki, the Commandant of the Cairo Police, and for several attempts on the life of Nahas Pasha. Although it was regarded as a fanatically Moslem body, it was believed to have been deeply penetrated by Communism. During the Palestine war the Brotherhood had made itself conspicuous for the enthusiasm of its members in personal service, in the fighting line, in the collection of patriotic subscriptions, in the organization of demonstrations, and in the hounding of Jews. This enthusiasm and single-mindedness were in marked contrast to official apathy, corruption, and incompetence.

National defeat almost always produces a revolutionary situation. Frustration, humiliation, and anger at the failure of those who had promised success combine to produce in many ardent spirits a desire for violence, destruction, and the overthrow of existing institutions which have proved themselves emotionally and materially unsatisfactory. In the case of Egypt this feeling was enhanced by disillusionment with the Arab League, and the feeling of hostility towards Egypt which was being manifested by many foreign powers. This feeling of hostility, attributed by Egyptians to the machinations of international Jewry, was largely undeserved. The war in Palestine led on the one hand to various restrictions on foreigners living in, or entering and leaving Egypt, and on the other hand to a certain amount of hooliganism directed against foreigners, both Jewish and non-Jewish. The restrictions were not always either intelligently or

351

courteously applied, and the hooliganism was not always effectively or energetically suppressed. All these things, inevitable and understandable in time of war with an inexperienced bureaucracy and an overworked police, were magnified and distorted both in Europe and the United States as a result of the unintelligent working of the Egyptian censorship, which made it necessary for the foreign Press to rely upon rumour and gossip from aggrieved persons instead of on the factual reporting of their accredited correspondents.

These circumstances all played into the hands of the Moslem Brotherhood. Palace, Government, and Opposition all gradually woke to the realization that aggressive nationalism was becoming a synonym for revolution, and that it was becoming more urgent to deal with the imminent menace of the Brotherhood than to continue making motions of defiance abroad.

The Palestine war fizzled out, but the restraints of martial law were retained as a means of dealing with internal terrorism. In spite of the fact that the Moslem Brotherhood was known to be the *fons et origo* of this terrorism, the Brotherhood had not yet been condemned as illegal, although the Communist Party, which represented no immediate menace, had been so condemned. At one time or another the Brotherhood had received assistance and support from most of the political factions in Egypt as a means of furthering their own party designs, and its rise to power and influence would not have been possible without this assistance and support. Any attack on the Moslem Brotherhood during its period of growth into a terrorist movement would probably have been widely stigmatized as an attack on Egyptian nationalism, as an act of tyranny against true patriots, as a deed almost of treason dictated by subservience to a foreign power. During the fighting period of the Palestine war, when there was no longer any doubt about the true aims and nature of the Brotherhood, it was as difficult politically to suppress it as it would have been for

352

Egypt's Zionist opponents to suppress the Irgun Zvai Leumi, who were playing in Israel a role similar to that of the Brotherhood in Egypt. But by the end of 1948, when the fighting was virtually over, and when it had become apparent that the existence of the Brotherhood represented a standing menace to the lives of all public men in Egypt, from King Faruq downwards, the Government felt that they had sufficient support from the Palace, from Parliament, and from public opinion generally to deal drastically with the Brotherhood without being accused of lack of patriotism. In December 1948, therefore, the Government decreed the suppression of the Brotherhood. Within a few days of this decision the Prime Minister, Noqrashy Pasha, was shot dead by an assassin. This deed had the effect of banishing any hesitation which might have been felt about the necessity of dealing immediately and drastically with a menace which threatened the whole structure of organized society in Egypt. Noqrashy was succeeded as Prime Minister by Irbahim Pasha Abdel Hadi, the Chief of the Royal Cabinet, who was attached to no political party, who had, as his position indicated, the confidence of the Palace, and who was respected by public opinion.

He succeeded to a dangerous inheritance. Two out of the last three Prime Ministers had been assassinated while in office. Egypt had been defeated in war, was unpopular abroad, and thoroughly demoralized at home. But the new Prime Minister enjoyed the advantage of complete freedom of action as far as Palace, Parliament, and the Wafd were concerned. It was generally felt that party politics, dilettante xenophobia, accusations of treason, and recriminations about the Palestine war could conveniently be postponed until the Moslem Brotherhood, which showed an uncomfortable disregard for the accepted rules of political controversy, had been removed from the scene.

Abdel Hadi Pasha got to work promptly, ruthlessly, and efficiently. The prisons were emptied of Zionist suspects and filled with members of the Moslem Brotherhood. Hassan al

M   353

Banna, the leader of the Brotherhood, was mysteriously murdered. Malcontents, whether belonging to the Brotherhood or not, were terrorized or terrified into silence. After six months of ruthless police activity, the country breathed again. Abdul Hadi Pasha's Government had made Egypt temporarily safe once more for the intrigues and manœuvrings of parliamentary democracy. But although the Government, by the use of forcible methods, had purged discontent of its violence, it had neither removed the causes nor the existence of widespread discontent.

The nationalist fanaticism characteristic of the Moslem Brotherhood had to a large extent been a method of expressing a more general and more deeply-rooted feeling of discontent. During and after the war a wave of revolutionary sentiment passed over the world. Sometimes it was confused with Communism, sometimes with nationalism, sometimes it was violent, sometimes it was peaceful, but everywhere its essential feature was a demand for more social justice and a demand for better living conditions for all workers. As in 1919–20, most of the countries of the West were able to exploit the fear and dislike of Communism as a means of stemming its growth. It was natural that Egypt should have been similarly affected and it was fortunate for Egypt's rulers that she escaped its full force.

Socially, in 1947, Egypt could be compared with pre-revolutionary France. There was a wealthy landowning class, privileged, undertaxed, dominating the two Houses of Parliament, who, with their professional and official associates and hangers-on, owned nearly all the wealth and exercised nearly all the influence and patronage in the country. There was a small class of industrialists and financiers, mostly of foreign extraction, wealthy, but much less influential politically and socially than the landowners. There was a growing middle class of professional men, Government officials, and commercial employees. This middle class was for the most part under-employed, hard-hit by the continually increasing cost of living and the

354

continually increasing incidence of taxation, politically conscious, and acutely critical both of Egypt's social structure and its administrative deficiencies. Lastly, there were the agricultural and industrial workers. The agricultural workers —the *fellahin*—consisted of small proprietors, tenant cultivators, and landless labourers, and were poor, for the most part illiterate, underorganized, undernourished, and apathetic. The industrial workers, much fewer in number than the *fellahin*, but growing both in number and importance, were on the whole better paid, better educated, and healthier. Those employed by large companies in the oilfields and in the bigger textile factories had already attained some degree of organization, by means of which they had succeeded in considerably improving their rates of pay and conditions of work. It was from the middle classes and the industrial workers that most of the active social discontent proceeded, and it was from these classes that the main strength of the Moslem Brotherhood had been drawn. The effective suppression of the Moslem Brotherhood had temporarily inhibited any violent manifestation of this discontent, but it was clear that this inhibition would only be temporary unless something were done either to remedy or to divert the discontent.

The suppression of the Moslem Brotherhood provided the Wafd with its opportunity. As usual, the years of opposition had enabled the Wafd to lick its wounds and to consolidate its forces. Under the Constitution an election had to be held at the beginning of 1950. Nahas and his colleagues had had no share in, and were therefore able freely to criticize, the policies which had resulted in the disappointments and humiliations of the previous three years. They were even able to criticize as 'tyranny' the methods of suppression which had given them their opportunity. It was almost certain that a 'free' election would return a large Wafdist majority; it was equally certain that any party government in power would so arrange matters as to provide an electoral majority for itself. A 'free' election could only be secured by

355

a 'neutral' government summoned to office for the sole purpose of holding, and without interest in the outcome, of elections. The principal obstacle to this course was the attitude of the Palace. As has been made clear in these pages, the political pendulum in Egypt oscillated between the personal rule of the Palace at one end of the swing and the party dictatorship of the Wafd at the other. When the Wafd was in office, the King was relegated to the status of a constitutional monarch; when the Wafd was out of office, the King became, in varying degrees, a personal ruler. It was unlikely that the Palace would willingly connive at the return of the Wafd to office as the result of 'free' elections. But it was becoming dangerous, from the point of view of the dynasty, for the Palace to continue to be closely associated with a régime which was becoming increasingly unpopular and which, however unjustly, was held responsible for Egypt's political humiliations and for her economic difficulties. As in February 1942, the time had come, in the interest of the dynasty, for the Palace to retire temporarily from active participation in politics. It was reasonable to suppose, on the basis of past performance, that a Wafdist Government would before very long provide ample opportunity for its dismissal.

In 1949, therefore, Abdul Hadi Pasha resigned from office with his Government, which was replaced by a 'neutral' Government under Hussein Pasha Sirry, which was charged with the conduct of a General Election to take place early in 1950.

Ibrahim Pasha Abdul Hadi had deserved well of his country. He had taken office at a very real and immediate risk to his life at a time when the Moslem Brotherhood was within measurable distance of paralysing the whole machinery of state. In less than a year of office he had restored the authority of the Government. He had undertaken no social reforms, but he had restored conditions in which the introduction of social reforms became possible. His methods had not been in accordance with the recognized methods of democracy, but he had made the practice of democracy possible for his successors.

Martial law was partially suspended for the benefit of the electoral campaign. It was a sign of the times that, in the course of this campaign, promises of social reform took precedence over promises about the fulfilment of national aspirations. The Wafd went to the country as a people's party. They would reduce the cost of living, they would institute social reforms, they would eliminate waste and corruption from government expenditure, they would put an end to martial law, they would do everything that the previous Government had failed to do, including, of course, the fulfilment of Egypt's national aspirations. Much of this could, of course, be written off as mere electioneering. But it was the first time that any political party in Egypt had shown itself conscious of the responsibilities of the government of a modern state. It really did seem as if the Wafd might be emerging from its sterile era of 'struggle' into an era of constructive statesmanship.

The Wafd, when it was returned with a large majority, carried with it into office the support of the vast majority of the people of Egypt, as well as a large measure of that international goodwill which Egypt had previously lost. In view of his advancing years and of his difficult relations with the Palace, there was at first some doubt as to whether Nahas Pasha would become Prime Minister. But honourable retirement is seldom palatable to prominent politicians, either in Egypt or elsewhere, and so Nahas Pasha became Prime Minister of Egypt for the fourth time at the head of a Wafdist Ministry, supported by an overwhelming majority in the Chamber of Deputies, and by the clamorous enthusiasm of a large section of the population.

We must now return to the theme of this book, which is Anglo-Egyptian relations. The factors governing these relations had changed rapidly during the thirty months which had elapsed between Noqrashy's denunciation of

Great Britain at Lake Success and the return of the Wafdist Government to office. Relations between Great Britain and the United States on the one hand and the U.S.S.R. on the other had deteriorated to an extent which had already made the likelihood of a third world war a theme of common conversation. The end of the British Mandate in Palestine and the establishment of the state of Israel had deprived Great Britain of a possible alternative military base in the Eastern Mediterranean, and had emphasized Egyptian inability to defend the Suez Canal without foreign assistance.

The same events which, in the eyes of the British Government, increased the desirability of retaining Egypt as a military base caused Egypt to become even less enthusiastic, not only about the presence of British troops, but also about the continuance of any form of alliance with Great Britain.

Previously the main weight of Egyptian objection to the military clauses of the Treaty had been concentrated, not on the principle of an alliance, but on the fact of the presence of British troops in Egypt. As the state of 'cold war' intensified this largely emotional objection tended to be reinforced by more practical considerations. The ruling class in Egypt, if it came to a choice between Great Britain and the United States on the one hand and the U.S.S.R. on the other, would unquestionably choose the former; they realized too that they would probably be unable to remain neutral if it came to a war between the two blocs. But, understandably, they did not wish to be committed in advance to a treaty which, in practice, meant the complete subordination of Egypt's wartime policy and strategy to those of Great Britain. Another powerful consideration was that the existence of a Treaty with Great Britain, and the presence of British troops in Egypt, deprived Egypt of the bargaining power which she otherwise would have had, and which was possessed by other Middle Eastern countries, such as Israel, Syria, and Lebanon, by reason of their not being bound by treaty to any European Power. If Egypt had been in a position to sell her favours, she could doubtless have obtained a good price for them in the form of arms, economic assistance, and so on; as it was, Great Britain and the United States tended to regard Egypt as being already 'in the bag', and to neglect her accordingly.

These considerations alone would have militated severely against the success of any new negotiations with Great Britain. But, in addition, developments in the Sudan since the hearing of the Egyptian case at Lake Success had interposed another, and equally intractable, obstacle. At Lake Success the British delegate, in answer to Egypt's case on the Sudan, had announced that Great Britain's policy in the Sudan was the development of self-governing institutions which would enable the people of the Sudan, in due course, freely to choose the form of government which they desired. Under the condominium, the British Government was bound to try to secure Egypt's consent to and association with the implementation of this policy. Egypt's objection was not to the policy itself, but to the fact that she was being asked passively to acquiesce in a British policy implemented by British officials. She was convinced that under cover of this policy the British Government was determined, irrespective of the real wishes of the Sudanese people, to separate the Sudan from Egypt, and considered that the implementation by Great Britain of a policy of progressive self-government in the Sudan would enable her to ensure this. Egypt was therefore unwilling to acquiesce in a policy which was designed, in her consideration, to defeat her aims and ambitions as regards the Sudan.

Although there was some substance in Egypt's contention, she had shown some political clumsiness in allowing herself to be manœuvred into a position in which she appeared, in the eyes of Sudanese and of world opinion, to be opposing self-government for the Sudan at a time when Great Britain was preaching and implementing such self-government. Her only chance of retaining a foothold in the Sudan was to insist on the fullest participation in Great Britain's plans for self-government. Instead, she chose the opposite course of refusing to associate herself at all with such plans.

In the autumn of 1947 the Khartum Government prepared a draft Constitution for the Sudan, and submitted it for approval to both the British and the Egyptian Governments. This Constitution provided for the election of a Legislative Assembly, and for the formation of a Legislative Council, whose business it would be to prepare and submit legislation for the approval of the Legislative Assembly. The Executive power still remained in the hands of the Governor-General and his Executive Council, but the draft Constitution did embody a substantial first instalment of self-government, and as such was approved by the Advisory Council for the Northern Sudan, which was at that time the only official organ of Sudanese opinion to which the draft Constitution could be submitted.

Egypt was now finally presented with the choice between co-operation with and opposition to Great Britain in the future administration of the Sudan. Her choice of opposition was probably dictated by the following considerations: (a) As had so often happened in the past, the members of the Egyptian Government and the leaders of Egyptian political opinion were limited in their freedom of choice by their own past declarations. Having at Lake Success and elsewhere denounced the 1899 Agreement, it was difficult formally to acquiesce in its continued operation. (b) The Egyptian Government suspected that the whole business of the Sudan Constitution was part of a plot concocted between Khartum and Whitehall to exclude Egypt from the Sudan, and that the invitation to Egypt was a means of trying to obtain Egypt's tacit consent to such exclusion. (c) The Egyptian Government feared that the participation of the Ashigga in Sudanese elections would give that party a minority status in the proposed Assembly and proclaim to the world the paucity of the support accorded by the Sudanese to the prospect of union with Egypt. This did not necessarily mean that the Egyptian Government realized that the Ashigga did not enjoy the support of a majority in the Sudan; it merely meant that no Egyptian Government is confident of winning any election of which it does not itself have the stage-management.

It is probable that Egypt's refusal was foreseen, as it was certainly welcomed, by the Khartum Government, who were anxious above all things that the new Constitution should become an efficient instrument of administration rather than a forum for nationalist politicians, which it certainly would have become in the event of Egyptian participation. Whitehall, on the other hand, would probably have been willing to accept some administrative deterioration in the Sudan as the price of removing the principal obstacle to the conclusion of a satisfactory military arrangement with Egypt.

After making every allowance for the strength of the reasons which decided Egypt to refuse participation, it can hardly be doubted that Egypt was mistaken in her decision. For by that decision she deprived herself of the chance of influencing the future development of the Sudan by means other than those of agitation and violence.

In spite of Egyptian protests, the Khartum Government, having received the British Government's approval, promulgated the draft Constitution, and proceeded with the elections for a Legislative Assembly. Egypt had condemned herself to gaze impotently at a process of ordered political development to which she had formally objected, but which she was unable effectively either to challenge or to impede.

Apart from the considerations about a military alliance and the future of the Sudan, there were various causes of friction and disagreement between Egypt and Great Britain arising from the Palestine war which provided additional obstacles in the way of a mutual understanding.

During the Palestine war Egypt had, so far as she was able, interrupted the supply of war material destined for Israeli ports. In practice, this principally involved a close check on oil tankers passing through the Suez Canal northwards, loaded with oil from the Persian Gulf. As Iraq had stopped the export of oil to Haifa through the I.P.C. pipeline, this meant that the Haifa Refinery was cut off from supplies of Middle East oil either by pipeline from Mosul or by tanker from the Persian Gulf. Egypt, in pursuance of the policy adopted by all Arab countries of non-recognition and economic blockade of Israel, continued to forbid the transit of Haifa-bound oil tankers through the Suez Canal long after the fighting in Palestine had come to an end. This affected Great Britain far more than it affected Israel, for whereas Israel suffered only by reason of having to import more expensive oil either from Rumania or from the New World for her internal requirements, Great Britain lost the considerable quantities of sterling exchange which were normally earned by the export of oil refined at Haifa. In spite of protests from Great Britain and, later, from the United States, Egypt continued to enforce a prohibition which was little more than an empty gesture as far as Israel was concerned, but which was a powerful and perpetual irritant to Great Britain. (For the legal aspect of Egypt's action, see Note on page 79).

Under the 1936 Treaty Great Britain had agreed to supply arms and equipment to the Egyptian forces. During the Palestine war Great Britain, acting on a U.N.O. decision to stop the supply of arms to both sides, had stopped the supply of arms to Egypt. This action, although it made no difference to the result of the war, left a legacy of bitterness which was later increased, when Great Britain's rearmament got under way, by a decision to suspend the supply of certain types of arms to Egypt. This decision was widely interpreted in Egypt as an attempt to put pressure on the Egyptian Government over the supply of oil to Haifa.

The aftermath of the Palestine war had also left Egypt with strategic problems of her own which overshadowed and, to some extent, conflicted with the common strategic problems which were the foundations of the 1936 Treaty. Until 1948, Egypt and Great Britain had a common interest in defending Egypt from invasion. The only powers likely to invade or to threaten Egypt were major powers to whom such an invasion would be part of a general war against Great Britain, and against whom Egypt would be quite unable to defend herself unaided. With the creation of the state of Israel this situation changed. On the one hand, Israel was a power with which Great Britain wished to be friendly, and which she wanted to include with the Arab states in a comprehensive scheme for the defence of the Middle East. On the other hand, Israel was a power whose hostility Egypt feared and whose destruction she desired. While Great Britain wanted Egypt to become reconciled with Israel and to dovetail her military preparations into a general plan for the defence of the Middle East against Russia, Egypt viewed her defence preparations as being primarily directed towards the possibility of a local war with Israel. Thus the main condition of a military alliance—identity of strategic purpose—no longer existed.

In spite of all these apparently insuperable obstacles, both Governments were anxious for an agreement. The Egyptian Government wanted the prestige of a successful negotiation with Great Britain; the British Government wanted the assurance of having a military base in a friendly Egypt in the event of war. But both Governments had severely limited the extent of the concessions which they were in a position to make. The Egyptian Government was committed to the slogan, 'Evacuation and the Unity of the Nile Valley'; the British Government, by its abandonment of Palestine, had deprived itself of a possible alternative Middle East base, and, by the grant of a Constitution to the Sudan, had placed its ultimate disposal in the hands of the Sudanese.

In these circumstances the negotiations which opened in the autumn of 1950 between Mr. Bevin and Mohamed Pasha Salah-ad-Din, the Egyptian Foreign Secretary, were almost foredoomed to failure. The East-West cold war was sufficiently serious to make Egypt unwilling to tie her hands, but not sufficiently serious to make Egypt realize the need for protection. The quarrel with Israel in which Egypt was a principal still loomed larger than the East-West quarrel in

363

which Egypt could only be a satellite. Although there was little doubt as to which side Egypt would choose in this quarrel, if she had to make a choice, she wished to avoid having to make a choice and if one became inevitable to exact a stiff price for her support.

Until Egyptian public opinion really felt the need for the advantages which an alliance with Great Britain would bestow, any Egyptian Government would negotiate merely as a means of demonstrating its patriotism by putting forward demands which Great Britain was either unable or unwilling to concede. If and when Egyptian public opinion felt the need for an alliance with Great Britain, it would not be difficult to devise a formula which would reconcile the needs of protection with the slogans of nationalism. Until such a need became apparent, the gap between Egyptian demands and the limit of British concessions was unlikely to be bridged.

CHAPTER EIGHTEEN

THE STRATEGIC IMPORTANCE OF EGYPT

WE have observed that in the course of the 150 years covered by this book Great Britain's interest in Egypt has been continuous, and that it has been motivated by varying considerations. Up to the time of the opening of the Suez Canal in 1869, Great Britain's principal aim, as regards Egypt, was to prevent France from obtaining a predominant influence in Egypt, as such influence was considered a potential threat to Great Britain's Indian possessions. The opening of the Suez Canal roughly coincides with, but does not wholly account for, the beginning of a more active and a more positive interest. By 1869 Ottoman influence in Egypt had declined almost to zero and European, and particularly French, influence in Egypt had correspondingly increased. Great Britain's traditional policy of 'neutralizing' Egypt, by inducing the powers to regard it as an integral part of the Ottoman Empire, had consequently become more difficult to pursue at a time when the opening of the Suez Canal route to India made it more vital than ever for Great Britain to pursue it. The weakness of the Ottoman Empire, French interest in the Suez Canal, and Egypt's indebtedness to European banking houses all greatly increased the possibility of unilateral French intervention in Egypt. Great Britain's influence in Europe, combined with French weakness as the result of the Franco-Prussian war, was sufficiently strong to prevent such unilateral intervention, and in the event it was Great Britain who occupied Egypt. Such intervention by a European power had been rendered almost inevitable by the events of the previous three years. After deposing Ismail, Great

365

Britain and France had virtually established a joint protectorate over Egypt. Arabi's rebellion was, to all intents and purposes, a rebellion against this Dual Control, and it was necessary for Great Britain and France to deal with it, either by compounding with it or by crushing it.

By reason of the accidents of French domestic policy, Great Britain crushed the rebellion and occupied Egypt without French assistance. Whether Great Britain welcomed the opportunity of acting alone, and whether France shrank from the odium of associating herself with Great Britain in an action which might have miscarried is uncertain. It is fairly clear that Great Britain's object at the time was not permanently to occupy Egypt, but to ensure for herself a dominant role in any future settlement of Egypt. The Drummond-Wolff Mission indicates that Great Britain still viewed such a settlement in terms of the neutralization of Egypt by reintegrating Egypt into the Ottoman Empire. But in view of the extent of European interests in Egypt, a policy of neutralization depended on the safeguarding of these interests, which, because of the difficulty of establishing a strong, indigenous government in Egypt, and because of the weakness of the Ottoman Empire, could only be secured by the continuance of the British occupation in Egypt.

In the early years of the twentieth century the imminent collapse of the Ottoman Empire, the German *Drang nach Osten*, and the growing menace of a European war all combined to change Great Britain's policy in Egypt from one of attempted neutralization to one of permanent occupation. This change of policy was facilitated by the 1904 Agreement with France, by which France, hitherto Great Britain's principal European rival in Egypt, recognized the British occupation of Egypt in return for British recognition of France's 'special rights' in Morocco.

After the First German War, Great Britain was faced with the void created in the Middle East by the disappearance of the Ottoman Empire. This void Great Britain endeavoured to fill by the creation of a belt of British-protected states whose existence would ensure the freedom of British communications with her Asian, African, and Australasian possessions and dependencies. The discovery of vast oil reserves in the Middle East increased Great Britain's interest in the control of the Middle East in general, but not in that of Egypt in particular. It was the Italian adventure in East Africa and the growing intimacy between Rome and Berlin which really brought Egypt into the front line of British imperial strategy. From 1935 on British strategic control of Egypt was the principal obstacle to the establishment of Mussolini's Roman Empire and the principal guarantee for the continued existence of the British Empire.

During the Second German War enemy aeroplanes and submarines all but closed the Mediterranean to Allied shipping, and so nullified the value of the Suez Canal as an 'imperial life-line'. But this fact enhanced rather than diminished the strategic importance of Egypt to Great Britain. As a result of the closing of the Mediterranean to Allied shipping, Suez was the one port at which Allied troops, benefiting from Great Britain's mastery of the seas, could be assembled to repel an enemy incursion into Africa, or to threaten an enemy incursion into Asia, or to enable an Allied advance into eastern or southern Europe. Egypt was the key to the Third Front, which led to the collapse of Italy, which nourished the resistance movements in Yugoslavia and Greece, which helped to prevent a German invasion of Turkey, and which finally sent Allied troops pouring over the Brenner Pass into the heart of Germany.

After the Second German War, the rivalries of the Western European powers ceased for the first time in 150 years to be a relevant factor in the consideration of Great Britain's Middle East strategy. As the Suez Canal had also lost most of its strategic value in wartime, Great Britain's original strategic reasons for interesting herself in Egypt had thus almost been eliminated. Great Britain's Middle East strategy had to be remodelled in the light (a) of the hostility of the U.S.S.R. and (b) of the independent status combined

367

with the political, economic, and military weakness of most of the States of the Middle East. The first phase of British Middle East strategy after the end of the Second German War may be said to have lasted from the middle of 1945 to the end of 1948. During this phase the menace from U.S.S.R. was regarded as being comparatively remote, and British policy concentrated on trying to build up the Arab states into a political and economic entity which would, with Anglo-American assistance, and with the co-operation of Turkey and Iran, develop into a political, economic, and military bulkhead against Communist penetration into Asia and Africa.

The creation of such a bulkhead was regarded as a replacement for rather than a supplement to British garrisons in the Middle East, since it was considered not only that the presence of British garrisons would militate against the attainment of the political and economic objectives of the plan, but also that the attainment of these objectives would make the maintenance of British garrisons unnecessary.

It was under the influence of this strategic conception that Great Britain, in 1946, agreed in principle to the evacuation of British forces from Egypt. The intention was to replace this base by a base in Kenya. This presupposed that a serious danger of war was unlikely to eventuate until the States of the Middle East had settled down into the pattern envisaged for them, by which time it would be possible to regard them as equal and effective partners in a co-ordinated scheme of defence, sufficiently stable politically to be faithful to their engagements, and sufficiently strong militarily to play an active part in the front line of defence.

By the end of 1948 it had become apparent, first, that the danger of war had become more imminent, and, secondly, that the Arab states of the Middle East were incapable of playing the role which had been assigned to them. The Arab League was collapsing under the strain of the Palestine war. The existence of the state of Israel and the dissensions between the various Arab states made it impossible to envisage any connected scheme of defence which depended on the active participation of the states of the Middle East. Prospects of economic rehabilitation were fading away, since the Arab states were unable, even with financial assistance, themselves to put the necessary schemes into effect, and were unwilling to accept the foreign supervision and control which would enable them to do so.

The idea of securing the Middle East by means of political integration and economic rehabilitation was therefore abandoned as a primary objective of policy. But it was impracticable at the same time to abandon the Middle East to its own resources. First, it was desirable not only to deny to any potential enemy the vast oil resources of the Middle East, but also to retain these resources for the use of the Western Allies. The possession of these resources might well decide the result of a world war. Secondly, it was desirable to retain strategic control of territory from which it would be possible to reach, either by land or by air, the industrial centres and oilfields of the U.S.S.R. It was therefore vital for Great Britain to make such dispositions as would ensure her freedom to accumulate supplies, move troops, and operate aircraft in the Middle East in the event of war. The Arab League policy was designed to secure this freedom by means of freely-negotiated alliances with states with a conscious objective towards which they were prepared freely to contribute and willingly to co-operate. The failure of the Arab League policy made it necessary to try to achieve the same result piecemeal by means of such diplomatic methods as were available. This failure, which involved, *inter alia*, the extrusion of active British influence from Palestine and from the Levant states, on the one hand made it all the more necessary for Great Britain to make the most of her treaty relations with Egypt, Jordan, and Iraq, and on the other hand caused these states to resent the commitments which bound them to Great Britain. In the case of Jordan, this resentment was mitigated by financial and military assistance received from Great Britain, without which Jordan

369

could not have existed as an independent state; in the case of Iraq, there were powerful vested interests who found it temporarily convenient to acquiesce in the British connexion. In the case of Egypt, there were no such mitigating factors. The alliance with Great Britain was regarded, not as a freely negotiated arrangement for mutual convenience, but as a residue of the Occupation, which carried with it no privileges and no advantages, but only humiliation and inconvenience. Great Britain was in the position of a husband imposing his marital rights on a reluctant wife.

CHAPTER NINETEEN

1922–50—A RETROSPECT

ARETROSPECT of Anglo-Egyptian relations during
the years 1882–1922—from the Occupation to the
Declaration of Independence—such as was attempted
in an earlier chapter, is mainly concerned with an assessment
of the British administrative record during those years. A
retrospect of Anglo-Egyptian relations during the next
twenty-eight years, from 1922 to 1950, must concern itself
primarily with the long-term results of that administration
as expressed both in the social, administrative, and economic
life of independent Egypt and in the social and political
relations between independent Egypt and Great Britain.

The depth and durability of British influence in Egypt was
limited by the conditions of the Occupation. Great Britain
imposed no administration of her own; she simply patched
up what she found. Her administrators did not, for the most
part, administer their own policy; they directed its administration by others. The legal systems of Egypt, both in the
mixed and the national courts, were quite uninfluenced by
British legal theory or practice; the system of taxation
developed by the British was conditioned rather by the
existing labyrinth of international agreements than by any
assessment of the needs of the country. The provincial
administration, which was the basis of British rule in India,
in the Sudan, and in the Crown Colonies, was hardly
influenced by British imperial practice. Great Britain's
abiding contribution to Egyptian life can be summed up in
three phrases—the development of perennial irrigation, the
instinct for political stability, and the use of the English
language.

371

The subject of perennial irrigation has been discussed in an earlier chapter: the effect of perennial irrigation has been to make of Egypt a rich country, to cushion her from the effects of inexperienced administration, and to provide her with the possibility of financing the social, administrative, and industrial developments appropriate to the requirements of an independent and progressive state.

The history of independent Egypt is remarkable in that there has been an almost complete absence of serious domestic violence. There has been a general instinct in favour of the rule of law, and there has been a general instinct against the grosser abuses of arbitrary government. When we consider the turbulent histories of, for example, Syria and Iraq during the short term of their independent existence, one is almost inclined to regard Egypt as a model of ordered and peaceful progress. It is perhaps not unreasonable to ascribe to British influence this instinct for political moderation, which shows itself in a comparative lack of vindictiveness towards political opponents, and in a reluctance to use violence as a short-cut to the attainment of political ends. There is much sound and fury in Egyptian—as in British— political life, but there is an overwhelming public opinion in favour of fighting political battles by means of the tongue and the pen only, instead of with more lethal weapons. In the midst of incompetence, corruption, nepotism, and extravagance, the decencies of debate have on the whole been preserved. Professional politicians have not been synonymous with gangsters, and execution has not been the normal penalty for political failure.

The use of the English language is perhaps the most potent and the most durable of the bonds which have been forged during the last seventy years of Egypt's association with Great Britain. Almost every educated Egyptian speaks, reads, and writes English well. This has been achieved, not through the medium of private English schools, of which there have been very few, but as a result of English having been a compulsory subject in Egyptian Government schools for the past sixty years. This Egyptian facility in English has greatly assisted business relations and social contacts between British and Egyptians, and has also helped to soften the inevitable acerbities of Anglo-Egyptian political disagreements. It has led to the employment of British rather than of other foreign experts, and has encouraged Egyptians to pursue their higher studies at British rather than other European universities. It has had other, and less tangible, effects. It has made accessible to Egyptians the wellsprings of English life and culture, and in this way has fundamentally conditioned the impact of the West upon educated Egyptians. In most of his intellectual, social, and cultural attitudes, the young Egyptian has been influenced by his English reading and by his knowledge of English ways and English people. For good or ill, and whether he likes it or not, the average educated Egyptian is deeply stained with the tincture of Englishness.

This continuing British influence, derived from long, and not always friendly, contact with British people, British policies, and British institutions has had an undoubted effect on the course of affairs in Egypt during the last thirty years. The strength of this influence has not seriously been affected by political disputes between Great Britain and Egypt. On the contrary, the way in which these disputes have been handled on the Egyptian side has been conditioned by the effect of British influences on the minds of Egyptian statesmen and public men. These influences have shown themselves in a readiness, on the whole, to compromise, in the appreciation of the difference between an argument and a quarrel, and in a general tendency to avoid precipitating serious crises. In short, the same instinct of moderation which has dictated the conduct of domestic affairs has also, on the whole, dictated the conduct of Anglo-Egyptian relations.

Essentially British influence in Egypt has consisted in the impact of upper- and middle-class British technical, administrative, educational, and cultural attainments on the

Egyptian upper and middle classes. It has been an influence of personalities rather than of ideas, and the influence has been communicated by methods rather than by theories. It has, imperfectly and partly unconsciously, communicated to a small though vastly influential body of educated Egyptians an attitude of mind which is rapidly disappearing in Great Britain itself. This attitude of mind can be defined as one of benevolent autocracy, expressed in the production of benefits for all as a result of the autocratic exercise of the aptitudes and wisdom of the few. Democracy, in this context, is merely a safety-valve for the ventilation of grievances.

The British practice and precept of benevolent autocracy within the framework of a parliamentary constitution was the only practicable political recipe for Egypt. The parliamentary constitution was a necessary concession to the twentieth-century *Zeitgeist*, but there could be no effective democracy in a country at Egypt's stage of social development. Autocracy was a condition of efficient administration; benevolence was a condition of the fruitful exercise of autocracy.

Unfortunately, Egyptian administration was not so efficient, nor was her ruling class so enlightened, as to make the exercise of a benevolent autocracy effective. In a calmer age, Egypt might have been given time, by the process of trial and error, peacefully to evolve a stable administrative and social system. But the repercussions of the Second German War set up subterranean pressures which the existing Egyptian social and political order, reinforced only with the diminishing heritage bequeathed by British rule, has proved unable to withstand.

The most serious of these pressures was that of inflation. Before the Second German War, the cost of living in Egypt was low, taxation light, and Government expenditure small. The annual Budget balanced at about £30,000,000 sterling. During the war years two things had happened to Egypt's economy. First, the cost of imports increased and the supply of imports diminished. Secondly, the demand in Egypt for goods was doubly accentuated by the requirements of the Allied forces and by the increased requirements of those who benefited from Allied military expenditure. An inflationary situation was therefore created in which the amount of money in circulation had increased without a corresponding increase in the amount of goods to be bought. (Allied military expenditure was mainly financed by the issue of currency notes against Treasury bills issued to Egyptian credit in London.) This inflation could only be corrected on the one hand by rationing consumption and on the other hand by withdrawing money from circulation. This withdrawal could only be achieved by a combination of saving and taxation. Like rationing, such measures could only be made effective by a government which had both the will and the power to combat and to control the orgy of profiteering and speculation into which the war plunged Egypt. By 1945, the cost of living had increased to some three and a half times its pre-war level. Agricultural and urban landlords and producers of all kinds had done and were continuing to do well; consumers were suffering correspondingly. During the war years, however, the evil results of this inflation were to some extent masked by the full and well-paid employment resulting both from the needs of the armed forces and from the impetus given to local production.

After the war Egypt had an opportunity to put her economic house in order. The country had been unravaged by war. Egypt had accumulated a sterling credit amounting to some £400,000,000 sterling as a result of goods and services supplied to the Allied forces. A number of large fortunes had been made by Egyptian citizens. The price of cotton, Egypt's principal export, was high. The necessities of war had given a great fillip to Egypt's industrial development, particularly in petroleum production and textile manufactures. The sterling credits could have been used to finance a programme of irrigation development in order to provide more cultivable land for Egypt's rapidly increasing population; there is little doubt that the British Government would have responded readily in releases of goods and dollars to implement such a scheme if one had been forthcoming. The enormous wealth which had been accumulated and the enormous incomes which were being enjoyed by agricultural landowners could have been tapped both by Government loan and by taxation in order both to finance social services and to withdraw from circulation some of the surplus money, concentrated in too few hands, which was continuing to push up prices in an economy where shortages of goods still continued.

None of these things was done. In spite of the fact that Egypt's current sterling and dollar exports were, by and large, sufficient to finance Egypt's essential dollar and sterling imports, no attempt was made to finance any capital development schemes by means of the sterling credits, which were, for the most part, frittered away as and when they were, rather grudgingly, released by the British Treasury. Taxation continued to be imposed on a hand-to-mouth basis without any attempt at redistributing incomes or combating inflation. Even in so far as taxation was nominally imposed on the well-to-do (as, for example, under the progressive tax on incomes of over £E.1,000 per annum), it was widely evaded by the wealthiest. The main weight of taxation continued to fall, by means of Customs duties, stamp duties, etc., on the middle and lower classes, whose standards were already being depressed by the increasing cost of living. Thus the rich got richer and the poor got poorer and the already large gap between rich and poor increased day by day.

Meanwhile, the expenses of government mounted, partly by reason of the high cost-of-living allowances which it was necessary to pay to the enormous and increasing army of Government officials, partly by reason of the military expenditure undertaken after the war with Israel, and partly as the result of reckless extravagance in such items as lavish official entertaining, an extraordinary multiplicity of official cars, expensive and numerous foreign missions and delegations, and thinly-disguised political bribery. It was necessary to meet this increasing expense by increased taxation, which was imposed in such a way as to give another turn to the inflationary screw, thus paving the way for more Government expenditure and another round of inflationary taxation.

Lack of Government initiative was not relieved by the resources of private enterprise. Wealthy Egyptians, in so far as they invested and did not spend their money, tended to concentrate their investments on urban and rural 'real estate'. Foreign enterprise and investment were hampered both by lack of confidence in Egypt's future and by a medley of laws and regulations which rendered such enterprise and investment unattractive. These laws and regulations were intended to ensure adequate Egyptian control of and participation in foreign enterprise and investment; in practice, they prevented such enterprise and investment from being embarked upon.

The extent to which the administrative functions of the government of a modern state have increased during the last thirty years is not always fully appreciated. The Egyptian administrative machine was simply not capable of supporting the burden of these increased functions. For example, so far from being able to devise a system of taxation fitted to the needs of the time, it was unable efficiently to collect the proceeds of existing taxes. Even if the rulers of Egypt had been able to devise suitable policies, they had not the machinery to implement them.

But more decisive than this technical inability was the unwillingness of the Egyptian ruling class to make any contribution either to the finances of the state or to the well-being of the people. Power was generally regarded as a means towards self-enrichment, self-aggrandisement, and as an opportunity for dispensing patronage among relatives, friends, supporters, and hangers-on. The responsibilities of power were only fulfilled in so far as was necessary in order to ensure the continued enjoyment of power. Such business

377

of state as was transacted was regarded as a necessary chore incidental to the enjoyment and maintenance of power. The dispensation of patronage on a large scale, combined with periodical orgies of emotional patriotism, was up to a point sufficient to satisfy enough of the people enough of the time to ensure a comparative absence of violent discontent, provided that the course of patronage was changed often enough to make a fairly large number of people feel that they were potential beneficiaries of the system.

Several factors contributed to discredit this time-honoured system. It had become habitual for Egyptian governments to discredit their rivals and predecessors by exposing the more flagrant of their corruptions; extended over a period of years, this practice had the not unnatural effect of undermining public respect for the ruling class and for the administration as a whole. It had also become habitual for governments and political parties to organize demonstrations and to subsidize movements either in support of themselves or in denunciation of whatever or whoever they wished to denounce. This created a form of organized public opinion which eventually ceased to be amenable to the instructions and directives of its paymasters. It could no longer be turned off at will, and had either to be pandered to or else bribed or coerced into silence.

The pressure of overpopulation, the increased cost of living, the influence of foreign ideas (of which British social democracy was probably more immediately subversive of established Egyptian practices than was Russian Communism), and the humiliation of the Palestine war with its attendant scandals of corruption and maladministration combined to complete the disillusionment and disgust of public opinion. For the first time, Egyptian domestic politics became something more than a matter of rivalries and disputes between various political factions. The spectators were swarming on to the pitch.

This was the situation at the beginning of 1949. Such attempts as the Noqrashy Government had made to appease

378

organized labour and to promote organized charity, and such efforts as it had made to divert public indignation on to the heads of the British or the Jews had proved quite inadequate as a means of rehabilitating the popular credit of the Government or of checking the growth of the Moslem Brotherhood, which was the outward and visible sign of popular discontent. The only immediate solution was repression—a solution rendered possible by the existence of the Emergency Regulations which had been promulgated in connexion with the Palestine war. Meanwhile, the Wafd, in so far as the Emergency Regulations permitted, took care not only to disassociate themselves from the Government's policies and methods, but also to create a precedent in modern Egyptian history by the advocacy of social reforms. With an eye to the General Election, which, under the Constitution, was due to take place the following year, Wafdist propaganda concentrated, not on the satisfaction of Egyptian national aspirations *vis-à-vis* Great Britain, but on the necessity for social welfare and social services. As usual, the Wafd in opposition was wiser than the Wafd in power, and they even carried their wisdom to the extent of veiling their social reform programme under a cloud of generalized benevolence.

As we have seen, the Palace found it advisable to acquiesce in the Wafd's return to power at the General Election which was held in January 1950. The Wafd, for their part, had no real intention of pursuing any radical policy of reform, and were by no means averse to making an arrangement with the Palace which would preclude the dangerous possibility of Palace and Wafd trying to outbid each other for popular approval. When it came to the point, the Wafd shrank from the implications of a 'popular' policy. With its retinue of rich landlords and prosperous, middle-aged lawyers, the Wafd was no longer a potentially revolutionary party; it was as firmly wedded to the *status quo* as was any other party in the state.

On the surface it seemed that all was going well. Nahas, as

379

avid for applause as an ageing *prima donna*, received satisfactory ovations whenever he appeared in public. It was still possible to raise popular enthusiasm over demands for evacuation and the unity of the Nile Valley. But there were rumblings beneath the surface. Examples of ministerial corruption, nepotism, and inefficiency, which previously had been accepted as matters of course, became subjects of common conversation and disapproving comment. Proposed increases in taxation were received with open criticism of Government extravagance. The old formula of bribery, patronage, and nationalism had lost its magic, and there was nothing to put in its place.

By the middle of 1950 two of Lenin's three prerequisites for a revolutionary situation already existed in Egypt. There was widespread discontent and there was Governmental impotence. The third prerequisite—an organization capable of taking advantage of the first two—did not exist. The Moslem Brotherhood had been temporarily broken. The Army had been weakened and humiliated by the failure in Palestine.

Four ultimate courses appeared to confront Egypt— reform, repression, a foreign occupation, or revolution. There appeared to be neither the will nor the means to accomplish the first. The successful accomplishment of the second depended on a strengthening of the loyalty and efficiency of the Army and the police and the administrative services generally. Foreign—that is to say British—occupation was likely only in the event of a complete breakdown of law and order. Revolution depended on the emergence of a revolutionary leader and a revolutionary organization.

CHAPTER TWENTY

REVOLUTION

W HEN the Wafd returned to power at the beginning
of 1950, it was obvious that it would, before very
long, have to justify itself both to its supporters and
to its opponents by an attempt to solve the Anglo-Egyptian
deadlock. As the months went by, the Wafd Government's
failure to deal with, or even seriously to approach, domestic
problems, together with increasing murmurs about corruption in high places, made the necessity for creating a patriotic diversion more and more evident. As had happened so
often before, the Wafd's power of manœuvre in negotiations
with the British was limited both by the utterances of its
leaders when out of office and by the readiness of their
opponents to accuse them of having betrayed their country.
Negotiations with the British Government, through the
British Embassy, were reopened in 1950 and dragged on
intermittently for the next eighteen months.[1] By the end of
the summer of 1951 increasing popular discontent with the
Government's domestic administration and increasing friction with the Palace determined the Wafd to rally the
country to itself through a spectacular attempt to solve the
Anglo-Egyptian problem by direct methods. Negotiations
with the British Embassy were broken off, and in October
the Wafd-dominated Parliament unanimously voted the
abrogation of the 1936 Treaty, the abrogation of the 1899
Sudan Convention, and the proclamation of King Faruq as
King of Egypt and the Sudan. This gesture was followed by
the attempted denial of Customs and other facilities to British
troops in the Canal Zone. The British forces took such
forcible action as was necessary to maintain themselves in

the Canal Zone. As might have been expected, there were frequent clashes; within a month there was a state almost of guerrilla war in the Canal Zone, with Egyptian 'liberation units', consisting partly of young enthusiasts and partly of professional thugs, encouraged and financed by the Government and overtly or covertly supported by the police, attacking British military installations, sniping at British military transport, and so on. The Egyptian Army took no part in these attacks. The Government was in a delicate position. A large part of the Egyptian Army was in the Sinai Desert, on the Israeli border, and could only be supplied from, or return to, Egypt by the Ferdan railway bridge or by the various ferries over the Canal, which could all be denied to them by the British. There was reason to believe that the Wafd Government could not entirely rely on the support of the Army. The functioning of normal life in Cairo and in the Nile Valley generally was dependent on the continued supply of petrol and heavy oils from the oil refineries at Suez, which the British forces could have cut off from the rest of Egypt. Lastly, there was no doubt that the British forces in the Canal Zone, reinforced as they had been, were in a position to occupy the whole of Egypt without serious difficulty.[2] On the other hand, the guerrilla campaign and, more important, the almost complete withdrawal of Egyptian labour from the British camps, which the Government had been able to enforce, must have made the British military authorities consider whether a base in the Canal Zone would be of any value in the face of determined Egyptian resistance to it.

In the Sudan the Egyptian Government's gesture had no effect on the *status quo*, since the Wafd did not enjoy sufficient support in the Sudan to make any direct action feasible by such supporters as they did have.

Events in the Canal Zone were accompanied by a tremendous orchestra of anti-British propaganda in the Press, in broadcasts, and in pronouncements by various members of the Government. In December all remaining British

382

officials in the service of the Egyptian Government (mostly schoolteachers in Egyptian Government schools) were summarily dismissed. There was an unofficial, and largely ineffective, boycott of British goods. On 25 January 1952 a battalion of armed Egyptian auxiliary police at Ismailia, who had been passively or actively assisting the 'liberation units' in their attacks on the British, were surrounded in their barracks by British forces and called upon to surrender their arms and ammunition. On direct orders from Fuad Serag-ed-Din, Minister of the Interior and Secretary-General of the Wafd, they refused to do so. Thereupon they were attacked with tanks and light artillery and lost about fifty killed before being overcome. The news of this event caused a serious outbreak of violence in Cairo, starting with the auxiliary police and extending to the hungry Cairo mob, augmented by thousands of unemployed ex-workers from the Canal Zone. Although the outbreak was in its origin anti-British, and although twelve Englishmen were massacred in the British Turf Club, which was burnt by the rioters, it soon developed into a general orgy of looting and destruction, in the course of which many of Cairo's restaurants, bars, cinemas and luxury shops were pillaged and burnt. Hunger, xenophobia, and the desperate hate of the 'have-nots' for the 'haves' in a country where the wide gap between rich and poor is a standing incitement to disorder appear to have been the dominating passions released on that day. Order was restored late in the afternoon by the Army; the situation had passed right out of the control of the police. In the small hours of the following morning the King dismissed the Wafd Government on the ground of its failure to maintain public order, and charged Aly Maher with the task of forming a Government. For the fourth time in his career, Nahas had been summarily dismissed from power.

To all appearance, history had once more repeated itself. The swing of the pendulum had carried the Wafd to power and in course of time had flung it out again in favour of a coalition of politicians brought into being by the Palace and

owing its continued existence to the Palace. On the surface
it appeared that the King was the master of the situation.
But in reality Faruq's prestige had suffered irreparably from
the scandals of his private life, from the corruptions of his
entourage, and in particular from the connexions of his
entourage with the scandals of the Palestine war. Discontent
with the King and his entourage was fairly general in the
Army, in view of the Palestine war scandals, and the Army,
by its successful intervention of 26 January, had demonstrated that it held the key to the situation.

For the time being all proceeded on orthodox lines. The
Palace and the pashas generally had been thoroughly
frightened by the events of 26 January. They realized the
danger of mass incitement as an instrument of policy, and
reverted to the less ambitious method of negotiation with
the British as a means of fulfilling national aspirations. But
they did not realize the extent to which Egypt's social fabric
had been weakened by the strains and stresses of the post-
war years, they did not realize the extent to which pashadom
had become discredited in the eyes of almost everyone except
its few beneficiaries, and they did not realize that Egyptian
nationalism had become, not only, or even mainly, a revolt
against the British, but a revolt against indigenous oppression
and corruption.

Aly Maher, with his Government of elderly 'independents', was a faithful reflection of the old order. They had
neither the will nor the means to institute any social reforms,
and Aly Maher himself, an old and adroit politician, was
mainly concerned to bring together a solid bloc of 'moderate'
politicians sufficiently strong on the one hand to resist
pressure from the Palace and on the other hand to keep the
mob quiet. Aly Maher's idea of a united front of pashas to
preserve the *status quo* did not appeal to Faruq, who wished
to drive home his advantage against the Wafd; at the
beginning of March he was replaced as Prime Minister by
Neguib Hilaly, a comparatively recent dissident from the
Wafd. One of the first acts of the Hilaly Government was

to advise the King to dissolve Parliament, which, at the time of Nahas's fall, had been prorogued, but which still remained in being. This act, which was regarded as being a direct blow at the Wafd, was followed by the house arrest of Fuad Serag-ed-Din, the Secretary-General of the Wafd and ex-Minister of the Interior.

The new Prime Minister took office at a disadvantage, in that he was little more than a nominee of the two most prominent Ministers in the previous Government, Mortada Maraghy and Zaki Motaal, who had both connived at Aly Maher's dismissal. The only thing which could have established Hilaly's independence of the Palace, on the one hand, and his position in the country, on the other, would have been an agreement with Great Britain on terms which were acceptable to Egyptian public opinion.

Prospects for such an agreement were not bright. In October 1951, almost simultaneously with the Egyptian abrogation of the 1936 Treaty, the Governments of Great Britain, France, and Turkey had offered Egypt a Four-power Pact of which Egypt was to be an equal member with the other three and under the terms of which the British forces on the Canal Zone were to be replaced by an international force provided by the signatories of the proposed Pact. This proposal was rejected by the Wafd Government, and it was most unlikely that any Egyptian government could afford to agree to any proposal for a regional pact which was not preceded by an unconditional withdrawal of British troops. From the British point of view, and indeed from the point of view of all the Western Allies, belief in the desirability of a strategic base in the Canal Zone had, during the events of the previous few weeks, been reinforced by a belief that the continued presence of British troops in the Canal Zone was in addition desirable as a means of protecting foreign interests in view of the troubled internal state of Egypt. On balance, the events leading up to 26 January had made British agreement to evacuation less likely, since any doubts that might have been created about the usefulness of a strategic base in the midst of a hostile population were more than outweighed by a determination not to abandon a potential means of influencing events in a country so patently teetering on the verge of chaos.

In the Sudan the 'constitution' proclaimed by the Wafd Government after the abrogation of the condominium, providing as it did for only limited Sudanese autonomy, was coldly received by all except the avowedly pro-Egyptian parties. In May 1952 a Self-Government Ordinance, presented to the Legislative Assembly by the Sudan Government, providing for general elections in six months and independence after a transition period of three years, was approved by a large majority. On the Egyptian side room for manœuvre was even more limited in the Sudan than in the Canal Zone, since the Wafd Government, by proclaiming Faruq as King of the Sudan, had made it almost impossible for any subsequent government to retreat without an affront to the royal prestige.

After three months of inconclusive negotiations with the British Embassy, Hilaly had nothing to show for his efforts. Harried on the one hand by the nationalist Press, who accused him of having too much patience with the British, and on the other hand by the King, who, with a strange insensitiveness to his growing unpopularity, was trying once more to edge himself into the centre of the stage, Hilaly resigned at the end of June, the immediate reason being his refusal to admit into his Cabinet a prominent and particularly disreputable member of the King's entourage. He was succeeded as Prime Minister by Hussein Sirry, an elder statesman who had more influence with the King than had Hilaly and who enjoyed an enviable reputation for being anti-British. Sirry reverted to Aly Maher's policy of conciliating the Wafd; he released Serag-ed-Din from *residence forcée* and announced his intention of preparing for new and free elections. (As Hussein Sirry had headed the caretaker Government which had presided over the 1950 elections, the Wafd were inclined to regard him as a sort of forerunner to themselves, and their spirits rose accordingly.) But the storm was now gathering fast over the heads of the Palace and the pashas. It was an open secret that there was grave discontent in the Army against the Palace. At the beginning of July Sirry attempted to appease the Army by asking Faruq's approval for the appointment of Brigadier Mohamed Neguib, leader of the dissident Army officers, as Minister of War. Faruq refused and demanded the appointment of one of the royal relatives in his place. Sirry thereupon resigned. The King turned once more to Hilaly, who, with singular imprescience, formed a Cabinet constituted in accordance with Faruq's wishes. The new Cabinet had barely taken office when, on 23 July 1952, Mohamed Neguib, at the head of a few battalions of troops, marched on Cairo. He took possession of the city and the administrative machinery without resistance or bloodshed and, in the course of the next few days, dismissed the Hilaly Government, demanded and obtained the abdication and departure from Egypt of King Faruq, established a Regency Council to represent Faruq's infant son, and arranged for a new Government under the premiership of Aly Maher.[3]

It soon became apparent that General Neguib and the Junta of young Army officers who advised and assisted him had not only achieved a successful coup, but aspired to accomplish a social revolution. The titles of 'bey' and 'pasha' were abolished as being symbolic of the old order. A decree was promulgated for the expropriation and redistribution of all landed estates of over 200 acres. A purge of corrupt and dishonest officials was put in hand. In all these measures the Army, acting through the civil Government, provided the motive power and, very often, the means of execution. Army 'liaison' officers were established in Government departments with wide powers to ensure that the wishes of the Army were carried out.

It was hardly to be expected that Aly Maher would prove to be either a willing or an efficient instrument for the administration of a social revolution involving, as its principal item, the destruction by expropriation of the Egyptian landed aristocracy. It was not long before General Neguib was forced to become ruler of Egypt in name as well as in fact and to displace Aly Maher as Prime Minister. The change took place peacefully and without apparent rancour.

A remarkable feature of the Neguib revolution was the good temper and lack of vindictiveness displayed by Neguib and his Junta. His seizure of power and the abdication of Faruq were accomplished literally without bloodshed. The numerous politicians and members of the Palace entourage arrested immediately after the coup were all subsequently released. Nahas himself (who, immediately after the coup, returned from Aix-les-Bains post-haste, like Falstaff from Gloucestershire, accompanied by Serag-ed-Din in the role of Pistol, to congratulate Neguib) was left at liberty. A prominent landowner who staged an armed demonstration against the land expropriation decree was tried by a military court and sentenced to imprisonment for life. The only execution during the first few months of the régime was that of a worker who had killed a policeman during a riot in a textile mill.

The new régime fired the popular imagination, and at the beginning enjoyed popular support. The departure of King Faruq pleased almost everyone. The old politicians were regretted by hardly anyone. The vast majority of decent middle-class Egyptians approved the measures taken against corruption and rejoiced at the emphasis placed on social reform. Egyptians with contacts abroad, who were aware of the extent to which their country's reputation had suffered by reason of the behaviour of Faruq and of the corruption which had made Egypt a byword, were acutely sensitive to, and delighted at, the general approval with which the new régime was regarded in foreign countries. Most important of all, perhaps, in consolidating the domestic position of the new régime was the personality of General Neguib himself, who, legitimately aided by the modern arts of publicity and propaganda, established in a very short space of time a remarkable dominion over the affections of the mass of the Egyptian people.

General Neguib's Government was to need all the popularity he had gained for them. They found themselves faced with four principal difficulties. First, the leaders of the old political parties (of which the Wafd was the only one to retain any influence) were by no means willing either to relinquish their political influence or abandon their personal fortunes without a struggle; secondly, they were faced with the difficulty common to all revolutionary governments of having to restrain the ardours and, to some extent, to disappoint the hopes of their most loyal supporters; thirdly, the Government had inherited from their predecessors a critical economic situation; fourthly, they had to face an inevitable popular demand for the settlement of the Anglo-Egyptian dispute on terms satisfactory to Egyptian national aspirations.

The release of the political detainees in November 1952 was followed by a brief period during which the Government attempted to harness the old political parties to the purposes of the new régime. This attempt was abandoned as the result of a Wafd-inspired plot to overthrow the régime by means of student riots and an Army revolt. This convinced the Government of the necessity of a decisive break with the past. The 1923 Constitution, which had up till then remained formally in force, was abrogated, the old political parties dissolved and their funds confiscated, any idea of immediate elections abandoned, and a five-year 'period of transition' announced. At the same time there were a number of arrests among Army officers and civilians. Among the latter was Fuad Serag-ed-Din. An Army Colonel was tried by court-martial, found guilty, and sentenced to death on a charge of having attempted to incite various Army officers to mutiny. These measures disposed of any immediate likelihood that the Neguib régime would be displaced by any movement from the Right.

389

The régime's left flank was guarded for the time being by the benevolence of the Moslem Brotherhood and by General Neguib's personal popularity with the masses. But it was clear that future pressure from the Left would be inversely proportional to the régime's success in dealing (*a*) with the country's social and economic problems and (*b*) with the Anglo-Egyptian dispute.

In 1951, when cotton prices began to fall from the high levels attained immediately after the outbreak of the Korean War, the Wafd Government attempted to keep prices up by continual intervention on the Alexandria Cotton Exchange and by the fixing of a minimum price at which the Government were prepared to buy cotton themselves. As a result of these manœuvres, cotton exports had practically ceased, and the Government had accumulated large stocks of cotton whose purchase had been financed by an inflationary increase in the fiduciary note issue. The governments which had succeeded the Wafd had made a half-hearted attempt to deal with the situation by permitting a controlled drop in the minimum prices of cotton, but had only slightly improved the situation. The Neguib Government was faced with the eventual large losses consequent on selling stocks of Government-purchased cotton at falling world prices, with the results of the inflation caused by the method of financing these purchases, and with the acute shortage of foreign, and particularly of sterling, exchange caused by the falling off of cotton exports. This immediate and probably temporary difficulty was accentuated by the more permanent difficulty of finding finance for the agricultural and industrial investment which was an essential condition of the attainment of the main object of the revolution—the raising of the living standards of the people.

The redistribution of the big estates, although a step in the right direction, was only a small contribution towards the solution of Egypt's basic social problems of poverty, land-hunger and overpopulation. These could only be remedied by an expansion of the irrigated area and an expansion of industry sufficient to provide for the needs of Egypt's rapidly growing population. Both the one and the other required capital. Egypt's Budget revenue, limited by inefficient methods of collection leading to evasion, diminished by falling Customs revenue due to shortage of foreign exchange, and largely committed to swollen military estimates, was quite insufficient to provide for any considerable capital expenditure. The Egyptian investor, inured to profitable speculation in land or commodities, was unlikely to be attracted by a Government loan at a low rate of interest. The foreign investor had been frightened off both by the antics of previous governments and by a welter of restrictive laws and regulations. The periodically released sterling balances, which might have provided at least part of the capital required, were, as a result of the lack of current sterling earnings, entirely devoted to the financing of current and essential sterling imports. Capital from one or other of the American-financed international organizations was only likely to be made available on any considerable scale on terms involving control and supervision which would not have been politically acceptable.

These economic limitations, combined with the inevitable difficulty of rapidly building up an efficient and honest new administration from the ruins of the old, made it all the more necessary for the Government to consolidate its domestic position by means of a successful solution of the Anglo-Egyptian dispute. It was apparent from the first that General Neguib, although unprepared to recede from Egypt's well-publicized national demands vis-à-vis Great Britain, at all events as regards evacuation from the Canal Zone, was prepared, up to a point, to pursue these demands by methods of negotiation. But the British Government moved with considerable caution in its approach to the new régime.

General Neguib was the first to make a decisive move. It will be remembered that in 1947 a Constitution had been promulgated unilaterally for the Sudan by Great Britain, after Egypt had refused to participate, and that a Legislative

Assembly, boycotted by the pro-Egyptian parties, had come into being. It was soon clear that a further advance on the road to self-government could not be long delayed. The pace of advance towards self-government was in fact set by Egyptian propaganda, which made it necessary for the Umma and other parties represented in the Legislative Assembly forcibly to advocate as attractive an alternative as possible to the pro-Egyptian parties' demand for union with Egypt. The Sudan 'Constitution' promulgated by the Wafd Government in October 1951, unsatisfactory as it was to Sudan political opinion in that it reserved all important powers in Sudanese affairs to Egypt, forced the Sudan Government to outbid the Egyptian offer. Consequently, the Self-Government Ordinance submitted to and approved by the Legislative Assembly in May 1952 provided for immediate elections, followed by a three-year period of self-government, subject to certain reserved powers in the hands of the Governor-General, and complete independence at the end of the three-year period. It was intended that the elections should be held within six months and that the new Ordinance should come into operation after the elections.

That was the position when General Neguib assumed power at the end of July. It seemed as though Egypt was effectively excluded from any decisive share in shaping the future destiny of the Sudan. The denunciation of the condominium by the Wafd Government had in fact been welcomed by the Sudan Government, which had always been unwilling to implement its effective existence. The Wafdist Government's action confirmed the Sudan Government in its determination to ignore Egyptian interests and desires in planning the future of the Sudan.

General Neguib and his Junta had the sense to realize that Egypt's principal and indeed vital interest in the Sudan was the question of access to Nile water. They realized, moreover, that this access was more likely to be secured through a friendly though possibly independent Sudan than through a subservient but probably hostile one. Faruq's removal facilitated the matter of prestige, and a visit by an Umma Party delegation to London in October 1952 to discuss elections with the British Government provided General Neguib with the opportunity for a smart diplomatic coup.

The Umma Party, led by Sir Sayed Abdul Rahman al-Mahdi, son of the Mahdi, the largest party in the Legislative Assembly, was opposed to union with Egypt, and advocated independence for the Sudan. Previous Egyptian governments, which professed to regard Sudanese independence as a thinly disguised euphemism for a British-controlled Sudan, had regarded the Umma Party as creatures of the British. It was therefore a bold stroke for General Neguib to invite al-Mahdi and his delegation to Cairo for consultations on their way to London. After these consultations, General Neguib was able to announce that he had come to an agreement with the Umma delegation on the future of the Sudan. This agreement was rapidly followed by an agreement with the pro-Egyptian parties, a delegation of which had been summoned to Cairo for the purpose. The Egyptian Government then addressed a note to the British Government embodying its proposals for the future of the Sudan based on the two agreements that had been arrived at, intimating at the same time that they were prepared to negotiate a settlement of the Sudan question separately from, and preliminary to, negotiations on evacuation from the Canal Zone.

Since the British Government had for the previous two years been maintaining, in effect, that they were prepared to accept any solution of the Sudan problem acceptable to the people of the Sudan, and since the two principal Sudanese parties had agreed with Egypt on a solution to the Sudan problem closely approximating to the Self-Government Ordinance, to which the British Government was already committed, it seemed that a solution of the Anglo-Egyptian conflict, as far as the Sudan was concerned, was in sight.

The Egyptian note was in substantial accord with, but

not precisely similar to, the agreements signed with the Sudanese political parties, and was based on the provisions of the Self-Government Ordinance. There were, however, differences, of which the most important were:

(a) The Egyptian note proposed that the Governor-General should, during the three-year transition period, be advised by a three-man Commission consisting of an Englishman, an Egyptian, and an Indian or Pakistani. According to the Egyptian proposal, this Commission would, in practice, exercise most of the powers of the Governor-General.

(b) The Egyptian note proposed that Sudanization of all Government services should be completed by the end of the three-year period.

(c) The Egyptian note proposed that the Governor-General's power of veto should only be effective if supported by both co-domini, instead of only one of the co-domini, as provided in the Ordinance.

(d) The Egyptian note proposed the abolition of the Governor-General's special powers over the Southern Sudan during the three-year period as provided in the Ordinance.

The subsequent negotiations between the British and Egyptian Governments were mainly concentrated on the question as to whether the Governor-General should have special powers over the Southern Sudan during the three-year period, and whether Sudanization of the Government services in the Southern Sudan should necessarily be completed during the three-year period. The British Government continued to insist on the necessity for the Governor-General's powers in the Southern Sudan and on the impracticability of Sudanization within three years as far as the South was concerned.

The people of the Southern Sudan—that is to say, the inhabitants of the White Nile, Bahr-al-Ghazal and Equatoria provinces—are non-Arabic-speaking pagans, while the

394

inhabitants of the rest of the Sudan are, for the most part, Arabic-speaking Moslems. Ethnologically and socially, the inhabitants of the Southern Sudan are akin to the inhabitants of the rest of Central Africa. Their inclusion within the boundaries of the Sudan is due mainly to the Franco-British rivalry in Africa during the nineties, which led Kitchener to turn Marchand back from Fashoda and annex the Upper Nile to the Sudan after the Battle of Omdurman. The Sudan Government did not attempt to assimilate the inhabitants of the South with the Arabs of the Northern Sudan, and in administering them relied on paternal rule, missionary education, and the influence of tribal custom, rather than on any attempt to introduce self-government on the Western model. The Egyptians have always criticized this policy as being designed eventually to separate the South from the North, and to assimilate the South with the British colonies of East Africa.

Under the 1947 Constitution, provision was made for representation for the South in the Legislative Assembly, but the South was unrepresented in the principal political parties. In view of the social and political backwardness of the South, there were good administrative reasons for reserving special powers to the Governor-General in respect of the South during the three-year period, as provided in the Self-Government Ordinance. The Umma Party's agreement with the Egyptian Government, involving the abandonment of these reserved powers, must be viewed in relation (a) to the fact that the Umma Party had already voted in favour of these reserved powers in the Legislative Assembly and (b) to the fact that the Umma Party was entirely composed of Northern Sudanese. It was also significant that a new Sudanese political party, the Socialist Republicans, which did contain representatives from the South, at first refused to sign an agreement with the Egyptian Government. Soon afterwards, however, as the result of a tour of the Sudan by Major Salem, a member of the Junta (which seems to have been marked by astonishing discourtesy on both sides), the Socialist

Republicans did join the other Sudanese parties in a united front with the Egyptian Government.

The British Government made it known that they would like to hold elections in the Sudan and to leave the points at issue to be decided by the new Sudanese Parliament. But it seemed probable that not only the Ashigga group of parties, but the Umma party also, would boycott elections unless the Self-Government Ordinance were amended in accordance with the terms of the agreements signed between the Egyptian Government and the various Sudanese parties.

After considerable negotiation, an Agreement was arrived at between the British and Egyptian Governments on 6 February 1953. This Agreement (Appendix IV) in effect made the condominium genuinely operative for the first time since its promulgation in 1899, constituting as it did a freely-negotiated Anglo-Egyptian instrument for the administration of the Sudan. The period of this administration was limited to a transitional period of three years, at the end of which it was provided that the Sudanese people should choose between sovereign independence and union with Egypt. The most important points in the Agreement were as follows:

(*a*) Elections for a Sudanese Parliament to be held as soon as possible and supervised by an international Commission.

(*b*) Powers of the [British] Governor-General to remain as provided for in the Self-Government Ordinance, but the Governor-General to be supervised and controlled by a five-member international Commission formally appointed by the Egyptian Government.

(*c*) Formation of a Sudanization Committee with the object of 'Sudanizing' the administrative services during the three-year period.

(*d*) Provision for the election of a Constituent Assembly within three years to make arrangements for self-determination.

(e) Withdrawal of British and Egyptian troops from the Sudan before the election of the Constituent Assembly.

Egyptian suspicions of the British Governor-General and the British administration generally were met by the provision of an international Commission to supervise the Governor-General. The British desire for the retention of the Governor-General's special powers over the South was met by leaving these powers substantially unchanged, but subject to the supervision of the international Commission.

The fruitful implementation of such an Agreement was obviously dependent on an improvement in the traditional attitude of suspicion which dominated relations between successive Egyptian Governments in Cairo and the British-controlled Administration in the Sudan. Soon after the signing of the Agreement, charges and counter-charges of bad faith began to be bandied about. At the administrative level, each side clearly regarded its primary duty as being the frustration of the real or imagined intrigues of the other side. Each side regarded the other as working for the ultimate control of the Sudan under the cloak of self-determination. In these circumstances, it was not to be expected that the Agreement, however it worked in the Sudan, would result in any noticeable improvement in Anglo-Egyptian relations as a whole. In this wider field the only effect of the Agreement was to concentrate Egyptian attention on the other, and seemingly more intractable, point at issue.

Negotiations on the future of the Canal Zone opened in Cairo some two months after the conclusion of the Sudan Agreement. In the interval, the Egyptian Government made it clear, in public and semi-public pronouncements, that their attitude towards the presence of British troops in the Canal Zone did not differ materially from that taken up by their Wafdist predecessors. They made it clear that they would require an unconditional British agreement to withdraw all troops from the Canal Zone within a stated period, expressed in months rather than in years, as a prelude to discussions about a possible new agreement for mutual defence. The British attitude, expressed in various negotiations which had taken place from 1948 onwards, was that they would be prepared to concede evacuation of combatant troops in return for the conclusion of a new mutual defence agreement. The difference between the two parties was really one of confidence. Neither trusted the other sufficiently to desert the entrenched positions in which they had dug themselves. Egypt maintained the right of a sovereign state to choose whether or not to have foreign troops on its territory; Great Britain took its stand on possession, on the 1936 Treaty, and on the necessities of the cold war.

There was no sign of any renewed confidence between the Governments of the two countries. The British Conservative Government had shown no sign of any desire to assist General Neguib to consolidate the new régime in Egypt; the Egyptian Government, whether because of domestic exigencies or because of disappointment at British coolness, showed no tendency, as it had done over the Sudan, to retreat from the attitude taken up by its predecessors. In these circumstances, the negotiations, which started in Cairo between Sir Ralph Stevenson, the British Ambassador, advised by General Sir Brian Robertson, towards the end of April seemed almost foredoomed to failure.[4]

In the event, negotiations were broken off on 6 May. It was made clear on both sides that the reason for the breakdown was the Egyptian Government's insistence that any British troops remaining to operate the base should be under Egyptian control, and replaceable by Egyptians, at Egyptian instance, as and when, in the opinion of the Egyptian Government, there were Egyptians trained sufficiently to take their places. The British view was that it was technically impossible to maintain the base under such conditions. But the real basis of disagreement was not a technical dispute as to the extent to and the speed at which British technicians could be replaced by Egyptians. Public utterances on both sides after the breakdown of negotiations made it clear that the pre-conditions of an alliance simply did not exist. The Egyptian Government did not feel the need for British help and protection; the British Government did not feel the need for Egyptian co-operation and friendship. Threats of violence came from the Egyptian side; expressions of determination to resist violence from the British. Anglo-Egyptian relations entered one of their periodical phases of crisis, characterized, as usual, on both sides by a readiness to wound combined with a reluctance to strike.

In the short run, British troops could not be ousted from Egypt by any force which the Egyptians could raise. In the long run, the base could not be maintained in the face of sustained Egyptian hostility. Ultimately, the choice before Great Britain was either to dismantle the base or to hand it over to Egypt as part of a new treaty of alliance. British policy was concerned to postpone the taking of this choice, Egyptian policy to force this choice upon Great Britain. The reason for British procrastination lay in the hope that future circumstances might induce Egypt to moderate her demand for complete evacuation or induce her to acquiesce in the denial of that demand. But Egyptian moderation or acquiescence was only likely in the event of the imminence or outbreak of a third world war. Any other supposition was Micawberish.

In the dispute little was said by either party about the 1936 Treaty. This Treaty had been denounced by the Egyptians and, at all events since its denunciation by the Egyptians, disregarded by the British, who, because of the Egyptian threat to the base, maintained in the Canal Zone a force some eight times greater than the maximum provided for in the Treaty. But the Treaty remained relevant in that, in accordance with its terms, Great Britain would have, on its expiry in 1956, to seek permission from the United Nations to maintain troops in Egypt after that date (except in the event of an agreement on the subject between Egypt and Great Britain). It was doubtful whether such permission would be forthcoming from the United Nations.

From the British point of view, there were therefore cogent reasons for trying to arrive at an amicable settlement before 1956. From the Egyptian point of view there were equally cogent reasons for standing firm and waiting for the access of diplomatic support which they could reasonably expect to receive on the expiration of the Treaty. From both points of view there were cogent reasons for keeping the situation 'off the boil' until 1956.

That was the position as it stood in July 1953. An agreement with Great Britain to transfer the base to Egyptian control, or even to remove the base from Egypt altogether, would go very far to secure the continued existence of the Neguib régime in Egypt, and also to release the latent reformist energies of that régime. While failure to secure such an agreement would not necessarily prove fatal to the continued existence of the régime, it would undoubtedly affect its popularity, and so encourage its recourse to dictatorial methods and, possibly, to violence. Whatever view be taken of the Neguib régime, there was no doubt that, from the Western point of view, any politically possible change, whether to the Right or to the Left, would be a change for the worse. The question for the British Government was whether the continued existence and relative friendliness of the Neguib régime was worth purchasing at the cost of transferring to Egyptian control or of abandoning a base which it might not be possible to continue maintaining for very much longer. The British Government, through the mouth of Sir Winston Churchill, answered this question with an emphatic negative.[5] Whether or not this was to be the final word probably depended on whether the British Government were prepared later to revise their estimate of the Neguib régime in Egypt.

In the eyes of the Neguib régime, the father of Egyptian nationalism is not Zaghlul but Arabi. General Neguib himself invites comparison with Arabi. Like Arabi, he is of comparatively humble birth. Like Arabi, he is an Army officer who led a military coup against the monarch and the pashas.

But Neguib's coup, unlike Arabi's, was successful. Arabi's coup was frustrated by British intervention in favour of the monarch and the pashas. The presence of British troops in the Canal Zone is, in the eyes of the Neguib régime, a remnant and reminder of the British occupation of 1882. As Arabi's successor and avenger, quite apart from any other aspect of the matter, General Neguib regards it as a sacred duty to procure the evacuation of these troops. The parallel with Arabi must be borne closely in mind by anyone wishing to try to understand the Neguib régime. The régime's consciousness of this parallel was probably heightened by the suspicion with which it was regarded by the British Government. There was even a legend that the British Government considered intervention in favour of Faruq at the time of Neguib's coup, and were only prevented from such intervention by the United States.

British suspicion of the Neguib régime was influenced by two independent factors. First, there was the traditional British mistrust of all military coups and military dictatorships. This mistrust also operated in the case of Arabi. Secondly, there was the reaction from the Arab League policy, which collapsed in ruins at the time of the Palestine war. This reaction took the form of an extreme scepticism towards any suggestion that anything good could possibly come out of the Arab world. The violence of the reaction was proportional to the extravagance of the original assumption that the Arab League could be erected into an Anglophile, economically viable, and politically integrated federation. 'Once bitten, twice shy.'

The opinion has been expressed that the British Government of the day made a mistake in restoring the Khedive instead of supporting Arabi. At that time the British Government had very little material, and that mostly unfavourable, with which to judge the potentialities of Arabi and his associates as rulers of Egypt. There is rather more material with which to judge the Neguib régime.

The Neguib régime must, in fairness, be judged by

comparison with its Egyptian predecessors and potential successors. In view of the corruption, the administrative inefficiency, and the economic chaos to which it succeeded, it must be judged, not by its achievements after a year of office, but by its potentialities. A cynic, surveying the Egyptian scene after a year of the new order is tempted to murmur: *'Plus ça change, plus c'est la même chose.'* Even a kindlier critic is impelled to reflect on the proverbial use which a cruel destiny makes of good intentions when unaccompanied by any machinery for implementing them. But a friend of Egypt, viewing the Egyptian scene with a dispassionate, if disillusioned, eye, discounting irritation at the appurtenances of an immature and inexperienced military dictatorship, and ignoring the crude propaganda with which the régime seeks to commend itself to the world at large, can discern the gradual disappearance of undesirable things which were there before and the gradual appearance of desirable things which were not there before.

The court, which, by its influence and example, encouraged habits of corruption, immorality, greed, and extravagance, has disappeared. The big landowners, who, for the most part, had no interest in their land and tenants except as a means of providing them with money for extravagant and, usually, gross living, are disappearing. The professional politicians, who regarded power primarily as a means of illicit gain, are no longer in the fashion. There are signs of a newly-born spirit of public service and sense of public obligation among members of the educated classes. There are signs that students are thinking of patriotism in terms other than the shouting of slogans and the burning of tramcars. There are evidences of a disposition to will the means as well as merely willing the ends of social reform.

It is true that these things have not yet blossomed forth into any sort of achievement. They may never so blossom forth. Newly awakened energies and enthusiasms are being diverted towards and may be lost among the sterile deserts of anti-British agitation. If this happens, the Egyptian revolution may either harden into wooden-faced and jack-booted authoritarianism or dissolve into a morass of fanaticism, xenophobia, and pseudo-Communism. Meanwhile, the hope and possibility of renaissance exist. This hope and this possibility could not have been brought to birth by democratic means. The Egyptian parliamentary system did not contain within itself the germ of reform. Any criticism of the Neguib régime based on its method of attaining power is absurd.

The British Government is faced with the necessity of making up its mind as to whether the Egyptian revolution is just another military *coup d'état*, or whether it is indeed the rebirth of a nation. On the rightness of Great Britain's choice depends not only the future of British influence in the Middle East, but also the future of Egypt. For Egypt, unreasonable though it may seem to Western eyes, is quite capable of strangling herself with the umbilical cord which, as Egypt sees it, still binds her unwillingly to Great Britain.

In the past Great Britain began by underrating Mohamed Ali and Ataturk; these errors of judgement were subsequently repaired without much difficulty or loss. Since then international politics have become more complicated, and such errors are less easily repaired. Errors of judgement over Palestine have exacted heavy forfeits. Another failure accurately to discern the shape of things to come in the Middle East could have dire consequences. In this matter Great Britain, whether she likes it or not, has a responsibility not only towards her own people and the people of Egypt, but towards the peoples of the whole world.

NOTES ON CHAPTER TWENTY

1. Sir Ralph Stevenson replaced Sir Ronald Campbell as British Ambassador in the summer of 1950.

2. The 1936 Treaty specified that the number of British troops in the Canal Zone should be limited to 10,000 in time of peace. It was understood that these would mainly consist of technical and administrative personnel. When the Egyptian Government denounced the Treaty, the base was heavily reinforced

by combat troops until the number of British troops in the Canal Zone rose to about 80,000.

3. Within a year, on 18 June 1953, the Regency and all royal titles were abolished, and a Republic proclaimed, with General Neguib as President.

4. General Sir Brian Robertson had formerly been C.-in-C. British Land Forces in the Middle East.

5. In a speech made by Sir Winston Churchill in a foreign affairs debate in the House of Commons in May 1953, Sir Winston (who was, at the time, acting Foreign Secretary as well as Prime Minister) reiterated the British intention of remaining in the Canal Zone until satisfactory alternative arrangements were made. He also took the opportunity to make some slighting references to General Neguib.

POSTSCRIPT
THE ROAD TO SUEZ

THE abrogation of the Egyptian Constitution in February 1953 and the announcement of a 'period of transition' had been followed by the setting-up of a Revolutionary Command Council (RCC), consisting of the thirteen members of the military 'Junta' under the chairmanship of Mohamed Neguib. The RCC was the supreme executive authority in Egypt, acting under the nominal authority of a mainly civilian Cabinet, of which Mohamed Neguib was Prime Minister and in which was vested supreme legislative authority. On 18 June 1953, a month after the breaking-off of negotiations with the British about the future of the Canal Zone, the end of the Egyptian Monarchy was proclaimed and a Republic set up. Mohamed Neguib became President of the Republic, as well as remaining Prime Minister and Chairman of the RCC, but the office of Commander-in-Chief of the armed forces, which he had previously held, was taken over by Abdul Hakim Amer, one of the young revolutionary officers, and an intimate of Gamal Abdul Nasir, who became Deputy Prime Minister and Minister of the Interior.

Gamal Abdul Nasir was the acknowledged leader of the group of young officers who had engineered the coup of July 1952. At the time of the coup he was in his middle thirties. He was of middle class origin, the son of a minor government official, and a Lieutenant-Colonel in the Army. He had fought with bravery and distinction in the Palestine campaign. He had been engaged in underground revolutionary activity since his student days and had for many years been busy organising a subversive group in the

405

Army, dedicated to the overthrow of the regime and to the liberation of Egypt from foreign control and from domestic corruption. In his first impact on the Egyptian public, after the proclamation of the Republic, he appeared as a saturnine, awkward-seeming figure by contrast with the good-natured Neguib. It was not until later that he developed the 'common touch' and the demagogic talents which were to make him famous.

It soon became apparent that Gamal Abdul Nasir was the real driving force behind the Revolution. Within nine months he was to become the real master of the country. These nine months were occupied in a struggle for power between Abdul Nasir and Neguib from which Abdul Nasir emerged completely victorious. It was waged bloodlessly and mainly behind the scenes. It was a struggle not of personalities but of principles. At the time of the July 1952 coup the military Junta had had no idea of setting up a permanent military dictatorship in Egypt. They simply aimed at removing the 'old gang' in the hope and expectation that this removal would liberate the forces of reform which, they assumed, were being stifled by the corruptions of the 'old gang.' Mohamed Neguib had been selected by the young officers as a respected senior officer to act as the titular leader of the coup. But it was not long before Abdul Nasir and the more radical and more perceptive members of the Junta realised that reform was not merely a matter of purging corruption. Slowly, probably reluctantly, but inevitably, they came to realise that there could be no reform without revolution. But Mohamed Neguib, who held great titular power in his hands and who, moreover, had won great popularity in Egypt in his role as a father-figure, and considerable respect abroad by his role in the Sudan negotiations with Britain, appears to have held to the original idea of the coup and to have continued thinking in terms of a fairly rapid reversion to constitutional life. He came to regard Abdul Nasir and the more radical members of the RCC as young hotheads and was no longer willing to accept his role as a figurehead. He began to claim the right to veto the decisions of the RCC. By the end of the year, there was more or less open disagreement between Neguib on the one hand and Abdul Nasir and the majority of the RCC on the other.

The first 'showdown' came on 24 February 1954 when it was announced by the RCC that Neguib had been relieved of the posts of President, Prime Minister, and Chairman of the RCC and that Abdul Nasir had replaced him as Prime Minister and Chairman, leaving the Presidency vacant. This announcement, which attributed Neguib's removal to his attempts to monopolize power, was greeted with widespread popular demonstrations of sympathy with Neguib. Within a few days, Neguib was invited by the RCC to return to the Presidency. He accepted and, almost immediately, announced dates for elections and for the convocation of a Constituent Assembly, abolished martial law and the Press censorship, and reinstated himself in the Premiership and in the Chairmanship of the RCC. Neguib had, to all appearance, won the day. The RCC announced its intention to dissolve itself, to grant full political rights, to hold free elections, and to allow an elected National Assembly to choose a President. All political internees (except for communists) were released.

But behind the scenes Abdul Nasir, organising his relationships with the Army, with the police, and with the workers' syndicates, was preparing to strike back. This was the decisive moment for the Egyptian Revolution. On 29 March the RCC rescinded all the liberal decisions they had taken only a few days before. A fortnight later, Abdul Nasir once more replaced Neguib as Prime Minister and Chairman of the RCC, leaving Neguib, for the time being, with the Presidency. Abdul Nasir accomplished this without opposition either from his colleagues in the RCC (except for one, who resigned) or from the Army, and without overt opposition from public opinion. From henceforth he was the real master of the country.

The first matter to which Gamal Abdul Nasir addressed himself was the conclusion of an agreement with Britain over the Canal Zone. He imposed security measures in the Zone and arrested many of those who had been causing trouble to British troops. The Press, once more under censorship, became more moderate in its references to Britain. In the improved atmosphere which resulted negotiations with Britain, which had been broken off in May 1953, were resumed. On 27 July, after several weeks of hard bargaining in Cairo between the RCC on the one hand and the British Ambassador, Sir Ralph Stevenson, and the British Commander-in-Chief Middle East, General Sir Brian Robertson, on the other, Heads of Agreement were initialled. They provided, (a) for the evacuation of all British forces from Egypt within twenty months of the signature of the Agreement; (b) for British bases in the Canal Zone to be maintained by British civilian contractors for a period of seven years; (c) for British forces to re-occupy the Canal Zone in the event of an attack by any outside power on Egypt, or on any other country which was a party to the Arab Collective Security Pact of 1950, or on Turkey. The Agreement was signed, and came into force, on 19 October 1954.

The Agreement was regarded with some scepticism in Britain, particularly by right-wing Conservatives. It was justified by the British Government on the grounds that technical and strategic developments had made the Canal Base less important than before and that it was a necessary act of faith in the future of Anglo-Egyptian relations. In Egypt, Abdul Nasir announced, rather ominously, that 'One stage of our struggle has ended and a new stage is about to begin.' Egyptian Press comment put more emphasis on 'final liberation from imperialism' than on future co-operation with Britain. The Anglo-Egyptian Chamber of Commerce in London expressed the hope that the way was now open for a rapid expansion of trade between the two countries.

It is convenient at this point briefly to refer to events in the Sudan after the conclusion of the Anglo-Egyptian Agreement over the Sudan in February 1953. The general elections in the Sudan provided for in the Agreement were held in the autumn of 1953 and resulted in a victory for the Ashigga group of parties, which took office in January 1954 under the Premiership of Ismail Azhari. The Ashigga's victory had undoubtedly been assisted by Egyptian money and Egyptian-inspired propaganda which alleged that the Umma party was supported by the British and played upon the alleged heresies and past atrocities of the Mahdiya. But subsequent attempts by the Egyptian Government to influence the Sudanese in favour of union with Egypt at the end of the three-year transitional period laid down in the Agreement were more and more resented by Sudanese opinion generally and even by the supposedly pro-Egyptian Sudanese Government. Abdul Nasir, with some statesmanship, realised that the prospect of an independent and friendly Sudan was better than the prospect of a subservient and hostile one; he therefore made an abrupt change in Egyptian policy, recognised the inevitability of Sudanese independence, and removed from the direction of Sudan affairs Salah Salem, a member of the RCC who had won international notoriety as the 'dancing Major' during one of his propaganda visits to the Sudan, and who was identified in the eyes of the Sudanese with the previous Egyptian policy of 'Unity of the Nile Valley.' In August 1955 the Sudanese Parliament passed a resolution demanding the withdrawal of foreign troops from the Sudan — a demand which was promptly complied with both by the British and Egyptian Governments. In December 1955 both Houses of the Sudanese Parliament passed unanimous declarations that the Sudan was 'to become a fully independent sovereign State.' These declarations by-passed the provisions in the Anglo-Egyptian Agreement for the election of a Constituent Assembly at the end of the three-year transitional period to make arrangements for self-determination, but neither Britain nor Egypt were disposed to make any objection and, on 1 January 1956, the Prime Minister of the Sudan, Ismail Azhari, read out at a joint session of the Sudanese Houses of Parliament declarations from the British and Egyptian Governments recognising Sudanese independence. Nineteen days later the Sudan was admitted to membership of the Arab League and, in November 1956, to membership of the United Nations. In December 1958 the Sudanese Constitution was overthrown as the result of a military coup which had, as one of its objects, the elimination of such Egyptian influence as still remained in the Sudan. The resultant military regime has, however, remained on reasonably good terms with Egypt and, in October 1959, concluded a Nile Waters Agreement with Egypt which superseded the 1929 Agreement and provided for a new allocation of irrigation water between the two countries. Relations between Britain and the Sudan have likewise been friendly, both under the constitutional and military regimes, although there is no military alliance or other 'special relationship.'

In the autumn of 1954 Abdul Nasir, having temporarily stabilised Anglo-Egyptian relations, turned his attention to domestic affairs and to Egypt's relations with the rest of the Arab world. On the domestic front, with the political parties dissolved and broken, and with Neguib sitting in the Presidency in innocuous desuetude, the only serious political opponents of the regime were the Moslem Brotherhood. The Brotherhood, which could be regarded as a rival revolutionary group, had at first welcomed the coup, but had become more and more critical both of the military regime's secularising tendencies and of its determination to treat the Brotherhood as just another political party, to be purged, controlled and emasculated in accordance with the requirements of what was beginning to emerge as a one-Party, dictatorial State. An attempt by a member of the Brotherhood to assassinate Abdul Nasir in

August 1954 was used as an occasion to put an end to the Brotherhood as an organised entity. Several thousand members were arrested, caches of arms, ammunition and propaganda material were unearthed and confiscated. Many of those arrested were tried and sentenced to terms of imprisonment; a few were hanged. The Brotherhood was broken up and ceased to count as a significant factor in the Egyptian scheme of things. Evidence given in the trials suggested that some members of the Brotherhood had intended to overthrow the RCC and invite Mohamed Neguib to assume supreme power. It is uncertain whether Neguib was privy to any plans which the Brotherhood might have had to this end, but the opportunity was taken to remove him from the Presidency and to place him under house arrest.

The assault on the Moslem Brotherhood momentarily shocked public opinion in other Arab countries, particularly in Syria, where many of the Brotherhood leaders obtained sanctuary, and in Saudi Arabia. This hostility made Abdul Nasir seek for some understanding with Iraq as the basis of his Arab policy. In pursuit of this Salah Salem went to Baghdad in August for discussions with Nuri Said, the Prime Minister of Iraq. In September Nuri Said came to Cairo. These conversations disclosed a radical disagreement between the two Governments in their approach to defence relationships between the Arab States and the non-Arab world. The Egyptian attitude which Abdul Nasir had inherited, without acknowledgement, from the old regime, was that the 'cold war' was no affair of the Arabs, that the communist threat from Russia was a British invention designed to perpetuate British control of the Middle East, and that the Arabs were quite capable of defending themselves from the only attack likely to be made upon them, which was from Israel. The Anglo-Egyptian Agreement, although it was, in form, a joint defence arrangement between Britain and Egypt against the possibility of communist aggression, was regarded by

Abdul Nasir simply as a means of securing the evacuation of British troops from the Canal Zone, and it is clear that he never paid any serious regard to the reciprocal obligations which Egypt had assumed under the Agreement. Immediately after the initialling of the Agreement, he began to develop that policy of Arab 'neutralism' with which he later became identified and, in so doing, came into immediate collision with Nuri Said. The Iraqi Government, which had seen at closer quarters than Egypt the Russian attempts to subvert Turkey and Iran, and which traditionally (e.g. in the pre-war Saadabad Pact) had closer ties with Turkey than did the rest of the Arab world, was not inclined to subordinate Iraq's defence needs to a conception of Arab solidarity which, if it came to the point, could do nothing to satisfy those needs, and was already thinking in terms of an association with NATO by means of a defence agreement with Turkey, which was already a member of NATO. This divergence in outlook between the two Governments, which became apparent at the talks held in Baghdad and Cairo during August and September, led Abdul Nasir, in October, to call a meeting of the Foreign Ministers of the member States of the Arab League with a view to trying to dissuade Iraq from allying herself with Turkey and so, indirectly, with NATO. This attempt was unsuccessful and, in January 1955, the conclusion of a defence pact between Turkey and Iraq was announced from Baghdad. Iraq's action was publicly criticised by the Egyptian Government which summoned the member States of the Arab Collective Security Pact to a meeting in Cairo. Iraq refused to attend. After this meeting Saudi Arabia, Yemen, and Syria publicly aligned themselves with Egypt against Iraq.

On 30 March 1955 the Turco-Iraqi Agreement—henceforth to be known as the Baghdad Pact — was enlarged and underlined by the adherence of Britain. (It was to be joined by Pakistan in September and by Iran in October.) Britain's adherence was evidence of a re-thinking by the

British Government about Middle East defence since the signature of the Anglo-Egyptian Agreement the previous October. The Baghdad Pact was seen, in British eyes, as an alternative to that Middle Eastern strategy which, up to the time of the 1954 Agreement, had been based on the British military presence in the Canal Zone. The British Government was still thinking in terms of a 'special position' in the Middle East. Previously, the existence of this 'special position' had been safeguarded by the existence of the Suez Base which preserved the possibility of rapid and effective British military intervention at any point in the Middle East and which ensured that British interests would not be neglected in any political dispositions which might be made in the Middle East. The Baghdad Pact was a British attempt to ensure that this 'special position' should survive the Suez Base by attracting a majority of Arab States, starting with Iraq, into an alliance with Britain based on that 'special position.' This attempt was seen by Abdul Nasir as a direct challenge to his crescent ambitions for leadership in the Arab world: similarly Abdul Nasir's ambitions were seen by the British Government as a threat to that 'special position' in the Middle East which they regarded as vital to British interests. Thus, within a few weeks of the signature of the Anglo-Egyptian Agreement, the stage was set for a struggle between Britain and Egypt for hegemony in the Arab world.

This atmosphere of mutual rivalry and resentment was accentuated by Abdul Nasir's tumultuous irruption into the field of Arab-Israeli conflict. Up to the beginning of 1955, the revolutionary Government of Egypt had avoided taking any leading part in Arab demonstrations against Israel. Although Egypt associated herself with the general Arab non-recognition and boycott of Israel, and although the Suez Canal remained closed to Israeli shipping, the Egyptian attitude towards Israel had, by Arab standards, been one of almost treasonable moderation. The Egyptian-administered Gaza strip had certainly been used by Palestinian refugees as a base for a certain number of not very well-organised, not very lethal raids into Israeli territory, but these raids, although probably connived at, had not been organised by the Egyptian Government. In February 1955, the Israeli Government, exasperated by these raids, retaliated with a large-scale, successful and destructive counter-attack, which penetrated deeply into the Gaza strip, destroyed quantities of Egyptian arms and ammunition, and killed and wounded a number of Egyptian troops.

It was already becoming apparent to Abdul Nasir that the leadership of the Arab world to which he aspired would demand some more positive evidence of Egyptian hostility towards Israel. The Israeli raid made it necessary, for prestige reasons, to take some immediate and resounding action in this direction. An attack on Israel was impracticable; Abdul Nasir had no illusions about the military results of such an attack. There was an alternative, which would not commit Egypt to fighting Israel, but which would both reinforce Egypt's neutrality propaganda vis-à-vis Britain and Iraq and which would demonstrate Egyptian hostility towards Israel.

After the armistices which had put an end to the Palestine war in 1949, Britain, France and the United States had, in 1950, issued a Tri-Partite Declaration in which they had expressed readiness to supply both Israel and the Arab States with arms for internal security and for self-defence and to take action 'both within and outside the United Nations' to prevent the violation by force of any Middle Eastern frontier or armistice line. In practice the implementation of this Declaration resolved itself into the application of a rationing system in the supply of arms both to the Arab States and to Israel with a view to trying to ensure that neither side had a preponderance of arms with which to attack the other. In September 1955, Abdul Nasir, complaining that this rationing system by the Western Powers was preventing Egypt from taking proper

measures of self-defence against Israel, announced the conclusion of an Agreement between Egypt and Czechoslo-
vakia by which Egypt would receive large quantities of war
equipment, including Russian aircraft and tanks, in exchange for rice and cotton. This announcement, which
evoked protests and warnings from Britain and the United
States, was greeted with tremendous enthusiasm in the
Arab world. Even the Iraqi Government commended it,
since it was directed against Israel, towards whom Iraq
had hitherto shewed a hostility much more uncompromising than that of Egypt.

This additional blow to Anglo-Egyptian relations was
followed, in October 1955, by the conclusion of a military
pact between Egypt, Saudi Arabia and Syria which replaced the by now moribund Arab Collective Security Pact
signed in 1950. With Iraq in the Western camp, Lebanon
and Jordan remained precariously perched on the fence.
Jordan was bound to Iraq by dynastic ties and to Britain
by indispensable grants-in-aid. In November 1955 the
Jordan Government made enquiries from the British Government about the possibility of joining the Baghdad Pact,
thus presenting Abdul Nasir with a direct and unmistake-
able challenge. In December, General Sir Gerald Templer,
the British Chief of the Imperial General Staff, went to
Amman for discussions. His visit was marked by serious
disorders throughout Jordan, and the Jordan Government
decided not to join the Pact. There can be no doubt that,
in coming to this decision, the Jordan Government was
influenced by pressure from the Egyptian Government
which, by radio propaganda and bribery, had incited the
disorders, and, by diplomatic pressure, had intimidated
the Jordan Government. The result was a considerable
diplomatic victory for Abdul Nasir and a corresponding
defeat for the British Government. Three months later, in
March 1956, King Husain, under strong popular pressure,
summarily dismissed General Glubb, the British Commander-in-Chief of the Jordan Army, together with such

415

few British officers as remained in the Jordan service. From then on Jordan was slowly sucked into the Egyptian orbit.

Meanwhile, Abdul Nasir was endeavouring to cope with Egypt's urgent domestic problems, foremost among which was the pressure of a rapidly increasing population on a limited area of cultivable land. The Agrarian Reform Law, which had expropriated the bigger landlords, redistributed their estates, limited agricultural rents, and made some attempt to fix minimum agricultural wages, had not of itself done much towards a solution of the problem which was one, not of redistribution, but of increasing agricultural and industrial production. Schemes for increasing production became concentrated on a proposal for the erection of a High Dam at Aswan which, by providing a reservoir for 130 milliards of water (as compared with 5 milliards stored by the existing Aswan Dam) would enable the cultivable area of Egypt to be increased by some 30%, would provide for flood protection, would insure against abnormally low Niles, and would provide for the generation of large quantities of cheap electricity for industry. Such a scheme would require enormous foreign currency expenditure which, as it appeared at the time, could only be financed by the provision of loans from the West. Abdul Nasir had already, in November 1954, received a loan of 40 million dollars from the United States Government for irrigation and general development and it seemed likely that a request for finance for the High Dam would be sympathetically regarded by both the United States and British Governments. It was the kind of development which both powers had been urging on the underdeveloped countries as a means of raising the standard of living of their populations and so of inoculating these populations against the allurements of communism. It might also have been felt in Washington and in London that this kind of peaceful development, which would absorb so much of Egypt's financial and administrative energies, might well divert Abdul Nasir from less peaceful

416

political adventures beyond Egypt's borders and might well bind Abdul Nasir with chains of gold to the Western powers. The United States Government, since the Czechoslovakian arms deal, and as a result of growing Egyptian trade relations with the Soviet bloc (in part the result of this arms deal, in part the result of a diminished British demand for Egyptian cotton) was concerned lest Egypt might become a Russian satellite. The British Government was concerned at Abdul Nasir's successful opposition to the Baghdad Pact. Both Governments saw the High Dam scheme as representing the Dr. Jekyll side of Abdul Nasir's character and, with varying degrees of scepticism, resolved to encourage it. Conversations were started between the Egyptian and United States and British Governments towards the end of 1955 and, in February 1956, a provisional agreement was announced. The World Bank would lend Egypt 200 million dollars on condition that the United States and British Governments would between them lend her 70 million dollars to pay for imported materials and services required for the High Dam: Egypt was to provide the equivalent of 900 million dollars in local currency for local services and materials, and the whole scheme was made dependent on the conclusion of agreements between Egypt and the other Nilotic States for the utilisation of the waters.

It was not long before the United States Government began to have second thoughts about this provisional agreement. In the first place Abdul Nasir, in an attempt to avoid that reliance on the West which a full implementation of the provisional agreement would have involved, began sounding Russia about the possibility of participation in the financing of the High Dam. In the second place the Czechoslovakian arms agreement, under which very large quantities of arms were being imported into Egypt, was diverting more and more of Egypt's trade to the communist bloc and appeared to provide evidence of Egypt's aggressive intentions against Israel. In the third

417

place, the China lobby in Congress (whose consent would be necessary for the implementation of the provisional agreement) was irritated at the recognition of communist China by the Egyptian Government. The British Government was irritated by the fact that the half-promised loan was not deterring Abdul Nasir either from his subversionary activities in Jordan, or from his attempted sabotage of the Baghdad Pact, or from his obvious determination to denounce the 1954 Agreement in the event of its ever being invoked by the British Government. The French Government was furious at the assistance being given by Abdul Nasir to the Algerian rebels.

In July 1954 the United States Government, having apparently received information to the effect that the Russian Government would not be willing to finance the High Dam in the event of no loan being forthcoming from the West, informed the Egyptian Government that they were withdrawing their provisional offer of a loan for the construction of the High Dam on the ground that Egypt's financial position had deteriorated since the provisional offer had been made to an extent which made the Egyptian economy unable to bear the Egyptian share of finance under the terms of the agreement. As a result of the United States Government's decision the World Bank and the British Government also withdrew their provisional offers. Sir Anthony Eden (Lord Avon), the British Prime Minister at the time, has since stated that the British Government, before the withdrawal of the United States offer, had come to the conclusion that 'they could not go on with a project likely to become increasingly onerous in finance and unsatisfactory in practice,' that they 'were informed but not consulted' about the manner of the United States Government's withdrawal of the provisional offer, and that 'we were sorry that the matter was carried through so abruptly, because it gave our two countries no chance to concert either timing or methods, though these were quite as important as the substance.' He adds, 'I would have preferred to play this long and not to have forced the issue.'[1]

By this time Gamal Abdul Nasir had become a considerable personage both in Egypt and in the world generally. In May 1956 the last British troops had left Egypt in accordance with the provisions of the 1954 Agreement. In June 1956 a new Constitution was promulgated for the Republic of Egypt. It declared Islam to be the religion of the State and recognised Egypt as a part of the 'Arab nation.' It provided for government by a President and a Council of Ministers and for a single Legislative Chamber, members of which would be elected democratically. (Elections to a National Assembly were held in July 1957. The Assembly met later in the year but was dissolved in February 1958 after the Union with Syria.) The Constitution was inaugurated by a Referendum in which the people were invited to vote 'yes' or 'no' for the Constitution and 'yes' or 'no' for Abdul Nasir as President. There were no other candidates. In each case the vote was over 99% affirmative. In the Arab world, with the pro-Egyptian alignment in Syria and, more lately, in Jordan, and with the continued subservience of the spendthrift King Saud, Abdul Nasir had become an herioc figure. Jordan had been regarded as a bastion and Glubb as a symbol of continuing British influence in the Middle East. The fall of that bastion and the abrupt disappearance of that symbol had had a profound effect in Iraq, in Lebanon and in the Persian Gulf Shaikhdoms, where opposition to the Western-orientated regimes became identified with Arab nationalism, just as support for the existing regimes became identified with imperialism. Even in North Africa Abdul Nasir was seen as a symbol of liberation. Arms and money were being given by Egypt to the Algerian rebels. Egyptian aid and comfort was being given to those nationalist elements in Tunisia who had not reconciled themselves with the 'collaborationist' regime of Habib Bourguiba. In the world at large Abdul Nasir had established close

relations with Nehru and Tito and, with them, was trying to lead the newly-independent nations of Asia and
Africa down a middle road which led neither to Washington nor Moscow.

When the news of the withdrawal of the United States'
provisional offer arrived in Cairo Abdul Nasir had just
returned from Brioni where he had attended a meeting
with Nehru and Tito. His reaction was swift and effective.
On 24 July he made a public speech attacking the United
States in particular and promised the Egyptian people that
the High Dam would be financed without Western assistance. On 26 July, in a speech at Alexandria which was
greeted with delirious enthusiasm by those who listened
to it, he announced the nationalisation of the Suez Canal
Company and stated that the profits from the Canal would
finance the High Dam. In this speech, which was delivered
mainly in colloquial Arabic, Abdul Nasir for the first time
displayed his talent as a rabble-rousing orator and for the
first time roused the Egyptian people to real enthusiasm.
He had moved a long way from the silent, gauche, rather
sinister figure of 1953 with 'a smile like the silver fittings
on a coffin.' Even as he was speaking, Egyptian police were
surrounding the offices of the Canal Company in Ismailia
and the new Council for the Administration of the Canal,
under the Chairmanship of Mahmud Yunis, was holding
its first meeting in Cairo. The Nationalization Law transferred to the Egyptian State all the assets of the Canal
Company, undertook to compensate shareholders, and
froze the funds of the Company in Egypt and abroad. The
Law also provided for the continued employment of Company employees and contained sanctions of imprisonment
against employees leaving their work without permission.

The act of nationalization produced a wave of enthusiasm throughout the Arab world comparable to, but even
greater than, the enthusiasm which had greeted the Czechoslovakian arms deal nearly a year before. It was one more
act of defiance, one more piece of vicarious satisfaction to

set against thirty-five years of frustration and humiliation. For the Egyptians themselves, it was both an assertion of Egypt's sovereign right to do what she liked on territory which, up to two months previously, had been occupied by British troops, and an assertion of Egypt's ability to return blow for blow in any argument which might develop with the West.

In Britain the reaction to the act of nationalization was violent. Right-wing Conservatives, who had opposed the 1954 Agreement, regarded Abdul Nasir's action both as a confirmation of their fears and as a justification of their opposition to the Agreement. But the furious British reaction was by no means confined to the right-wing Conservatives. For Englishmen of all classes and all political beliefs, the Suez Canal had a great emotive significance as 'Britain's Imperial life-line.' Disraeli's purchase of the Canal shares in 1875 had an honoured place in the British Imperial mythology. Apart from this significance, freedom of passage through the Canal, which was still identified in many British minds with British control of the Canal, was vitally important to British interests. Once the gateway to the British Indian Empire and to the British possessions on the shores of the Indian Ocean, the Suez Canal was now principally important as the channel through which most of Britain's, and Western Europe's, oil supplies were transported from the oilfields of the Persian Gulf. Three-quarters of Britain's, and of Western Europe's oil supplies came from the Persian Gulf. Of this three-quarters, two-thirds, or about sixty-seven million tons a year, came through the Suez Canal, and the remaining third was pumped to the Mediterranean by pipelines passing through Syria, a country in close alliance with Egypt. Apart from the extra cost, there were not enough tankers afloat to maintain the existing flow of oil from the Persian Gulf round the Cape route. Therefore, as many people in Britain saw it, Abdul Nasir stood between Western Europe and a raw material vital for the Western European economy. He had in his hands a blackmailing weapon of immense power which could only be neutralised by the threat, or if necessary by the use, of armed force. Everything in Abdul Nasir's past record suggested that he had every intention of using that blackmailing weapon, trusting that Great Power rivalries and UN Resolutions would prevent the application of the only effective sanction. Furthermore, there seemed, in British eyes, reason to suppose that Abdul Nasir's ambitions extended to the control, not only of the transport lanes but of the oil itself, and that the nationalization of the Suez Canal had to be viewed together with the subversion of Jordan and the Egyptian intrigues and propaganda in Iraq and the Persian Gulf, as part of a grand design for obtaining control of the sources of Middle East oil as a preliminary to playing a game of power politics between Russia and the West.

The French reaction was at least equally violent. In France, as in Britain, anxiety over the future of oil supplies was enlarged by powerful emotive considerations. The Suez Canal had been constructed by French enterprise, was largely owned by French capital, was directed by a French Company, and was managed by a largely French staff. French public opinion was also extremely incensed with Abdul Nasir over the assistance which he was giving to the Algerian rebels and was, in general, far more opposed than British public opinion to the whole concept of Arab nationalism which was regarded as having sabotaged the concept of a French 'civilizing mission' in the Eastern Mediterranean.

The Americans were concerned, but far less so than the British and French, and indeed far less than the generality of Western European countries, all of whose economies were more or less dependent on continued freedom of passage through the Suez Canal. The American economy was not so dependent and, while taking into account the legitimate concern of their European allies — who were inclined to blame the United States Government for having precipitated the crisis by withdrawing from the provisional agreement over the High Dam — tended to take a detached view of the matter. After all, Suez was not Panama and the Canal Company Concession, which Abdul Nasir had so abruptly terminated, could be regarded as a survival of nineteenth century 'colonialism.'

The immediate reaction of the British and French Governments was to claim that the act of nationalization was a breach both of the 1888 Suez Canal Convention and of Egypt's committments under the Suez Canal Company's Concession. Egyptian assets in Britain and France were blocked and all Egypt's sterling and franc operations put under exchange control. On 30 July Eden, the British Prime Minister, told the House of Commons that Britain was strengthening her military forces in Cyprus as a precautionary measure and insisted that vital British interests demanded that the Canal should be put under international control.

The Anglo-French attitude was only doubtfully founded in international law, was emotive in content and excessive in form. Abdul Nasir's control of the Canal had been secured, not by the nationalization of July 1956 but by the Anglo-Egyptian Agreement of October 1954. The act of nationalization was not a breach of the 1888 Convention in which it was specifically stipulated that the Convention was neither founded upon, nor co-terminous with, the Suez Canal Company's Concession. It was an act analogous to the Iranian Government's nationalization of the Anglo-Iranian Company in 1951 in that it was a sovereign act arbitrarily cutting short a Concession granted by a sovereign State to a foreign Company. So long as the 1888 Convention providing for freedom of passage was observed the act of nationalization was one which only concerned the Government of Egypt on the one hand and the Canal Company shareholders on the other. (The British Government were in fact the largest shareholders in the Canal Company, but their attitude was only minimally, if at all, affected by

423

this consideration.) In fact, the 1888 Convention had been repeatedly breached since the Palestine war, since when Egypt (with the connivance of Britain up to the time of the Anglo-Egyptian Agreement) had, in defiance of a Security Council Resolution, denied passage through the Canal to Israeli ships and Israeli cargoes. After nationalization, Abdul Nasir was scrupulously careful not to breach the Convention (other than by continuing the Israeli ban) in spite of the payment of Canal dues by British and French ships into blocked accounts and in spite of the provocative behaviour of the Canal Company, which did its best to discourage pilots from working for the nationalized Canal Administration with the avowed intention of bringing traffic through the Canal to a standstill. (This display of 'canalmanship' was unsuccessful in that the nationalized Administration had little difficulty in recruiting sufficient pilots to replace those who had left; it appeared that the mysteries surrounding the art of navigation through the Canal had been greatly exaggerated.)

At the end of July, four days after the act of nationalization, and immediately after Eden's statement in the House of Commons, Dulles, the American Secretary of State, flew to London. According to Eden he expressed his attitude to the British Government in the following words: 'A way had to be found to make Nasser disgorge what he was attempting to swallow . . . We must make a genuine effort to bring world opinion to favour the international operation of the Canal . . . It should be possible to create a world opinion so adverse to Nasser that he would be isolated. Then, if a military operation had to be undertaken, it would be more apt to succeed and have less grave repercussions than if it had been undertaken precipitantly.'[2]

As a result of Dulles' advice the British Government convened a Conference of all those nations whose ships used, or whose trade depended on the free use of, the Canal. Representatives of 22 out of the 24 nations invited (all except Egypt and Greece) attended the Conference, and 18 of these 22 (all except Russia, India, Indonesia and Ceylon) agreed to a Resolution calling for the creation of an international Suez Canal Board which would be responsible for the management of the Canal. This Resolution was presented to Abdul Nasir on 3 September by a delegation from the Conference headed by Menzies, the Australian Prime Minister. Abdul Nasir, fortified no doubt by Russia's abstention from the Resolution, rejected it, pleaded that its implementation would be a derogation from Egyptian sovereignty, and reiterated his intention of observing the 1888 Convention, of developing the Canal to meet future requirements, of keeping tolls equitable, and of operating the Canal efficiently.

On 12 September Eden told the House of Commons that Britain, France and the United States had agreed to form a Suez Canal Users' Association (SCUA) which would employ pilots, co-ordinate traffic and generally act on behalf of users of the Canal. If Egypt refused to co-operate, Eden implied that force would be used. Immediately after this speech Dulles, in Washington, made it clear that, in the United States Government's view, SCUA was simply a means of enabling negotiations to continue with Egypt and stated that American ships would not be permitted to 'shoot their way through the Canal.' From this time onward it was clear that there was a basic difference in view between the United States Government on the one hand and the British and French Governments on the other. The United States Government was unalterably opposed to the use of force in connection with the dispute and insisted that any modification of the act of nationalization would have to be negotiated. The British and French Governments were determined to compel Abdul Nasir, by force if necessary, to accept some effective form of international control.

On 23 September the British and French Governments formally requested the United Nations Security Council to consider the situation created by the Egyptian act of nationalization. The matter came before the Security

Council on 5 October. By that time the Suez Canal nationalization, as seen from UN Headquarters, was no longer a burning international issue. For over two months the nationalized Canal had been working efficiently. There had been no accidents due to inexperienced pilotage, no delays due to inefficient administration, no discrimination (except against Israel), and no increases in tolls. The UN. Secretary-General brought the British, French and Egyptian Foreign Ministers together to discuss the possibility of an amicable settlement. But the British and French continued to insist on, and the Egyptians to reject, effective international control. So no progress was made. An Anglo-French proposal for international control submitted to the Security Council was vetoed by Russia.

In the meantime, two sets of military preparations, each unconnected with the other, but soon fatally to converge, were going forward. For several months, Egypt had been stockpiling military equipment near the Israeli border in Sinai, stepping up commando raids into Israel from the Gaza strip, and emitting raucous anti-Israeli propaganda over the Egyptian radio, propaganda which justified and boasted about the commando raids and continually threatened Israel with full-scale war. At the same time Egypt was developing her system of Arab alliances. The process of Egyptian subversion in Jordan resulted, at the beginning of October, in the advent to power of a Jordanian Government, headed by Suleiman Nabulsi, which was pledged to the abrogation of the Anglo-Jordanian Treaty of Alliance. Two days after Nabulsi assumed office the existing military alliance between Egypt and Syria was extended to provide for a Joint Military Command which put the armies of Egypt, Syria and Jordan under an Egyptian Commander-in-Chief. It seemed a reasonable possibility, to put it at its lowest, that Abdul Nasir was preparing for an attack on Israel as soon as he had got the Suez Canal question behind him.

The British and French Governments were still deter-

426

mined to be satisfied with nothing less than effective international control of the Canal, and had not been deterred from this either by American lack of enthusiasm, or by the Russian veto, or by Abdul Nasir's apparent reasonableness over the operation of the Canal. Joint Anglo-French military preparations had been proceeding on the island of Cyprus (where there was a British military base) ever since the act of nationalization, and it may be that Abdul Nasir's circumspect behaviour was influenced by his knowledge of these preparations. But this circumspect behaviour, accompanied as it was by complete intransigeance over effective international control, was not sufficient to persuade the British and French Governments to halt or to reverse these preparations. They felt that a dispersal of their military concentration would immediately result in some further aggressive act by Abdul Nasir, thus necessitating an immediate re-concentration. It became clear that the two Governments were waiting for Abdul Nasir either to climb down or to commit some provocative act providing a justification for the use of the force which had been assembled against him. An Egyptian attack on Israel would have provided such a justification. In the event it was Israel that attacked Egypt. In face of the commando raids, the broadcast threats, the stockpiling in Sinai, and the announcement of the Joint Military Command, the Israeli Government ordered general mobilisation on 27 October. On the evening of 29 October Israeli forces crossed the Egyptian frontier into Sinai in what the Israelis regarded as a preventive war to forestall the apparent Egyptian intention to invade Israel.

It seems clear that both the British and French Governments had some foreknowledge of what the Israelis were about to do and that they had decided to use the Israeli invasion as an occasion for occupying the Canal Zone. Eden, in his Memoirs, states: 'On October 25 the Cabinet discussed the specific possibility of conflict between Israel and Egypt and decided in principle how it would react if this occurred. The Governments of France and the United Kingdom should, it considered, at once call on both parties to stop hostilities and withdraw their forces to a distance from either bank of the canal. If one or both failed to comply within a definite period, then British and French forces would intervene as a temporary measure to separate the combatants. To ensure this being effective, they would have to occupy key positions at Port Said, Ismailia and Suez. Our purpose was to safeguard free passage through the Canal, if it were threatened with becoming a zone of warfare, and to arrest the spread of fighting in the Middle East. To realise this we would put into operation the plan for occupation of the Suez Canal Zone prepared by the Anglo-French military staff which had been studying the problem since the end of July. An advantage of this course was that we did not need to recast our military preparations. The same plan that had been intended to deal with Nasser's seizure of the canal fitted equally well with our new objective.'³

On 30 October, the day after the Israeli invasion, British and French Ministers met in London to concert their plans. As a result of this meeting an Anglo-French Note was sent to the Egyptian and Israeli Governments calling upon them to cease hostilities and to withdraw their forces to a distance of 10 miles from the Canal within twelve hours, failing which Anglo-French forces would 'intervene with whatever strength may be necessary to ensure compliance.' The Israelis, who had already overrun the Egyptian forces in Sinai and whose vanguards were approaching the Canal, accepted the ultimatum (since the principle object of their invasion — the destruction of the Egyptian armed forces and military establishments in Sinai — had been achieved) and halted their vanguards outside the stipulated 10-mile limit. The Egyptians, who were being required, not to halt their invading army, but to withdraw their forces from their own territory which was being invaded, rejected the ultimatum and began to extricate such of their forces as they could

428

from the Sinai Peninsula.

On the same day — 30 October — the Security Council met to debate the situation created by the Israeli invasion. Henry Cabot Lodge, the United States representative, determined to try and forestall the threatened Anglo-French intervention in the Canal Zone, put forward a Resolution demanding an immediate cease-fire, and the withdrawal of Israeli forces behind the armistice line, and urged all United Nations members to refrain from the use, or from the threat, of force and to avoid giving any assistance to Israel in the event of her failing to comply with the Resolution. Lodge pressed this Resolution to a vote. Observers then had the unusual spectacle of a Resolution sponsored by the United States and supported by Russia being vetoed by Britain and France. The breach with the United States was open and complete.

An immediate and ruthless Anglo-French attack against the Canal Zone, whether from the air or from the sea, would probably not have been vigorously resisted by the Egyptian forces and would have faced the United Nations and the world with a fait accompli. It would probably have forestalled the blocking of the Canal (an important consideration, since the ostensible object of the operation was to safeguard free passage through the Canal). It might have led to Abdul Nasir's overthrow. But, in the event, twelve hours elapsed between the expiry of the ultimatum and the beginning of aerial bombing. Forty-eight hours elapsed between the beginning of the bombing and the landing of the first paratroops. Another forty-eight hours elapsed between the first paratroop landing and the first sea landing. During all this time opposition to the Anglo-French operation had been steadily building up. The Egyptians blocked the Canal by sinking a number of ships in the fairway. In Syria one of the Iraq Petroleum Company's pumping stations was blown up by a unit of the Syrian Army, thus cutting off the flow of oil through the pipeline to the Mediterranean. Egypt, Syria and Saudi Arabia broke off diplomatic relations with Britain and France; Iraq, Sudan and Jordan with France only. Jordan refused to allow her bases to be used, under the Anglo-Jordanian Treaty, for operations against Egypt. None of these measures were of any serious inconvenience to the British and French except for the cutting of the IPC pipeline which, combined with the blocking of the Canal, completely disrupted the flow of oil supplies to Western Europe. Much more important were the hostile reactions of the non-Arab world. The strength of these reactions caused the British and French to abandon their operation a few days after having started it and before its primary objective had been achieved. The British decision to withdraw from Egypt (followed by a reluctant French decision to withdraw as well) was taken immediately after the capture of Port Said by a sea-borne force from Malta, and before the occupation of the Canal along its whole length had been achieved. It was taken as the result of four converging threats, of unequal strength, directed against the operation. None of these threats emanated from Abdul Nasir, nor from any Arab source.

The least immediately important of these threats was the Russian threat to attack London with rocket missiles and the Russian promise to send volunteers to fight in Egypt. Only slightly more important was the attitude of the British Labour Opposition which, after some initial hesitation, condemned the whole operation. Considerably more important was a vote in the United Nations Assembly on 2 November, two days after the expiry of the Anglo-French ultimatum and three days before the sea-borne landing at Port Said, which, by 64 votes to 5, condemned the Anglo-French action and called for a cease-fire. But the really decisive threat came from the United States Government which, after having voted with the majority in the Assembly Resolution on 2 November, appears to have made it quite plain to the British Government that every sanction short of, and perhaps even including, armed force would be used against Britain and France if the Resolution were not promptly complied with.

Immediately after the British decision to withdraw, Eden, who had suffered a nervous breakdown, resigned as Prime Minister and as leader of the Conservative Party, and was succeeded by Harold Macmillan.

Abdul Nasir's high-handed (to put it at its lowest) action in nationalizing the Suez Canal literally at the point of the bayonet and without previous warning or negotiation, and his aggressive behaviour towards Israel during the previous several months, was effectively masked as the result of Egypt becoming the first nation to have been rescued from aggression by United Nations action. For some months Abdul Nasir was a kind of UN mascot and, by a judicious moderation both in word and deed, he was able to extract the maximum of advantage from his position. Under pressure of the UN Assembly, which was acting in an executive capacity through the medium of the Secretary-General, Britain, France, and Israel were compelled unconditionally to evacuate Egyptian territory, handing over their positions to units of the United Nations Emergency Force (UNEF) which, with Egyptian permission, started to arrive in Egypt within a few days of the cease-fire. The Israelis, victors in a lightning campaign which had ended before the Assembly Resolution had been debated, tried to insist on some safeguards against future Egyptian aggression before withdrawing. But, for the time being, there was no limit to United States and to United Nations compliance towards Abdul Nasir. The United States Government made a veiled threat of economic sanctions against Israel in the event of their not evacuating Egyptian territory immediately and unconditionally. Israel reluctantly complied.

Meanwhile, Abdul Nasir had seized without effective protest and without payment all the British bases in the Canal Zone which, under the 1954 Agreement, had been placed in the care of civilian contractors. He had also, without effective protest, either sequestrated or nationalized all British and French property in Egypt. Diplomatic relations between Egypt on the one hand and Britain and France on the other had of course been broken off at the time of the Anglo-French invasion, and most British and French subjects had subsequently been expelled from Egypt. There was a gratifying and creditable absence of violence against the many British and French residents in Egypt during the course of the invasion and no British or French civilians appear either to have lost their lives or suffered serious physical injury. There was no looting and the procedures of sequestration, internment and expulsion were carried out in an orderly way. If Abdul Nasir had not taught his army to fight, he had at least taught his police to keep order.

The Canal was re-activated by and at the expense of the United Nations in an operation from which all British and French nationals were, on the insistence of the Egyptian Government, debarred.

Egypt had been able to conceal the fact of military defeat by Israel underneath the laurels of a diplomatic victory against Britain and France. The Canal had been nationalized. There was no more question of international control. The 1954 Anglo-Egyptian Agreement had, in effect, been torn up. All remaining British and French property in Egypt was either sequestrated or nationalized. A British Prime Minister had been driven from office. An Anglo-French invasion had been stopped in its tracks.

This book has recorded some examples of Egyptian humiliations suffered at the hands of Great Britain and France. Suez 1956 did much to redress the balance. 'Thus the whirligig of time brings in his revenges.'

NOTES ON POSTSCRIPT

1. Eden, Sir Anthony—*Full Circle: The Memoirs of Anthony Eden,* London, 1960, pp. 421-22.

2. *ibid,* p. 437.

3. *ibid,* p. 523.

BIBLIOGRAPHY

CHAPTERS ONE AND TWO

History of the Egyptian Revolution (2 vols.). Paton, Truebner, 1863.
The Beginnings of the Egyptian Question and the Rise of Mohamed Ali.
    Ghorbal. Routledge, 1928.
The Founder of Modern Egypt. Dodwell. Cambridge University
    Press, 1931.
Ibrahim of Egypt. Crabites. Routledge, 1935.
Bonaparte's Adventure in Egypt. Elgood. Oxford University Press,
    1936.
The Awakening of Modern Egypt. Rifaat. Longmans, 1947.

CHAPTER THREE

The Suez Canal. A. T. Wilson. Oxford University Press, 1933.
The Spoliation of Suez. Crabites. Routledge, 1940.
Suez and Panama. Siegfried. Cape, 1940.

CHAPTER FOUR

The Khedive's Egypt. de Leon. Sampson, Low, 1877.
England and Egypt. Dicey. Chapman and Hall, 1881.
Court Life in Egypt. Butler. Chapman, 1887.
The Story of the Khedivate. Dicey. Rivington, 1902.
Modern Egypt (Vol. I). Cromer. Macmillan, 1908.
The Mixed Courts of Egypt. Brinton. Yale University Press, 1930.
Ismail, the Maligned Khedive. Crabites. Routledge, 1933.
The Khedive Ismail, 1863–79. Shukry. Renaissance (Cairo), 1937.

CHAPTERS FIVE TO SEVEN

The Egyptian Campaigns, 1882–85 (2 vols.). Royle. Hurst and Blackett, 1886.

England in Egypt. Milner. Arnold, 1892.

England, Egypt, and the Sudan. Traill. Constable, 1900.

Secret History of the English Occupation of Egypt. Blunt. Martin Secker, 1906.

The Making of Modern Egypt. Colvin. Seeley, 1906.

Modern Egypt (2 vols.). Cromer. Macmillan, 1908.

Gordon at Khartoum. Blunt. Swift, 1911.

An Englishman's Recollections of Egypt. de Kusel. Bodley Head, 1914.

Abbas II. Cromer. Macmillan, 1915.

Lord Cromer. Zetland. Hodder and Stoughton, 1932.

CHAPTERS EIGHT TO TWELVE

Egypt and the Army. Elgood. Oxford University Press, 1927.

Egypt Since Cromer (2 vols.). Lloyd. Macmillan, 1932.

Lord Kitchener. Hodges. Thornton Butterworth, 1936.

Allenby in Egypt. Wavell. Harrap, 1943.

Life of Lord Lloyd. Adam. Macmillan, 1948.

Royal Institute of International Affairs Survey, 1928 and 1930.

CHAPTERS THIRTEEN TO NINETEEN

Royal Institute of International Affairs Survey. 1936 and 1937.

L'Egypte et la Deuxieme Guerre Mondiale. Lugol Schindler (Cairo), 1945.

The Middle East. Fisher. Methuen, 1948.

Britain and the Arab States. Seton-Williams. Luzac, 1948.

The Middle East. Royal Institute of International Affairs, Chatham House, 1950.

Seven Fallen Pillars. Kimche. Secker and Warburg, 1950.

Britain and the Middle East. Bullard. Hutchinson, 1951.

GENERAL

Egypt in Transition. Low. Smith, Elder, 1914.

The Egyptian Problem. Chirol. Macmillan, 1920.

Great Britain in Egypt. Polson Newman. Cassel, 1928.

The Egyptian Enigma. Marshall. Murray, 1928.

The Transit of Egypt. Elgood. Arnold, 1928.

The Monetary System of Egypt. Rifaat. Allen and Unwin, 1935.

The Anglo-Egyptian Sudan from Within. Various. Faber and Faber, 1935.

Americans in the Egyptian Army. Crabites. Routledge, 1938.

The Economic Development of Modern Egypt. Crouchley, Longman, 1938.

The Development of Modern France. Brogan. Hamish Hamilton, 1940.

Independent Egypt. Amin Yussef. Murray, 1940.

Egyptian Service, 1902–1946. Russell. Murray, 1949.

THE SUDAN CONVENTION OF 1899

Whereas certain provinces in the Sudan which were in rebellion against the authority of His Highness the Khedive have
now been reconquered by the joint military and financial efforts
of Her Britannic Majesty's Government and the Government of
His Highness the Khedive;

And whereas it has become necessary to decide upon a system
for the administration of, and for the making of laws for, the said
reconquered provinces, under which due allowance may be made
for the backward and unsettled condition of large portions thereof,
and the varying requirements of different localities;

And whereas it is desired to give effect to the claims which have
accrued to Her Britannic Majesty's Government, by right of conquest, to share in the present settlement and future working and
development of the said system of administration and legislation;

And whereas it is conceived that for many purposes Wadi
Halfa and Suakin may be most effectively administered in conjunction with the reconquered provinces to which they are respectively adjacent:

Now, it is hereby agreed and declared by and between the
undersigned, duly authorized for that purpose, as follows:

Article 1. The word 'Sudan' in this Agreement means all the
territories south of the 22nd parallel of latitude, which—

1. Have never been evacuated by Egyptian troops since the
   year 1882; or
2. Which, having before the late rebellion in the Sudan been
   administered by the Government of His Highness the
   Khedive, were temporarily lost to Egypt, and have been
   reconquered by Her Britannic Majesty's Government and
   the Egyptian Government acting in concert; or
3. Which may hereafter be reconquered by the two Governments acting in concert.

Article 2. The British and Egyptian flags shall be used together both on land and water, throughout the Sudan, except in the town of Suakin, in which locality the Egyptian flag alone shall be used.

Article 3. The supreme military and civil command in the Sudan shall be vested in one officer, termed the 'Governor-General of the Sudan.' He shall be appointed by Khedivial Decree on the recommendation of Her Britannic Majesty's Government, and shall be removed only by Khedivial Decree, with the consent of Her Britannic Majesty's Government.

Article 4. Laws, as also orders and regulations with the full force of law, for the good government of the Sudan, and for regulating the holding, disposal, and devolution of property of every kind therein situate, may from time to time be made, altered, or abrogated by Proclamation of the Governor-General. Such laws, orders, and regulations may apply to the whole or any named part of the Sudan, and may, either explicitly or by necessary implication, alter or abrogate any existing law or regulation.

All such proclamations shall be forthwith notified to Her Britannic Majesty's Agent and Consul-General in Cairo, and to the President of the Council of Ministers and His Highness the Khedive.

Article 5. No Egyptian law, decree, Ministerial arrêté, or other enactment hereafter to be made or promulgated shall apply to the Sudan or any part thereof, save in so far as the same shall be applied by Proclamation of the Governor-General in manner hereinbefore provided.

Article 6. In the definition by Proclamation of the conditions under which Europeans, of whatever nationality, shall be at liberty to trade with or reside in the Sudan, or to hold property within its limits, no special privileges shall be accorded to the subjects of any one or more Powers.

Article 7. Import duties on entering the Sudan shall not be payable on goods coming from Egyptian territory. Such duties may, however, be levied on goods coming from elsewhere than Egyptian territory; but in the case of goods entering the Sudan at Suakin, or any other port on the Red Sea littoral, they shall not exceed the corresponding duties for the time being leviable on goods entering Egypt from abroad. Duties may be levied on goods leaving the Sudan at such rates as may from time to time be prescribed by Proclamation.

Article 8. The jurisdiction of the Mixed Tribunals shall not extend, nor be recognised for any purpose whatsoever, in any part of the Sudan, except in the town of Suakin.

Article 9. Until and save so far as it shall be otherwise determined by Proclamation, the Sudan, with the exception of the town of Suakin, shall be and remain under martial law.

Article. 10. No Consuls, Vice-Consuls, or Consular Agents shall be accredited in respect of nor allowed to reside in the Sudan without the previous consent of Her Brittanic Majesty's Government.

Article 11. The importation of slaves into the Sudan, as also their exportation, is absolutely prohibited. Provision shall be made by Proclamation for the enforcement of this Regulation.

Article 12. It is agreed between the two Governments that special attention shall be paid to the enforcement of the Brussels Act of the 2nd July, 1890, in respect of the import, sale, and manufacture of firearms and their munitions, and distilled or spirituous liquors.[1]

Done in Cairo, 19th January, 1899. CROMER.
BOUTROS GHALI.

[1] Article 8 of the Brussels Act prohibits importation of firearms and ammunition into territories between 20° north latitude and 22° south latitude and extending westward to the Atlantic Ocean, and eastward to the Indian Ocean and its dependencies, &c., save under certain conditions defined in Article 9.

Articles 90-95 are restrictive measures concerning traffic in spirituous liquors, prohibition of importation and manufacture of such for native use in regions of this zone where either on account of religious belief or from other motives the use of distilled liquors does not exist or has not been developed.

DECLARATION OF THE PROTECTORATE

Proclamation by the General Officer Commanding-in-Chief the British Forces in Egypt announcing the Establishment of a British Protectorate over Egypt. *Cairo, December 18, 1914.*

His Britannic Majesty's Secretary of State for Foreign Affairs gives notice that, in view of the state of war arising out of the action of Turkey, Egypt is placed under the protection of His Majesty and will henceforth constitute a British Protectorate.

The suzerainty of Turkey over Egypt is thus terminated, and His Majesty's Government will adopt all measures necessary for the defence of Egypt, and protect its inhabitants and interests.

British note addressed to His Highness Prince Hussein Kamal Pasha respecting the Establishment of a British Protectorate over Egypt, and his Acceptance of the Khediviate, with the title of Sultan of Egypt.

MR. CHEETHAM TO HIS HIGHNESS PRINCE HUSSEIN KAMAL PASHA

December 19, 1914.

YOUR HIGHNESS,

I am instructed by His Majesty's Principal Secretary of State for Foreign Affairs to bring to the notice of your Highness the circumstances preceding the outbreak of war between His Britannic Majesty and the Sultan of Turkey and the changes which the war entails in the status of Egypt.

In the Ottoman Cabinet there were two parties. On the one side was a moderate party, mindful of the sympathy extended by Great Britain to every effort towards reform in Turkey, who recognised that in the war in which His Majesty was already engaged no Turkish interests were concerned, and welcomed the assurance of His Majesty and his Allies that neither in Egypt nor elsewhere would the war be used as a pretext for any action injurious to Ottoman interests. On the other side a band of unscrupulous military adventurers looked to find in a war of aggression, waged in concert with His Majesty's enemies, the means of retrieving the disasters, military, financial, and economic, into which they had already plunged their country. Hoping to the last that wiser counsels might prevail, His Majesty and his Allies, in spite of repeated violations of their rights, abstained from retaliatory action until compelled thereto by the crossing of the Egyptian frontier by armed bands and by unprovoked attacks on Russian open ports by the Turkish naval forces under German officers.

His Majesty's Government are in possession of ample evidence that ever since the outbreak of war with Germany His Highness Abbas Hilmi Pasha, late Khedive of Egypt, has definitely thrown in his lot with His Majesty's enemies.

From the facts above set out, it results that the rights over Egypt, whether of the Sultan, or of the late Khedive, are forfeit to His Majesty.

His Majesty's Government have already, through the General Officer Commanding His Majesty's Forces in Egypt, accepted exclusive responsibility for the defence of Egypt in the present war. It remains to lay down the form of the future government of the country, freed, as I have stated, from all rights of suzerainty or other rights heretofore claimed by the Ottoman Government.

Of the rights thus accruing to His Majesty, no less than of those exercised in Egypt during the last thirty years of reform, His Majesty's Government regard themselves as trustees for the inhabitants of Egypt. And His Majesty's Government have decided that Great Britain can best fulfil the responsibilities she has incurred toward Egypt by the formal declaration of a British Protectorate, and by the government of the country under such Protectorate by a Prince of the Khedivial family.

In these circumstances I am instructed by His Majesty's Government to inform your Highness that, by reason of your age and experience, you have been chosen as the Prince of the family of Mehemet Ali most worthy to occupy the Khedivial position, with the title and style of the Sultan of Egypt; and, in inviting your Highness to accept the responsibilities of your high office, I am to give you the formal assurance that Great Britain accepts the fullest responsibility for the defence of the

441

territories under your Highness against all aggression whencesoever coming; and His Majesty's Government authorize me to declare that after the establishment of the British Protectorate now announced all Egyptian subjects wherever they may be will be entitled to receive the protection of His Majesty's Government.

With the Ottoman suzerainty there will disappear the restrictions heretofore placed by the Ottoman firmans upon the numbers and organisation of your Highness's army and upon the grant by your Highness of honorific distinctions.

As regards foreign relations, His Majesty's Government deem it most consistent with the new responsibilities assumed by Great Britain that the relations between your Highness's Government and the representatives of foreign Powers should henceforth be conducted through His Majesty's representative in Cairo.

His Majesty's Government have repeatedly placed on record that the system of treaties, known as the Capitulations, by which your Highness's Government is bound, are no longer in harmony with the development of the country; but, in the opinion of His Majesty's Government, the revision of those treaties may most conveniently be postponed until the end of the present war.

In the field of internal administration, I am to remind your Highness that, in consonance with the traditions of British policy, it has been the aim of His Majesty's Government, while working through and in the closest association with the constituted Egyptian authorities, to secure individual liberty, to promote the spread of education, to further the development of the natural resources of the country, and in such measure as the degree of enlightenment of public opinion may permit, to associate the governed in the task of government. Not only is it the intention of His Majesty's Government to remain faithful to such policy, but they are convinced that the clearer definition of Great Britain's position in the country will accelerate progress towards self-government.

The religious convictions of Egyptian subjects will be scrupulously respected as are those of His Majesty's own subjects, whatever their creed. Nor need I affirm to your Highness that, in declaring Egypt free from any duty of obedience to those who have usurped political power at Constantinople, His Majesty's Government are animated by no hostility towards the Caliphate. The past history of Egypt shows, indeed, that the loyalty of

442

Egyptian Mohammedans towards the Caliphate is independent of any political bonds between Egypt and Constantinople. The strengthening and progress of Mohammedan institutions in Egypt is naturally a matter in which His Majesty's Government take a deep interest and with which your Highness will be specially concerned, and in carrying out such reforms as may be considered necessary, your Highness may count upon the sympathetic support of His Majesty's Government.

I am to add that His Majesty's Government rely with confidence upon the loyalty, the good sense, and self-restraint of Egyptian subjects to facilitate the task of the General Officer Commanding His Majesty's Forces, who is entrusted with the maintenance of internal order, and with the prevention of the rendering of aid to the enemy.

I avail, etc.
MILNE CHEETHAM.

THE ANGLO-EGYPTIAN TREATY OF 1936

Article 1. The military occupation of Egypt by the forces of His Majesty the King and Emperor is terminated.

Article 2. His Majesty the King and Emperor will henceforth be represented at the Court of His Majesty the King of Egypt, and His Majesty the King of Egypt will be represented at the Court of St. James's, by Ambassadors duly accredited.

Article 3. Egypt intends to apply for membership to the League of Nations. His Majesty's Government in the United Kingdom, recognising Egypt as a sovereign independent State, will support any request for admission which the Egyptian Government may present in the conditions prescribed by Article 1 of the Covenant.

Article 4. An alliance is established between the High Contracting Parties with a view to consolidating their friendship, their cordial understanding and their good relations.

Article 5. Each of the High Contracting Parties undertakes not to adopt in relation to foreign countries an attitude which is inconsistent with the alliance, nor to conclude political treaties inconsistent with the provisions of the present treaty.

Article 6. Should any dispute with a third State produce a situation which involves a risk of a rupture with that State, the High Contracting Parties will consult each other with a view to the settlement of the said dispute by peaceful means, in accordance with the provisions of the Covenant of the League of Nations and of any other international obligations which may be applicable to the case.

Article 7. Should, notwithstanding the provisions of Article 6 above, either of the High Contracting Parties become engaged in war, the other High Contracting Party will, subject always to the provisions of Article 10 below, immediately come to his aid in the capacity of an ally.

The aid of His Majesty the King of Egypt, in the event of war, imminent menace of war, or apprehended international

444

emergency, will consist in furnishing to His Majesty the King and Emperor on Egyptian territory, in accordance with the Egyptian system of administration and legislation, all the facilities and assistance in his power, including the use of his ports, aerodromes and means of communication. It will accordingly be for the Egyptian Government to take all the administrative and legislative measures, including the establishment of martial law and an effective censorship, necessary to render these facilities and assistance effective.

Article 8. In view of the fact that the Suez Canal, while being an integral part of Egypt, is a universal means of communication as also an essential means of communication between the different parts of the British Empire, His Majesty the King of Egypt, until such time as the High Contracting Parties agree that the Egyptian Army is in a position to ensure by its own resources the liberty and entire security of navigation of the Canal, authorises His Majesty the King and Emperor to station forces in Egyptian territory in the vicinity of the Canal, in the zone specified in the annex to this Article, with a view to ensuring in co-operation with the Egyptian forces the defence of the Canal. The detailed arrangements for the carrying into effect of this Article are contained in the Annex hereto. The presence of these forces shall not constitute in any manner an occupation and will in no way prejudice the sovereign rights of Egypt.

It is understood that at the end of the period of 20 years specified in Article 16 the question whether the presence of British forces is no longer necessary owing to the fact that the Egyptian Army is in a position to ensure by its own resources the liberty and entire security of navigation of the Canal may, if the High Contracting Parties do not agree thereon, be submitted to the Council of the League of Nations for decision in accordance with the provisions of the Covenant in force at the time of signature of the present treaty or to such other person or body of persons for decision in accordance with such other procedure as the High Contracting Parties may agree.

Article 9. The immunities and privileges in jurisdictional and fiscal matters to be enjoyed by the forces of His Majesty the King and Emperor who are in Egypt in accordance with the provisions of the present treaty will be determined in a separate convention to be concluded between the Egyptian Government and His Majesty's Government in the United Kingdom.

Article 10. Nothing in the present treaty is intended to or shall in any way prejudice the rights and obligations which devolve, or may devolve, upon either of the High Contracting Parties under the Covenant of the League of Nations or the Treaty for the Renunciation of War signed at Paris on August 27, 1928.

Article 11. While reserving liberty to conclude new conventions in future, modifying the agreements of January 19 and July 10, 1899, the High Contracting Parties agree that the administration of the Sudan shall continue to be that resulting from the said agreements. The Governor-General shall continue to exercise on the joint behalf of the High Contracting Parties the powers conferred upon him by the said agreements. The High Contracting Parties agree that the primary aim of their administration in the Sudan must be the welfare of the Sudanese. Nothing in this article prejudices the question of sovereignty over the Sudan.

Appointments and promotions of officials in the Sudan will in consequence remain vested in the Governor-General, who, in making new appointments to posts for which qualified Sudanese are not available, will select suitable candidates of British and Egyptian nationality.

In addition to Sudanese troops, both British and Egyptian troops shall be placed at the disposal of the Governor-General for the defence of the Sudan.

Egyptian immigration into the Sudan shall be unrestricted except for reasons of public order and health.

There shall be no discrimination in the Sudan between British subjects and Egyptian nationals in matters of commerce, immigration, or the possession of property.

The High Contracting Parties are agreed on the provisions set out in the annex to this Article as regards the method by which international conventions are to be made applicable to the Sudan.

Article 12. His Majesty the King and Emperor recognizes that the responsibility for the lives and property of foreigners in Egypt devolves exclusively upon the Egyptian Government, who will ensure the fulfilment of their obligations in this respect.

Article 13. His Majesty the King and Emperor recognizes that the capitulatory régime now existing in Egypt is no longer in

446

accordance with the spirit of the times and with the present state of Egypt. His Majesty the King of Egypt desires the abolition of this régime without delay. Both High Contracting Parties are agreed upon the arrangements with regard to this matter as set forth in the annex to this Article.

Article 14. The present treaty abrogates any existing agreements or other instruments whose continued existence is inconsistent with its provisions. Should either High Contracting Party so request, a list of the agreements and instruments thus abrogated shall be drawn up in agreement between them within six months of the coming into force of the present treaty.

Article 15. The High Contracting Parties agree that any difference on the subject of the application or interpretation of the provisions of the present treaty which they are unable to settle by direct negotiation shall be dealt with in accordance with the provisions of the Covenant of the League of Nations.

Article 16. At any time after the expiration of a period of 20 years from the coming into force of the treaty the High Contracting Parties will, at the request of either of them, enter into negotiations with a view to such revision of its terms by agreement between them as may be appropriate in the circumstances as they then exist. In case of the High Contracting Parties being unable to agree upon the terms of the revised treaty, the difference will be submitted to the Council of the League of Nations for decision in accordance with the provisions of the Covenant in force at the time of signature of the present treaty, or to such other person or body of persons for decision in accordance with such procedure as the High Contracting Parties may agree. It is agreed that any revision of this treaty will provide for the continuation of the Alliance between the High Contracting Parties in accordance with the principles contained in Articles 4, 5, 6, and 7. Nevertheless, with the consent of both High Contracting Parties, negotiations may be entered into at any time after the expiration of a period of 10 years after the coming into force of the treaty, with a view to such revision as aforesaid.

Article 17. The present treaty is subject to ratification. Ratifications shall be exchanged in Cairo as soon as possible. The treaty shall come into force on the date of the exchange of ratifications, and shall thereupon be registered with the Secretary-General of the League of Nations.

447

THE SUDAN AGREEMENT OF 1953

The Egyptian Government and the Government of the United Kingdom of Great Britain and Northern Ireland (hereinafter called the 'United Kingdom Government'), firmly believing in the right of the Sudanese people to Self-Determination and the effective exercise thereof at the proper time and with the necessary safeguards have agreed as follows:

Article 1. In order to enable the Sudanese people to exercise Self-Determination in a free and neutral atmosphere, a transitional period providing full Self-Government for the Sudanese shall begin on the day specified in Article 9 below.

Article 2. The transitional period, being a preparation for the effective termination of the dual Administration, shall be considered as a liquidation of that Administration. During the transitional period the sovereignty of the Sudan shall be kept in reserve for the Sudanese until Self-Determination is achieved.

Article 3. The Governor-General shall, during the transitional period, be the supreme constitutional authority within the Sudan. He shall exercise his powers as set out in the Self-Government Statute with the aid of a five-member Commission, to be called the Governor-General's Commission, whose powers are laid down in the terms of reference in Annex I to the present Agreement.

Article 4. This Commission shall consist of two Sudanese proposed by the two contracting Governments in agreement, one Egyptian citizen, one citizen of the United Kingdom and one Pakistani citizen, each to be proposed by his respective Government. The appointment of the two Sudanese members shall be subject to the subsequent approval of the Sudanese Parliament when it is elected, and the Parliament shall be entitled to nominate alternative candidates in case of disapproval. The Commission hereby set up will be formally appointed by Egyptian Government decree.

Article 5. The two Contracting Governments agree that, it being a fundamental principle of their common policy to maintain the unity of the Sudan as a single territory, the special powers which are vested in the Governor-General by Article 100 of the Self-Government Statute shall not be exercised in any manner which is in conflict with that policy.

Article 6. The Governor-General shall remain directly responsible to the two Contracting Governments as regards:

(*a*) external affairs;

(*b*) any change requested by the Sudanese Parliament under Article 101 (1) of the Statute for Self-Government as regards any part of that Statute;

(*c*) any resolution passed by the Commission which he regards as inconsistent with his responsibilities. In this case he will inform the two Contracting Governments, each of which must give an answer within one month of the date of formal notice. The Commission's resolution shall stand unless the two Governments agree to the contrary.

Article 7. There shall be constituted a Mixed Electoral Commission of seven members. These shall be three Sudanese appointed by the Governor-General with the approval of his Commission, one Egyptian citizen, one citizen of the United Kingdom, one citizen of the United States of America, and one Indian citizen. The non-Sudanese members shall be nominated by their respective Governments. The Indian member shall be Chairman of the Commission. The Commission shall be appointed by the Governor-General on the instructions of the two Contracting Governments. The terms of reference of this Commission are contained in Annex II to this Agreement.

Article 8. To provide the free and neutral atmosphere requisite for Self-Determination there shall be established a Sudanization Committee consisting of:

(*a*) an Egyptian citizen and a citizen of the United Kingdom to be nominated by their respective Governments and subsequently appointed by the Governor-General, together with three Sudanese members to be selected from a list of five names submitted to him by the Prime Minister of the Sudan. The selection and appointment of these Sudanese members shall have the prior approval of the Governor-General's Commission;

449

(*b*) one or more members of the Sudan Public Service Commission who will act in a purely advisory capacity without the right to vote.

The function and terms of reference of this Committee are contained in Annex III to this Agreement.

Article 9. The transitional period shall begin on the day designated as 'the appointed day' in Article 2 of the Self-Government Statute. Subject to the completion of Sudanization as outlined in Annex III to this Agreement, the two Contracting Governments undertake to bring the transitional period to an end as soon as possible. In any case this period shall not exceed three years. It shall be brought to an end in the following manner. The Sudanese Parliament shall pass a resolution expressing their desire that arrangements for Self-Determination shall be put in motion and the Governor-General shall notify the two Contracting Governments of this resolution.

Article 10. When the two Contracting Governments have been formally notified of this resolution the Sudanese Government, then existing, shall draw up a draft law for the election of the Constituent Assembly which it shall submit to Parliament for approval. The Governor-General shall give his consent to the law with the agreement of his Commission. Detailed preparations for the process of Self-Determination, including safe-guards assuring the impartiality of the elections and any other arrangements designed to secure a free and neutral atmosphere shall be subject to international supervision. The two Contracting Governments will accept the recommendations of any international body which may be set up to this end.

Article 11. Egyptian and British Military Forces shall withdraw from the Sudan immediately upon the Sudanese Parliament adopting a resolution expressing its desire that arrangements for Self-Determination be put in motion. The two Contracting Governments undertake to complete the withdrawal of their forces from the Sudan within a period not exceeding three months.

Article 12. The Constituent Assembly shall have two duties to discharge. The first will be to decide the future of the Sudan as one integral whole. The second will be to draw up a constitution for the Sudan compatible with the decision which shall have been taken in this respect, as well as an electoral law for a permanent

Sudanese Parliament. The future of the Sudan shall be decided either:

(a) by the Constituent Assembly choosing to link the Sudan with Egypt in any form, or

(b) by the Constituent Assembly choosing complete independence.

Article 13. The two Contracting Governments undertake to respect the decision of the Constituent Assembly concerning the future status of the Sudan and each Government will take all the measures which may be necessary to give effect to its decision.

Article 14. The two Contracting Governments agree that the Self-Government Statute shall be amended in accordance with Annex IV to this Agreement.

Article 15. This Agreement together with its attachments shall come into force upon signature.

P   453

INDEX

Legislative Council, 133, 186, 196, 199, 201, 205, 290
Leopold, King, 159
Lesseps, Ferdinand de, 62, 96; British occupation of Egypt, 125; concession granted, 63; Disraeli's purchase of Canal shares, 75; French attitude to, 67, 73; Said, friendship with, 62-3, 67; Suez Canal, defence of, 136; Suez Canal, policy of Lesseps, 76; Suez Canal, shares in, 67
Levant, French interests in, 40-1, 48, 60, 253, 321
Liberal Constitutionalists, 264, 272
Liberals, Egyptian party policy, 295
Libya, Turkish-Italian War, 205
Liquidation, Law of, 108-11, 114, 116, 127, 130, 159, 161-2, 194
Lloyd, Clifford. See CLIFFORD LLOYD.
Lloyd, Lord, High Commissioner in Egypt, 275; British control and Egyptian independence, 307; *Liwa, al*, newspaper, 201; British officials in Egyptian Service, 278; *Egypt since Cromer*, 288; elections and Wafd, 276-7; Nationalism, attitude to, 279; policy of, 279, 283-4, 308; resignation of, 284
Loans, negotiations for, 98
London Conventions, 154, 159, 161-2, 175-6, 191
Loraine, Sir Percy, High Commissioner, 285, 293
Lupton Bey, Governor of Bahr-al-Ghazal, 142, 153, 159

MacDonald, Ramsay, Prime Minister, 265
MacMahon, Sir Henry, High Commissioner in Egypt, 219, 225
Magellon, M., French Consul in Egypt, 13-14
Magnates, 290
Mahdi, 141-2, 145, 151
Mahdism, 157-8
Maher, Ali, Prime Minister, 313, 316, 383-5, 387; attitude to General Neguib's revolution, 387-8
Mahmud II, Sultan of Turkey, 39, 45
Mahmud Pasha, 278, 281-6, 288, 291, 295-6, 313
Mahmud, Pasha Fahmy, Prime Minister, 198

Mahmud Sami, Prime Minister, 115, 119
Mahmudieh Canal, 48, 54, 56, 60
Maize, cultivated, 53
Makram Pasha Ebeid, 291, 333, 336, 349
Malaria, 208, 257
Malet, Sir Edward, British Agent and Consul-General in Egypt, 117, 135-6, 144-5, 160
Malta captured by the French, 14
Mamelukes, 24, 28; Assembly of, 10; British assistance to, 28; British policy towards, 24-7; Circassian Mamelukes, 9; defeated at Battle of Pyramids, 14; government of Egypt by, 7-10, 12, 25; Mameluke Amir-al-Hajj, 10; Mameluke Shaykh-al-Balad, 10; military measures by, 21; military organization, 14; origin of, 7; power of, 10-11; revolt against Turkish Pasha, 30-1; slaughtered by Mohamed Ali, 34-5
Mamurs, 59
Marabout, 21
Maraghi, Sheikh Mustafa al, 294
Marchand, Captain, Fashoda incident, 156
Mariut Lake, 21
Mariut Railway, 211
Marriott, Colonel, 95
Martial law, 214, 218-20, 222-3, 248, 250, 262, 350, 352
Massawa, 139-40, 142, 153-4
Maxwell, Sir Benson, British Procureur-Général, 164, 182, 218
Maxwell, Sir John, British Military Commander in Egypt, 214, 221
Mediterranean Fleet, headquarters planned for Alexandria, 294
Menou, French commander in Egypt, 20
Merowe, 151
Middle East, 309; Balkanization of, 332; British garrisons in, 368; British interest in control of, 367; British policy, 321; British position in, 1941-2, 316; British strategy, 367; oil resources, 369; political integration and economic rehabilitation, 368-9; strategic control of, 321, 369; strategy based on co-operation of Arab League, 331

461

Military alliance with Great Britain, 300, 303
Military forces in Egypt. *See* BRITISH POLICY.
Military operations, 1914 War, 220-1
Milner, Lord, 102, 250; Mission to Egypt, 237-44, 260
Milner-Zaghlul Memorandum, 241-4, 247, 249-50
Miri, tribute, from land tax, 10
Misset, Major, British Agent in Cairo, 28, 30-4
Mixed Courts. *See* COURTS (MIXED).
Mixed interest cases, 309
Modernization of Egypt, Mohamed Ali and, 48
Mohamed Abdu, 112, 197
Mohamed Ahmed, 142, 152, 157
Mohamed Ali (1769-1849), 22, 289, 298; British proposals for his submission, 46-7; General Fraser's expedition, 33-4; French influence discredited, 47; French overtures to, 42-5; Great Britain and, 30-59; Greek revolt against Turkey, 1821, 36-7; Mamelukes slaughtered by, 35; Mediterranean policy, alliance with Mohamed Pasha, 40; Pasha of Egypt, 32, 47; policy of, 35; Powers, military action, 1840, 45-6; Sudan trade, 139; Suez Canal, 62, 72; tribute withheld by, 44; Turkey, military action against, 39; Turkey, rewards required from, 39-40; Viceroy over Sudan, 139
Mohamed Ali (1876-), 298
Mohamed Farid, Leader of the Hizb-al-Watani, 201
Mohamed Mahmud, 229, 233, 313
Mohamed Pasha Said, Prime Minister, 203, 210-11, 236-8
Mohamed Pasha Salah-al-Din, Egyptian Foreign Secretary, negotiations, 1950, with Bevin, 363
Moncrieff, Captain, R.N., 158
Monopolies, state, 54
Montreux Convention, 1937, 303, 310, 347
Moratorium, August, 1914, 213
Morice Bey, 158
Morier, J. P., Egyptian future, 25

Morocco, Anglo-French Agreement, 1904, 167
Mortada Maraghy, 385
Moslem Brotherhood, 334-5, 337, 341, 350-3, 355-6, 379, 390
Moslem fanaticism, 17, 201
Moslem law of inheritance, 255
Mudirs, 59
Mukhtar Pasha, 163
Multazimin, 10, 13, 28, 51, 59
Muqabala Loan, 92, 99, 107-8, 111
Murad Bey, 11-12, 14, 18-19, 24, 26
Mussolini, Egypt and, 298
Murray, General Sir Archibald, 221
Mustafa Kamal, leader of the nationalist movement, 168, 197, 201, 210, 289
Mustafa Pasha Fahmy, Prime Minister, 165-7, 210
Myos Hormos, 29

NAHAS PASHA, PRIME MINISTER, 280-1, 293-4, 297, 302, 318-19, 333, 357, 379-80; Arab League and, 325; Arab unity, 322; attempts on life of, 351; British intervention, 286; demands of, 334; dismissed, 282, 324, 383; elections and, 291; Neguib and, 388; policy during Second German War, 315; Policy of, towards an Axis or Allied victory, 317; position and power of, 312; resignation, 286, 312; Treaty negotiated with Henderson, 285, 296-7; United Front policy, 295-6
Napoleon I, Egyptian expedition, 13, 41; England, invasion of, 14; policy of, in Egypt, 17-18; return to France, 1799, 18; Syrian expedition, 1799, 17; Treaty of Tilsit, 34
Napoleon III, 66, 73, 75, 84
Napier, Commodore, 46-7
Nashaat Pasha, Chief of Royal Cabinet, 275-6
Nasir, al, Sultan, 8-9
National Bank of Egypt, 213
National Council, meeting in Cairo, 124